NATIONAL CAPITALISMS, GLOBAL COMPETITION,
AND ECONOMIC PERFORMANCE

Advances in Organization Studies

Advances in Organization Studies includes cutting-edge work in comparative management and intercultural comparison, studies of organizational culture, communication, and aesthetics, as well as in the area of interorganizational collaboration — strategic alliances, joint ventures, networks and collaborations of all kinds, where comparative, intercultural, and communicative issues have an especial salience. Purely theoretical as well as empirically studies are included.

General Editors

Stewart Clegg
School of Management
University of Technology Sydney
Quay Street, Haymarket
P.O.Box 123
Broadway, NSW 2007
Australia
s.clegg@uts.edu.au

Alfred Kieser
University of Mannheim
D 68 131 Mannheim
Germany
kieser@bwl.uni-mannheim.de

Volume 3

Sigrid Quack, Glenn Morgan and Richard Whitley (eds)

National Capitalisms, Global Competition, and Economic Performance

National Capitalisms, Global Competition, and Economic Performance

Edited by

SIGRID QUACK
Wissenschaftszentrum, Berlin

GLENN MORGAN
University of Warwick

RICHARD WHITLEY
NIAS, The Netherlands

JOHN BENJAMINS PUBLISHING COMPANY
AMSTERDAM/PHILADELPHIA

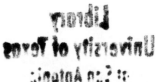

™ The paper used in this publication meets the minimum requirements of American National Standard for Information Sciences — Permanence of Paper for Printed Library Materials, ANSI Z39.48–1984.

Library of Congress Cataloging-in-Publication Data

National capitalisms, global competition and economic performance / edited by Sigrid Quack, Glenn Morgan, Richard Whitley.

    p.   cm. -- (Advances in organization studies, ISSN 1566-1075 ; 3)

  Includes bibliographical references and index.

    1. Corporate culture--Europe--Case studies. 2. Management--Europe--Case studies. 3. Capitalism--Europe--Case studies. 4. Competition, International--Case studies. I. Quack, Sigrid. II. Morgan, Glenn. III. Whitley, Richard. IV. Series.

HD58.7.N38   1999

338.094--dc21   99-051376

ISBN 90 272 3300 4 (Eur.) / 1 55619 746 2 (US) (Pb: alk. paper)   CIP

John Benjamins Publishing Co. · P.O.Box 75577 · 1070 AN Amsterdam · The Netherlands

John Benjamins North America · P.O.Box 27519 · Philadelphia PA 19118-0519 · USA

Table of Contents

List of Contributors

Elizabeth Campagnac, Ecole Nationale des Ponts et Chausses, Paris, France

Steven Casper, Economic Change and Employment Group, Wissenschaftszentrum, Berlin, Germany

Francesco Curto, Warwick Business School, University of Warwick, UK

Simon Deakin, Faculty of Law and ESRC Centre for Business Research, University of Cambridge, UK

Owen Darbishire, Said Business School and Pembroke College, University of Oxford, UK

Bob Hancke, Economic Change and Employment Group, Wissenschaftszentrum, Berlin, Germany

Marko Hocevar, Faculty of Economics, University of Ljubljana, Slovenia

Ad van Iterson, Faculty of Economics and Business Administration, University of Limburg, The Netherlands

Marko Jacklic, Faculty of Economics, University of Ljubljana, Slovenia

Christel Lane, Faculty of Social and Political Sciences and ESRC Centre for Business Research, University of Cambridge, UK

Mark Lehrer, Dept of Management, University of Rhode Island, USA

Kari Lilja, Helsinki School of Economics, Finland

Yuh-Jye Lin, Richard Rogers Partnership, Tokyo

Ray Loveridge, Said Business School, University of Oxford

Michael Mayer, Dept. of Management Studies, University of Glasgow

Glenn Morgan, Warwick Business School University of Warwick, UK

Frank Mueller, School of Management, Royal Holloway, University of London, UK

Matti Pohjola, Helsinki School of Economics, Finland

Sigrid Quack, Organisation and Employment Group, Wissenschaftszentrum, Berlin, Germany

Danielle Salomon, CSO-Paris, CNRS, France.

Risto Tainio, Helsinki School of Economics, Finland

Grahame F. Thompson, the Open University, UK

Richard Whitley, Manchester Business School, UK

Richard Whittington, Said Business School and New College, University of Oxford

Frank Wilkinson, Dept. of Applied Economics and ESRC Centre for Business Research, University of Cambridge, UK

Graham M Winch, Bartlett School of Architecture, Building, Environmental Design and Planning, University College, London, UK

Acknowledgement

The European Science Foundation is an association of its 56 member research councils, academies and institutions devoted to basic scientific research in 20 countries. The ESF assists its Member Organizations in two main ways: by bringing scientists together in its Scientific Programmes, Networks, and European Research Conferences, to work on topics of common concern; and through the joint study of issues of strategic importance in European science policy.

The scientific work sponsored by ESF includes basic research in the natural and technical sciences, the medical and biosciences, the humanities and social sciences.

The ESF maintains close relations with other scientific institutions within and outside Europe. By its activities, ESF adds value by cooperation and coordination across national frontiers and endeavours, offers expert scientific advice on strategic issues, and provides the European forum for fundamental science.

This volume arises from the work of the ESF Scientific Programme on European Management and Organisations in Transition (EMOT).

Further information on ESF activities can be obtained from:
European Science Foundation
1 quai Lezay-Marnésia
F-67080 Strasbourg Cedex
France
Tel. (+33) 88 76 71 00
Fax (+33) 88 37 05 32

Preface

This book resulted from a workshop organised as part of the series of European collaborative meetings planned as Theme A on *Changing Forms of Economic Organizations* in the European Science Foundation's Programme on *European Management and Organisations in Transition* (EMOT). This series of workshops focused on how different systems of economic coordination and control developed, and are changing, interdependently with key institutional sectors, such as political, financial, labour and cultural systems, across Europe. Results of previous workshops resulted in the publication of *The Changing European Firm: Limits to Convergence* (London: Routledge, 1996) and *Governance at Work. The Social Regulation of Economic Relations* (Oxford: Oxford University Press, 1997), both edited by R. Whitley and P. H. Kristensen. The present volume brings together contributions from the last workshop in this series, organised at the Wissenschafts-zentrum Berlin in 1997, which focused on the interrelationships between national institutions, globalisation and economic performance outcomes.

The contributions in this volume seek to understand the institutional foundations of economic performance outcomes in different European nation states. The papers provide a comparative framework for the analysis of the regulative, normative and cognitive factors which shape the performance of firms within specific sectors, encompassing manufacturing industries as well as different service activities, and national as well as international markets. The results demonstrate how different kinds of economic coordination which develop interdependently with nationally based social institutions give rise to distinct patterns of firm competences and capabilities. These competences and capabilities influence firms' ability to adapt to changing business environments and pressures from global competition with consequent effects for their own economic perform-ance, the performance of their sector, and last but not least that of their home nation state. The globalisation of economic activity generates pressures for standardisation and homogenisation; but it also reinforces existing sectoral and national differences in economic coordination, economic goal setting and related perceptions of performance outcomes which are linked to different institutional legacies and structures. Globalisation, thus, needs to be understood as a dynamic interplay of distinctive competitive advantages, derived from different national models of organisation.

We would like to thank the European Science Foundation for the financial support of this workshop, and the Wissenschaftszentrum, Berlin (WZB) for providing its excellent conference facilities for this meeting. Much of the final editing of the volume together with the drafting of the introduction was carried out at the department "Organisation and Employment" at the WZB. Sue Grey at Manchester Business School and Sylvia Pichorner at the WZB, have undertaken the major task of producing all the chapters in the appropriate format and solving all the queries arising from such a book production. Both deserve our sincere thanks for their patient help and excellent assistance. Finally, our thanks are due to the contributors and the other participants in the workshop for helping us to produce this volume.

Berlin, Warwick and Manchester

Sigrid Quack
Glenn Morgan
Richard Whitley

PART I

Introduction

CHAPTER 1

National Capitalisms, Global Competition and Economic Performance

An Introduction[*]

Sigrid Quack   Glenn Morgan

1. Introduction

Recent debates on internationalisation and globalisation have led to a renewed interest in questions of competitiveness and economic performance. Whereas some believe that in increasingly globalised markets it is only the ability of the individual firm to compete which matters, others contend that success in these markets is also related to the geographical location of a firm, or in other words, the comparative advantages generated by a firm's societal and institutional environment at the national level (i.e. Porter 1990; Sorge 1991; Streeck 1992; Hollingsworth et al. 1994; Lane 1995; Boyer and Drache 1996; Berger and Dore 1996; Whitley 1999).

Between these two schools of thought, which crudely can be labelled as neoliberal versus institutionalist approach, perceptions of what constitutes competitiveness and economic performance could not be more different. In the world of neoliberalism, the performance of firms is judged through market processes which select the efficient and deselect the inefficient. At the centre is the very simple idea that firms maximise profits (or, in a wider version, returns) by allocating scarce resources to the most efficient use. In pursuing this goal, firms are assumed to enter and exit easily different markets in response to relative changes of (real or expected) returns, the most efficient co-ordination of economic resources and optimal outcome at the system level being guaranteed by the working of the 'invisible hand' of market competition. According to this view, organisations are governed by universal principles, variation being allowed only

* We would like to thank Dorothee Bohle, Jacqueline O'Reilly, Dieter Plehwe, Arndt Sorge and Richard Whitley for their helpful comments on an earlier version of this chapter.

in relation to the specific technological requirements of their task environment and contingency factors. Even though factors such as bounded rationality, organisational inertia, etc. can impede perfect competition, in the long run the hidden hand of the market will push organisations to converge on an 'ideal profile' of 'best practice' if they want to succeed in world markets.

In this book, a different notion of competitiveness and economic performance will be adopted. The alternative argument explored here is that markets do not exist separately from social contexts. In contrast to the rhetoric of 'best practice', various comparative studies suggest that depending on the institutional context in which they operate, firms develop different patterns of capabilities and performance profiles (Whitley and Kristensen 1996, 1997; Hollingsworth and Boyer 1997; Berger and Dore 1996). These capabilities and capacities reflect the different ways in which performance is judged in different national contexts. For example, the dominance of 'shareholder value' performance criteria in Anglo-American capitalism is distinctive from the 'stakeholder capitalism' models of Germany and Japan where obligations to employees, suppliers and customers are part of the context within which overall firm performance is judged (see e.g. the discussions in Crouch and Streeck 1997). These differences impact on the ways in which firms grow and evolve. This reflects the general point that there are, in fact, many ways of measuring, monitoring and judging the performance of organisations in market societies. What is good and bad performance is not predefined but socially constructed by various groups and actors in particular national contexts. Whereas institutionalist approaches tend to argue that this national context still remains dominant, it is characteristic of neoliberal accounts that they assume a convergence of performance standards towards that enacted by Anglo-American capital markets and driven by the growth of global financial markets.

However, a closer examination of studies which have been undertaken in the tradition of the 'national business systems' and 'varieties of capitalism' approach reveals that compared to the richness of empirical evidence that has been provided on national differences in business organisation, surprisingly little has been said explicitly about how these relate to issues of performance. Instead, many of these studies undertaken in the 1980s and early 1990s seemed to embody a set of implicit assumptions about the relationships. In particular, the argument was implied that certain national institutional contexts were proving more effective in producing firms which could compete in global markets than others. This was often presented as a contrast between the 'failings' of Anglo-American capitalism and the 'successes' of Japan and Germany. Thus global competition was seen as paradoxically undermining firms from those countries which were most ideologically committed to it, i.e. the USA and the UK. Furthermore, it was assumed that these institutional frameworks derived from a long-term path dependent trajectory of the societies under examination and there would therefore be no simple convergence on a single model of economic organisation.

From the perspective of the late 1990s, however, this simple dualistic contrast seems increasingly inadequate in order to understand what is happening in different parts of the world under the impact of global competition. German unemployment, for example, has been well above that of the UK and the USA for most of the 1990s, whilst in Japan, industrial production has been stagnating and the financial system has been on the edge of breakdown for some years. For proponents of neoliberalism, this turn in fortunes which appears to have occurred is further proof of the inexorable march of global market forces into the heartland of 'regulated' capitalisms. The response of institutionalist theorists to these changes, on the other hand, has to be more complex. In this book, we seek to develop one set of responses by considering in more detail than has previously been the case the nature of the links between institutional conditions, market competition and performance outcomes. We would argue that three key points need to be considered and further developed if instititutionalist theory is going to develop an adequate response to the changing global economy at the turn of the millenium: performance as a process over time, the multiple dimensions of performance, and the links between firm performance, sector specialisation and national performance outcomes.

2.   Performance as a Process over Time

Firstly, we believe that institutionalism needs to examine performance not at a given point in time, but performance as a process over time. Societal configurations unfold their enabling and constraining potential for economic development over long periods in circumstances that can be greatly affected by what, within the context of this discussion, we may call contingent factors (such as war, long-term economic and technological cycles, inter-state rivalries and pacts, revolutions and social breakdowns). Thus the implications of social institutions for economic performance can be only assessed from a longitudinal perspective. What appears highly effective at one point in the development of the national and the international economy may appear less so at a later point. Failure to recognise this leads to over-simple, ahistorical generalisations about the relationship between types of institutions and particular performance outcomes. This requires two further elements.

There needs to be a more explicit theorisation of the nature of the international economic and political context and how this relates both to patterns of trade and capital flows and to nationally based systems of production. Hirst and Thompson (1996) have provided an invaluable first step in this process by revealing the degree of integration in the international economy at various stages of the last 150 years (see also Thompson's contribution in this book). Djelic (1998) has argued that the international environment should be conceptualised as a "concrete political and geopolitical arena, characterised by multiple, multilateral, and context dependent cross-national interactions." (Djelic 1998: 8). Within this context, nations take different roles at particular times (see e.g. Morgan's discussion of the inter-relationship between the international and national contexts for financial systems, Morgan 1997). In particular, some nations act to define and defend the 'rules of the game', in terms of who can participate in international trade and on what terms. Thus the post-war US dominance, and the Marshall plan in particular, has made an important impact on the evolution of different national systems of production in Western Europe. Post-war US dominance within the framework of the Cold War was also a crucial factor in providing the space for certain East Asian countries (first Japan, but later South Korea and Taiwan) to develop their industrial base, by providing both cheap capital and opportunities to protect home markets that were not made available to other countries. As this post-war order broke down, the rules of the game changed for many countries (see e.g. the chapters in this book by Tainio et al. and Whitley et al. which both deal with countries significantly affected by the breakdown of the Soviet system). Thus institutionalist theories need to see performance as a process which unfolds over time in a changing international economic and political context.

This is also relevant to the way in which national economies as a whole evolve over time — again, a theme which institutionalists have not considered in detail. In Adam Smith's (1937) model of the developing world economy, there was expected to be a division of labour based on the comparative advantage of particular areas in producing certain types of goods and services. In international terms, this underlay the division between agricultural and manufacturing areas but in national terms, it also reflected the idea that for historical reasons, certain countries had developed a particular expertise in certain goods and/or services. Within this inter-linked national and international process of development, therefore, nations had different patterns of sectoral specialisation (Kitschelt 1991; see also Quack and Morgan in this book for a more detailed discussion). This historical pattern of sector specialisation in a particular country creates a path dependency which can have varying effects depending on the broader context. For example, Britain traditionally had a very highly developed engineering sector with high employment and skill levels, as well as vibrant export markets throughout the 19th and much of the 20th century. The 'success' of British engineering was one of the foundations of the British economy. However, from the 1970s onwards, many of these markets were lost, firms went bankrupt and employees lost their jobs. This related to changing international conditions of competition and the growing challenge of Japanese and German firms, amongst others, in markets traditionally dominated by the British. A sector specialisation which had broadly benefitted Britain became one that caused major economic and social dislocation during its decline in the 1980s though more recently, some revival in British engineering and manufacturing generally may be detected (Delbridge and Lowe 1998). In other contexts, sector specialisation may provide a continued basis for economic development even when the international context changes (see e.g. the discussion of sector specialisation in the Netherlands by Van Iterson in this book).

Over time, types of sectoral specialisation have differential impacts on performance outcomes. A particular issue occurs as new sectors arise and old ones mature and decline. These sectoral changes may arise from changing international competition which allows the relocation of production facilities to lower wage areas. They may arise from changing technologies which open up new avenues for production and service. What becomes crucial is the ability of actors within national business systems to adapt to these changes, either by up-grading within existing sectors or developing new ones. Institutionalist analysis in the 1980s tended to emphasise the ability of some contexts to manage this up-grading process more effectively than others. However, in the 1990s, there has been a sense that the limits of this process may have been reached, e.g. in the German case (see Schienstock 1997; also the contribution by Lehrer and Darbishire in this book) and that institutional (as opposed to organisational) change may be necessary (e.g. restructuring the welfare state, see, for example, the discussions in Streeck 1997 and Esping Andersen 1997). The capacity to recombine existing sectors or to develop new sectors also seems to be differentially distributed (see e.g. the chapter of Loveridge and Mueller in this volume). Institutional environments which in the past enabled up-grading under conditions of gradual change in traditional sectors do not necessarily show the same virtues in sectors which are exposed to radical technological and competitive change in world markets. This may be a disadvantage of national contexts in which there is a tight fit between institutional systems and organisational and firm structures. Such a tight fit may then make transitions into new sectors or even into new ways of working in old sectors difficult to achieve.

Institutionalism therefore needs to take seriously how firms and industries evolve over time in both national and international contexts. What is successful at one point may not be so at another point. The difficult task for researchers is to unravel these connections and make sense of them in specific sectoral and national contexts. A number of contributions to this book attempt to do just this.

3. The Multiple Dimensions of Performance

The idea of tracking performance across time needs, however, to be accompanied by a much more complex view of what is meant by performance. In his useful review article entitled '*Measuring Performance in Economic Organizations*', Meyer states that "performance measures have increased with measurers" (Meyer 1994: 562). He describes what he terms 'the rapid growth of the performance measurement industry' and shows how different performance measures have arisen and then declined in perceived usefulness (see also Power 1994 for a similar argument). Both free market economists and, perversely, some institutionalist researchers have focused primarily on success in world markets as the key performance indicator. Failure to succeed in such markets is perceived almost as failure per se on the assumption that there is a tight feedback loop from this measure of performance to the survival of the firm as a whole. However, this is rarely the case even from a strictly economic point of view as firms are agglomerations of resources and capabilities that can survive and evolve for a number of years even in the light of falling market share for certain products (Meyer and Zucker 1989; Lazonick 1991). On top of this, it is necessary to note firstly, that not all products and services are traded internationally because their conditions of production and consumption make them specifically local. Secondly, the shift of products and services into the category of internationally tradeable is a historical process; it is only in the last two decades that professional services such as accounting have become global. The local/national nature of many products and services plus the loose coupling between performance on international markets and survival opens up a space within which a range of performance criteria can be considered.

Moreover, firms exist within national institutional contexts where social and political coalitions of interest have created particular systems of order based on compromises and agreements between different groups, for example, about the relative allocation of economic resources between capital and labour, between the public and the private sectors, between the national state and the local level. These sorts of historical compromises become reflected and reproduced in the expectations of how firms should act and how and when stakeholders such as the state, customers, suppliers, shareholders, banks etc. should have a right to involvement, participation or consideration in the decisions of the firm even if at specific moments of crisis for particular firms, the terms of this compromise may be re-negotiated.

Institutionalist theorists have implicitly recognised this process. However, in our view, this needs to be recognised explicitly. We label this as the social construction of performance standards to emphasise the point that performance standards are multiple and what occurs is a socially contested process in which various economic actors articulate and negotiate about their goals and interests. 'Success' in world markets (however this in itself may actually be measured) may or may not be high on the agenda that emerges from this process. What is needed therefore is more detailed research on different types of performance measures and how and why they become institutionalised in particular contexts (see Quack and Morgan in this volume for a more extensive discussion).

This is not to deny that certain implications follow according to how performance criteria are constructed and prioritised. Firms can place non-economic performance criteria high on their agenda but maintaining survival in the face of poor economic performance is then likely to be a continuing source of problems, particularly if they are in a sector and national context which is open to outside competitors. However, to re-emphasise the point, contrary to the ideologies of globalisation, not all sectors are in this situation and even where they are, the degree of tight coupling between performance in global markets and firm survival will vary, not least because of the ways in which governments still continue to intervene in an attempt to sustain political goals (see e.g. Weiss 1998; Boyer and Drache 1996). Institutionalist approaches therefore need to develop further down this avenue of research to reveal the ways in which social and political interests become embedded in performance standards (see e.g. the contributions by Morgan and Quack, Salomon and Hancké and Caspar in this book).

4. Links between Firm Performance, Sector Specialisation and National Outcomes

Thirdly, performance relates actors, processes and outcomes at multiple levels of society to each other. It is obvious that there is no simple one-to-one relationship between societal institutions, capabilities and performance profiles developed by companies, and performance outcomes at the company, intermediary (sectoral/regional) or national level. The contributions in this book point to some of these complexities which have been under-estimated by institutionalist approaches so far. The results show that the performance of individual companies depends on a great number of influences, ranging from its managerial and other capabilities to sometimes unforeseeable changes in the business environment. Institutional influences which support or hamper the development of certain competences and capabilities are a necessary but not sufficient condition for the success of individual companies. 'Tight' institutional systems may help to diffuse 'best practice' more rapidly than loose ones so that the average performance is closer to the best in the former. But this does not stop companies in 'loose' institutional systems from being successful in national and world markets; it is just that they are followed by a much longer tail of low performing companies (see the contributions of Deakin et al. and Campagnac et al. in this book).

Furthermore, the success of one particular sector of the economy in world markets can affect other sectors in varying ways and thereby have complex effects on the 'wealth of the nation' as a whole. One obvious example is the way in which the City of London's success as a centre for international financial dealings has arguably been at the expense of its linkages with the manufacturing sector. Hutton, for example, argues that the impact of this goes deep into the social fabric, justifying various sorts of inequalities and social attitudes that inhibit the modernisation of the British economy as a whole (Hutton 1995). Thus success in one sector may be at the expense of other sectors within the same national or regional space, though, as the debate on industrial districts has demonstrated, the process can also work the other way, i.e. the success of one firm or group of firms in world markets can help up-grade other firms (most obviously those in the supply chain, but also those in service-type roles, such as marketing).

Specialisation in specific economic sectors and the development of firms with embedded skills and competences as well as supportive institutional contexts has in general been regarded as necessary for success in national and international markets. There are, however, also examples of how over-specialisation can lead to institutional lock-in of companies, sectors and nations and hamper their ability to adapt to new business environments (see e.g. Weick 1979; Grabher 1993). As has been pointed out by Grabher and Stark (1997), amongst others, heterogeneity of forms of economic coordination within national business systems can become a source of adaptability because it provides the basis for a greater variety of alternative development paths. This is exemplified by Herrigel (1996) who identified the coexistence of two distinctive, but closely interlinked industrial orders as one of the main sources of German industrial power. In contrast, the concentration on a few economic sectors, as well as a strong uncoupling of coexisting economic activities, can become significant obstacles for successful adaptation to changing international business environments (see the contributions of Tainio et al. and Whitley et al. in this book.)

The impact of sector success or failure on 'the wealth of nations' is extremely complex, yet this is of crucial interest and importance to politicians and policy-makers. Success in world markets may depend on reducing labour costs, either directly through shedding workers or indirectly through changing the composition of the workforce towards temporary and/or part-time employment. In terms of its impact on the broader social and economic context, such 'success' may contribute to a growing sense of 'social' failure as unemployment rises, inequalities increase, taxes to fund welfare rise and the impotence of the political system is exposed. And yet, the individual firm which has restructured and relocated is 'successful' from the point of view of shareholder returns. Conversely, government intervention to support employment in a 'failing' firm may 'succeed' in the short-term in maintaining some sort of social peace in society more broadly, whilst storing up longer term problems in terms of financing the state's debt, with consequent impact on interest rates, inflation and firm competitiveness.

It is therefore crucial to identify more specifically the mechanisms which connect the different levels to each other, and to differentiate more clearly between the performance of the individual company and performance outcomes at aggregate levels, such as the sector and the national economy, as well as performance outcomes from the point of view of social and political order. Institutionalist theorists have tended to conflate a number of these levels when, in our view, it is crucial to unravel them and consider their interaction in a more detailed way.

5.   The Contributions in this Book

The studies presented in this book, by considering the key points stated above, seek to contribute to a better understanding of the links between institutional conditions, market competition and performance outcomes. All the chapters are concerned in varying ways with the adaptability of economic actors to changing economic and institutional environments. How do comparative advantages of national sectors and economies change over time, and which institutional settings favour or hinder such changes? The authors in this volume analyse this question from theoretical viewpoints which emphasise the interactions between the strategies and behaviour of economic actors, the forms of economic coordination which emerge between them and the broader societal and institutional environment in which they are embedded. Whereas the neoclassical paradigm assumes that economic actors are sovereign in setting and pursuing their goals, the authors in this book see economic action, and particularly different forms of adaptability to changing business environments, as societally and institutionally enabled or limited. This does not mean that all authors subscribe to the same conception of institutions and economic action: Whereas some of the contributions start from sociologically orientated approaches which have become known as national business systems (Whitley 1992; Whitley and Kristensen 1997) or social systems of production theories (Hollingsworth and Boyer 1997), others try to combine 'transaction cost theory' (Williamson 1975, 1985) with national business system theory, and others again follow a Chandlerian historical approach towards management and business (Chandler 1962, 1990) which — with often contradictory assumptions — is contesting similar terrain as the above mentioned theories. This book does not claim to present a coherent theory of institutions, economic change and performance outcomes. Rather, the contributions were written as an attempt to identify some of the unexplored and underdeveloped questions in this field of research and to present tentative approximations towards a more systematic conceptualisation of these questions. In this sense, the contributions in this book are an invitation to intensify the discourse between adjacent fields in sociology, economics, law, history and political sciences, in order to benefit from each others' advances in the understanding of various aspects of the relations between institutions, economic change and performance outcomes.

Most of the contributions in this book follow a cross-national comparative approach. The chapters provide a rich collection of empirical evidence for the variety of forms of business organisation which developed within Europe, the particular conceptions of how business should be structured and developed in order to be 'successful', and the variety of definitions of what has become considered as 'successful' or 'good performance' in different institutional contexts. These systematic cross-national comparisons provide deepening, and in some instances even surprising, insights into the effects of institutional settings on the capabilities of economic actors to deal successfully with changing economic and institutional environments. Some of the contributions transcend the limits of traditional cross-national comparisons and investigate the linkages and tensions between the role of certain economic actors within their national business system and their position in international alliances, international trade and global markets. They ask whether and to what extent national models of economic organisation and coordination can be successfully exported to international and global arenas, what are the 'rules of the game' in these arenas and what are their repercussions for the position of certain players in their national context.

The volume also goes beyond what has recently been criticised as 'manufacturing bias' and extends the institutional analysis of economic performance to service sectors. The results show that such an encompassing approach puts into question many of the taken-for-granted assumptions about the strength and weaknesses of certain national business systems. The contributions in this book suggest that 'loose' compared to 'tight' institutional systems might favour innovations in specific types of services (Morgan and Quack, in this volume), provide their economic actors with the ability to adapt more quickly to radical changes in their business environment (Lehrer and Darbishire, in this volume) and to compete more successfully in certain international business environments with a low degree of social embeddedness (Campagnac, Lin and Winch, in this volume). Taking on board developments in the expanding service sector, thus, makes visible what Lehrer and Darbishire (in this volume) call 'the need for a micro-foundation of institutional approaches to performance'. The contributions suggest that a given institutional setting can have very different impact on the adaptability of companies and economic actors in different sectors.

The book is organised in four parts. The first part attempts to identify the processes by which institutions and social groupings in different societies shape sectoral adaptation to changing business environments. The second part investigates how the socially constructed meanings of economic actors influence selections between alternative and sometimes conflicting performance goals and how these 'socially' constructed performance standards are affected by internationalisation. The third part comprises studies on the role of national business systems in shaping the performance of corporate actors in globalising markets. The last part analyses how, in specific geopolitical constellations, the institutionally shaped evolution of sector specialisation has contributed to the success of national business systems whereas in other constellations it seriously impeded adaptation to changing world market conditions.

5.1 *Changing Business Environments and National Patterns of Organisational Innovation and Adaptation*

This first part of the book is concerned with the question of how institutions influence national patterns of organisational innovation and adaptation, and how these patterns match with ongoing changes in the business environment of specific groups and clusters of firms. Quack and Morgan, in the first chapter, suggest the sector as a useful starting point for an investigation of economic performance. The authors examine in detail institutional structures within national business systems which shape the emergence and the decline of specific sectors, and thereby contribute to the development of certain types of sector specialisation in different nations. In opposition to neoliberal conceptions of the market as ultimate selection mechanism of 'the fittest', the authors argue that processes of restructuring of sectors within and across national boundaries are more likely to reflect a complex inter-mixing of political, social and economic considerations. The reasons why sectors emerge, are sustained and developed in particular contexts, as well as the reasons why sectors are restructured or even abandoned in other contexts, need to be related to distinctive socially constructed perceptions of what constitutes socially desired types of efficiency and performance of firms and sectors.

The following chapters provide detailed empirical analyses of how different national business systems influence the adaptability of companies — within certain sectors as well as those acting across sectoral boundaries — to changing business environments. Deakin, Lane and Wilkinson investigate the role of supplier relations for successful adjustment in sectors whose market and task environment in the 1980s and 1990s was characterised by gradually increasing competition on both, quality and price. Based on their comparison of the German, British and Italian mining machinery and kitchen furniture industry the authors argue that institutional factors play a significant role in raising the general performance of firms within a sector, even though no direct link can be established to the adoption of particular practices by individual firms and the enhancement of their performance. They conclude that social systems of production with 'thick' and/or 'tightly coupled' institutional settings (such as Germany and the third Italy) raise the general standards of performance for continuous upgrading and incremental innovation, and thereby facilitate adaptation to changing business conditions.

Increasing internationalisation — at least in these traditional industries — has not weakened the distinctiveness of production systems and their comparative advantages in terms of performance outcomes, but has rather served to perpetuate it in only slightly altered forms.

The sectors on which Lehrer and Darbishire report on in their German-British comparison represent an interesting contrast to the above mentioned study. Both, the airline and the telecommunication sector have been faced during the 1980s and 1990s with rapid changes in technology which together with deregulation and new demand patterns altered drastically the nature of competition. In this changed industry environment, the institutional structure in the UK was able to facilitate greater organisational experiments, innovation and radical restructuring whereas German institutions acted as a constraint and inhibited realignment to the new strategic and organisational demands. The authors conclude that under specified types of industry conditions, the dynamic efficiency of Anglo-Saxon firms can be superior to that of firms in Northern Europe's 'coordinated market economies' (Soskice 1999). The explanation is that the UK 'transaction order' facilitates flexibility and learning in industry environments where the required direction of strategic and organisational adaptation is uncertain, and where this change cannot be easily accommodated for by contracts conceding a high level of procedural rights to employees. By contrast, the German 'transaction order' favours flexibility and learning in industry environments where change is gradual, capability-enhancing, and can be accommodated within a framework of strongly codified procedural rights.

The results of these two studies, apparently contradictory in the first instance, in fact demonstrate how different national business systems generate distinct capabilities for adaptation. Whereas some contexts facilitate adjustment to incremental changes, others favour abilities for radical change. The same societal and institutional context, thus, is likely to affect the development of sectors with contrasting task environments differently. The same societal and institutional context might also have distinct effects on the adaptability of the actors in a given sector during periods of relative stability compared to periods of rapid change. For example, it is not yet clear whether the superior adaptability of the British champions in the air transportation and telecommunication sectors will continue to benefit them once that the sector has gone through its current period of turbulence and entered a more stable period of development (though one may doubt when or whether this will happen in the foreseeable future).

Whereas the above mentioned studies are located within well-defined sectoral boundaries, the contribution of Whittington, Mayer and Curto follows a rather different approach. In the centre of their interest is the large multi-business firm which operates across sectoral — and often also national boundaries — and its development during the post-war period in Western Europe. The power and influence of large industrial corporations makes it likely that their strategies and structures, and the related economic performance outcomes, will have a significant impact on the development of sectoral and national economies. Following a Chandlerian approach, the study reveals that corporate strategies and structures have only slight and ambiguous statistical relationships with performance at both corporate and national level. What they find, however, is an increasing spread of diversification in European large firms bringing together increasing amounts of different sectoral activities under the control of common hierarchies of management. The authors see these large multi-business firms as important transmission mechanisms, spreading capital, personnel and management practices across sectors — in analogy to the role of multinationals in transferring these assets between nations. In the future there might be increasing tensions arising from the relative, and growing autonomy of these large multi-business corporations and the institutionally embedded sectors in which these corporations are pursuing their business. According to the authors, the management of these tensions, and learning from experiences at both levels, will be an important source of competitive advantage in the coming decade.

5.2 *Societal Performance Standards and their Internationalisation*

There exist many different ways of measuring, monitoring and judging the performance of organisations in market societies. Different standards of performance emerge within nations and sectors as a result of historical institutional features of industrial development. Standards of performance have to be implemented and enforced by particular social actors, whether those be shareholders, regulators, the government or other categories of stakeholders. Morgan and Quack, in their contribution, suggest the notion of a social structure of performance standards as an analytical tool. This notion refers to both the mechanisms and processes which shape the way in which organisations are judged and the agents who play a central role in this. Following this framework of analysis, the authors compare the emergence, dissemination and changes in dominant performance standards in the British and German banking sector during the post-war period. The results show that until the 1970s, the expectations about what sort of performance was required from banks differed considerably between the two countries. In the German system, there were formal rules about how banks could act laid down by law and enforced by formal and informal agreements between the industry associations and the regulators. In Britain, the rules were informal, dependent on co-operation between the Bank of England and the inner core of City of London organisations. As international financial markets developed, performance standards themselves began also to change. However, the nature of these changes was not to discard entirely the previous system but rather to evolve into a new structure. New balances were being created partly by action at the international level to create standards of regulation that can guard against systemic disorder at this level and partly by the action of regulators and firms at national level.

In the following chapter, Salomon applies and extends this approach to an analysis of recent changes in the performance standards in the French banking system. Within the French state planned economic system of the post-war period, the key performance standards for the actors within the various banking subsectors was first of all conformity to the planning objectives of the state. Since the gradual extension of attempts to create a Single European market beginning in the mid-1980s and the growing internationalisation of financial markets, this highly regulated system has begun to be transformed. The result has been that competing priorities have emerged from different actors following their own interests, often in contradiction with one another, without the state being able to assert a single dominant policy. Tendencies towards standardising performance measures around financial criteria are supported and reinforced by international capital markets as well as the international regulatory regime. However, the local specificity of the French system means that there are multiple other performance criteria which continue to influence the banking sector. Salomon, like Morgan and Quack in the German case, argues that there is a strong element of path dependency in the transformation of social performance standards in the French banking industry. The French state will confront any new problems in the financial sector with a continued preference for intervention in spite of its adherence to deregulation; and the major banks know that one key performance criteria remains their ability to meet the state's objectives, no matter what the preferences of their other stakeholders are.

Whereas the above papers deal with the question of how performance standards defined within different national financial systems are affected by the external influences of internationalisation, the following contribution discusses the diffusion process of standards set at international level into different national business systems. Hancké and Casper analyse how ISO 9000, which is purported to be a universal quality management system, was implemented in very different ways, with very different effects, in the French and German car industry. Despite the fact that this industry can be regarded as a critical case for the argument of convergence, the authors reveal distinct differences in the ways in which ISO 9000 became established in both countries. In Germany, skilled workers took over quality control tasks and re-appropriated them as part of their new job descriptions. In France, on the contrary, those elements of ISO 9000 were given emphasis which fitted and reinforced the hierarchical organisation of the workplaces and the existing division of work between technicians and workers. The study shows that ISO 9000 norms were not really imported from outside into the systems, but that they were truly redefined and re-constructed by the crucial actors within each of the countries to fit their own views of what they could contribute to their industries and production systems.

5.3 National Business Systems and Corporate Performance in Globalising Markets

The chapters in this part are concerned with the changes occuring in the international division of labour and the linkages between national business systems and corporate performance in globalising markets. Forms of economic organisation which are considered as particularly relevant for processes of internationalisation serve as a starting point for this investigation. In the first chapter, Thompson deals with the role of multinational corporations (MNCs) in internationalisation and questions whether the advance of MNC activity has been quite so rapid and widespread as to undermine the functioning of national or local business systems. He uses quantitative data to demonstrate that the economic activity of MNCs is predominantly confined to the larger economic region in which the home country of the MNCs is located. In the aggregate, he concludes that international companies are still predominantly MNCs (with a clear home base to their operations) and not transnational companies (which represent footloose stateless companies). But even then, internationalisation might effect the functioning of national business system through the influence of MNCs as leading corporate actors exerting pressures on national governments. Available case study evidence, reviewed by the same author, however, suggest that MNC's strategies are deeply entrenched in the socio-economic institutional characteristics and cultures of the home countries. In so far as MNCs seek to tap into the advantages offered by particular locations and develop sophisticated networks of specialisation in order to strengthen their overall competitive performance they tend to strengthen the local innovative and business system, rather than undermine it.

Loveridge and Mueller, in their contribution, are concerned with the role of international strategic alliances in the rapid technological and organisational changes which are occurring in the telecommunication sector. Until well into the 1980s, the global telecommunication sector represented a relatively stable inter-organisational network with its vertically ordered roots in the supply of equipment within each national economy. Leading national suppliers were both collaborating and competing in the telecommunication markets that stretched beyond their parent country. Since then, however, the convergence of new technologies has brought about major changes in products, and in the firms supplying the various industrial markets on a global basis. The analysis shows that within major industrialised countries there has been a general acceptance of the market mechanism (e.g. privatisation) in transforming national telecom infrastructures in response to these exogenous changes. At the same time, the results demonstrate how problem formulation, agenda setting, and implementation of an appropriate policy response have been still largely shaped by domestic stakeholders and ruling coalitions in the national context, resulting in nationally divergent modes of deregulation. Loveridge and Mueller, like other authors in this volume, emphasise the tensions arising for the leading corporate actors from acting in different, and only partly overlapping national and international arenas with distinct rule systems. Managers in large telecommunication companies are increasingly confronted with discrepancies between their own strategic goals, the demands directed towards them by national actors (e.g. governments) and the expectations to which they are exposed from foreign partners in international alliances and joint ventures. As a result, the authors see an increasing erosion of normative boundaries and subscribe an increasingly important role to the corporate actor as creators of new identities within changed sectoral boundaries.

The study of Campagnac, Lin and Winch reinforces the impression created by the previous contributions that the inter-linking between national and international structures of economic coordination are rather intricate and far from following a simple direction of replacing the former by the latter. Studying the performance of French and British companies in the international construction sector — a sector in which goods and services are otherwise largely produced and traded domestically — the authors identify two different models of organisation which developed within the French and British context: the industrial model in France and the professional model in Britain. On the one hand, their analysis shows that very different models of organisation with distinctive competitive advantages can achieve similar levels of performance in different subsegments of international markets. Globalisation is not, therefore, an homogenising process, but a dynamic interplay of distinctive competitive advantages, derived from different national models of organisation. On the other hand, the results indicate that the capacities developed in a specific national context cannot always be transferred easily to international markets. Professional governance, even though being a weak trust mechanism, can nevertheless generate a major source of competitive advantage in certain subsegments of global markets, particularly in services where the model of organisation itself has to be exported to the point of consumption by the buyer. The authors conclude that corporate actors originating from 'tight' business systems might have competitive advantages in world trade in markets for finished goods and services such as the provision and operation of urban services, whereas those with a home base in 'loose' institutional systems could have more of an advantage in other service and intermediate goods sectors.

5.4 *Institutional Legacies and Performance Outcomes in National Business Systems*

The last section consists of longitudinal studies of the emergence of sector specialisation and the impact of these historical legacies on the further development of national business systems. The papers in this section refer to national economies in Europe that developed a distinctive sector specialisation which, faced with increasing world market competition, generated specific opportunities and constraints. Van Iterson explores the history of the Dutch business system and shows how the socio-institutional context has favoured a sector specialisation in elementary but highly modernised activities such as the processing industries, transport, distribution and financial services. Origins for this specific sector formation can be found in the divergent path and — compared to the UK — retarded evolution of industrialisation in the Netherlands. Another characteristic of the Dutch business system is that within these sectors a few large public limited companies, often with considerable multinational activities, shape the national image. The author shows that the success of these companies in an open world economy is, among other factors, related to the capability to build consensus across heterogeneous management teams and thereby combine the advantages of efficiency and effectiveness. Again, this capacity can be traced back to the formation of collective actors competing about social and economic space in modern Dutch organisations. The limited role of governmental and financial institutions in industrial development, according to the author, underlines the significant role that traditional rules of action and governance principles have played in the development of the modern business system. The consensual rules of action and the stakeholders' concept of business, however, have changed with the social groups which have expressed themselves through these structures at later stages of the historical development. In this sense, the emergence of national business systems and their performance outcomes can be traced back to earlier historical configurations without assuming deterministic path dependencies.

Whereas in the Dutch case, social relations and the formation of social groups were identified as important, the following contribution underlines how international political and power relations can shape the directions of sector specialisation and economic development of nations. Tainio, Pohjola and Lilja analyse how structural problems in the Finnish economy, and its vulnerability in the early 1990s, can be traced back to the post-war institutional setting which originated from Finland's uncertain political position between the Eastern and Western power blocks. After World War II, the desire for national unity and independence led to a foreign policy driven economic system based on state-led large long-term investment in heavy industries combined with internal cartellisation, protection from foreign competition and strong reliance on stable and planned demand markets in the Soviet Union. Even though politically successful, this strategy had far-reaching economic consequences. What was a successful expansion strategy and made Finland the 'Japan of the North' in the 1980s, resulted in severe problems for the Finnish economy in the 1990s. The Finnish economy and institutions had gradually become locked-in to a centralised, policy-led mode of economic coordination which after the breakdown of the Eastern Bloc no longer fitted with the emerging new global political and economic configuration. The Finnish case, thus, provides an example of how political power relations can favour a distinct sector specialisation that then generates structural inertia and hinders the development of new managerial capabilities required for new economic and political realities.

Historical legacies are also an important factor in explaining the economic success and failure of Eastern and Middle European transformation economies as Whitley, Jaklic and Hocevar show in their contribution. The high level of political and economic decentralisation in Slovenia coupled with substantial exposure to Western markets and a dominant role in the domestic market have led to the development of a considerable number of autonomous and competitive firms in this country. These firms have been able to introduce new products and processes in rather narrow market segments without radical changes in the macro- or micro-economic context. The legacies of Yugoslav late state socialism, however, enable also a continuity between old economic and new political elites which contributed significantly to the stability of the institutional context, and thereby to the success of the Slovene economy. The conditions for this success, however, might constrain the development of new capabilities necessary to deal with current environmental shifts. The idiosyncrasies of the Slovene region during the pre-Yugoslav period, with agrarian communities existing largely isolated from each other, have resulted in a particular economy which combines considerable cooperation between workers and managers within specialised firms with adversarial connections between business firms. The difficulties that many Slovene firms have in developing cooperative relations with business partners other than employees might well lead to a lock-in if firms do not develop more inter-firm cooperation in the fields of research, development and distribution which will be necessary to gain access to new market segments.

In sum, the processes leading to performance outcomes of nations, and changes in these outcomes are, as the contributions in this part suggest, complex and often idiosyncractic. The emergence and development of certain patterns of economic coordination which contribute to the success and failure of national economies can be traced back to past contellations in social group formation, institutional structures, national and international power relationships — but these legacies are not deterministic in the sense that one could have foreseen what the future development would have been.

5.5 *Conclusions of the Book*

The contributions in this volume subscribe to a view which perceives institutions as crucial to the long-term performance of sectoral and national economies. The results demonstrate how social institutions which have evolved over long periods give rise to distinct patterns of firm competences and capabilities with consequent effects for their own economic performance, the performance of their sector, and that of their home nation state. The directions of economic development of different sectoral and national business systems are thus dependent on historically evolved institutional legacies. Individual companies may be able to choose different paths of development, but for the actors of a system as a whole, it is — apart from exceptional historical constellations such as war, revolution or changes in international power balances — very difficult to achieve a "paradigm shift" to alternative institutional trajectories towards economic performance.

The chapters in this volume, however, cast severe doubts on the accuracy of earlier institutional accounts which tended to contrast the 'failings' of Anglo-American capitalism with the 'successes' of coordinated capitalism. The results presented here suggest that these conclusions were based on an over-generalisation of findings from certain manufacturing sectors, and that a more complex picture will emerge when the focus is shifted to other manufacturing sectors and service industries. The contributions in this volume show that in some circumstances 'loose' (as opposed to 'tight') institutional systems might provide a more appropriate base for specific forms of technical, organisational and product innovation. The studies show that this seems to be particularly the case in those sectors which are currently undergoing radical changes and increasing internationalisation. There are also indications that forms of economic coordination which developed within 'loose' institutional systems might be more easily exported to world markets than those originating from 'tight' systems.

The results furthermore indicate that the role of corporate actors in reproducing and transcending national business systems has been misperceived by both neoliberal and institutional accounts. The contributions in this volume paint a more differentiated picture of large multi-business and multi-national companies. They are both still tethered to the institutional basis of their home country or region, and yet also capable of going beyond that basis by explicitly seeking to reap benefits from other institutional contexts. Several chapters in this book argue that the management of tensions and contradictions arising for corporate actors from operating in multiple national and international business environments with different 'rules of the game' might become increasingly important for the performance of individual companies, and aggregate performance outcomes at the sectoral and national level.

The chapters in this book provide numerous examples which contradict the neoliberal version of performance measures and selection processes just being a matter of the market. They show that performance is a relative concept in so far as economic goal setting and the perceptions of what is considered as desirable economic coordination reflect the objectives of the various social actors involved in the economic coordination of a certain firm, sector or national business system. As economic activity becomes increasingly internationalised, the contest about competing and conflicting performance standards becomes transnational. Whereas some contributors see this internationalisation resulting in a dominance of objectives of corporate survival at the expense of wider communitarian goals, other authors expect that the phenomenon of path dependency will lead pure market criteria of corporate survival to become combined with socially embedded performance standards at the national and sectoral level.

The globalisation of economic activity, by creating new and complex divisions of labour between economic actors originating from different national business systems, generates pressures for standardisation and homogenisation, but it also reinforces existing specialisations in economic activity, goal setting and related perceptions of desired performance outcomes which continue to be linked to different institutional legacies and structures. Globalisation, thus, needs to be understood as a dynamic interplay of distinctive competitive advantages, derived from different national models of organisation. The question is not whether there is convergence or diversity, but how these contrasting tendencies become articulated in specific locations at specific times, and how their performance implications feed back into more long-term processes of institutional change at the national and international level.

Overall, the contributions in this book show that the rejection of the neo-liberal model with its emphasis on convergence and its replacement by the idea of 'varieties of capitalism' is not in itself sufficient to understand the dynamics of modern economies. The next crucial step in the evolution of the institutionalist approach requires more sustained attention to the social construction, development and evolution of performance criteria since by definition these act as the mechanisms through which societies, firms and individuals monitor and change what they are doing. It also requires a more detailed attention to the way in which the international economic context evolves and 'rewards' or 'punishes' specific types of firms with specific effects in national institutional contexts. The studies in this book represent only a first step and will hopefully stimulate further research in this direction.

References

Berger, S. and R. Dore (eds.). 1996. *National Diversity and Global Capitalism*. Cornell: Cornell University Press.

Boyer, R. and D. Drache. 1996. *States against Markets: the limits of globalization*. London: Routledge.

Chandler, A. D. 1962. *Strategy and Structure: Chapters in the History of American Industrial Enterprise*. Cambridge: MIT Press.

Chandler, A. D. 1990. *Scale and Scope: the Dynamics of Industrial Capitalism*. Cambridge, Mass: Harvard University Press.

Crouch, C. and W. Streeck (eds.). 1997. *Political Economy of Modern Capitalism*. London: Sage.

Delbridge, R. and J. Lowe (eds.). 1998. *Manufacturing in Transition*. London: Routledge.

Djelic, M.-L. 1998. *Exporting the American Model. The Postwar Transformation of European Business*. Oxford: Oxford University Press.

Esping Andersen, G. (ed.). 1997. *Welfare States in Transition*. London: Sage.

Grabher, G. (ed.). 1993. *The Embedded Firm: On The Socioeconomics of Industrial Networks*. London: Routledge.

Grabher, G. and D. Stark (eds.). 1997. *Restructuring Networks in Post-Socialism. Legacies, Linkages, and Localities*. Oxford: Oxford University Press.

Herrigel, G. 1996. *Industrial constructions: The sources of German industrial power*. Cambridge: Cambridge University Press.

Hirst, P. Q. and G. F. Thompson. 1996. *Globalization in Question: The International Economy and the Possibilities of Governance*. Cambridge: Polity Press.

Hollingsworth, J. R., P. C. Schmitter and W. Streeck (eds.). 1994. *Governing Capitalist Economies. Performance and Control of Economic Sectors*. Oxford: Oxford University Press.

Hollingsworth, J. R. and R. Boyer (eds.). 1997. *Contemporary Capitalism. The Embeddedness of Institutions*. Cambridge: Cambridge University Press.

Hutton, W. 1995. *The State We're in*. London: Jonathan Cape.

Kitschelt, H. 1991. Industrial Governance Structures, *International Organization* 45(4): 453–93.

Lane, C. 1995. *Industry and Society in Europe*. Aldershot: Edward Elgar.

Lazonick, W. 1991. *Business Organization and the Myth of the Market Economy*. Cambridge: Cambridge University Press.

Meyer, M. W. 1994. Measuring Performance in Economic Organizations. In: N. Smelser and R. Swedberg (eds.), *The Handbook of Economic Sociology*, 556–80. New York: Princeton University Press.

Meyer, M. W. and L. G. Zucker. 1989. *Permanently Failing Organizations*. London: Sage.

Morgan, G. 1997. The Global Context of Financial Services: National Systems and the International Political Economy. In: G. Morgan and D. Knights (eds.), *Regulation and Deregulation in European Financial Services,* 14–41. London: Macmillan.

Porter, M. E. 1990. *The Competitive Advantage of Nations*. New York: Free Press.

Power, M. 1994. The audit society. In: Hopwood, A. G. and P. Miller (eds.), *Accounting as social and institutional practice*, 299–318. Cambridge: Cambridge University Press.

Smith, A. 1937. *An Inquiry into the Nature and Causes of the Wealth of Nations.* New York: Modern Library.

Schienstock, G. 1997. The Transformation of Regional Governance: Institutional Lock-ins and the Development of Lean Production in Baden-Württemberg. In: Whitley, R. and P. H. Kristensen (eds.), *Governance at Work: The Social Regulation of Economic Relations,* 190–208. Oxford: Oxford University Press.

Sorge, A. 1991. Strategical Fit and Societal Effect: Interpreting Cross-National Comparisons of Technology, Organization and Human Resources, *Organization Studies* 12(2): 161–190.

Soskice, D. 1999. Divergent Production Regimes: Coordinated and Uncoordinated Market Economies in the 1980s and 1990s. In H. Kitschelt, P. Lange, G. Marks, J. D. Stephens (eds.), *Continuity and Change in Contemporary Capitalism,* 101–134. Cambridge: Cambridge University Press.

Streeck, W. 1992. *Social Institutions and Economic Performance. Studies of Industrial Relations in Advanced Capitalist Economies.* London: Sage.

Streeck, W. 1997. German Capitalism: Does it Exist? Can it Survive? In: C. Crouch and W. Streeck (eds.), *Political Economy of Modern Capitalism,* 33–54. London: Sage.

Weick, K. E. 1979. *The Social Psychology of Organizing.* Reading: Addison-Wesley.

Weiss, L. 1998. *The Myth of the Powerless State: Governing the Economy in a Global Era.* Oxford: Polity Press.

Whitley, R. (ed.). 1992. *European Business Systems. Firms and Markets in their National Contexts.* London: Sage.

Whitley, R. 1999. *Divergent Capitalisms: The Social Structuring and Change of Business Systems.* Oxford: Oxford University Press.

Whitley, R. and P. H. Kristensen (eds.). 1996. *The Changing European Firm. Limits to Convergence.* London: Routledge.

Whitley, R. and P. H. Kristensen (eds.). 1997. *Governance at Work: The Social Regulation of Economic Relations.* Oxford: Oxford University Press.

Williamson, O. E. 1975. *Markets and Hierarchies: Analysis and Anti-Trust Implications.* New York: Free Press.

Williamson, O. E. 1985. *The Economic Institutions of Capitalism.* New York: Free Press.

PART II

Changing Business Environments
and National Patterns of Organisational
Innovation and Adaptation

CHAPTER 2

Institutions, Sector Specialisation and Economic Performance Outcomes[*]

Sigrid Quack   Glenn Morgan

1. Introduction

In this chapter, the sector is suggested as a useful starting point for an investigation of economic performance. Various authors have identified the sector as an important arena in which social and economic actors coordinate, co-operate and compete with each other within the national and international sphere (Porter 1990; Hollingsworth et al. 1994). The literature, however, has rarely addressed directly the issue of how institutions shape the evolution of and changes in the sector portfolios that constitute different national business systems. The sector will be understood here as a historical formation of complementary, interlinked and co-evolving economic activities of business organisations which produce a range of similar or related products and services, together with those who regularly transact with them in supplying, servicing, regulatory or customer roles (see e.g. Räsänen and Whipp 1992).

There are several reasons why sector specialisation provides a useful starting point for the analysis of the relationship between national institutions, global competition and economic performance. The emergence, evolution and decline of distinct forms of sector specialisation can, on the one hand, exemplify how national institutions shape over time collective capabilities and specific business recipes of companies in different national contexts, and thereby influence performance outcomes of sectoral and national economies. On the other hand, the sector provides a scene to study how economic actors are involved in the definition and re-definition of rules of business conduct and performance expectations which over time become engraved in the particular structures of competition and coordination. Finally, sectors have been drawn to a different extent and at

* We would like to thank Dorothee Bohle, Jacqueline O'Reilly, Dieter Plehwe, Arndt Sorge and Richard Whitley for their helpful comments on an earlier version of this chapter.

different times into international markets. Thus the development of sector specialisation can exemplify how global competition feeds back into the economic organisation and performance of national business systems.

The chapter falls into three sections. We first review arguments about the relationship between the structural characteristics of national business systems and sector specialisation. In the following section, we move from the structural to the processual level and consider sector specialisation as an emergent process, e.g. how sectors emerge historically and how existing sectors adapt, transform or decline in response to changing business environments. In the last part, we ask what is the driving force behind processes of sector restructuring. We examine critically the notion of 'market performance' as selection criteria and suggest that performance depends on a more complex set of economic, social and political factors.

2. National Institutions and Sector Specialisation

The literature on 'national business systems' (Whitley 1994; Whitley and Kristensen 1996, 1997) and 'varieties of capitalism' (Hollingsworth et al. 1994; Berger and Dore 1996; Hollingsworth and Boyer 1997) demonstrates how national institutions influence business organisation and economic coordination in different countries in distinct ways. The results of this literature are in line with earlier work by researchers related to the Aix-school (Maurice et al. 1980, 1986; Sorge 1991; for a recent review of the approach see Maurice and Sorge 1999) indicating that business organisations tend to concentrate on certain economic activities which have a close fit with their societal environment. This 'closeness of fit' argument can be applied to the relationship between institutions and sector specialisation in two directions: Firstly, it can be shown that the societal context provides an envelope of opportunities and constraints which tends to influence the development of capabilities and competencies of firms. Capabilities and competences of firms are here understood as sets of organisationally specific experiences, knowledge and expertise that enables them to carry out particular economic activities. Correspondence between firms' capabilities on the one hand and technological and organisational task requirements in certain industries and market segments on the other hand, then, can explain why firms in one country tend to cluster in certain sectors whereas in other countries they do so in other sectors. Secondly, it has also been shown that different societal contexts have distinct affinities to the social and political formation of collective actors which often play an important role in the institutionalisation of sectors. In the following, we examine how national systems of finance and innovation, labour market institutions, demand conditions and the role of intermediate/sectoral institutions correspond to distinct patterns of sector specialisation.

2.1 *Financial Systems and Sector Specialisation*

Several studies have underlined the impact of national systems of finance and corporate governance on the time horizon of companies' investment and commitment of their resources to particular activities (Zysman 1983; Hutton 1995; Vitols 1997). Since the 1970s, the management of companies in Anglo-Saxon countries has, as a result of strong and liquid capital markets, become increasingly subject to strong pressures of outside stakeholders. These are mainly shareholders and institutional investors controlling dispersed share ownership which are predominantly interested in liquidity and short-term dividend growth (Lazonick and O'Sullivan 1996). In other European countries, the availability of long-term bank-based and/or state-controlled finance and considerable family and/or state ownership in companies, together with relative protection from hostile take-over through small or legally restricted markets for corporate governance, means that the management of companies can develop and pursue more long-term goals and strategies. Even though the interests and goals of the various stakeholder groups can vary widely in the latter systems, they tend to converge more easily towards medium- and long-term returns.

Since the 1970s, the increasing pressures for liquidity in Anglo-Saxon market-based financial systems have favoured mass production strategies which focus on short-term cost reduction and can be organised with large numbers of semi-skilled workers (Lane 1995; Porter 1990). Furthermore, it has been argued that the focus of Anglo-Saxon countries on short-term returns encourages the commitment of resources to activities which have low entry and exit costs (Whitley 1994) whereas it limits their readiness to invest in company specific R&D activities (Lazonick 1991; Whitley 1999). In contrast, the more long-term incentives of bank-based or state administered financial systems in continental European market economies have been related to their stronger commitment to capital-intensive industries (Whitley 1994). This context also favours flexible production strategies which focus on improvements in product and process quality. It facilitates the emergence of sectors which require long-term investment in company internal R&D and the development of company specific human resources (Sorge 1991; Streeck 1992). More recent studies, however, indicate that the links between financial systems and sector specialisation might be more complex. Service activities which are organised on a project basis, as is, for example, often the case in finance and construction, seem to flourish more easily under the 'time bound' investment rules of Anglo-Saxon countries than in continental European countries (Christopherson 1998; Campagnac et al. in this volume). Market-based financial systems seem also be more beneficial to the establishment of newly emerging firms in high-tech sectors with high uncertainty than bank-based systems (see Vitols 1995 for a comparison of Great Britain and Germany).

2.2 *Labour Market Institutions and Sector Specialisation*

Various studies have shown links between labour market institutions, such as the system of training and education and the industrial relations system, and competitive strategies of companies from different countries (Maurice et al. 1980; Lane 1989; Whitley and Kristensen 1997). The success of German manufacturing sectors following flexible specialisation and diversified quality production strategies in the 1970s and 1980s, for example, has been regarded as closely related to the high level of qualification and polyvalent skill profile of their labour force (Sorge 1991; Streeck 1992). The limited success of these production strategies in the corresponding British and French sectors can — among other factors — be attributed to the fact that the societal pattern of organising human resources did not fit to the same extent to the task requirements inherent in these productions patterns as the German one (Sorge 1991). The concentration on competitive advantage in manufacturing, however, has as Christopherson (1998) argues, led to a neglect of aspects of training and employment policies which influence sector specialisation in the service sector. The strength of financial and legal services in the US reflects, among other factors, the specific organisation of the educational system which generates a large number of highly qualified professionals who carry their skills with them on an individual basis from project to project (see Porter 1990 for a similar statement with regard to the basis of success of the British finance industry).

National and labour market institutions also matter with regard to the ways in which companies make use of their employees' skills and seek their active participation in product and process development. Together with the industrial relations systems they influence how collective learning processes and innovation can be organised at the company and at the sectoral level. Employers associations and unions acting as 'discursive institutions' at the sectoral level can help to overcome what Sabel (1994) has called the 'dilemma of economic development'. A continued dialogue between corporate actors and interest organisations can help them to elaborate a new common understanding of changes in their environment. The presence of strong intermediate organisations, however, can make radical change also more difficult, exactly due to the need for extensive negotiations. This might be particularly the case when the transformation has a strong distributive element (see Lehrer and Darbishire in this volume).

2.3 *Demand Conditions and Sector Specialisation*

A further factor which influences sector specialisation, but has not received much attention in the institutional literature, is the role of demand conditions and vertical relationships among industries in stimulating sector specialisation. These factors have been assigned particular attention in Porter's (1990) work on the competitive advantage of nations. He shows that not only the size of the home market, but also the composition and pattern of growth of national demand influences sector specialisation. Demand patterns are related to specific geographic and climatic conditions (e.g. the Swiss tunnelling or the US heavy truck industry), social, political and legislative considerations (e.g. the environmental industries in Sweden and Denmark, and the low level of regulation in the City of London), and cultural conditions (e.g. the Italian textile and garment sector, and the Japanese focus on compact and multifunctional consumer electronics). Similarly, demand patterns interconnect developments in supplier and related industries. Demand patterns in Porter's view contribute not only to competitive advantage through economies of scale (e.g. size of the US American market), but also through pressures to upgrade products and improve productivity of production processes over time. National demand patterns which turn out to anticipate a broader shift of demand in international markets, can generate an important comparative advantage for the companies which are located in this country. The absence of such demand, on the other hand, can hinder the development of internationally successful sectors. According to Sorge (1991: 178) this was exactly what happened in the French machine tool industry which — despite having the necessary capabilities — could not fully exploit the comparative advantages of flexible specialisation because their customers continued to order products along the more standardised lines.

Financial systems, labour market institutions and demand factors together can explain quite well the differences in sector specialisation which have been observed between different industrialised countries (see Porter 1990; Kitschelt 1991). In both the US and UK, manufacturing tends to concentrate on large-scale production of consumer goods, and within the service sector, industries such as finance, legal advice, media and entertainment, etc. are strongly developed. The German institutional context, in contrast, has led to the flourishing of many specialised manufacturing equipment industries which focus on the high-quality end of the market, whilst the Japanese economy developed strength in consumer electronics. Within certain sectors, companies from Anglo-Saxon countries tend to focus more on the lower price end, whereas German firms tend to cover the more customised demand and Japanese firms combine low-cost with high-quality aspects.

2.4 *Institutions, Innovation and Sector Specialisation*

A number of authors have underlined the importance of innovation for sustained success of companies and sectors in international competition (Nelson and Winter

1982; Porter 1990; Lazonick 1991). This applies not only to technological but also to organisational innovation. The impact of national institutional systems on technological innovation has been analysed in detail in the economic literature on 'national innovation systems' which cannot be referred to here in length (see e.g. Lundvall 1992; Nelson 1993; Storper 1996). The results indicate that institutions are of particular significance with regard to the rapid appropriation of knowledge, the organisation of collective learning and the management of uncertainties throughout the innovation process.

In general, institutional contexts which encourage collective investment in knowledge generation and use, both within and between firms, have been regarded as more likely to lead to stronger innovation than those that reproduce adversarial and spot market type relationships between economic actors. This argument, however, cannot explain the innovativeness of certain manufacturing sectors such as the computer and software industry in the US, and certain service sectors such as financial and legal services in both the US and UK context. It seems more appropriate to perceive of liberal market economies as not impeding innovation as such, but favouring certain types of innovation over others. This leads to the need to differentiate the impact of national business systems according to different types of technology (see e.g. Kitschelt 1991) and types of innovation (see e.g. Langlois and Robertson 1995). Sectors are likely to vary with regard to the level of complexity, the tightness of coupling, and the uncertainty involved in the innovation process (the latter, for example, leading to decentralised networks of innovation in sectors with high uncertainty such as gene technology). It also matters whether innovations depend on the development of company resources, or can be achieved through the integration of advances in basic research and science undertaken in universities or research centres outside of the firm. Whereas in some sectors large industrial and services firms might be the nexus of innovation, in others innovation will be brought about through a high rate of new entrepreneurial firm creation (Porter 1990; Whitley 1999).

Liberal market economies, for example, provide a range of incentives to entrepreneurs seeking to establish new companies (including substantial amounts of venture capital). These features, together with a high degree of employee mobility, are likely to favour the type of radical product and organisational innovation which is characteristic of industries and services which have developed a certain strength in the US and/or UK (Christopherson 1998; Hall 1997; Soskice 1997). In contrast, the long-termism inherent in the financial system and employment relationships in co-ordinated market economies favours strategies of incremental process and product innovation that build on the development of company internal resources (see e.g. Deakin et al. in this volume). The latter systems can mitigate against radical innovation. For example, it can be difficult to recruit experts from outside the firm or to change rapidly the skill profile of the employees. The limitation of CEOs by boards, works councils, etc. raises more problems for radical organisational innovation to be implemented than in Anglo-Saxon systems (Lehrer and Darbishire in this volume).

2.5 Variations in the Institutionalisation of Sectors

According to Hollingsworth et al. (1994: 9) there are two different sources for the historical development of sectors: Sectors can emerge from below through the independent interaction and cooperation between companies and their trading partners. Sectors can also be created from above through the imposition of boundaries and rules by public authorities. Between these two extremes, however, there is also the possibility of strong intermediate sectoral institutions (such as employers' associations, workers' unions, professional bodies, sector specific training institutions and research institutes) to evolve which provide a social fabric in which actors can develop a strong sectoral identity (Räsänen and Whipp 1992). Thus, a line can be drawn from the institutional context and historical processes of group formation to the degree and forms of sector specialisation in different societies. An institutional context that constitutes firms as isolated and self-sufficient actors, and in which the state refrains from direct intervention, as in the case of the UK, for example, is unlikely to generate a strong inter-sectoral specialisation with deep intra-sectoral clustering. In contrast, an institutional context which favours long-term, reciprocal obligations between firms and the evolution of intermediary organisations which take part in the co-ordination of flows and strategies will contribute to the emergence of strong and deeply clustered sectors such as in Germany. Finally, there are those countries, in which the state takes a strong interventionist role in the economic process (e.g. France and South Korea). In this case, the state tends to sponsor a small number of large companies with whom it has close relations.

   This leads to the general point that sectoral identities and members vary in their institutionalisation across national contexts. The structure of sectors varies both within and across countries along a range of dimensions. Table 1 provides one conceptualisation of this variety based on studies reported in Whitley and Kristensen (1996, 1997). It distinguishes between economies in which there are a large number of sectors in operation and those characterised by a few dominant sectors. It also distinguishes between those societies in which most sectors tend to be dominated by large firms and those in which sectors show a higher degree of variation in firm size and patterns of interaction.

   Differences in the structure and institutionalisation of sectors are likely to influence the nature of sector adaptation and innovation in response to new technology and globalising markets. Whereas in some techno-organisational task environments the dominance of a few large companies might facilitate the

Table 1: *Sector Specialisation and Organisation*

Characteristics of the Economy as a whole	Characteristics of Sectors	
	Small number of large firms	Highly integrated complex of firms
Large number of sectors	France	Germany
Small number of sectors	Finland	Denmark

accumulation and application of new knowledge, entrepreneurial activity of small companies can be more appropriate for innovation in other task environments. Faced with changing technological and organisational paradigms, large companies might become caught in their own routines and inertia while the innovations achieved by entrepreneurial firms can lead to a complete redefinition of sectoral identities and boundaries. This is exemplified by the changes occurring over the last decades in the computer industry. The structural evolution in this sector (as described by Malerba and Orsenigo 1996) also highlights that the role of actors other than firms (such as universities and research laboratories, the government, financial institutions, suppliers and consumers) undergoes significant changes over time, and that country differences in structural evolution lead to distinctive performance outcomes.

Sectors dominated by large companies are also more likely to be drawn to a greater extent into international markets and vice versa. The experiences and actions of large companies which are operating in national and international markets, and are often also combining a wide range of different business activities, are likely to feed back not only into the organisation and performance of national sectors (see Loveridge et al. and Whittington et al. in this volume) but also to reshape sectoral boundaries. Sectors, thus, do not have a once and for ever fixed shape but are rather fluid entities with changing identities over time.

3.   Sector Specialisation as an Emergent Process

The previous discussion illustrated the relationship between the structural characteristics of national business systems and sector specialisation. The institutional environment provides an envelope of constraints and incentives but within them there is a variety of solutions possible. This raises the necessity of shifting from the structural level to the processual level in which one examines the ways in which certain opportunities for sectoral development are or are not taken. From this vantage point, the different economic actors with their strategies, goals and actions are the starting point of analysis to see how a) sectors emerge historically,

b) adapt to changing business and market environment, and c) the role socially constructed performance standards play in this process.

In order to explain why specific sectors emerge in certain countries while other fail to develop we need to refer to historical macro-variables such as the timing of industrialisation and pre-existing social and political institutions. These national conditions supported and constrained learning processes of specific new sectoral capabilities and governance structures. It would be, however, a misconception to believe that the historical emergence of specific national sectors occurred independently from developments in other countries and the power relations between different nations (see e.g. Gerschenkron 1962). Whereas in some countries the evolution of specific sectors may have been largely insulated from events in other parts of the world, in other countries it clearly was not. The account of Van Iterson (in this volume), for example, demonstrates how the evolution of specific sectors in Netherlands was from the beginning linked to the integration of the country's largest companies in the world economy (see also Morgan 1998 for an account of the impact of the Colonial past on the emergence of specific sectors in Britain).

In many cases sectors have evolved around new basic technologies which had a certain fit to pre-existing national institutions and governance structures. Kitschelt (1991), for example, argues that countries seize their opportunities in new technologies primarily at junctures when national institutional endowments permit the development of efficient sectoral governance structures matched to the properties of the newly emerging technology. The British market-oriented society with its weak state, for example, could seize most energetically the opportunities offered by loosely coupled technologies emerging in the First Industrial Revolution whereas national economies in which the state was more strongly involved in industrial development provided more appropriate governance structures for the development of sectors with tightly coupled technologies requiring high investments (see e.g. the emergence of certain heavy industries and the chemical industry in Germany).

Business historians such as Gerschenkron (1962), Landes (1969), and more recently, Lazonick (1991) have also directed attention to how the emergence of and shifts in the relative importance of leading sectors have contributed to the rise and decline of national economies such as those of Britain, the US, Germany and Japan over the last two centuries. These authors, however, rather than focusing on technology as such, give more weight to the impact of national institutions on the development of specific organisational and managerial capabilities which became the basis for 'success' and 'failure' in specific economic sectors. In Germany, financial and educational institutions, as well as the involvement of the state, favoured the development of new science-based industries during the Second Industrial Revolution which required a more sophisticated managerial control of high-throughput processes. In contrast, the backwardness of the old industries in Britain retarded the development of appropriate institutions, and the persistence of family control and the rigidities of British class structure thwarted the development of organisational capabilities required for success in these new sectors.

Once sectors have come into being, the further development of their capabilities is often regarded as following path dependencies. With North (1990) path dependence can be defined as "a way to narrow conceptually the choice set and link decision making through time. It is not a story of inevitability in which the past neatly predicts the future." (North 1990: 98f). This means that the institutional factors outlined above plus internal routines which firms and organisations have established within the possibilities and constraints of their institutional framework will influence the type, speed and direction of change processes in which companies engage. For most of the time, learning and innovation will be of an incremental nature directed by institutional legacies and organisational routines. There is, however, some disagreement between different authors about how narrowly this corridor is defined by the institutional environment and how much autonomy individual firms and sectoral actors have to break out of existing organisational routines and to engage in 'revolutionary' (un-)learning. Very roughly, three approaches towards path dependency can be distinguished: a coherent, a dialectic and an experimental view.

In the *coherent version of path dependency* it is assumed that adaptation strategies of companies in a given sector take nationally distinct directions because, as a result of their institutional and societal context, they will develop different problem definitions, draw on distinct resources to manage the change process and are part of a nationally distinct logic to negotiate changes. This version of path dependency emphasises continuity and stability. The corridor which defines possible alternative developments is rather small. Change occurs merely through incremental learning and innovation. Only on rare occasions will industrial innovation sharply diverge from the path-dependent learning of institutional governance structures in new technology sectors. Economic depression, victory or loss in a major war, or a fundamental change in a country's position in the international system can serve as catalyst of a 'paradigm shift' yielding new technological trajectories and governance structures (see e.g. Kitschelt 1991).

The *dialectic approach towards path dependence* considers to a larger extent the variety, contradictions and tensions inherent to national business systems. It follows that the institutional and societal context gives shape to the basic patterns of companies' strategies, but does not determine them in detail. Companies have to some degree a choice which elements of their institutional environment they will enact in order to develop new strategies to cope with changes in their environment. The variety of institutionally supported forms of economic organisation within a national business system, thus, becomes an important resource for the ability of companies to adapt and innovate. Elements for such an analysis can be found in the work of Sorge (1991) who has suggested that business strategies and organisational/human resource patterns are enacted from a wider range of distinct and contrasting elements, and that the success of business strategies might lie in their

> "ability to combine, albeit selectively, distinct alternatives. Such alternatives to be combined may be, for instance, cost leadership and differentiation of the product range, production efficiency and product quality, (…) economies of scale and scope, (…)." (Sorge 1991: 184).

Herrigel's (1996) analysis of German industrial power as based on the evolving interactions between two competing industrial orders provides another example of such a dialectical approach towards path dependencies.

The *experimental view of path dependency* is quite common in evolutionary economics. In the tradition of Schumpter's concept of innovation as 'carrying out new combinations', various scholars have underlined the uncertainties which companies face when they have either to adapt existing or to develop new strategies. Some choices may be better than others, but no choice is clearly best ex ante. A diversity of responses of firms is regarded as good, since they explore the potential range of possible answers. Over the long run, competition would promote firms which chose well on the average and eliminate firms which consistently make mistakes. "In this view, the market system is (in part) a device for conducting and evaluating experiments in economic behaviour and organisation" (Nelson and Winter 1982: 277). This view highlights that diversity and pluralism of economic forms are a precondition for successful adaptation, innovation and selection. It points to the often unpredictable directions which sector specialisation takes as a result of complex interactions between national institutions, global markets and organisational choices.

Underlying these different versions of path dependency are not only distinct views of how much autonomy firms have to choose and experiment with alternative elements of organisational, human resource and product market strategies. These views also differ with respect to how much variety is allowed for within a national business system. Obviously, not all the firms within a given economy will correspond to the ideal profile identified as characteristic for this society; and not all companies will cluster in those sectors assumed to flourish particularly in a given society. Pockets of flexible specialisation production in the UK/US, for example, indicate that there is also an organisational beside the societal effect (Mueller 1994) and that even within arms-length systems it is possible to mobilise close and trustful relationships in certain localities. More recently, Hirst and

Zeitlin (1997) have tried to allow for this variety by developing the notion of 'mixed' or 'hybrid' systems of production. They underline that hybrid forms of production embedded in so-called dominant social systems of production have always existed. Social systems of production focusing on the customisation of products are dependent to some extent on the standardised production of components and parts; and social systems of production which centre on standardised production require customised machines. According to their view, firms in most countries and periods deliberately mix elements of mass production and craft or flexible specialisation. The resulting interpenetration of elements of flexible specialisation and mass production also means that firms often find it easier to shift strategies from one pole to another than abstract considerations of the models might suggest.

4.   Performance Standards and Sector Specialisation

The previous sections examined the process of sectoral specialisation and why certain contexts favour particular types of sectors. What has not yet been clearly identified, however, is the underlying source of this process of sector specialisation. From a traditional economic perspective, one might assume that what is occurring is a process of market selection, i.e. certain firms/sectors located in particular institutional contexts out-perform those from elsewhere. In other words, it becomes possible to link institutionalist analysis at this level to traditional market economics. In this section, we critically examine the notion that 'market performance' can provide this explanatory framework.

4.1 *Competitive Advantage and Market Selection in Economics and Organisational Theory*

For neo-classical theory, the driving force behind the increasing division and specialisation of economic activity is the most efficient allocation of scarce resources to competing ends. This allocation is achieved through the 'invisible hand' of the market in which firms seek efficiency to survive. Positive profits are treated as the criterion of natural selection — the firms that make profits are selected or 'adopted' by the environment, and others are rejected or disappear. The concern of neo-classical approaches with matching demand and supply leads — even in applied competition theory — to a preoccupation with the question of how competitive prices can be achieved in equilibrium situations. Imperfect information and the use of market power are seen as important impediments to a socially efficient allocation of resources.

    Within economics, however, there is a long history of complaints about the shortcomings of the neo-classical approach with regard to explanations of competitive advantage and performance. Authors from different theoretical backgrounds such as Hayek (1948) and Schumpeter (1942), or more recently Nelson and Winter (1982) and Langlois (1986) have pointed out that economic phenomena are in large measure the result of learning over time by economic agents. Competition, thus, cannot be accounted for by Walrasian general equilibrium models but should be analysed as a dynamic (and, as some argue, evolutionary) process. Institutionalists argue that the coordination of economic activity is not merely a matter of price-mediated transactions in the markets, but is supported by a wide range of economic and social institutions that are themselves an important topic of theoretical economic inquiry. Particular attention is given to how institutions shape the expectations, information systems and interpretative frameworks which are used by economic actors (see e.g. Loasby 1991). Taking into account more complex and uncertain environments and longer time horizons, the neo-classical perception of conscious maximisation of explicit objectives within the constraints of well-defined alternatives cannot be maintained any longer and needs to be replaced by other conceptions of rationality which allow for imperfections of knowledge under uncertainty (Shackle 1958), opportunism and bounded rationality (Williamson 1975, 1985), and learning from experience (Langlois 1986).

The accounts within new institutional economics of processes of competitive advantage and performance, however, are often still bound to the notion that in the end, it is the market which decides about the 'success' or 'failure' of individual business organisations or whole sectors. Transaction costs economics, for example, has relaxed a number of assumptions inherent in neo-classical orthodoxy. But it still maintains that the efficiency properties of alternative organisational forms determine their success or failure — even if it is only the fitter, and not necessarily the fittest in some absolute sense that is selected in 'weak form selection'.[1] Politically imposed impediments and disadvantaged parties may be able to delay transaction cost economising. These exceptions, however, are treated as 'noise' that will disappear in the long run (Williamson 1994). The hypothesis maintained is that firms producing products at the least cost drive out high-cost producers since markets favour low prices, and firms cannot withstand losses of profits or of customers, at least not for a long time.

As the business historian William Lazonick (1991:214) critically states, "Williamson's theory is a theory of an organisation that can only adapt to changes in the environment but does not offer a conception of how innovative organisations might attain and sustain competitive advantage by differentiating the quality and cost of their products from their competitors." Lazonick's work directs attention to the structures, behaviour and strategies of business organisations which generate the basis for what he calls value-creation. These issues, while often neglected in economic accounts of organisations as 'black boxes', have attracted increasing attention in organisational and management theory (for an overview of theoretical approaches towards organisational performance, see Clark 1996 and Meyer 1994). Performance implications, however, have often been dealt with only implicitly (see e.g. Whittington et al., in this volume, for an overview of the treatment of performance in the Chandler-ian approach to structure and strategy approach) or, again, been referred to as a matter of market selection. The economist Edith Penrose (1959), for example, while being among the first to stress the importance of managerial organisation and organisational learning for performance still maintained that the selection between 'successful' and 'failing' organisations was merely a question of profitability and market selection.

A more recent example of these arguments can be found in Porter's (1990) theory of competitive advantage. In this version, the market is subdivided into segments in which competition works through different criteria: for example, price, quality at lowest price, customisation, delivery and/or technologically excellence at the cost of price, etc. It is up to companies' strategies to decide in which of these segments of the world market they want to position themselves. Within this market segment then again, competition will select the more efficient, qualitative, more customised or technologically excellent producers and drive out badly performing companies. These arguments assume that there are a variety of bases on which competition occurs; nevertheless, they remain wedded to the idea that it is through the market that performance is differentiated and selection occurs, leading to the development of strong firms and strong sectors, as a result of the theory of comparative advantage.

Furthermore, this approach assumes a relatively seamless transition between competition within the nation and competition in world markets, in the sense that, as trade barriers come down, firms utilise their home-based advantages in the larger international market. International competitive advantage of sectors or nations thus can be measured in terms of their exports and foreign investment to other nations. Success and failure in international markets feeds back into the national context, forcing some sectors and firms to close and enabling others to grow and expand. Processes of sector formation and reproduction in national contexts are therefore reconstituted under the impact of international competition. As particular markets for goods and services become opened up for international trade, selection mechanisms operate to restructure sector specialisation processes within national business systems.

4.2 Institutionalist Approaches to Competitive Advantage and Market Selection

It is characteristic of many institutionalist approaches towards comparative business organisation that their main concern, rather than challenging the notion of market selection per se, is to elucidate the variety of ways in which economic success can be achieved. In other words, they reject the notion that there is one best way to organise and propose instead the concept of 'functional equivalence'.[2] Their argument is that firms and sectors develop characteristics based on their national institutional context. In international markets, firms and sectors from different contexts may be equally successful even though their structures are different. Thus whilst some firms will be de-selected, there is no need to assume that those firms which survive and prosper need to have the same structure.

Sorge (1991), for example, argues that the primary requirement for a firm is to fit its task and societal environment, and that the degree of fit is essential for performance. But the success of a business strategy may also rest on its own impurity, i.e. on the selective combination of opposing contingent task requirements, and the institutional ability to reconcile conflicting contingencies. Despite this differentiated approach toward the links between institutions and performance, however, once more the market is identified as the selection mechanism which decides about the survival or disappearance of organisations, and thereby the emergence or disappearance of sectors: "...(T)he mentioned affinities are likely to come out in the process of a quasi-Darwinian selection in the intensifying international division of labour." (Sorge 1991: 168).

Sorge's argument reflects the ambivalence of the tradition of the 'societal effect' approach to sectoral specialisation and the role of performance. Maurice et al. (1986), in one of the first studies in the societal effect tradition, refused to give explicit performance judgements. According to their argument, firms with similar task environment may have very different organisational forms and organisational goals in different societies and still perform equally well. Nevertheless, the French-German comparison of Maurice et al. contains a subtext underlining the relative merits of the German system and the idea that competition on world markets between the two types of firm will lead to the de-selection of the French model. Equivocally they conclude that if "... different forms of the division of labour may lead to comparable levels of efficiency, it is none the less true that certain systems seem to be more efficient than others." (Maurice et al. 1986: 23). Thus the notion of functional equivalence seems to reach its limits when the two 'equivalents' are placed directly in competition (see Rose 1985). The implicit assumption is that at this point market selection will operate, causing the decline of certain firms and sectors from the less 'efficient' institutional context. Sorge attempts to reconcile these apparently contradictory elements:

"The German model is definitely not the only or best model of operating within the respective product market segment, for instance, and the mass or the continuous process mode is not identical with French-style practices. The principle of functional equivalence, of different socio-organisational goals (Child 1972), still appears pertinent. However, the above discussion also points to the limits of the functional

equivalence perspective. Arrangements that are institutionalised and therefore transcend a functional purpose (...), have an affinity, nevertheless, with tasks, markets and overall strategies. The question of to what extent, and where, an institutionalized arrangement is not functionally neutral, is fairly open."
(Sorge 1991: 168).

4.3 *Performance and Institutional Contexts: Against Market Fundamentalism*

The ambiguities within the 'societal effects' approach to the question of market selection and performance point to the need to pursue further the question of what drives sector specialisation. The assessment of organisational performance makes sense only with regard to the attainment of objectives or goals — which raises the question of whose objectives and goals are the benchmarks against which performance is assessed. Goal setting and assessment of economic performance do not follow universal laws, but are influenced by socially constructed standards, rules and norms through which economic actors shape their environment. This means that performance standards may differ in time and space. Dominant standards are the result of selections between alternative and sometimes conflicting performance goals that are negotiated between different groups of social actors, which to a certain extent reflect influences of the national institutional context (see Morgan and Quack in this book). Thus the creation of sectoral specialisation and firm survival within national contexts cannot be simply read off as an outcome of neo-classical market selection.

If we compare the perception of desired performance outcomes in different societies we find variations which are related to differences in ownership patterns, governance principles and market relations. Whitley (1999) discusses the relative influence of owners, managers, different kinds of employees, business partners, and other groups in deciding upon dominant firms' objectives and performance standards. Four dominant goals and performance standards can be distinguished: personal and family wealth accumulation; high returns to portfolio managers and shareholders; growth in assets, turnover and markets; increasing technical excellence and reputation. In practice, these goals are always combined but usually one tends to dominate as a result of different interest groups' control over the strategic priorities of firms and the nature of the broader institutional environment. For example, the Anglo-Saxon business systems are likely to give priority to increases in share prices and dividends compared to the other goals; in contrast, business systems in which managers have a high degree of control over company development, and particularly when combined with strong employee and business partner influence, are likely to favour growth goals because salaries and rewards of managers are regarded as tied to the firm, and employees and business partners gain more from the expansion of the firm than from increased profits.

National business systems are not only likely to influence the relative power and influence of different stakeholder groups. The formation of these social groups and their interests as such will also differ depending on the historical and social context (Kristensen 1997). For example, members of the highly mobile work force in the US, described above, should have much less interest in the development of the individual company they are working for than their counterparts in the German, and even more, in the Japanese system which focuses on long-term employment relationships. Differences in the educational and social background of British, French and German managers have been shown to lead to distinct management styles and a focus on generalist versus technical issues (Lane 1989). The social formation of supplier and business partner relations, and as a consequence, the type of interest they take in companies, has also been demonstrated to differ considerably depending on the national context (Lane 1997; Deakin et al. this volume).

These considerations mean that the driving force of sector specialisation in particular contexts cannot be simply ascribed to market selection mechanisms. Processes of selection and deselection are social constructions in the sense that actors have to decide on the goals which they want to achieve in particular contexts. These goals are not necessarily about short-term economic survival. Key stakeholders such as the state, lenders, shareholders and employees are involved in complex ongoing and conflictual decisions about the terms on which their own requirements are going to be met through the current strategy and structure of the firm and sector. Thus states can support the development of certain sectors, e.g. aerospace and defence, for straightforward political reasons. Such decisions do not negate market mechanisms but rather displace them to other parts of the social order, in the process restructuring and redefining the nature of survival and growth for firms. Similarly, lenders can evolve more complex goals than short-term profit maximisation, particularly when as with the case in Germany, a substantial part of the banking system is collectively, as opposed to privately, owned.

In this context it is important to underline that performance is always a multi-dimensional phenomenon — a construct in which certain aspects can become an issue for the actors involved in economic activity or not. Economic actors in sectoral or national business systems cannot maximise all dimensions of performance at the same time. In order to examine trade-offs between performance objectives, Traxler and Ungerer (1994) have suggested grouping them along four dimensions: Allocative efficiency represents the ability of an organisation to employ most efficiently the available resources at a given point in time. Dynamic efficiency (also referred to as 'adaptive efficiency' by North 1990: 80) describes the ability of organisations to adapt successfully to changing environments (see also Klein 1984; Lazonick 1991). Distributional performance deals with considerations of social peace and the egalitarian distribution of economic outcomes.

Stabilisation, finally, refers to the resources and capabilities on which an organisation can draw to overcome periods of economic difficulties.

These four dimensions of performance lead to conflicting goals. In evolutionary economics, tensions between allocative and dynamic efficiency have become known as 'Schumpeterian trade-off' (e.g. Nelson and Winter 1982; Langlois 1986). Authors from the institutionalist camp have referred to it as the conflict between achieving short and long-term profitability (Boyer and Hollingsworth 1997). Anglo-Saxon market capitalism has been in general ascribed a high propensity to maximise allocative efficiency whereas continental European capitalisms, and more recently Japan, with 'thick' institutional settings have been regarded as providing superior conditions for long-term success through higher developed capacities for adaptability to changing business environments (Aoki 1988; Katzenstein 1989; Streeck 1992).

Patterns of sectoral specialisation within national contexts, therefore, do not reflect a simple logic of market selection. Which sectors survive, how they develop and how they are structured can only be understood by examining the ways in which various groups of actors reach agreements and compromises on their economic, social and political interests within the particular institutional structure of their own society. These agreements are subject to periods of tension and instability which may result in restructuring and change or stasis and continuity. However, they certainly cannot be reduced to a process of neo-classical market selection.

4.4 *Markets as Social Structures: An Institutionalist Approach towards Market Selection*

By arguing against neo-classical market fundamentalism, as we have done in the previous section, we do not intend to deny the important role that markets play in shaping and selecting performance outcomes. We do, however, maintain that the market is not the only, and possibly not the most important site in which performance is assessed and performance outcomes are selected. Furthermore, we contend that the process of Darwinian selection with which the market is ascribed under the perfect competition model in orthodox economics constitutes a rare exception to what actually tends to happen in real markets (see Boyer 1997 for a more extensive discussion). Old and new institutionalist theory has pointed out that most markets for commodities call for sophisticated institutional arrangements as a prerequisite for their functioning (e.g. the state as guarantor of property rights, or non-price mechanisms to achieve market clearing, see e.g. Campbell and Lindberg 1990). We would argue that it is necessary to go one step further and to perceive of markets as consisting of social structures which emerge from recurrent exchange between different economic actors and are often shaped by power struggles over access to resources and choices of performance outcomes (see e.g. Swedberg 1994 for an overview on sociological approaches to markets). Boyer (1997) suggests that in studying the role of socially constructed markets as selection device, particular emphasis should be given to:

> "[T]he list of institutions, organizations, legislation, or associations that are organising the functioning of (…) markets, with detailed description of their responsibilities, objectives, tools and enforcement tools or incentives. (…) A characterisation of the forms of competition, according to the number of traders, the distribution of ownership, the distribution of market power, the possible explicit or implicit coordinating mechanisms, in order to solve overcapacity problems or to respond to uncertainty and/or structural changes." (Boyer 1997: 70).

Even though attempts to fill this research programme are still in their infancy, there is already considerable evidence for the existence of a variety of social market structures with distinct effects on the selection of 'successful' and 'unsuccessful' business organisations and corresponding effects for the development of different economic sectors. Interestingly enough, it is particularly in globalised financial sectors which are often regarded as prototype of anonymous and price-coordinated market selection that social and cultural aspects have been demonstrated to affect the workings of the market. Baker (1984), for example, demonstrated that price volatility in US securities markets was strongly influenced by the nature of networks operating in these markets. He showed that fragmented and larger networks of participants caused much more price volatility than smaller, more intense networks. Furthermore, it has been demonstrated by Podolny (1993, together with Philipps 1996) that market exchanges between US investment banks often involve not only the manifest transfer of goods and resources, but also a latent transfer of status. Status transfer has a significant impact on the resources which market participants can acquire, and thereby influences their performance. Thus, as far as the emergence, development and decline of sectors is influenced by market selections these selections should be regarded as the result of social and power relations between different market participants and their contest about different performance standards.

4.5 Towards 'Dis-embedded' Performance Standards in Global Markets?

It is tempting to suggest, as a number of institutionalist authors imply, that markets as social structures and socially constructed performance standards may work within tightly controlled national borders (as was characteristic of the golden age of Keynesianism) but once these borders are reduced in efficacy, then the global market 'red in tooth and claw' operates as a brutal form of selection between firms and nations, causing some sectors to disappear in particular countries and others to strengthen and grow. Three broad mechanisms are assumed to translate these market imperatives into action. The first is quite simply market competition itself which places firms from different institutional context into direct confrontation. Thus cheaper and/or more reliable products from one country cause the decline of that sector in another country. The second mechanism derives from global financial markets, which allows firms to shift resources out of their home base into other contexts offering better comparative advantage for the production of certain goods or services. The latter process allows firms to survive and prosper by outward investment but this destroys national sectors and the ties which link them together. From this perspective, whatever might have been the role for socially differentiated performance goals and outcomes under the accumulation regime of 'national Keynesianism', the situation in the era of globalisation is considerably different. Firms are measured by a single criterion of performance on the global market and failure to adjust to this leads to the decline of firms and sectors. The third mechanism which relates to this is the idea of the transfer of standards of performance across countries via multinational corporations (MNC), transnational corporate networks and international standard setting agencies.

This view, however, over-estimates the degree to which markets and firms can ever be completely 'dis-embedded' from national contexts or state or international regulation. Thus the terms on which firms compete in international markets have to come from somewhere: either national or regional or international bodies of some sort continue to regulate trade. What is at issue is not regulation per se but a series of practical questions such as what is the most appropriate level for regulation in particular sectors, what is the extent of regulation which is compatible with broader economic and political goals, who should have responsibility for implementing and monitoring regulation and who should pay for it. Whilst proponents of the free market might start from the presupposition that the market should rule, they recognise that in practice, this still requires some sort of framework. This framework therefore opens up the possibility of just the sort of bargaining over goals which has always existed at the national level. The fact that international institutions tend to be dominated by proponents of the free market only reinforces the point that power is used to make the market work by forcing countries to open up their boundaries; it is not inconceivable that it could therefore be used with more (or, perhaps, a different) political direction (see the arguments in Hirst and Thompson 1996; Boyer and Drache 1996; Berger and Dore 1996).

Similarly, the process of transfer of best practice always tends to be affected by different social contexts. Firstly, universal standards such as for example the ISO 9000 norms of product quality are likely to be implemented and enacted differently by social actors in distinct national and sectoral environments (see Hancké and Casper in this volume). Secondly, international regimes often delegate monitoring responsibilities back to the authority in the home country and are based on home-country control (Hirst and Thompson 1996; Lütz 1996). Thirdly, organisational procedures within multinational corporations still need to articulate different local, sectoral and national logics of action in order to be successful. The interesting question, thus, is not so much whether standards of performance are defined domestically or globally, but how the transfer processes work, how national, international and global rules of the game are articulated with each other and what changes in power are involved in these processes (see Loveridge and Mueller's chapter in this volume).

The fact that the last decade has seen the decline and in some cases loss of certain manufacturing sectors from advanced industrial societies or the systematic restructuring of others in the light of global competition should clearly not be under-estimated. However, nor should the significance of this be over-estimated. There remain considerable differences in the way in which sectors are opened up to international competition and the terms of this opening-up as well as the way in which firms and sectors adapt to this process. Governments and international regulators still play a role in the terms on which this occurs. Thus all Western governments continue to protect their agricultural sectors from cheaper foodstuffs from the developing world. Many of them continue to support certain key industries such as defence, energy, air transport and telecommunications (see the discussion in this volume by Lehrer and Darbishire, and Loveridge and Mueller) whilst at the same time encouraging them to become globally competitive. Even classically globally competitive sectors such as automobiles remain of central concern to governments, many of whom will seek to support home firms in this sector in order to sustain employment and the host of suppliers dependent on the sector. Service sectors are notoriously difficult to open up to international competition not just for purely technical reasons but because of entrenched professional groups. Thus certain patterns of sector specialisation which have been established historically are likely to continue long in to the future whatever the proponents of globalisation argue.

5. Conclusions

In this chapter, we have examined in detail the issue of sector specialisation. We have shown how institutional structures such as the nature of financial systems, innovation strategies, labour market institutions, demand conditions and patterns of intermediary associations influence sectoral specialisation in different national business systems. However, these structural factors exercise their influence through shaping the ways in which firms and individuals respond to opportunities and threats in their environment. This led us to consider whether ultimately the key issue was the process of market selection as assumed in neo-classical theory. Here, we argued that some institutionalists do in fact accept that this type of Darwinian market selection is at work between what they term 'functionally equivalent' aspects of business systems. Thus institutionalism can be linked to market economics ultimately through the recognition that there are various alternative forms of organising which have functional equivalence but it is likely that in particular circumstances one form will be more 'efficient' than another.

In this chapter, however, we have questioned this market fundamentalism. Instead, we have followed others in arguing that just as there are multiple functionally equivalent structures, there are multiple performance standards which are set for firms. Shareholder dominance is only one such standard and there are many examples of more complex balances of interest between different groups, creating performance standards that reflect social, political and economic interests. Therefore, the reasons why firms and sectors are sustained and developed in particular contexts needs to be related to the way in which certain performance standards are put in place by specific social actors in particular arenas. There are many arenas in which different choices for performance goals are negotiated and contested. The market — reconceptualised as a social structure — is only one of them. We also reject the idea that the opening up of national borders implies a declining significance for these sorts of processes and the final triumph of neo-classical markets. For the free market theorists, the decline of borders will lead inexorably to the creation of an international division of labour which reflects comparative economic advantages between countries and areas. Thus firms and sectors within countries which are unable to compete on the global market will decline whilst others will grow. In our view, this both over-generalises from a limited number of examples and under-estimates the continued role of political and social intervention at national, regional and global levels. There remain ways in which sectors can be protected or encouraged which will not disappear as a result of globalisation per se, though it may be that global institutions influenced by free market ideology may insist in the case of certain less powerful countries that they do not use these mechanisms. In general, however, it is important to examine the specific processes through which sectors within and across national boundaries are being restructured. It would be our expectation that this will reflect a complex inter-mixing of political, social and economic considerations, rather than some pure form of market selection (see e.g. the studies on financial services industries in Europe in Morgan and Knights 1997 as well as the discussions in this volume).

Notes

1. Other proponents of new economic institutionalism, like Langlois (1986: 13) ascribe a more far-reaching influence to social institutions. In this view, social institutions set the boundary conditions and provide filtering and selection mechanisms which shape the process of

competition. In contrast to sociological conceptions described elsewhere in this article, however, social institutions are still regarded as distinct from the economic processes under consideration.

2. A distinction needs to be drawn between the notion of functional equivalence as used in contingency theory (referring to the use of different means to achieve identical goals), and a more broadly defined notion of 'functional equivalence' according to which not only the means, but also the goals pursued by economic actors can vary across countries (as referred to in this chapter).

References

Aoki, M. 1988. *Information, incentives and bargaining in the Japanese economy*. Cambridge: Cambridge University Press.

Baker, W. 1984. The Social Structure of a National Securities Market, *American Journal of Sociology* 89: 775–811.

Berger, S. and R. Dore (eds.). 1996. *National Diversity and Global Capitalism*. Cornell: Cornell University Press.

Boyer, R. 1997. The Variety and Unequal Performance of Really Existing Markets: Farewell to Doctor Pangloss?. In: Hollingsworth, J. R. and R. Boyer (eds.). 1997. *Contemporary Capitalism. The Embeddedness of Institutions*, 55–93. Cambridge: Cambridge University Press.

Boyer, R. and D. Drache. 1996. *States against Markets: the limits of globalization*. London: Routledge.

Boyer, R. and J. R. Hollingsworth. 1997. The Variety of Institutional Arrangements and Their Complementarity in Modern Economies. In: Hollingsworth, J. R. and R. Boyer (eds.). 1997. *Contemporary Capitalism. The Embeddedness of Institutions*, 49–54. Cambridge: Cambridge University Press.

Campbell, J. and L. Lindberg. 1990. Property Rights and the Organization of Economic Activity by the State, *American Sociological Review* 55: 634–647.

Clark, P. 1996. Organizational Performance. In: Warner, M. (ed.), *International Encyclopedia of Business and Management*. Volume 4, 3943–3955. London: Routledge.

Christopherson, S. 1998. Why do national labor market practices continue to diverge in a global economy? Paper presented to the EGOS Conference, July 1998, Maastricht.

Gerschenkron, A. 1962. *Economic Backwardness in Historical Perspective*. Cambridge, MA: Harvard University Press.

Hayek, F. A. 1948. *Individualism and Economic Order*. Chicago: University of Chicago Press.

Hall, P. 1997. The Political Economy of Adjustment in Germany. In: W. Zapf and M. Dierkes (eds.), *Institutionenvergleich und Institutionendynamik*, WZB-Year Book, 293–348, Berlin: Edition Sigma.

Herrigel, G. 1996. *Industrial constructions: The sources of German industrial power*. Cambridge: Cambridge University Press.

Hirst, P. Q. and G. F. Thompson. 1996. *Globalization in Question: The International Economy and the Possibilities of Governance*. Cambridge: Polity Press.

Hirst, P. and J. Zeitlin. 1997. Flexible Specialization: Theory and Evidence in the Analysis of Industrial Change. In: Hollingsworth, J. R. and R. Boyer (eds.), *Contemporary*

Capitalism. The Embeddedness of Institutions, 220–239. Cambridge: Cambridge University Press.

Hollingsworth, J. R., P. C. Schmitter and W. Streeck (eds.). 1994. *Governing Capitalist Economies. Performance and Control of Economic Sectors.* Oxford: Oxford University Press.

Hollingsworth, J. R. and R. Boyer (eds.). 1997. *Contemporary Capitalism. The Embeddedness of Institutions.* Cambridge: Cambridge University Press.

Hutton, W. 1995. *The State We're in.* London: Jonathan Cape.

Katzenstein, P. J. 1989. *Industry and Politics in West Germany: Toward the Third Republic.* Ithaca: Cornell University Press.

Kitschelt, H. 1991. Industrial Governance Structures, *International Organization* 45(4): 453–93.

Klein, B. 1984. *Prices, wages and business cycles. A dynamic theory.* New York: Pergamon Press.

Kristensen, P. H. 1997. National Systems of Governance and Managerial Prerogatives in the Evolution of Work Systems: England, Germany, and Denmark Compared. In: Whitley, R. and P. H. Kristensen (eds.), *Governance at Work: The Social Regulation of Economic Relations,* 3–46. Oxford: Oxford University Press.

Lane, C. 1989. *Management and Labour in Europe. The Industrial Enterprise in Germany, Britain and France.* Aldershot: Edward Elgar.

Lane, C. 1995. *Industry and Society in Europe.* Aldershot: Edward Elgar.

Lane, C. 1997. The social regulation of inter-firm relations in Britain and Germany: market rules, legal norms and technical standards, *Cambridge Journal of Economics* 21: 197–215.

Landes, D. 1969. *The Unbound Prometheus: Technological Change and Industrial Development in Western Europe from 1750 to the Present.* Cambridge: Cambridge University Press.

Langlois, R. N. (ed.). 1986. *Economics as a process. Essays in the New Institutional Economics.* Cambridge: Cambridge University Press.

Langlois R. N. and P. L. Robertson. 1995. *Firms, Markets and Economic Change.* London: Routledge.

Lazonick, W. 1991. *Business Organization and the Myth of the Market Economy.* Cambridge: Cambridge University Press.

Lazonick, W. and M. O'Sullivan. 1996. Organization, Finance and International Competition, *Industrial and Corporate Change* 5(1): 1–50.

Loasby, B. J. 1991. Equilibrium and evolution. *An exploration of connecting principles in economics.* Manchester: Manchester University Press.

Lundvall, B. A. (ed.). 1992. *National Systems of Innovation.* Pinter: London.

Lütz, S. 1998. The revival of the nation-state? Stock-exchange regulation in an era of globalized financial markets. *Journal of European Public Policy* 5: 153–168.

Malerba, F. and L. Orsenigo. 1996. The Dynamics and Evolution of Industries, *Industrial and Corporate Change* 5(1): 51–87.

Maurice, M., A. Sorge and M. Warner. 1980. Societal Differences in Organizing Manufacturing Units. A Comparison of France, West Germany and Great Britain, *Organization Studies* 1(1): 59–86.

Maurice, M., F. Sellier and J.-J. Silvestre (eds.). 1986. *The social foundations of industrial power. A comparison of France and Germany.* Cambridge, MA: MIT Press.

Maurice, M. and A. Sorge (eds.). 1999. *Embedded organizations. Societal analysis of actors, organizations and socio-economic context.* Amsterdam: John Benjamins.

Meyer, M. W. 1994. Measuring Performance in Economic Organizations. In: N. J. Smelser and R. Swedberg (eds.), *The Handbook of Economic Sociology,* 556–580. New York: Princeton University Press.

Morgan, G. 1998. Varieties of Capitalism and the Institutional Embeddedness of International Economic Coordination. Paper presented to EGOS Conference, July 1998, Maastricht.

Morgan, G. and D. Knights (eds.). 1997. *Regulation and Deregulation in European Financial Services.* London: Macmillan.

Mueller, F. 1994. Societal Effect, Organizational Effect and Globalization, *Organization Studies* 15(3): 407–428.

Nelson, R. R. and S. G. Winter. 1982. *An Evolutionary theory of Economic Change.* Cambridge, MA: Harvard University Press.

Nelson, R. R. (eds.). 1993. *National Innovation Systems: A Comparative Analysis.* Oxford: Oxford University Press.

North, D. C. 1990. *Institutions, Institutional Change and Economic Performance.* Cambridge: Cambridge University Press.

Penrose, E. T. 1959. *The Theory of the Growth of the Firm.* Oxford: Oxford University Press.

Podolny, J. M. 1993. A Status-based Model of Market Competition, *American Journal of Sociology* 98: 829–872.

Podolny, J. M. and D. J. Phillips. 1996. The Dynamics of Organizational Status, *Industrial and Corporate Change* 5(2): 453–471.

Porter, M. E. 1990. *The Competitive Advantage of Nations.* New York: Free Press.

Räsänen, K. and R. Whipp. 1992. National Business Recipes: a Sector Perspective. In: R. Whitley (ed.), *European Business Systems. Firms and Markets in their National Contexts,* 46–60. London: Sage.

Rose, M. 1985. Universalism, culturalism and the Aix group: promise and problems of a societal approach to economic institutions, *European Sociological Review* 1(1): 65–83.

Sabel, C. 1994. Learning by Monitoring: The Institutions of Economic Development. In: N. J. Smelser and R. Swedberg (eds.), *The Handbook of Economic Sociology,* 137–165. Princeton, NJ: Princeton University Press.

Schumpeter, J. 1942. *Capitalism, Socialism, and Democracy.* New York: Harper and Brothers.

Shackle, G. L. S. 1958. *Time in Economics.* Amsterdam: North-Holland Publishing Company.

Sorge, A. 1991. Strategical Fit and Societal Effect: Interpreting Cross-National Comparisons of Technology, Organization and Human Resources, *Organization Studies* 12(2): 161–190.

Soskice, D. 1997. Innovation Strategies of Companies: A Comparative Institutional Approach of Some Cross-Company Differences. In: W. Zapf and M. Dierkes (eds.),

Institutionenvergleich und Institutionendynamik, WZB-Year Book, 271–289, Berlin: Edition Sigma.

Storper, M. 1996. Innovation as Collective Action: Conventions, Products and Technologies, *Industrial and Corporate Change* 5(3): 761–789.

Streeck, W. 1992. *Social Institutions and Economic Performance. Studies of Industrial Relations in Advanced Capitalist Economies.* London: Sage.

Swedberg, R. 1994. Markets as Social Structures. In: N. J. Smelser and R. Swedberg (eds.), *The Handbook of Economic* Sociology, 255–282. Princeton, NJ: Princeton University Press.

Traxler, F. and Ungerer, B. 1994. Industry or Infrastructure? A Cross-National Comparison of Governance: Its Determinants and Economic Consequences in the Dairy Sector. In: J. R. Hollingsworth, P. C. Schmitter and W. Streeck (eds.), *Governing Capitalist Economies. Performance and Control of Economic Sectors,* 183–214. Oxford: Oxford University Press.

Vitols, S. 1995. German Banks and the Modernization of the Small Firm Sector: Long-term Finance in Comparative Perspective. WZB-Discussion Paper FS I 95–309. Berlin: Wissenschaftszentrum Berlin für Sozialforschung.

Vitols, S. 1997. Financial Systems and Industrial Policy in Germany and Great Britain: The Limits of Convergence. In: D. Forsyth and . Notermands (eds.), *Regime Changes: Macroeconomic Policy and Financial Regulation in Europe from the 1930s to the 1990s,* 221–55. Providence, RI: Berghahn Books.

Whitley, R. 1994. Dominant Forms of Economic Organization in Market Economies, *Organization Studies* 15(2): 153–182.

Whitley, R. 1999. *Divergent Capitalisms: The Social Structuring and Change of Business Systems.* Oxford: Oxford University Press.

Whitley, R. and P. H. Kristensen (eds.). 1996. *The Changing European Firm. Limits to Convergence.* London: Routledge.

Whitley, R. and P. H. Kristensen (eds.). 1997. *Governance at Work: The Social Regulation of Economic Relations.* Oxford: Oxford University Press.

Williamson, O. E. 1975. *Markets and Hierarchies: Analysis and Anti-Trust Implications.* New York: Free Press.

Williamson, O. E. 1985. *The Economic Institutions of Capitalism.* New York: Free Press.

Williamson, O. E. 1994. Transaction Cost Economics and Organisation Theory. In: N. J. Smelser and R. Swedberg (eds.), *The Handbook of Economic Sociology,* 77–107. Princeton, NJ: Princeton University Press.

Zysman, J. 1983. *Governments, Markets and Growth.* Financial Systems and the Politics of Industrial Change. London: Cornell University Press.

CHAPTER 3

Performance Standards in Supplier Relations

Relational Contracts, Organisational Processes
and the Institutional Environment
in a Cross-National Perspective[*]

Simon Deakin   Christel Lane   Frank Wilkinson

1. Introduction

Numerous studies have pointed to the distinctive institutional properties of
'productive systems' or 'industrial orders' at national and/or regional level. These
have shown that strong divergencies persist between countries and regions in the
framework for labour and product market regulation and for corporate governance
(see Whitley 1992 and 1994; Berger and Dore 1996; Hollingsworth and Boyer
1997; Crouch and Streeck 1997). At the same time, it is widely accepted that in
so far as particular institutional structures provide a basis for superior economic
performance, this is so only in a cluster of core industries and in certain international market environments, rather than bestowing competitive advantage across
the board. This phenomenon has been referred to as the existence of a strategic
fit between certain institutional constellations and production/product strategies
(Sorge 1991: 187). Claims that the growing inter-dependence of national economies, as well as the rise of transnational regulatory bodies, might be leading to
institutional convergence (Crouch and Streeck 1997) are countered by the
suggestion that such strategic fit leads to specialisation by national production
systems which becomes more rather than less pronounced with growing economic
interdependence (Sorge 1991; Berger and Dore 1996).

There has been a strong tendency in the literature on institutional effects to
assume that tightly coupled systems and socially deeply embedded firms yield

* The support of the Economic and Social Research Council (award number L114251016, Vertical
Contracts, Incentive and Competition) is gratefully acknowledged. We are grateful to our colleagues
Alessandro Arrighetti, Reinhard Bachmann, Tom Goodwin and Alan Hughes for permission to draw
on joint work, referred to in the text, in the completion of this paper.

superior performance outcomes across a larger range of industries. More recently, this has been questioned on both theoretical and empirical grounds. Theoretically, it has been argued that tight coupling can lead to both cognitive and organisational lock-in which has adverse consequences for product diversification and managerial autonomy (Grabher 1993), as well as for radical innovation (Kern 1998). The lack of organisational flexibility implied in both cases is empirically well illustrated in the analysis of the German telecommunications industry by Lehrer and Darbyshire (this volume). But rather than demonstrating that the survival chances of the German production system are severely impeded (see the only partly polemical claim by Streeck 1997) this merely illustrates the relatively poor strategic fit between the current German national institutional environment and *some*, albeit important industries.

The nature of the link between institutional structures and economic performance remains elusive and controversial. Indeed, the comparative study of economic institutions is in many respects a field which is still 'in its infancy' (Mayer 1997: 171). Such comparative analysis has many theoretical strands, but there is a certain amount of agreement on some fundamental aspects of the relationship between institutions and business organisations which have implications also for the study of performance. Few institutionalists in organisation studies claim that institutional structures *determine* organisational activity and ensuing performance outcomes. It is rather assumed that a given institutional framework sets limits on what performance standards are viable and what outcomes feasible, and that product strategies diverging from the societally predominant paradigm are adopted at higher costs to individual enterprises. Managerial agency is not denied but rather viewed as institutionally circumscribed, and social embeddedness (Granovetter 1985) of managerial action is given some weight.

The level of organisational diversity within national or regional productive systems, implied by the non-determinist stance adopted in this paper, depends on the nature of the institutional environment. The more tightly coupled are the elements of a given productive system and the more cohesive an industrial order the stronger is the influence of the institutional environment and the slower and more incremental any process of institutional and organisational change (Lane 1994; Whitley 1994). In the words of DiMaggio and Powell (1991), such cohesive systems bestow greater legitimacy on adopting organisations, and isomorphism becomes more pronounced. Conversely, loose coupling and lack of cohesion lead to fragmentation between subsystems and a wider range of organisational responses within the overall system (see Lane 1994, on the British case). Thus, while a range of performance outcomes can be achieved in both tightly and loosely coupled systems this range will be larger in the latter type of productive system.

The present paper aims to cast further light on these issues by reporting the findings of a comparative study of supplier relations in two traditional industries

— mining machinery and kitchen furniture — in Germany, Britain and Italy. We report on how managements of buyer firms in the different countries and sectors viewed market pressures for new product strategies, how these pressures were transmitted to suppliers, and to what extent and how suppliers responded to these pressures. The evidence we present suggests ways in which supplier relations are both socially and institutionally embedded. Although all the firms studied were being subjected to growing competitive pressures in both domestic and overseas markets, their responses to such pressures were strongly conditioned by industry-specific and, above all, nation-specific factors.

We also consider how far the different responses of firms led to divergent outcomes in terms of economic performance. On the evidence presented here, there is not necessarily a direct link between the institutional framework, the adoption of particular practices by individual firms, and the enhancement of the performance of those firms. The capacity of a *single firm* to survive and prosper depends on a number of factors; its approach to contracting and the nature of its linkages with other firms is only one. However, a clearer link between the institutional framework and competitive outcomes may be observed when we consider *groups of firms* as defined by industry, region or country of operation. This suggests that institutional factors may play a significant role in raising the *general* level of performance within a given population of firms. Such a claim is not only consistent with the theoretical framework outlined above but also is highly plausible in the light of empirical evidence about the firms in our sample. The majority of our cases were supplier firms which sold diverse components to customer firms in more than one industry and hence had highly divergent market chances. At one end of the scale, a firm might supply only highly customised components to the shrinking markets of one industry, whereas at the other end, a supplier of more standardised parts might do business with firms in several industries and hence be more shielded from the adverse effects of sudden conjunctural or politically influenced changes in market size.

2.   Defining Performance Standards

Economic concepts specifying performance goals include the notions of allocative (or static) efficiency and dynamic efficiency. The former refers to the allocation of scarce resources to their most productive uses while the latter has a broader connotation which is related to the capacity of a productive system to survive external shocks through innovation and adaptation to a changing external environment (Deakin, Goodwin and Hughes 1997). At the level of the individual firm, the notion of operational efficiency is used to refer to how effectively the various inputs into the firm are combined together to produce its outputs. In the context of buyer-supplier relations, a broad interpretation of *inputs* would allow for the incorporation of social criteria and would acknowledge that systems of production and exchange are socially and institutionally embedded. Such social criteria include those implied by the concept of relational contracting, that is, cooperation and reciprocity. *Outputs* may then be understood to include improvements in the quality and/or technological sophistication of products, as well as in the reliabilty of their delivery. This suggests the hypothesis that where relational contracting remains poorly developed and arm's length relations persist, allocative efficiency receives greater emphasis and may be enhanced in the short run, in that frequent changes of suppliers may result in cost savings. But it is also suggested that relational contracting achieves better performance outcomes in the longer run. It facilitates the development of enhanced dynamic efficiency, particularly technological updating of products or processes or incremental innovation. This, in turn, enables nations and/or regions better to compete on international markets and, in particular, to adapt to changing market demands.

Although the present paper gives most emphasis to assessing inputs into production systems, namely the various characteristics of supplier relations, we have also developed some measures of output. These permit us to draw some conclusions on performance standards and outcomes. We assess the relative importance given to the performance standards of price, quality, reliable delivery and technological improvement by individual firms' managers, as well as their perceptions of any change in importance in these standards over a five-year period. We additionally investigate the procedures which firms put into place to achieve quality, reliability and technological improvement. Finally, we assess firms' success in achieving these performance goals by exploring their link to export performance. Ability to compete on foreign markets may be taken as a proxy measure of the ability to adapt to and fulfill the new market demands of cost-efficient quality and continual technological updating. We also make use of indicators based on turnover and number of employees.

3.   The Social and Institutional Embeddedness of Performance Standards

Performance standards can be seen as socially and institutionally embedded in the sense that inputs into production include the social aspects of production and exchange; outputs are equally socially influenced by the various business goals pursued in different institutional contexts. This process by which performance standards are constructed therefore has deep historical roots and is shaped by national and also regional institutional environments, giving rise to distinctive social systems of production/business systems (Whitley 1992).

Formalised institutions — the legal-regulatory system, governmental bodies, collective organisations and associations — play a particularly important role in concretising norms, practices and conventions which govern performance standards. This role becomes clear when considering those substantial divergencies which exist at the level of the institutional framework, even between systems which are otherwise close together in terms of their fundamental approach to the regulation of industry.

In the present context, important differences exist at the level of the legal and regulatory framework which governs inter-firm relations (see Lane 1997). In German commercial law, a prominent role is accorded to notions of good faith, there are active trade associations, and there are extensive, substantive quality standards which receive the backing of the state. In Italy, by contrast, the legal system is perceived to be expensive, rigid and of little use; there is widespread reliance on institutions below the level of the central government (trade and artisanal associations and local and regional governmental entities) in supporting networks of firms. In Britain, on the other hand, there is a strong tendency towards 'voluntarism' in commercial law and inter-firm relations, with both the state and producers' associations playing a comparatively minimal role in organising and regulating private-sector business relations.

The most striking difference at the level of legal doctrine between the three systems concerns the absence from English law of a generalised principle of good faith in contractual dealings. The English courts have difficulty in formulating an acceptable version of the good faith doctrine, and have insisted instead on the need to preserve the notion that commercial parties deal, for the most part, at arm's length. As a consequence, certain doctrines which are well known in civil law systems, such as requirements of pre-contractual duties of disclosure and the possibility of relief for commercial impracticability, have remained underdeveloped; this is also the case, although to a lesser extent, by way of comparison to the commercial laws of the United States. In Germany, by contrast, the doctrine of good faith has gradually been expanded and refined in the commercial context, not least in the light of the post-war philosophy of the social market. Similarly, in Italy, legal doctrine formally stresses the links between the duty of contractual cooperation and the concept of 'social solidarity' under the 1949 Constitution.

We would suggest that the most important differences in the institutional framework relate not simply or even principally to the substance of various rules, but *to the relationship between the different levels of normative and cognitive regulation*. In Germany there is an exceptionally high degree of interdependence between the separate levels, resulting in a tightly coupled and cohesive production system. Contract law doctrine recognises the importance of industry-level regulation through the notion of legally-binding general conditions of business, and the content of the latter, in turn, is affected by the overarching legal requirement of good faith as well as by specific legislation regulating the terms of standard form contracts (Lane and Bachmann 1996, 1997; Lane 1997). The links extend to the trade associations which operate at the level of the sector and chambers of commerce at the level of the locality; the official, state-sponsored bodies which are responsible for the promulgation of technical standards (in particular the Deutsche Institut für Normung); and the federal and regional state bodies which are concerned with the formulation and conduct of industrial policy. The effect has been to lend a powerful degree of stability to industry-level norms which is lacking in Britain, where legal regulation of standard form contracts is less extensive. The role of collective institutions is weak, in the sense that trade associations play a more limited role. In some sectors membership is very low. This was the case, for example, with the kitchen furniture sector in our own study; in mining equipment there had been a tradition of strong, industry-level organisation, but with privatisation and the rapid decline in the market for coal the role of the trade association had considerably diminished (see Lane 1997). In Britain, substantive standards relating to product form and quality are given less emphasis than process-related standards designed to enhance quality assurance within organisations (principally BS 5750 and ISO 9000).

In Italy, as we have suggested, the importance of legal notions of good faith is offset by the perceived ridigity and inefficiency of the court system. The principal role of industrial trade associations is to represent their member firms in relations with local and national government; in addition, the associations representing the smaller, 'artisanal' firms provide extensive business services to their members (Best 1990: 209–211). Trade associations and other national systems of formal regulation are said to be weak in Italy and are easily circumvented. But, in the case of the Third Italy, there exist compensatory communitarian mechanisms of regulation (Regini 1997: 106). Regini (1997: 107) holds them to be very effective, but also notes that their voluntaristic character makes them very unstable. There is a greater stress than there is in Britain on quality standards operating at the level of particular regions, localities and products. However, in contrast to Germany, there is less of a tendency for these standards to be supported by law or otherwise backed up by the state; nor do trade associations play such a prominent role in setting, codifying and enforcing standards as they do in Germany (Interview Notes). There is evidence of a strong degree of social pressure in favour of dealing in good faith within business communities, backed up by the threat of exclusion as a sanction against opportunism (Burchell and Wilkinson 1997).

The suggestion that there exists, at a general level, a relationship between institutional influences and the form taken by supplier relations is supported by evidence of recent changes in the organisation of supplier relations in the economies studied here. While Piore and Sabel (1984) drew a sharp distinction between 'mass production' and 'flexible specialisation' (FS), more recent writing has expanded the typology to include additional types (Streeck 1992; Hollings-worth and Boyer 1997; Regini 1997). The German social system of production, combining large volume with diversity, quality and technological ingenuity, is widely typified as Diversified Quality Production (DQP), but FS may be found in some industries, dominated by *Mittelstand* firms. The Third Italy, due to the smaller scale of production, simple organisational structures and entrepreneurial managerial style, less formal modes of regulation and a more developed capacity to exercise versatility and to respond to changed market demands, is usually associated with FS (Regini 1997: 104). Both are based on performance standards which privilege quality, technical excellence and in the Italian case, design and style, over costs. The British system, in which firms continue to adhere to the production of price-sensitive, relatively standardised goods, and make extensive use of numerical flexibility underpinned by fairly lax rules governing hiring and firing, is perhaps best typified as flexible mass production.

Both the German and the Italian production systems, although very different in nature, presuppose 'relational' contracting in the context of a congenial organisational environment, and a strong reliance on collectivised factor inputs (Streeck 1992; Dei Ottati 1996). Both DQP/FS and relational contracting are facilitated by "joint, collective, obligated and regulated provision of vital, non-appropriable production inputs" (Streeck 1992: 25). Traditionally, these social inputs are largely absent in the British production system, and the social supports for relational contracting are considered to be weak, on the whole. This leaves individual firms more isolated but also enhances managerial autonomy which may result in greater organisational flexibility — the phenomenon highlighted by Lehrer and Darbishire (this volume).

However, by the early 1990s it had become evident that because of intense international competition in their core markets, German firms were straining to achieve cost-efficient quality, whereas their British counterparts had intensified efforts to increase product quality. In the German case, this reorientation in product strategy has been accompanied by efforts to introduce greater flexibility into organisational structures and patterns of labour utilisation (Lane 1995), as well as reducing the cost of outsourcing. The latter has been pursued by both appointing suppliers in the lower-wage neighbouring Eastern European countries and by attempts to make German suppliers achieve cost savings (Cooke 1993). But, by and large and with variation between industries, attempts to save costs have focused more strongly on increasing process automation than on extracting one-sided sacrifices from either employees or suppliers. The strategy of buying components from lower-wage countries, although much increased, has remained marginal in proportional terms (Dörre 1996). In sum, although German managers are now more aware of the necessity to achieve cost-efficient quality the steps taken to attain it have remained modest, and the pursuit of dynamic efficiency based on quality and continual updating of products has not been abandoned.

In Britain, where an orientation to price competition has long been well established (Hodges and Woolcock 1993), the new pressures are diametrically opposed to those experienced in Germany. The predominant concentration on low-tech industries and the ability of new market entrants from Asia Pacific and Eastern Europe to undercut British prices have resulted in a concerted push by many firms to become both more specialised and to shift products towards the higher quality end of the spectrum. These efforts have been supported by selective government policies and campaigns to raise skill levels, encourage the adoption of quality management standards and even to strengthen trade associations (Lane and Bachmann 1997; Lane 1997). But all these measures have been enacted within the old framework of 'thin' institutions and, instead of institutionalising mutual obligation, have continued to rely on voluntarist participation. While these measures have not been without success, the shift to new performance standards has been accomplished only selectively and precariously. Moreover, government support for such measures has been seriously undermined by the much more dominant set of policies, orientated towards deregulation and the destruction of collectivistic institutions which, in any case, did not possess the strength to enforce constraints on opportunistic behaviour. The impact on supplier relations has been an increased pressure to provide quality and reliability, without, however, relinquishing the insistence on competitive prices. Moreover, the pursuit of dynamic efficiency continues to find insufficient institutional support.

This set of circumstances makes it just as difficult as in Germany to achieve the widespread and sustained shift to a new set of performance standards. Although it may be easier to rally the various industrial actors behind the banner of higher product quality the structures to attain this goal, we will demonstrate, remain incompletely developed. In Germany, where the task of lowering production costs is much more divisive and hence apparently more formidable the challenge is to develop a new consensus without destroying the 'thick' institutions which are a precondition for implementation.

In Italy, the 'industrial district' model of close inter-firm cooperation and regional clustering has also come under pressure from international competition on both quality and price. On the whole, the export performance of particular industrial districts has remained high and high rates of innovation are also reported; a fall in manufacturing employment in some areas has been more than offset by a rise in related services employment (see Brusco et al. 1996; Dei Ottati 1996). A recent assessment is therefore that the industrial district experience "has demonstrated that competitiveness on global markets is not a contradiction to high labour costs, high incomes and a fair distribution of income; on the contrary, we would claim that a fair income distribution is a necessary condition (although not sufficient), for consensus, and consensus and participation are an indispensable prerequisite for economic success" (Brusco et al. 1996: 35).

Since it is a feature of the Italian system that performance relies to a large extent upon local reputational effects and upon the diffusion of good practice rather than upon formal norms and standards, it is significant that the intensification of international competition and the increasing pace of technological change should have led to calls for a *strengthening* of institutional intervention aimed at maintaining the conditions for effective cooperation: "an effective institutional support is required both (a) for the accelerated renewal and upgrading of localised pools of industrial knowledge and know-how; and (b) for ensuring a more conscious and predetermined cooperation among the many competing actors (individual and collective, as well as private and public) that populate the district" (Dei Ottati 1996: 61). It has been suggested that this might take the forms of greater decentralisation of governmental powers, reforms to the structure of representative institutions, and the strengthening of links between SMEs and the science base of research and development (Cossentino 1996).

4.   The Industry-Level Environment

In order to examine more closely the hypothesis of a link between performance standards and economic performance outputs, it is necessary to consider in more detail the role of industry-specific factors and how they interact with the wider institutional environment in influencing firm-level strategies. The sectors studied here (mining machinery and kitchen furniture) are traditional, primarily production-oriented industries, making products of medium- to high-complexity which necessitate careful coordination of a large variety of inputs but require only incremental updating of product and process technology. Firms in these industries have a history of private-sector ownership and are highly attuned to market competition. They operate in both home and export markets which, since the early 1990s, have exhibited far-reaching changes in the level of demand (mining machinery) and an increasing shift to cost-effective quality as a factor of competitiveness (kitchen furniture).

There is a contrast here with studies of British and German firms which have been recently privatised and which are still relatively highly regulated and primarily service-oriented (see Lehrer and Darbishire, this volume). The latter operate in a much more turbulent business environment where either new technology (telecommunications) or a fundamentally changed structure of demand (air transport) have put a premium on high organisational flexibility and a capacity for fast response to external changes.[1] What these industries share in common with those in more traditional production sectors are demands for cost savings in response to intensified competitive (and/or regulatory) pressures, and the British strategy to achieve such savings through employment cuts is also evident in both sets of industries.

The differences between Britain, Germany and Italy in the two industries covered by our research largely, though not completely, reflect those in national/ regional social systems of production outlined above.[2] In the kitchen furniture industry, German and Italian firms have both pursued diversified quality production, aiming at the high quality/high price end of the market. Whereas German firms compete on technological ingenuity/solidity of products (Döhl et al. 1989), Italian firms are known for the highly individual style and elegance of their products. Both sell on European markets and compete with each other. There is a high degree, in each case, of regional concentration of firms which assists in the development of networks of cooperation (Ostwestphalen in Germany, and parts of Tuscany and Emilia-Romagna in Italy).

Many British kitchen furniture firms, by contrast, have been more focused on the low price, standardised and often self-assembly end of the market, and have been unable until recently to make inroads into foreign markets or to respond effectively to import penetration.[3] The market is divided into a small number of large manufacturers and a fringe of small firms, many of which are unstable; between 1990 and 1992 10 per cent of all firms in the furniture and timber industry in Britain entered into formal insolvency proceedings. The demand for kitchen furniture has been subject to the general instability of the British housing market. In 1988 sales were £681 million but during the recession in the housing market they fell again to £531 million.

Mining machinery, in all three countries, is produced in a production system close to flexible specialisation, demanding solutions customised to specific geological conditions, as well as a high degree of reliability and technical capacity. Whereas such a product strategy fits well into the social system of production of Germany and the Third Italy, it is less well adapted to the British industrial order. In Germany and Britain, due to the decline of domestic mining capacity, mining machinery firms have become highly dependent on sales in global markets, whereas the Italian firms surveyed for the research reported here, which had not specialised so exclusively in deep-mine machinery, could still rely on a substantial home market.

The decline of domestic mining production was particularly sharp in Britain (Department of Trade and Industry 1993). Until 1991, British Coal (formerly the National Coal Board, a nationalised corporation) was the largest single buyer of mining equipment in any developed country; the number of coal faces worked in Britain was greater than in the whole of the United States. However, between 1987 and 1991, 70 per cent of UK mines were closed. During this period, both British Coal and the electricity generators who were its major customers were undergoing a process of privatisation, and government policy encouraged the introduction of competition into energy markets with the result that stable demand for coal was no longer guaranteed. Electricity privatisation was completed in 1990. The privatised generators agreed a contract with British Coal for the delivery of coal at prices substantially above those available on world markets. At the same time, new use was made of gas as a source of power; this was expected to take out the equivalent of 25 to 30 million tonnes of coal from the generation market at a time when British Coal supplied 77 million tonnes of a total of 101 million tonnes consumed in the UK. British Coal's supply contracts with the generators were due to expire in 1993; by October 1992 it had failed to agree contracts for more than a few months ahead and was forced to make a rapid reduction in capacity. It announced that 31 of the remaining 51 pits would shut with immediate effect and, despite a public outcry and legal challenges, all pits deemed to be uneconomic had closed by December 1994. On 24 December all mines owned by British Coal were handed over to private ownership, with RJB Mining taking over 14 out of the 15 remaining deep mines and 14 of 32 open cast sites.

The effects of the decline in the domestic market for coal in the 1980s and 1990s were directly transmitted to the UK mining machinery sector (Trade and Industry Select Committee 1993). In real terms the market for mining machinery declined in value by 50 per cent between 1982 and 1992. In 1982 machinery sales amounted to £824,000; in 1992 this figure had fallen to £393,800. In 1992, the trade association ABMEC (the Association of British Mining Equipment Companies) estimated that the effect on its member companies of reducing the number of mines from 50 to 20 would be to reduce turnover by 36 per cent and employment by two thirds (from 22,000 to around 7,000).

In Germany, by contrast, the relationship between the coal industry and electricity generation was stabilised during the same period by the so-called Century Contract, agreed in 1980. This guaranteed the mining industry rising annual sales to the generators at cost price until 1995, with prices being subsidised from government expenditure raised by a special tax. The steel industry was also required through long-term contracts to buy a fixed amount of German coal, with an element of public subsidy. In 1991 both the electricity and the steel contracts were renegotiated. The electricity agreement planned for a reduction in the demand for coal from 70 million to 50 million tonnes by the year 2000, to be achieved in gradual annual stages; an element of public subsidy was retained despite doubts as to its legality under the EC Treaty. In effect, the mining machinery firms were thereby given notice that their dependence on Ruhrkohle AG (the principal coal producer) was coming to an end, and that they should seek out markets overseas. However, neither the speed nor the scale of this contraction was comparable to that being experienced by British firms during the same period. In 1991, the German mining machinery sector employed 18,500 workers, mainly concentrated in the Ruhr region; Ruhrkohle, 50 per cent of whose business remained in the coal sector, employed 109,000 workers in 1994 (for further information see Kienitz 1987; Lehner et al. 1989; Korfmann 1992; Weber 1992).

5. Competitive Pressures and Relational Contracting

We now turn to an analysis of information on the contracting strategies of firms in the industries in question which were surveyed in 1994 and 1995 (for details on the methodological design of the study see Deakin, Lane and Wilkinson 1997). Respondents were asked, firstly, about the nature of the competitive pressures facing them (see Table 1). 71 per cent of the firms said that price was important for competitive success, 77 per cent referred to quality, 71 per cent cited ability to deliver on time, and 32 per cent believed product development/improvement to be important. The highest proportion of firms stressing price (80 per cent) were British, the highest per cent emphasising quality were Italian (89 per cent), while German firms were the most likely (41 per cent) and British firms the least likely (20 per cent) to put emphasis on product development/improvement. Firms in all sectors and countries reported that a considerable intensification of competition had occurred since in the late 1980s and early 1990s. In terms of changes over time, price, quality and delivery on time, in that order, were seen by substantial proportions of firms as having increased in importance; smaller proportions of firms cited design, product development and product improvement (see Table 2). The largest proportion of firms, by a small margin, attributing an increase in importance to price, were again the British, and for quality the Italian firms were again leading. But concerning product development/improvement, this time Italian and British firms attributed increased importance for competitiveness more often than did German firms.

The impact on the vertical supply chain of the intensification of competition is suggested by the fact that 59 per cent, 33 per cent, 54 per cent and 34 per cent

Table 1: *Firms' Perceptions of Which Factors Were Important for Competitive Success*

% of firms:	By Country			
	Germany	Britain	Italy	All
Price	61	80	70	71
Design	22	55	32	35
Quality	70	75	89	77
Product development	43	20	21	32
Product improvement	39	20	26	29
Delivery on time	65	75	74	71

Source: Comparative survey of supplier relations in Germany, Britain and Italy, 1993/4.

Table 2: *Firms' Perceptions of Which Factors Were Becoming* **More** *Important for Competitive Success*

% of firms:	By Country			
	Germany	Britain	Italy	All
Price	59	60	47	56
Design	5	20	21	15
Quality	23	45	63	43
Product development	9	15	16	13
Product improvement	0	5	11	5
Delivery on time	23	50	37	36

Source: Comparative survey of supplier relations in Germany, Britain and Italy, 1993/4.

of firms, respectively, reported that the control exercised by customers over prices, batch size, delivery dates, and credit terms had increased, compared with 14 per cent, 12 per cent, 20 per cent and 14 per cent, respectively, who considered that customer control over these matters had declined. All the German and British respondents and half the Italian respondents reported having problems with their trading partners. The most important complaints in all three countries were over price, quality and delivery, and although a similar proportion of customer and supplier firms complained about prices, 80 per cent of the customer firms identified quality and delivery as problems compared with less than half the suppliers. Customer firms told us they were more likely to change suppliers over poor quality and delivery than prices, while few suppliers claimed they would switch customers if they made quality and delivery demands which were too high. 66 per cent of the supplier firms said that they would switch from customers over low prices but less than 20 per cent of customer firms gave prices being too high as reasons for changing suppliers. Together, these findings suggest that the balance of power clearly lay with customer firms. An increasingly competitive buyers' market was requiring firms to supply improved products at keener prices.

However, despite the hard trading environment, the large majority of buyer and supplier firms we interviewed preferred long-term business relationships to short-term relations. Almost all the firms were interested in such links with 80 per cent of the German and 55 per cent of the British saying they were interested in forming long-term relations in all circumstances. The Italian firms were more specific. Half looked for long-term relationships when the products being traded were customised and half said they were interested in such relationships when they yielded mutual benefits. Other motives for forming long-term relationships between firms included security, strategic reasons, specific investments and the exchange of confidential information. However, despite the clear advantage they saw in long-term links, 84 per cent of the Italians, 42 per cent of the British and 30 per cent of the German saw advantages in short-term relations. These were seen as having potential to utilise spare capacity, to exploit price advantages, to exploit the economic position of other firms and as a means of retaining independence.

In short, firms across the range of industries and countries were interested in building long-term trading relationships as a response to growing demands from customers for competitiveness on both quality and price. However, where divergencies in terms of outcomes emerge is in the degree to which these concerns were translated into stable and durable relationships which could be described as 'relational', in the sense of being based on close links of trust and cooperation.

6.   Contract Form and Trust

The use of formal contracts to build trust between firms is an important, if often neglected, aspect of the development of relational strategies (see Deakin, Lane and Wilkinson 1997; Deakin and Wilkinson 1998). The survey evidence on which we are drawing here suggests that the forms inter-firm contracts take are more heavily influenced by country-specific aspects of the institutional framework than by industry-specific environments, although the latter are also important. Across the two sectors studied here, a greater degree of contractual formality was observed in the mining machinery industry than in kitchen furniture. Mining machinery firms almost all made use of exclusion or limitation clauses to cover themselves against the risk of extensive liability for the costs of lost production if one of their machines broke down. Few furniture firms were faced with potential costs of this kind, and use of exclusion clauses and other complex risk allocation devices was rare. But apart from this, there were no statistically significant differences by sector in the use by firms of written documentation, in their use of legally-binding agreements, in the use of particular contractual clauses, in their understanding of the likely costs of legal action, in the likelihood of legal action against another firm for breach of contract (see, for further detail, Arrighetti et al. 1997).

However, significant differences in all of the above factors were found at the level of the cross-country comparisons. In relation to the level of contractual formality, German firms in both sectors were much more likely to make use of clauses indicating a high level of inter-dependence and of formal planning for contingencies. Contracts in Germany tended to be longer-term, in the sense of spanning a number of discrete exchanges. In both Britain and Italy, most agreements tended to be order-specific or, at best, were loose 'framework' or 'requirement' contracts under which the buyer could place orders as required. British firms were the least likely to have formal performance standards based on audits and rating systems incorporated into contracts.

German and British agreements were found to be significantly more likely than Italian ones to contain clauses providing for a degree of exclusive dealing, protection of intellectual property rights, and retention of title over property after sale. In relation to planning, German firms were most likely to have hardship clauses requiring the parties to renegotiate the contract in the event of an unforeseen contingency. By contrast, British firms reported finding such terms 'confusing'. German firms were also more likely to have clauses governing the duration of the contract and allowing for termination for breach of condition or by way of notice; as all these are terms which are only necessary in contracts of a certain duration and covering more than one exchange, their presence is an indicator of the greater length and complexity of German contractual arrangements. Numerous German companies also reported making use of gentlemen's agreements; but their function was one of supplementing the more formal agreements. No German respondents used non-binding agreements or understandings to the exclusion of a formal agreement. Italian firms reported the lowest level of formality of contract terms, with little provision for contingencies and very little use of terms indicating a high degree of inter-dependence. The British firms occupied a middle position; this is largely accounted for by an important difference between the two sectors, with the kitchen furniture firms relying on contract formality far less than firms in mining machinery.

Table 3 contains details of two procedurally-related performance standards which firms used to monitor the quality of components supplied, namely formal quality audits and rating systems. Both of these were much less likely to be relied on by British firms than by their German and Italian counterparts. Table 4 shows that in relation to mechanisms for developing long-term and stable inter-firm relations, British firms were most prone to stress personal contacts (the latter were also regarded as important by the German respondents). German firms made use of quantity guarantees, and a high degree of interdependence among German firms was also indicated in their much greater mention — 50 per cent of German as

Table 3: *Performance Standards and Inter-Firm Linkages*

% of firms with:	By Country		
	Germany	Britain	Italy
Formal quality audits*	76	37	74
Rating systems*	87	35	72
No of Firms	(21)	(19)	(19)

* inter-country differences significant at the 1% level using the Chi-square test
Source: Comparative survey of supplier relations in Germany, Britain and Italy, 1993/4.

Table 4: *Additional Bases for Inter-Firm Linkages*

% of firms with:	By Country		
	Germany	Britain	Italy
Quantity guarantees[a]	61	25	53
Financial arrangements[a]	47	25	5
Technical assistance[b]	56	65	32
Personal contacts[b]	86	95	68
Visiting for product development[c]	50	22	–
No of Firms	(23)	(20)	(19)

[a] inter-country differences significant at 5% level, using the Chi-square test.
[b] inter-country differences significant at the 1% level, using the Chi-square test.
[c] Figures for Italy not available on this item. The total number of firms answering was 20 for Germany and 18 for Britain.

Source: Comparative survey of supplier relations in Germany, Britain and Italy, 1993/4.

opposed to 22 per cent of British firms — of joint product development/improvement as a reason for frequent visiting. (We have no comparable figure for the Italian sample.) Not surprisingly, German firms also attributed greater importance than did British and Italian firms to joint product development as conducive to the development of mutual trust (the respective scores were 7.2, 5.5 and 5.8 out of a possible 10) although the Italian firms scored slightly higher (5.4) than the German (4.8) and British (4.1) firms in connecting joint development of new production technology with the building of trust. Joint product development is significant not only as an indicator of close links between firms but also signals dedication to the promotion of dynamic efficiency, singled out in the introduction as one important performance goal in the new competition.

The survey also found evidence of important differences in respondents' attitudes in general towards the legal system, trading standards and the role of trade associations in the sectors and countries studied. In Germany, respondents commented that their contracts were shaped by the general law as well as by the 'general conditions of business' applying in their industry. Both the Civil Code and the general conditions were seen to apply 'as a matter of course', as did quality standards laid down by the DIN and by trade associations. These findings, when taken together with the results of the questions on contract form and duration, suggest that German firms were not simply aware of the legal and regulatory framework for exchange, but made active use of it in constructing long-term trading relationships. There is a strong contrast here with Italy, where firms were unable to estimate the costs and outcomes of legal action and did not rely extensively on contractual form to shape their relationship. This appears to reflect a system in which the court system is seen as slow, expensive and uncertain in terms of outcome. In addition, the impact of formal standard setting and regulation by the state and by sectoral bodies alike was seen as limited. In Britain, there was a sectoral divide. Most mining machinery contracts were detailed and sophisticated, but a large proportion of firms in the kitchen furniture sector reported that informal understandings were common, with some firms conducting business over a long period without either legally binding or written agreements.

A clear inter-country difference also arose with regard to methods of dealing with untrustworthy behaviour. When asked how they dealt with untrustworthiness in business relationships, more than 50 per cent of all firms surveyed said they ended relationships immediately, 21 per cent made contractual arrangements to cover the risk and 14 per cent made more informal efforts to sort things out. All but two (88 per cent) of the Italian respondents to this question claimed that they would terminate relations immediately. Such immediate action would also be taken by 50 per cent of British respondents while 25 per cent tried to sort out differences, and 25 per cent made contractual provisions to cover risk. An even smaller proportion of German firms said that they would respond to untrustworthiness by ending relationships (32 per cent), and a much higher proportion (41 per cent) responded by making contractual provisions to cover risk (Burchell and Wilkinson 1997)

Elsewhere (Deakin, Lane and Wilkinson 1997) we have described the predominant British strategy in terms of *flexibility outside contract*, because the informal contacts and understandings on which the parties relied to do business most often arose independently of, and sometimes even in contradiction of, the terms of a formal agreement. In Germany, on the other hand, *flexibility beyond contract* meant that flexibility took account of the contract in the sense of filling in gaps or providing for additional elements of performance. In Italy, the absence of 'hard' standards and the cost of using the legal system to enforce contracts was made up for, in part, by the presence of widely-accepted social norms governing quality and reliability and by collective provision of public goods, as well as by an implicit threat to cease trading with any firm which failed to match up to these expectations.

Did the voluntaristic approach of the British firms lead to reduced reliance on costly legal procedures for enforcing agreements? There was no evidence that this was the case, indeed, there was evidence to the contrary. German respondents made frequent references to the role of normative influences, in particular the standard form contracts of industry-level trade associations, in shaping contractual practice; but they expressed the greatest confidence in their ability to predict the level of legal costs; and they were the most likely to carry insurance against legal liability. They were also the least likely to take legal action for breach of contract, even to recover debts. By contrast, legal action for non-payment of the price was regarded as highly likely in Britain in both the sectors studied, but in particular in the kitchen furniture sector which exhibited the lowest level of contract formality of any of the industries studied, in the sense that several firms in this sample reported that they dispensed with contractual documentation altogether in favour of informal understandings. A number of British firms in both sectors complained about the practice of late payment of debts and many looked on legal action to claim the price as a matter of first, rather than last, resort.

On this basis, there is some evidence to suggest that the presence of a formal legal contract may be part of a strategy of building a 'trusting' relationship in which the parties are able to avoid the use of the courts (Germany); alternatively, in the absence of effective court-based ordering, firms rely on intermediate institutions and on a widely shared commercial morality, as well as the availability of alternative sources of supply, to achieve cooperation (Italy). By contrast, a strategy of basing the exchange on loose understandings and 'give and take', while it has certain advantages from the point of view of encouraging close personal dealings, may also lead both to distrust and to frequent recourse to the courts (Britain). In Britain, then, the relatively limited role for system trust did not necessarily entail a greater role for inter-personal or processual trust. Rather, the weakness of collective institutions resulted in an environment in which the formation of trustworthy relations was inhibited by the tendency of the more powerful firms to pursue their market advantage for all it was worth. Consider, for example, the following statement, made by a British respondent in the mining machinery industry:

> "There has been a fundamental change. In the old days of standard form conditions it was easy to place subcontracting work. Now that customers are varying their terms and conditions so quickly, there are enormous costs monitoring this and of customising terms with our own subcontractors. The whole process is much more difficult and twice the cost of before."

British respondents reported that it was becoming common for larger customers to seek to customise the normal industry-level terms, often insisting on the insertion of terms which exposed their subcontractors and suppliers to a high level of risk. Suppliers reported that they were obliged to accept this practice as a condition of continuing to do business with these customers. Instability in this aspect of the institutional framework was put down to the effects of the sharp recession of the early 1990s and also to privatisation in the electricity and mining industries, which had led to a reassessment of previously established standard form agreements.

7.   Performance Outcomes

How far are the different strategies adopted by firms reflected in different performance outcomes? Tables 5 and 6 summarise evidence concerning changes in turnover and employment between 1988 and 1994 in the sample of firms surveyed, by country and by sector. Sectoral factors are evident in the much greater level of job loss, and reduced rates of employment growth, in mining machinery for the period in question, a pattern which is also repeated for turnover. Differences by country are less marked; nevertheless, only 39 per cent of the British firms reported growth of turnover in real terms in the period of question as opposed to 61 per cent of German and 50 per cent of Italian firms. In relation to employment, 27 per cent of British firms reported a rise, compared to 53 per cent of German firms and 67 per cent of Italian firms. Across the British sample as a whole, performance with regard to employment was polarised between a substantial group reporting rapid growth, at one extreme, and one reporting rapid decline at the other. Another interpretation of the British data would be that improved turnover was often accompanied by downsizing of the workforce.

The survey data do not reveal a strong link between the adoption of practices which would indicate a high degree of close cooperation, and superior firm-level performance. No significant correlations were found between the adoption by *individual* firms of one of the features of close cooperation listed in Tables 3 and 4, and their performance as measured by increases in turnover and/or employment in the five years before the date of the interview. Both within the sample as a whole and within individual countries, the incidence of relational contracting was more or less randomly distributed among successful and less successful firms.

However, this is not the whole story, since the data in Tables 5 and 6 also indicate that the location of a firm makes an important difference to its performance in terms of employment and turnover. The British pattern is the exception here: a small group of highly successful firms at one extreme is set against a long tail of underperformers at the other.

A more useful indicator of performance than either employment or turnover is that provided by the export performance and orientation of firms which, we suggested earlier, can be taken as proxy for capacity to adjust to changed market

Table 5: *Change in Turnover 1988–1994 (1988 prices)*

% of firms with:	All Firms	By Country			By Product	
		Germany	Britain	Italy	Mining Machinery	Kitchen Furniture
Rapid decline	21	14	39	11	31	11
Stagnant or slow decline	33	33	28	39	31	36
Slow growth	26	29	11	39	21	32
Rapid growth	19	24	22	11	17	21
No of Firms	(57)	(21)	(18)	(18)	(29)	(28)

Source: Comparative survey of supplier relations in Germany, Britain and Italy, 1993/4

Table 6: *Change in Employment 1988–1994*

% of firms with:	All Firms	By Country			By Product	
		Germany	Britain	Italy	Mining Machinery	Kitchen Furniture
Rapid decline	21	19	39	6	34	7
Stagnant or slow decline	33	38	33	27	38	29
Slow growth	24	24	0	50	17	32
Rapid growth	21	19	27	17	10	32
No of Firms	(57)	(21)	(18)	(18)	(29)	(28)

Source: Comparative survey of supplier relations in Germany, Britain and Italy, 1993/4.

demands. Table 7 shows that a far larger percentage of British firms than in either of the other two countries had no overseas customers, although, at the opposite end of the scale, a sizeable group of British firms had more than half of their customers overseas. Industry-level data confirm this contrasting picture as far as Britain and Germany are concerned. Import penetration was lower and the proportion of domestic production exported was higher in Germany than in Britain in the period covered for both the industries in the survey. In 1987 imports formed over 20 per cent of UK domestic sales in kitchen furniture, and although this figure had dropped to less than 11 per cent by 1993, it compares unfavourably to import penetration of only 2 per cent in Germany during this time. In mining machinery, the export ratio (or value of exports as a proportion of production) in Britain touched 22 per cent in 1984 but fell back to as little to 8 per cent in 1990, rising again to 14 per cent in 1992; in Germany it was 46 per cent in 1991 Korfmann 1992; Department of Trade and Industry 1993). Comparable data for Italy for the 1990s have not been available, but data for the 1980s, cited by Regini (1997: 105, Table 5.1) suggests that the Italian situation in the two industries has been nearer to the German than to the British situation.

In this context, the relative performance of the British and German mining machinery industries since the early 1980s provides a useful point of comparison. The UK mining machinery industry has a long and successful history of exporting its products. In the early 1990s it was thought that 50 per cent of roof supports and face conveyor equipment in the United States was of UK origin, 80 per cent in Mexico, 80 per cent in South Africa, 90 per cent in Australia and 100 per cent in Japan. However, between 1982 and 1992 the value of exports fell by 40 per cent while the value of imports rose by a corresponding amount. In the mid-1990s, following the privatisation of British Coal and the rapid reduction in domestic coal production, the two principal final equipment suppliers (or 'orginal equipment manufacturers', OEMs) were taken over, in successive stages, by an American competitor. The US conglomerate, Harnishfeger Industries, which had previously

Table 7: *Firms with Overseas Customers*

% of firms	All Firms	By Country			By Product	
		Germany	Britain	Italy	Mining Machinery	Kitchen Furniture
0	23	14	45	11	13	33
1–25	33	32	10	58	29	37
24–50	34	45	30	26	45	23
51 and over	10	9	15	5	13	7
No of Firms	(61)	(22)	(20)	(19)	(31)	(30)

Source: Comparative survey of supplier relations in Germany, Britain and Italy, 1993/4.

taken over Joy, the US owner of one of the two principal UK OEMs, completed a hostile takeover of Dobson Park Industries, the UK owners of Longwall International, in October 1995. Thus only one or perhaps two sizeable OEMs remain. Although similar moves towards concentration have taken place in Germany, there are still a dozen or more large independent companies and altogether the industry in the Ruhr alone (the principal region) contains around 100 firms. It remains to be seen which strategy is the most successful in enabling the industry to survive through diversification and expansion into new export markets (such as Iran, China and the countries of the former Soviet Union). However, what is clear is that the process of rationalisation which was set in train by the rapid running-down of UK coal production has reduced the UK mining machinery industry to a shadow of its former self in a very short space of time.

8.   Conclusions: Institutions and Competitiveness

There is evidence that relational linkages which, in different forms, exist in Germany and Italy, have raised the *general* level of performance of firms in those systems, by requiring firms, as an effective precondition of entry, to come up to a certain threshold. Performance in the two traditional industries investigated in this chapter has been viewed as the attainment of dynamic efficiency, i.e. the ability to conform to new market demands for cost-efficient quality and incremental product innovation. The preconditions for the achievement of dynamic efficiency — the adoption of measures to maintain product quality and constant technological updating — were significantly more developed among German and Italian than British firms, and the superior export performance, on average, among the former additionally has confirmed their superior adjustment to the new market demands. This suggests, in turn, that the performance of firms is linked to two key features of national-level environments, namely a stable domestic market and an institutional framework which provides incentives for strategies based on high quality production and incremental innovation.

The variations in performance *within* each system which our data reveal reflect, in addition to varying economic contexts of supplier firms, differences in the managerial and other capabilities of individual firms; the institutional influences which serve to promote quality and technological ingenuity in a given system are necessary but not sufficient conditions for its achievement *at the level of the firm*. But even if individual firms vary in their capacity to compete, it is still the case that such institutional support is a prerequisite for the enhanced competitiveness of the system (or group of firms, defined by industry, region or country) as a whole. The fact that the degree of variation was particularly high among British firms bears out the claim, made in the introduction, that weak coupling and low cohesion in the institutional framework permit greater managerial autonomy and hence a higher degree of diversity within the productive system.

Krugman (1994) has argued that the 'competitiveness' of a nation or industry is a meaningless concept, in the sense that it is only the ability to compete of individual firms which matters. Our comparative findings, however, suggest that institutional features which are found at national, regional and sectoral level can have a bearing, firstly, on the form in which the elements of inter-firm relations, including performance standards, are constructed and, secondly, on performance outcomes. Supposedly 'rigid' performance standards, based on long-term contracts and quality thresholds, can have the effect of raising the general level of performance in a given sector, as can less formal 'social' norms which operate at a conventional or customary level. By contrast, the absence of norms or conventions governing inter-firm cooperation may adversely affect the degree to which an industry generates high-quality and technologically sophisticated products; although their absence does not preclude the emergence of successful individual firms, these tend to be the exception in industries which are characterised by the survival of a large number of low cost, low quality producers. Such exceptional firms may have compensated for their low degree of institutional embeddedness by relying more strongly on social embeddedness to create governance mechanisms.

We have argued that close, trust-based cooperation in supplier relations is not necessarily conducive to raising general performance levels in all industries but instead have suggested that there is a strategic fit between relational contracting and gradual adaptation to changed market demands, including incremental innovation. Whether, conversely, arm's length contracting, which gives managements of both supplier and buyer firms more manoeuvring space, is therefore more conducive to higher performance in highly volatile sectors, requiring a high degree of organisational flexibility (Lehrer and Darbishire, this volume), is still under debate. A longer history of sustained superior performance in such sectors will be required to settle this question. Finally, our data have clearly demonstrated that increased international competition and greater interconnectedness between national economies have not weakened distinctiveness in production systems but have rather served to perpetuate it in only slightly altered forms.

Notes

1. It should also be noted that differences in the regulatory framework for telecommunications in, for example, Germany on the one hand and the United Kingdom and the United States on the other, have affected the strategies adopted by telecommunications firms in those countries, and that this has had implications for the sharing of costs and benefits between different 'stakeholder' groups (see Batt and Darbishire 1997).

2. The following description mainly applies, in each industry, to final equipment producers; there is greater variation among suppliers, depending on the components they supply.

3. Information in this paragraph is based on trade sources and on UK official statistics, in particular the Business Monitor Series of the Central Statistical Office.

References

Arrighetti, A., R. Bachmann, and S. Deakin. 1997. Contract law, social norms, and inter-firm cooperation, *Cambridge Journal of Economics* 21: 171–195.

Batt, R. and O. Darbishire. 1997. Institutional determinants of deregulation and restructuring in telecommunications: Britain, Germany and the United States compared, *International Contributions to Labour Studies* 7: 59–79.

Berger, S., and R. Dore (eds.). 1996. *National Diversity and Global Capitalism.* Ithaca, NY: Cornell UP.

Best, M. 1990. *The New Competition: Instructions of Industrial Restructuring.* Cambridge: Polity Press.

Brusco, S., G. Cainelli, F. Forni, M. Franchi, A. Malusardi, and R. Righetti. 1996. The evolution of industrial districts in Emilia-Romagna. In: F. Cossentino, F. Pyke, and W. Sengenberger (eds.), *Local and Regional Response to Global Pressure: The Case of Italy and its Industrial Districts.* Geneva: IILS.

Burchell, B., and F. Wilkinson. 1997. Trust, business relationships, and the contractual environment, *Cambridge Journal of Economics* 21: 217–237.

Cooke, P. 1993. The experience of German engineering firms in applying lean production methods. In: IILS (ed.), *Lean Production and Beyond: Labour Aspects of a New Production Concept.* Geneva: International Institute of Labour Studies.

Cossentino, F. 1996. The need for a new regulatory and institutional order. In: F. Cossentino, F. Pyke, and W. Sengenberger (eds.), *Local and Regional Response to Global Pressure: The Case of Italy and its Industrial Districts.* Geneva: IILS.

Crouch, C., and W. Streeck (eds.). 1997. *The Political Economy of Modern Capitalism.* London: Sage.

Deakin, S., T. Goodwin, and A. Hughes. 1997. Cooperation and trust in inter-firm relations: beyond competition policy?. In: S. Deakin, and J. Michie (eds.), *Contracts,*

Cooperation and Competition. Studies in Economics, Management and Law, 339–369. Oxford: OUP.

Deakin, S., C. Lane, and F. Wilkinson. 1997. Contract law, trust relations and incentives for cooperation: a comparative study. In: S. Deakin, and J. Michie (eds.), *Contracts, Cooperation and Competition. Studies in Economics, Management and Law*, 105–142. Oxford: OUP.

Deakin, S., and F. Wilkinson. 1998. Contract law and the economics of interorganizational trust. In: C. Lane, and R. Bachmann (eds.), *Trust within and between Organizations. Conceptual Issues and Empirical Applications*, 146–172. Oxford: OUP.

Dei Ottati, G. 1996. The remarkable resilience of the industrial districts of Tuscany. In: F. Cossentino, F. Pyke, and W. Sengenberger (eds.). 1996. *Local and Regional Response to Global Pressure: The Case of Italy and its Industrial Districts*. Geneva: IILS.

Department of Trade and Industry. 1993. White Paper, *Prospects for Coal* (Cm. 2235. London: HMSO.

DiMaggio, P. J., and W. W. Powell. 1991. The iron cage revisited: institutional isomorphism and collective rationality, in W. W. Powell, and P. J. DiMaggio (eds.), *The New Institutionalism in Organizational Analysis*. Chicago, London: University of Chicago Press.

Döhl, V., N. Altmann, M. Deiss, and D. Sauer. 1989. *Neue Rationalisierungsstrategien in der Möbelindustrie. I. Markt und Technikeinsatz*. Frankfurt/Main: Campus.

Dörre, K. 1996. Globalstrategien von Unternehmen — ein Desintegrationsphänomen? Zu den Auswirkungen grenzüberschreitender Unternehmensaktivitäten auf die industriellen Beziehungen, *SOFI Mitteilungen* 24, November: 15–28.

Grabher, G. 1993. Rediscovering the social in the economics of interfirm relations: the weakness of strong ties. In: G. Grabher (ed.), *The Embedded Firm*, 1–31. London, New York: Routledge.

Granovetter, M. 1985. Economic action and social structure: the problem of embeddedness, *American Journal of Sociology* 91: 481–510.

Hodges, M., and S. Woolcock. 1993. Atlantic capitialism versus Rhine capitalism in the European community, *West European Politics* 16(3): 329–44.

Hollingsworth, J. R., and R. Boyer (eds.). 1997. *Contemporary Capitalism: the Embeddedness of Institutions*. Cambridge: CUP.

Kern, H. 1998. Lack of trust, surfeit of trust: some causes of the innovation crisis in German industry. In: C. Lane, and R. Bachmann (eds.), *Trust within and between Organizations*, 203–213. Oxford: OUP.

Kienitz, K.-P. 1987. Die Ruhrkohle AG — eine unternehmerische Antwort auf die Strukturkrise der Steinkohle in den 60iger Jahren. In: L. Neumann (ed.), *Die Ruhrkohle AG: Sozialökonomische Unternehmensbiographie eines Konzerns*, 12–41. Bochum: Germinal.

Korfmann, H.-D. 1992. Die deutsche Bergbaumaschinenindustrie vor neuen Herausforderungen, *Glückauf* 128(5): 348–58.

Krugman, P. 1994. Competitiveness: a dangerous obsession, *Foreign Affairs* 73: 28–44.

Lane, C. 1994. Britain: a Stalled Social System of Production?, Paper prepared for the Workshop on Social Systems of Production, May Manchester, Mimeo, University of Cambridge, UK.

Lane, C. 1995. *Industry and Society in Europe*. Aldershot: Edward Elgar.

Lane, C. 1997. The social regulation of inter-firm relations in Britain and Germany: market rules, legal norms and technical standards, *Cambridge Journal of Economics* 21: 197–215.

Lane, C., and R. Bachmann. 1996. The social construction of trust: supplier relations in Britain and Germany, *Organization Studies* 17: 365–95.

Lane, C., and R. Bachmann. 1997) Cooperation in inter-firm relations in Britain and Germany: the role of social institutions, *British Journal of Sociology*, 48: 226–255.

Lehner, F., J. Nordhause-Janz, and K. Schubert. 1989. *Probleme und Perspektiven des Strukturwandels der Bergbau-Zulieferindustrie*. Bochum: Arbeitsgemeinschaft für angewandte Sozialforschung und Praxisberatung, University of Bochum.

Mayer, C. 1997. Corporate governance, competition and performance, *Journal of Law & Society* 24: 152–176.

Piore, M., and C. Sabel. 1984. *The Second Industrial Divide*. New York: Basic Books.

Regini, M. 1997. Social institutions and production structure: the Italian variety of capitalism in the 1980s'. In: C. Crouch, and W. Streeck (eds.), *Political Economy of Modern Capitalism*, 102–116. London, Thousand Oaks, New Delhi: Sage.

Sorge, A. 1991. Strategic fit and the societal effect: interpreting cross-national comparisons of technology, organization and human resources, *Organization Studies* 12(2): 161–190.

Streeck, W. 1992. *Social Institutions and Economic Performance*. London: Sage.

Streeck, W. 1997. German capitalism: Does it exist? Can it survive?. In: C. Crouch, and W. Streeck (eds.), *Political Economy of Modern Capitalism*, 33–54. London: Sage.

Trade and Industry Select Committee. 1993. *UK Energy Policy and the Market for Coal*. Cm. 237-xiv, Session 1992–93. London: HMSO.

Weber, H. 1992. Strukturwandel des Bergwerksmaschinenbaus und innovative Beschäftigungs- und Qualifizierungspolitik. Final Report of a special study for the Metal Industry's Innovation and Coordination Bureau in the Ruhr Area. Gelsenkirchen: Institut für Arbeit und Technik.

Whitley, R. 1992. Societies, firms and markets: the social structuring of business systems. In: R. Whitley (ed.), *European Business Systems*, 5–45. London: Routledge.

Whitley, R. 1994. Dominant forms of economic organization in market economies, *Organization Studies* 15(2): 153–82.

CHAPTER 4

Comparative Managerial Learning in Germany and Britain

Techno-Organisational Innovation in Network Industries

Mark Lehrer   Owen Darbishire

1. Introduction

Economies can, to a significant extent, be distinguished by the 'richness' of their respective institutional contexts. Continental European economies can be characterised as offering a dense pattern of networks between firms, industry associations, unions, and banks, alongside what many argue as government-provided frameworks for collective thinking and planning that have been beneficial to firms and employees alike. By contrast, the more decentralised economic organisation in the UK and US has incorporated a greater focus on individual entrepreneurship and an atomistic view of economic behaviour anchored in the sacrosanct principle of autonomous decision-making by firms.

During the 1970s and 1980s, widespread interpretations of the economic performance of Germany led many to the conclusion that rich institutional networks amounted to more than simply promoting positive social gains to stakeholders. Rather, gains in economic performance were perceived as deriving from the stability the system provided, from its ability to facilitate adaptation through the reduction in risk and uncertainty to stakeholders, a consensual approach to implementing change, and the clear acceptance of technological advance. However, a reassessment of this analysis suggests that the success of German socio-economic institutions has depended on a particular constellation of market conditions and technological changes that may have receded in the 1990s (see Streeck 1997; and the essay by Deakin et al. in this volume). In at least certain industries, new sets of market conditions and technological options appear to favour Anglo-Saxon institutional patterns, owing to globalisation, more rapid rates of market change, and opportunities for technological substitution.

Two core service industries, airlines and telecommunications, illustrate this changing, and contingent, comparative advantage of national institutions. In both industries techno-organisational innovation has proceeded more rapidly at the British competitors (British Airways and British Telecom) than at their German counterparts (Lufthansa and Deutsche Telekom respectively) (Darbishire 1997a; Lehrer 1997a,b). In both the airline and telecommunications industries, substantial technological change has altered the nature of competitive strategy and organisational demands, necessitating radical restructuring rather than incremental adaptation. Under these new dynamic environmental conditions the managerial autonomy afforded by the British institutional structure has helped the UK national champions respond more rapidly than their consensus-oriented German counterparts in the adoption of key technologies — with a significant impact on commercial profitability (airlines) or ability to lower costs and offer a higher level of service (telecommunications).

The cross-national institutional comparison in this paper illustrates the importance of different forms of 'learning'. German institutions both facilitate and encourage 'technical learning', which is particularly suited to environments where the knowledge base is stable and predictable, and progress incremental. As the results from the airline and telecommunications industries demonstrate, the comparative institutional advantage of Britain is not simply that the principle of managerial autonomy has enabled the UK national champion to engage in more rapid shifts of business policy by utilising a top-down implementation approach that their consensually oriented German competitors could not. Rather, the managerial autonomy in the airline and telecommunications industries was a key factor promoting a particular pattern of trial and error, or 'experimental learning'. In contradistinction to the 'technical learning' of German institutions, it is this 'experimental learning' that is encouraged by British institutions.

Both civil aviation and telecommunications are industries where experimental learning has been important. In particular, these industries involve the management of large networks and as such companies in these industries are subject to constant competing pressures for centralisation and decentralisation. New technology has, furthermore, exacerbated these conflicting pressures. Consequently, determining the optimal organisational structure and the optimal incorporation (and configuration) of new technology into the organisation is apt to require constant experimentation. The following case studies strongly illustrate this, and reveal how the British national champions distinguished themselves through their capacity to experiment and learn through successive iterations of techno-organisational reform.

Beyond the tension between centralisation and decentralisation in their respective industries, the airlines and telecommunications companies had to manage a second duality: the conflict between an operations-based and a market-based business approach. Here the trend was more clear-cut: the market-based approach was unquestionably more appropriate in the altered environment. In what may seem like a paradox, it was principally the nature of technological change in the 1980s and 1990s which rendered the operations-based approach outdated, and favoured the market-based approach. Indeed, the nature of new technological opportunities was substantially more significant than deregulation and privatisation. The early privatisations of both British Telecom (in 1984) and British Airways (1987) in what had previously been heavily regulated markets undoubtedly increased the commercial acumen of these firms. Yet their impact should not be overstated. Privatisation was certainly valuable in allowing BT and BA to reduce headcount through voluntary departure programmes (though neither company has had to resort to lay-offs).[1] Yet in neither industry was the essential nature of the market altered as a result of either deregulation or privatisation. Far more important has been the changing nature of technology, and the impact that this has had on optimal competitive strategies in the two respective industries.[2]

Detailed analyses of airlines and telecommunications highlight that a deeper understanding than privatisation alone is required to explain the greater techno-organisational innovation undertaken by BT and BA vis-à-vis their European counterparts. Comparisons with Deutsche Telekom and Lufthansa illustrate just how far the British national champions have advanced, and show that within the changing parameters of these industries BT and BA did considerably more than simply cut costs and personnel. Lufthansa, which had been a leader in European aviation for almost three decades, declined and was overtaken by BA in the 1980s in a series of technological and organisational innovations (Lehrer 1997a). Deutsche Telekom, which had technologically and organisationally out-performed its British rival, was similarly surpassed by BT in the development of a market-based organisational structure, while it also lost its historic lead in a rapidly changing technological and competitive environment (Darbishire 1997a).

Although the concept of performance underlying the present analysis is centred on key techno-organisational innovations in the industries studied (and certain economic repercussions of these innovations), some of the distributional consequences will likewise be evident. In general, the capacity of the British firms to reorganise themselves more rapidly than their German counterparts has included the authority of management to effectively impose losses unilaterally on groups within the firm who stand to lose from reorganisation. Nonetheless, the non-negligible benefits to British consumers and shareholders deriving from their national champions' more rapid pace of techno-organisational learning makes it difficult to derive unambiguous judgements about social welfare and fairness.

The balance of this article falls into three parts. Empirical evidence of the air transport and then telecommunications industries is presented to shed light on the precise nature of the innovative activities observed in each case. Subsequently, these findings will be placed into a larger theoretical context. It is argued that of substantial importance has been that in both industries technology has altered the nature of competition, and introduced new forms and elements of competition. Within this radically altered industry environment we argue that the institutional structure within which UK firms operated was able to facilitate greater organisational and operational experiments, innovation, and restructuring of activities to enhance performance. The German firms followed later along a path that had already been trodden by the UK leader because of institutional constraints upon their ability to engage in organisational experiments, rather than to implement incremental adjustment along a historically well-established competitive trajectory.

2.   British Airways versus Lufthansa

The 1980s witnessed a period of rapid technological change and market liberalisation in European civil aviation. The ascendancy of British Airways from 'Bloody Awful' to leading European carrier during the course of the 1980s contrasts with the relative decline of Lufthansa in that decade, and with the financial disaster of carriers like Air France. Figure 1 presents a comparison of the British and German carriers' financial performance in the years 1987–1995. Detailed research in the industry reveals techno-organisational innovation as explaining a surprisingly large part of the variance, estimated at about £300m (Lehrer 1997b). However, this innovative activity was of a nature not at all apparent to casual observers of the industry — and, for a long time, not even to managers in competing European airlines.

Techno-organisational innovations at BA amounted to a 'paradigm shift,' and in implementing these changes British Airways had, by the mid-1980s, built up

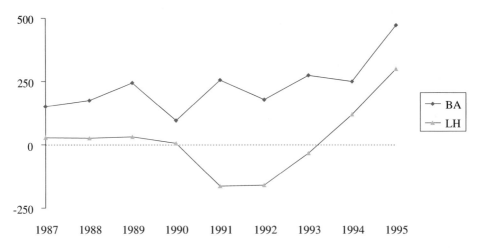

Figure 1. *Group Profits (£ millions)*

Source: Calculated by authors from company annual reports

a 5–10 year lead over its rivals in the areas of information systems, organisational structure, hub planning, flight scheduling, and global selling across its network. A key component of the paradigm shift was in its 'revenue management' system, that is, in forecasting, capacity-adjusting, and price-setting tools. An indication of BA's innovative prowess can be gauged by the fact that it was able to install successive generations of revenue management systems by means of in-house development, whereas airlines like Lufthansa and Air France had to depend on American vendors of revenue management technology (Lehrer 1997b). In other words, Lufthansa did not actually innovate at all, but simply emulated British Airways once the lag in commercial practices had become manifest and the know-how for implementing key IT components became commercially available. Yet whether they innovated or simply imitated, all major European airlines were obliged to implement the new paradigm. Although the complexity of the issue is too great to cover at any length here, a list of the essential changes is contained in Figure 2.

The difference between the old and new paradigms in European civil aviation corresponded to the shift from point-to-point and hub-and-spokes configurations in the US only to a certain extent. While the new paradigm adopted by British Airways (and much later by Lufthansa) did indeed mean intensifying the strategic centrality of the hub airports at London (and Frankfurt), it also required a number of other adjustments which were not entirely obvious merely from observing the behaviour of US carriers. These included overhauling information systems to optimise pricing structures ('revenue management'), transferring control over the planning functions to the marketing department, and centralising the sales organisation so that sellers optimise revenue across the airline's whole network of routes rather than just their own geographical profit centre.

System	Old Paradigm	New Paradigm
View of market and corresponding number of markets	100–200 markets: Separate markets to and from home country	10,000–20,000 markets: Intensified use of main airport as international hub
Optimization of prices and schedule	On route by route basis (segmented network)	On O&D basis (Origin and destination of passengers)
Planning of scheduling, pricing, selling	Separate, sequential tasks in different departments	Tightly integrated by a central network department under control of marketing
Sales organisation	Decentralised	Centralised to optimise network benefits

Figure 2. *Paradigm Shift*

Collectively, these changes serve the purpose of 'optimising the network,' which became a battle cry of airline managers when they realised the need to do so. However, none of the changes make sense in isolation, and nor could they be made incrementally. Rather, to 'optimise the network' the whole set of airline systems had to be changed in step, and a 'big bang' in top management recognition had to take place for the process to start. This interdependence among systems and the difficult-to-recognise character of the new paradigm helps to explain why, after BA adopted the paradigm in the mid-1980s, competitors such as Lufthansa and Air France failed to do so until well into the 1990s — by which time Lufthansa managers estimated that their tardiness was costing them about DM 700m in foregone revenue (Lehrer 1997b).

Although BA's profitability in the late 1980s had been ascribed by some to factors like lower wages, social security charges, slot congestion at Heathrow, or greater protection from competition in the UK-US bilateral aviation agreement, by the early 1990s it became clear that the British carrier had achieved technical dominance in certain key systems. For example, in late 1992 when Lufthansa CEO Weber was asked at a company 'town meeting' in Frankfurt what BA did differently to make high profits, he replied that there were three reasons:

– BA's well established and sophisticated yield management system, with 20 booking classes, gave it a seat-load factor (i.e. percentage of the plane filled) of 14 per cent higher than Lufthansa.
– BA operated a centralised hub structure in London, whereas decentralised services [such as those at Lufthansa] were becoming less profitable.[3]
– Profitable North Atlantic operations, thanks to the UK-US bilateral, were much more favourable than the Germany-US bilateral (*Der Lufthanseat*, 16 Oct 1992: 2).

Figures 3 and 4 give an approximate indication of BA's technological lead in the first area mentioned by Weber: the evolution of the number of booking classes and the implementation of four generations of revenue management that emerged in the 1980s and 1990s (for a more in-depth analysis see Lehrer 1997b). The achievement of BA's competitive advantage over Lufthansa, which resulted from its technological dominance and superior organisational structure and reforms, had its foundations in the differing national institutional contexts within each country.

The institutional features within Britain that proved particularly advantageous in adapting to the paradigm shift within the industry were the high discretion of the CEO, high managerial mobility, and a national culture of generalist (as opposed to specialist) managers (Lane 1989; Lehrer 1997b). These institutional traits were crucial enabling conditions in allowing British Airways' management to orchestrate the organisational experiments and manage the intra-firm power shifts that were needed to break with an operations-oriented approach that was

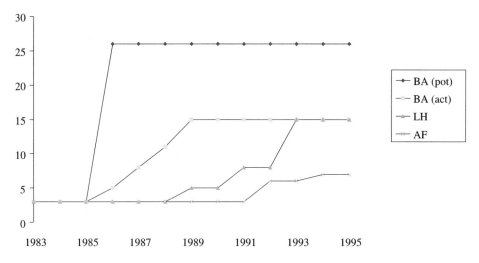

Figure 3. *Booking Classes. BA: pot(ential) vs. act(ual) in IT systems*

Source: Lehrer (1997b)

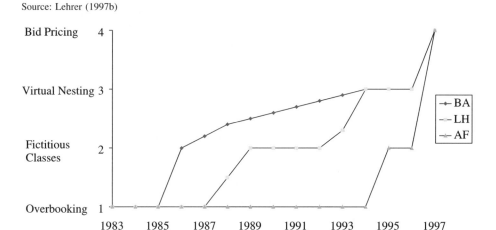

Figure 4. *Generations of Revenue Management*

Source: Lehrer (1997b)

typical in the industry. Up until 1983, British Airways, like Lufthansa, operated under the traditional division of labour between operations and marketing managers: the former were responsible for planning and execution of airline services whereas the job of the latter was to sell the capacity supplied by the operations people.

Even prior to privatisation, BA had the ability to restructure itself rapidly, and such reforms of organisational structure facilitated experimentation and learning of a particular kind: in learning more about markets and the way in which techno-organisational changes could improve BA's position in these markets. Thus, in May 1982 British Airways restructured itself into three divisions (International Services Heathrow, European Services Heathrow, and Gatwick Services). Yet by July 1983 all three division heads had been 'retired,' and an entirely new airline structure had been designed and put into place, this time based around eleven profit centres: eight geographic 'market centres' for passenger operations, plus cargo, charter, and package tours. During the legendary Night of the Long Knives (11 July 1983), 161 of BA's top managers were sacked and the newly formed profit centres were entrusted to a group of managers in their thirties and forties, often promoted three to four levels overnight. All profit centres reported to a powerful, newly appointed, marketing director. The 1983 reorganisation was planned in total secrecy by a handful of selected managers and announced as a total surprise, enabling BA to appoint young new managers to positions of power within the company. By 1986, and after a number of innovative experiments, BA was in a position to change its organisational structure once again, this time implementing the network-optimising paradigm described earlier. It cemented this by creating a centrally controlled world sales organisation guided by state-of-the-art information systems.

Although the cause of this flurry of activity was the appointment of Colin Marshall to chief executive in early 1983, of more importance institutionally was the enabling condition of formal authority vested in the chief executive under the UK system of corporate governance. With the assured backing of the board (which Marshall had), Marshall could unilaterally dictate policy and alter top management appointments. The role of the CEO was critical in orchestrating two very different processes simultaneously — the one open and public, the other hidden and a private company matter. Outwardly, Marshall professed a religion of customer service, of people, of staff as the greatest company asset, of the need to boost staff morale in order to boost the quality of customer service and company prosperity. However, inside the company and hidden from public view, Marshall reshuffled the managerial hierarchy drastically and put a completely different spin on his professed conviction that BA's 'most important assets are its people.'

Though openly advocating a 'market-driven' approach from the start, Marshall, as a former Hertz and Avis top executive, was at first very vague about what being 'market-driven' actually meant in an aviation context. Instead, his immediate policy was the promotion of young promising managers to positions they could never have obtained under the previous organisation. Less than three weeks after Marshall took office, four internally promoted managers, all in their 30s, were named to a core marketing team which became the all-important Marketing Policy Group, the key spawning area for BA's marketing innovations in the 1980s. The top managerial ranks were systematically screened during

Marshall's first months for 'set-in-their-ways' managers to be dismissed and younger, fresher talent to be promoted to run an entirely reorganised airline. The result was a flurry of fresh ideas and experimentation from 1983 on. The 1983 reorganisation which radically altered the company's internal power structure allowed experimentation to take place, while it was the 1986 reorganisation which cemented the adoption of the network-optimising paradigm on the basis of insights gained from the variety of novel practices that had been tried out. Both reorganisations were imposed in a very top-down way by Marshall and his key personal consultant Michael Levin. Though he never held an official position, Levin, who did most of the screening of managers within BA and conceived both reorganisations, essentially acted as Marshall's right arm, with almost unlimited discretion.

The rapidity with which Marshall was able to restructure operations within BA, and the ability to learn through progressive iterations of organisational reform, contrasts with what is possible within the German institutional context. German institutions strongly promote consensual decision-making in the top boards, while additionally encouraging hierarchies of career specialists. These institutional features made it difficult for Lufthansa to match many of BA's moves (Lehrer 1997a). Constrained from a hire-and-fire approach which paralleled BA's, Lufthansa's strategy was essentially to conceive of itself as the aviation equivalent of Porsche, BMW, and Mercedes. Indeed, in the face of the progressive liberalisation of the European market from 1987, Lufthansa actually *enhanced* the centrality of 'German quality' in its strategic thinking — and indeed mistook this emphasis for a genuine marketing strategy. It took the parallel with car manufacturers so seriously that it appointed a BMW marketing man to a newly created *Vorstand* (executive board) position in the executive board for product development and marketing in May 1989, and after the *Vorstand* member in sales resigned in early 1990, Lufthansa eyed VW's illustrious Daniel Goeudevert (executive responsible for sales) as a replacement candidate.

Lufthansa's focus on technical excellence was similarly reflected in other dimensions. While the industry was changing, and the critical competitive parameters were moving away from mastery of *aircraft* technology and towards the mastery of new *marketing* techniques, Lufthansa's focus on technology remained. As such, Lufthansa remained a 'typically German' company. Its particularly prestigious and large maintenance division (*Technik*) supplied a disproportionate number of influential top managers in the executive board. These included the highly respected Reinhardt Abraham as deputy chairman (*stellvertretender Vorstandsvorsitzender*) in the 1980s, and Jürgen Weber, the chairman of the executive board since 1991. Whereas the sales and marketing side of Lufthansa has struggled to find able members in the 1980s and 1990s, the maintenance division has provided a steady stream of orderly internal successions throughout this period. Accompanying its indisputable expertise in aircraft matters,

Lufthansa persisted in maintaining one of the youngest fleets in the world with the latest aviation technology, partly achieved through taking advantage of rapid depreciation provisions of the German tax code.

In contrast to the kind of 'experimental learning' evidenced by BA, Lufthansa engaged in a process which might be called 'technical learning'. The term technical learning applies in two senses: first, Lufthansa remained wedded to a focus on modern aircraft technology more than modern marketing methods; second, although the company could and did reorganise itself, the emphasis was not on experimentation but on optimisation in order to correct for noted difficulties with the prior form of organisation. Remarkably, Lufthansa managed to reorganise its sales and marketing operations both in 1986 and in 1991 without discovering the need to optimise its network.

Thus, in 1986, the year when BA decided to centralise its sales organisation, the executive board of Lufthansa voted to *decentralise* its marketing and sales operations. Although this reform was explicitly designed to sharpen the company's ability to respond to different markets, a weakness noted by many interviewed Lufthansa managers was that the reform changed only the structure, but not the people. For example, hierarchies of product planners in Frankfurt were recast as route managers responsible for deciding the appropriate cabin configurations and service levels for their respective geographic markets. Yet the people were the same and indeed they remained cloistered in Lufthansa's headquarters as before. The result was that operations-based thinking continued as before but was simply less coordinated. When Lufthansa reorganised its sales and marketing operations again in 1991 into more centralised areas (Europe, America, Asia/Africa), it did not do so because of any commercial learning — the company still had not discovered the network-optimising paradigm. Rather, it did so mainly to put a halt to excessively uncoordinated decision-making. This had resulted in a proliferation of cabin configurations and unforeseen complexity costs (in the hundreds of millions of DM) because of difficulties in efficiently scheduling the heterogeneous fleet of aircraft that had resulted from the reorganisation decided in 1986 (INSEAD 1995).

Lufthansa suffered — and its management openly complained about — institutional rigidities in being able to divest itself of staff whose operations-oriented thinking had become increasingly out of tune with the more dynamic and commercially competitive environment in the industry. This was not the only institutional obstacle, however. To understand at a deeper level Lufthansa's difficulties in experimentation and learning, it is necessary to explore the impact of institutional constraints based in the German system of corporate decision-making in German joint stock companies.

The institutional constraints within which management at Lufthansa and other large German companies (including Deutsche Telekom) operate emerge first by considering the role of the supervisory board (*Aufsichtsrat*). Following the Co-Determination Act of 1976, appointments to the executive board normally require a two-thirds majority of the supervisory board. Moreover, the latter normally deliberates on the best candidate for each position on the executive board individually; the CEO (*Vorstand* chairman) of a German corporation is not usually free to install his or her own team. At Lufthansa, the man heading the scouting searches for able managers to fill executive positions was always the chairman of the supervisory board. This contrasts with the role and power of the CEO at British Airways.

Furthermore, within the executive board itself, decision-making is not concentrated in the hands of the chairman, again in significant contrast to the powers of the CEO in Anglo-Saxon companies. Instead, the rule is one-person, one-vote majority voting decision-making. In practice, this meant that a newly appointed Lufthansa CEO did not have great unilateral power that equated with that held by Colin Marshall at BA. In the case of the last two Lufthansa CEOs, Heinz Ruhnau (1982–91) and Jürgen Weber (1991–present), they often had phenomenally little power compared to their American or British colleagues. For example, the 1986 decision to reorganise came only after a difficult 5–2 vote in the executive board, and considerable strain for the CEO Ruhnau. These institutional factors highlight the difficulties reorienting intra-company power structures, organisational structures, and corporate strategy in Lufthansa.

Lufthansa's CEO in the 1980s, Heinz Ruhnau, knew he had to do something to upgrade the marketing side of Lufthansa. But the problem was that German corporate governance institutions, with majority-based decision-making, gave him little scope to do more than to propose new heads of sales and marketing. As it was, the marketing seat on the executive board turned into an ejection seat, a ten-year succession of appointment misfits. The 1984 appointee turned out to be largely an administrator and was forced into resignation in early 1990. He had not been able to revitalise Lufthansa's marketing strategy, and in 1989 his division had been split into separate sales and marketing divisions, with the new head of the latter being Falko von Falkenhayn from BMW, who went on to earn the unflattering nickname 'Wirro von Wirrenkopf' ('Muddle von Muddlehead'). The search for a new head of sales lasted for the first nine months of 1990, with no winning and willing candidate emerging. Ultimately the supervisory board elected to promote Lufthansa's corporate strategy director, acceding to the preferences of the employees' representatives and against the preference of Ruhnau (interview sources; also mentioned in *Wirtschaftswoche*, 27 Sept 1991: 75). Yet he too did not work out, and announced his resignation in 1992.

By this time, Lufthansa's losses plunged to critical levels and put Lufthansa in the throes of a do-or-die turnaround challenge. At this point, consensus decision-making began to work in the airline's favour and allowed a comprehensive turnaround plan to be executed rapidly (INSEAD 1995). This plan included implementation of the network-optimising paradigm. Discovery of the new paradigm was mainly the act of outside consultants and its (rapid) implementation was by this time, again, not an innovation, but an imitative process of catch-up, that is, based on technical rather than experimental learning.

3. British Telecom versus Deutsche Telekom

An analysis of the telecommunications industry both parallels and extends that of the airline industry, in a manner that corresponds to the greater technological and strategic changes that have occurred. Similarly, the performance outcomes, which reflect a significant relative deterioration of the German national champion and a rapid advance by its British counterpart, at least correspond to those in the airline industry. Nevertheless, the substantial degree of strategic reorientation required in this industry, and the break from past practices, has meant that the same set of institutional constraints that hindered the performance of Lufthansa vis-à-vis British Airways, also hindered Deutsche Telekom vis-à-vis British Telecom. Yet since the required radical restructuring extends deeper into the workplace, so the institutional constraints inherent in the German system have had a greater impact. In contradistinction, the British institutional structures which perform less favourably in times of incremental corporate adjustment have performed comparatively better when a substantial techno-organisational realignment has been required.

The increased application of digital technology to the telecommunications industry has massively raised the potential for new products and services, while increasing global pressures for deregulation and competition (see also the contribution of Loveridge and Mueller in this volume). Nevertheless, the core of the industry has remained nationally based, and the strategic reorientation of Deutsche Telekom and British Telecom considered here similarly has a national base. Within this domestic market, however, the potential of new technology has greatly increased the strategic dimensions on which companies can compete — including cost, quality, reliability, speed and flexibility of service, differentiation between market segments, software configuration in the use of both PABXs (private branch exchanges) and the network, the available range of value added network services (VANS), and the level of technical support (including consultancy activities and sales) by office or field technicians. Added to this are a broad range of new interactive services that are becoming feasible, many of which reflect the blurring of the computer, publishing, and cable television broadcasting markets.

The feasible dimensions of strategy within the industry facilitated by new technology require a sharp discontinuity with the past: Adapting from a bureau-cratic, public service, technological focus to being commercially and consumer driven and a shift from a universal service requirement (characterised by mass production of simple dial tone) to a significantly differentiated market. Additional-ly, this strategic reorientation, and the nature of the new technology in telecom-munications, implies a radical re-evaluation of previous craft skills (that have long been protected in Germany) and functional organisational barriers (among both white and blue collar workers), as well as having significant employment (downsizing) implications.

Far from being at a strategic disadvantage to BT (perhaps as a result of the lateness of privatisation), Deutsche Telekom has in fact possessed a significant strategic advantage owing to its ownership of both basic telecommunications and cable TV networks. This contrasts with the asymmetric regulatory structure in the UK which has prohibited BT from this latter market. The cross-ownership at Deutsche Telekom facilitated the integration of services over both networks, as well as the development and provision of substantial new, high value-added services. Yet, in spite of the world's most extensive ISDN and cable TV networks, Deutsche Telekom was slow to develop new services. Furthermore, although digitalisation began in 1985, by 1994 only 30 per cent of the network was digital, in contrast to over 85 per cent in BT (Darbishire 1997a; Batt and Darbishire 1997). Furthermore, the slow rate of digitalisation at Telekom was in spite of it having invested substantially more than other telecommunications companies in capital equipment: Between 1985–1990 45–47 per cent of turnover was invested, 10–15 percentage points more than BT and benchmarked US regional Bell operating companies (RBOCs). Furthermore, Telekom's capital productivity failed to increase during this period (Gerpott and Pospischil 1993). Deutsche Telekom also under-performed relative to BT with low levels of service (including the under-development of data transmission and itemised billing), high prices (with basic calls 20 per cent above OECD averages, and leased lines up to ten times higher), long waiting lists, and high fault rates (Darbishire 1997a). These problems were compounded by the basic absence of integrated computer systems to provide enhanced customer service — illustrated by the failure to have a computerised customer records system before the end of 1993. The contrast with the historically poor performance of BT (Carter 1977) is sharp.

Of equal significance to the poor service levels provided by Telekom is that it has performed well in much of its underlying technology, network structure, and the high technical competence of its staff. However, the explanation for Telekom's comparatively weak performance lies in the fact that it is precisely these traditional advantages that are being diminished in importance by the changing nature of the industry which is becoming more software and customer service driven. Yet institutional constraints have inhibited a realignment to a new strategic and organisational paradigm.

At an organisational level there are many parallels with the airline industry analysed above, including the underlying constraints imposed by decision making structures in the executive and supervisory board.[4] When Telekom undertook a major series of reforms in 1989, which were associated with its creation as a company formally separate from the German postal services, it did so in an example of structural inertia, with the old organisation defining the new. This included the separation of switching and telephone services on the one hand, and transmission services on the other. While this suited a technological orientation in an analogue environment, the failure to reform this structure until 1992 inhibited the effective planning of the digital network. This was because operational requirements suggested the integration of switching and transmission in order to gain economies of scope, and to plan effectively the digitalisation of the network given that returns to the technology are considerably enhanced when technological updates occur in both operational areas (Darbishire 1995). However, both the old and new organisational structures hindered their integration at centralised planning levels, and local operational levels. As in the airline industry, an important reason for this failure to implement necessary organisational reforms was because the Chairman of the *Vorstand* lacked significant authority, being *"primus inter pares*; but [with] no line authority vis-à-vis the other members of the management board" (Pospischi 1993: 610). Digitalisation was consequently slowed, and in spite of beginning the digitalisation programme in 1985, emphasis was given (up until 1992 especially) to optimising the use of existing analogue technology.

A prominent feature of the transformation of the telecommunications industry has been the conflicting pressures between the centralising tendencies of an increasingly integrated technological system on the one hand, and the decentralising pressures of providing differentiated services (and quality of service levels) to customers on the other. This conflict is also manifested in the pressure to give consistent levels of service to national business customers in particular, and the flexibility seemingly implicitly required in operational management to meet the varied product base. The overwhelming compromise observed internationally is a realignment of corporate structures from their previously functional organisation to one based on three principal divisions — residential customers, business customers, and the management of the network infrastructure.

In the case of Deutsche Telekom, this restructuring has been both late in coming, and slow in its implementation. In addition to difficulties experienced within the *Vorstand* because of intra-organisational power shifts, the case of Telekom also highlights the constraints imposed by workers' representatives in works councils and on the supervisory board. Although there are no codetermination rights on either organisational structure or the introduction of new technology, the central works council has utilised its codetermination rights on the *consequences* of these decisions to bargain the underlying strategy of change. For a range of reasons (including, in particular, concerns about the impact of divisionalisation on working conditions, and conflicts between operational demands and union organisational structures), the works councils and union within Deutsche Telekom opposed the managerially proposed (divisional) organisational reforms. The final impact was to amend and delay, rather than fully impede, the development of a new organisational structure. However, this included the introduction (or prevention) of over 180 management proposals, affecting the organisation and delineation of work, and the structure of tasks within local areas. The result was that although bargaining for reform began in 1991, the reorganisation did not begin until 1993, and lasted into 1997. This slow pace was in spite of the fact that the proposed structure is fundamentally similar to (and drawn from) those previously instituted in BT and several RBOCs in the US.

The contrast with BT is substantial. The authority of the CEO, and the absence of worker rights to influence organisational structures, has meant that BT has (at least in practice, if not strategically) used substantial *instability* of corporate structures as a mechanism to promote improvements in organisational performance, by continually altering the organisational structure to correct the most significant perceived organisational performance barriers. After privatisation in 1984 BT sought to use decentralisation and the creation of local profit centres to increase productivity. However, this structure conflicted with requirements for consistent national performance levels within an integrated network, and led first to a recentralisation, and subsequently a divisionalisation in 1991. Substantial additional changes to this structure have followed, including the merger of two divisions in 1994.

The complex pattern of organisational instability and reforms has followed process improvements within the company, and the identification of additional process flaws in each structure. Of particular significance, however, has been that BT has been able to rapidly experiment, innovate, and develop alternative structural forms in an attempt to match the contradictory demands of new technology and emerging strategic requirements. Furthermore, with some of these massive reorganisations having been planned in secret, BT has been relatively unhindered (at least in this process) by the ensuing intra-organisational power realignments within senior management ranks. This can be witnessed by the greater success BT has had over Deutsche Telekom in shifting to a customer facing, sales and marketing driven organisation, with a reduced emphasis on the historically pre-eminent role played by technical operations. In a parallel with Lufthansa, Deutsche Telekom has found this shift far harder to achieve, and its characteristically German emphasis on technology has remained in spite of the strategic shift of the industry to sales and marketing operations guided by sophisticated information management systems in a customer-oriented service environment.

The depth of institutional constraints on Deutsche Telekom can also be contrasted with British Telecom through an analysis of the ability of each company to reorganise work in a rapidly changing technological environment. The detailed web of institutions in Germany has previously been held to be a significant comparative advantage in fostering or facilitating the introduction of new work organisation (Katz and Sabel 1985). Institutional structures in Germany that confer procedural rights on stakeholders have been argued to create greater (internal) flexibility, owing to the absence of threats from workplace change. Such procedural rights are generated by the juridified system of codetermination in Germany, which

> "gives the workforces effective means to protect themselves from the negative effects of technical change....The result is a pattern of sometimes considerable rigidities in the external labour market going together with high flexibility of internal markets" (Streeck 1988: 25).

Job demarcations and restrictive practices have been deemed unnecessary, since employees' own institutionalised position, working conditions, and the skills of workers are protected.

In contrast to this picture, the countering of managerial prerogative by custom-and-practice rules (possibly built around craft unionism) in the workplace in Britain (or contractual job control unionism in the US), are threatened by changing work organisation and high internal labour market flexibility. Thus, while institutions have been perceived as systematically facilitating cooperative behaviour and change in Germany, they have been regarded as hindering such change in the UK and US.

Evidence drawn from the 1980s supports this contention. However, a primary difference in the telecommunications industry has been the extent of the transformation underway, where fundamental changes in the nature of many jobs are occurring. Work in the telecommunications industry has historically been organised in 'functional silos' (Batt and Keefe 1997), with departmental specialities such as network construction, installation, and repair; operator services; and accounting and billing. Strong hierarchies and internal labour markets have developed within each of these functional areas (Batt 1995). The nature of the transformation of the telecommunications industry, however, is such that a fundamental change in the nature of many jobs is occurring, which has rapidly undermined the rationale for these functional distinctions.

Furthermore, change in the telecommunications industry is not that of an incremental addition to existing skill sets in a potentially integrative bargain. Technical jobs are becoming increasingly software and clerically based, with a reduction in the direct maintenance and repair of switching equipment, the expansion of remote monitoring, and with the movement of customer service jobs to mega-centres which make use of integrated computer records. Furthermore, the new technology and wide-scale re-engineering have had a correspondingly substantial downsizing effect. These changes have combined to undermine the effectiveness of substantive rights (based in British custom-and-practice rules) to resist change. By contrast, even in the face of workplace changes which significantly threaten the underlying interests of workers, procedural rights (derived from German codetermination legislation) remain effective. Yet under these circumstances procedural rights do not appear necessarily to promote flexibility. And although substantive rights may not do so either, their influence is greatly diminished.

The fundamental nature of change in the telecommunications industry serves, therefore, to undermine these substantive rights. Thus, in BT employee leverage in work reorganisation has consequently been reduced, enhancing the degree of managerial prerogative. It has not been primarily a change in employment legislation or managerial attitudes following privatisation that facilitated the reassertion of managerial prerogatives, but the radical nature of the new technology, which has meant that many craft jobs have changed fundamentally in nature (for example, with diagnostic testing of switching equipment having changed from a skilled, manual, 'hands-on' task, to a remote, part-clerical, software based task). The radical nature of this change served to undermine the traditional basis of job-control, and craft-based custom-and-practice rules. When combined with the substantial employment consequences of this technology this has greatly enhanced the extent of managerial prerogative in the introduction of new work organisation. In turn, and when combined with the corporate reorganisations into customer facing divisions, it has allowed a reduction in the focus on the network, a significant increase in the commercialisation and consumer orientation of both the company and the workforce, and the introduction of significant reorganisations of work through new technology, including cross-functional reorganisations which transgress traditional work boundaries.

By contrast, in Germany, procedural rights (for example on the relocation of existing workers, the introduction of technology, and the re-grading of work) have given worker representatives *greater* voice precisely because the changes occurring are so substantial, and are subject (at least in part) to codetermination rights. In the face of technological changes which represent a fundamental challenge to workers, both in terms of employment and traditional craft-based skills, worker representatives have been reluctant to accept work reorganisation. Indeed, as in German industry more generally, work organisation in the telecommunications industry has been strongly founded on craft-based skills. In manufacturing, negotiated adjustment in the 1980s centred around enhancing those broadly defined skills, frequently together with the introduction of new technology in pursuit of an up-market, high value-added approach (Streeck 1989; Jürgens et al. 1991). In the telecommunications industry, however, the transformation of work reflects the more radical nature of new technology, where potential gains derive from new skills sets and cross-functional organisational integration, rather than building on existing craft skills. This critical difference has been reflected in highly detailed programmes of work reorganisation in Deutsche Telekom, which have both significantly slowed adjustment and limited the degree of local experimentation.

The cautious negotiations and implementation of change has thus arisen because new technology does not build on existing craft skills. The focus consequently remained for longer on optimising the use of existing analogue technology, rather than promoting digitalisation. That is, work continued to be specialised around technology types, with a corresponding slow development of digital skills. This combined with a resistance to the centralisation of operational tasks implicit in digitalisation and 'computerisation' processes, and a continuation of the traditional functional organisational structure — which itself more generally reflects the traditional German emphasis on functional specialisation. However, this is in sharp contrast to a strategy that de-emphasises technology in favour of a customer focus, and illustrates the difficulty Deutsche Telekom has had in making this transformation in a company (and German) tradition of management steeped in technology, not service.

The highly centralised nature of change in Deutsche Telekom, together with the continuing technological functionalism and clear hierarchical lines, mitigates against flexible experimentation of alternative structures. The incremental and bureaucratic process of change has thus helped to ensure stable strategies, but in doing so has relied on 'borrowing' models of transformation (developed in the course of the 1980s and early 1990s in Britain and the US), without experimentation or innovation. Workplace consensus in the implementation of change in Telekom has come at the expense of the slow and restricted introduction of new technology and development of computerised service capabilities, lack of experimentation, and significant constraints on what structural and work reorganisation have been possible.

4. Implications of Case Studies

The case studies of the airline and telecommunications industries focus on how company adaptations have occurred in response to rapidly changing market opportunities and market risks arising from technological change. The focus of the change has included the managerial and corporate organisational level, and (in the case of the telecommunications industry where the impact of technological changes has been more far reaching) the restructuring of work processes. When contrasted with prior research, both of these mutually consistent case studies suggest a similar conclusion: Even allowing for differences in state control and market reform (for more details see Lehrer 1997a and Darbishire 1997a), the performance impact of economic governance institutions within Britain and German industry depends on the nature of change in the industry environments.

The argument that institutions themselves are key to understanding the process and outcome of adaptation is not new. However, we argue that, previously, insufficient attention has been paid to environmental context. As such, the analysis here reassesses the conventional wisdom that the 'stable flexibility' of German institutional structures is a clear source of economic advantage. Certainly German institutions are capable of adjusting to changed environmental conditions. Indeed, Katzenstein (1989) identifies 'institutional adaptation' as a source of competitive advantage, derived through a reduction in risk and uncertainty, a consensual approach to implementing change, and an acceptance of technological change within existing craft (and perhaps functional) structures. However, by its very nature, the success of incrementalism is founded on the ability to make minor, but progressive, adjustments to existing strategy, corporate structure, and work organisation. Such changes do not challenge the underlying relationships within the companies — whether those be the role of functional departments, managerial ranks, or skilled (craft) workers.

Where a more fundamental break is occurring in the industry, however, the 'stable flexibility' implied by incrementalism can be slow in producing significant innovations, experimentation, and reorganisation in corporate strategy. This can be further compounded where the nature of the change involves a significant distributive element, such as intra-organisational power shifts, the downplaying of particular skill sets, or substantial employment reductions. The strategic dynamism of the airline and telecommunications industries highlights precisely these institutional limitations. In both the civil aviation and telecommunications industries, the critical change during the 1980s was a new industry environment that rewarded rapid innovation, experimentation, and a reconfiguration to organisational structures which emphasised cross-functional working and the development of new (individual and organisational) skill sets.

The significant changes that the air transport and telecommunications industries underwent in technologies and market opportunities was a shift to the advantage of the British national champion. On the one hand, it was significantly easier to initiate the work and organisational restructuring demanded in this new environment by managerial fiat in the UK. More importantly, however, in a market environment characterised by a high degree of uncertainty, it was not necessary in the UK context to fully determine in advance the exact nature of the changes required, thus allowing for flexibility and learning in the course of longer-term experimentation and implementation. The iterative organisational reforms in both British Airways and British Telecom highlight this capacity in their respective highly uncertain and contingent market places. Conversely, Lufthansa and Deutsche Telekom were penalised by an industry environment which no longer generated programmable productivity increases, where the costs and benefits of reform could not be fully calculated in advance, and where the nature of the reforms required was highly uncertain.

Although recent typologies of European business systems (Whitley 1996) capture a wealth of dimensions along which national institutions vary in their effects, there is a need for a set of microfoundations to help explain why national institutions that work well under certain environmental conditions work better or worse when in particular industries these conditions change. Equally, there is a critical need to develop the microfoundations to explain under which conditions Anglo-Saxon business institutions may provide a competitive advantage — beyond just the interplay of market forces.

The findings from the aviation and telecommunications case studies presented here do not accord well with the conventional wisdom which, crudely stated, is that although Anglo-Saxon labour and capital institutions facilitate downsizing, industry exit, and diversification as means of industrial adjustment, they are less apt in facilitating innovation or experimentation in work practices. Yet our findings are precisely that managerial prerogatives were actually key factors in experimentation and innovation in work practices. It is, therefore, necessary to develop a perspective of Anglo-Saxon institutional competitive advantage that is based not only on the allocative efficiency of free markets, but precisely on the notions of 'adaptive efficiency' (North 1990: 80) or 'dynamic efficiency' (Klein 1984; Carlsson 1989) that have been hypothesised as a particular virtue of more negotiated Continental European institutional contexts (Hollingsworth et al. 1994).

The finding that, under specified types of industry conditions, the adaptive or dynamic efficiency of Anglo-Saxon firms can be superior to that of firms in Northern Europe's 'industry-coordination' economies can be brought under the umbrella concept of 'comparative institutional advantage' (Soskice 1994; Lehrer 1997b). The notion is that the performance impact of capital and labour institutions depends critically on the nature of the economic tasks to be performed and the exogenous industry environment in which they have to be performed. Although alternative theoretical framings of our empirical findings are imaginable, one way of conceiving of Anglo-Saxon institutions is in terms of *incomplete contracts*, commensurate with the ease of 'exit' as an adaptive response in 'free' markets. Notwithstanding dismissive treatments of the transaction cost perspective (Powell 1990; Sabel 1994), it can be argued that business institutions are embedded in national 'transaction orders' — to be contrasted with Sabel's 'constitutional orders' — which vary systematically between countries, in particular with respect to the completeness of contracts. There are consequently systematic differences in how risk and uncertainty are dealt with, and thus how institutions promote technological innovation, work restructuring, and corporate organisational change in the face of uncertain environmental conditions.

In the transaction cost perspective (Williamson 1975), business institutions are seen to mediate 'market failures' arising from the 'lumpy' distribution of information in the economy at large, and within the firm in particular, and the costs associated with learning about, transacting for, and monitoring economic activity. There are consequently systematic differences in how alternative institutional arrangements deal with risk and uncertainty, and thus how institutions promote or retard technological innovation, work restructuring, and corporate organisational change. These systematic differences facilitate certain forms of organisational flexibility (Klein 1984; Carlsson 1989), while hindering others. The hypothesis developed here from the experience of two major network industries is that the UK 'transaction order' actually facilitates flexibility and learning in industry environments where the required direction of strategic and organisational adaptation is uncertain, and where this change cannot be easily accommodated for by contracts conceding a high level of procedural rights to employees. By contrast, the German 'transaction order' favours flexibility and learning in industry environments where change is gradual, capability-enhancing, and can be accommodated within a framework of strongly codified procedural rights.

A paradox raised by this point is that low-trust Anglo-Saxon institutions essentially allowed BA and BT to perform those tasks which Sabel (1994) credits the high-trust social-economic institutions of Japan with facilitating. In Sabel's view, 'contrarian regimes' (as particularly widespread in the West) make it difficult for firms to reconcile learning with the monitoring of existing contracts between parties, because true learning results in an undoing of the production routines upon which prior contracting was based. In Sabel's stylised view of trust-based relationships, the identities of cooperating actors are fluid enough to transcend a rigid interpretation of prior agreements and continually reforge the identities and agreements between cooperating parties in the learning process. As Sabel (1994: 145) puts it:

"In a contrarian world ... there is no joint exploration of novelty and still less any redefinition of identities through persuasion. The world is presumed to be well understood....Each party, moreover, has settled interests in the form of ranked preferences for particular outcomes, and pursues them strategically."

Crudely put, the empirical finding here for the high-trust German model corresponds more closely to the outcomes in Sabel's ideal type of a 'contrarian regime' than the low-trust British model disclosed in BA and BT. The stasis observed in Lufthansa and Deutsche Telekom was seen to emanate, at least in part, from the rigidity of actors' identities. This derived from the blocking effect of fixed board seats on the consensus-based *Vorstand* in the case of Lufthansa, and also from the German post workers union's resistance to changes that would alter the identities and interest constellations of employees at Telekom.

What the analysis shows is that Anglo-Saxon institutional patterns, in contrast, offer opportunities for altering the identities and interests of actors. High levels of managerial prerogative and high unilateral decision-making discretion of the CEO in Anglo-Saxon companies make it feasible for top managers, middle managers, and workers alike to be shifted around (not to mention outright replaced). The nature of 'substantive' rights of unions in the UK means that identities and interests are by no means as clear-cut as the notion of a 'contrarian world' implies. Indeed, fluid UK labour markets for CEOs, managers, and workers alike mean the 'completeness' of contracts will always be limited. To say this is, of course, not to deny the system's negative distributional effects for certain employee groups nor even potentially hindering some of the 'incremental' productivity improvements that German companies appear to excel in.

Although the evidence from the air transport and telecommunications industries demonstrates that 'low-trust' contractual relations are compatible with fluid identities, flexibility and experimental learning in certain industry contexts, a full institutional analysis extends beyond just the comparative completeness and incompleteness of contracts. First, the British training and educational system encourages the development of less specialised skills and a more generalist orientation among employees and especially managers (Lane 1989). Consequently, employees in UK firms have less of their human capital invested in a particular skill set, and hence are less likely to combat techno-organisational changes which downgrade the value of their prior activities. By the same token, of course, they are possibly less apt to embrace activities which upgrade their previous skills. Second, the stronger and more fluid external labour market in Britain facilitates employment adjustment, and thus potentially reduces the degree of risk-aversion amongst (at least younger) managers in particular. This is reinforced by the education and training system. Third, trust can be difficult to maintain in any system where the nature of changes underway are substantially distributive, and impose significant costs on particular groups. Employee attitude surveys have consistently shown poor results in BT, and declines in Deutsche Telekom during the 1990s as more fundamental restructuring has occurred. Similarly, although BA had successful trust-building programmes in the 1980s ('Managing People First'), in the mid to late 1990s both BA and Lufthansa have had to cope with growing employee discontent and strikes as management has tried to impose more drastic cost-cutting measures.

5. Conclusion

The process of transformation of the telecommunications and air transport industries has clearly differed substantially between Britain and Germany, a difference we have attributed to different 'transaction orders' in the business system of the two countries. New technologies have been adopted more quickly in the British champions, the firms have reoriented themselves more rapidly from a technological objective to a consumer one, and there has been substantially more experimentation with new work practices than in Germany.

It is the fundamental nature of the transformation of the air transport and telecommunications industries that explains the differing adjustment paths. In the Anglo-Saxon case, the significant effects of new technologies have not hindered, and to some extent assisted, management in overcoming inflexibilities in traditional craft divides (as in telecommunications) and in the balance of power between functional units (marketing and operations, as in the aviation flag carriers). There have, furthermore, been no restrictions on management altering corporate structures, or substantially reducing employment. By contrast, it is precisely the radical nature of the transformation that is showing the limitations of incrementalist adjustment in Germany.

The process of reform in Germany demonstrates that where adjustment does not build upon traditional units of technical excellence or existing craft skills, there is indeed a resistance to change. Furthermore, the functional organisation of work has been slow to change and a consumer orientation has been slower to develop in place of technological fascination. In Lufthansa, consensus decision making at the *Vorstand* level appeared to retard management's ability to make the dramatic shifts of power between functions that the competitive environment appeared to demand. In Deutsche Telekom, in addition to similar difficulties in organisational reforms, the union and works council have utilised codetermination rights, and the broader institutionalisation of worker representatives, to limit the degree and pace of change.

In Britain, by contrast, on-going experimentation and innovation in corporate structures and work organisation actually reflects the low level of institutionalised representation by employees and their difficulties in constraining business strategies. Amongst the stakeholders, shareholders have in particular benefited substantially and employees borne the brunt of costs of transformation.

The analysis derived from these cases suggests the necessity of distinguishing more carefully the sources of gain and performance limitations of institutional structures. The competitive challenges involved in the transformation of the telecommunications and air transport industries are highlighted by the difficulty in securing a climate in which integrative bargaining is possible, and suggest that many of Germany's institutional advantages do not always extend to industrial environments outside the shop-floors of manufacturing industries. A principal source of gain in Germany has been from building upon existing structures and skills, and promoting the implementation of strategies that do that. The competitive advantages often associated with German institutional structures may thus dissipate in fast-changing non-shopfloor industry contexts, though Germany may retain a strength in a robust implementation of new structures, even if only able to do so with a significant time lag. Nevertheless, and even then, industry context does matter, and innovative flexibility and experimental learning in a rapidly changing environment are not empirically borne out as institutional strengths of the German business system.

Notes

1. BT reduced its employment from 235,100 in 1984 to 133,000 by 1994, with the vast majority of this reduction coming during the 1990s. BA reduced its headcount from a high of 58,000 in 1979 to a low of 37,000 in 1983, while it also demonstrated its numerical flexibility after the Gulf War in 1991 when it shed 4,600 positions through an emergency cost-cutting programme.

2. This is not to suggest that there is one dominant, best competitive strategy. It is to argue, however, that the appropriateness of particular strategic approaches (or paradigms) changed as a result of altered technological conditions.

3. This remark is particularly surprising in view of the fact that Lufthansa's hub airport at Frankfurt is in many ways superior to Heathrow, having three runways compared to only two at Heathrow. A crucial component of Lufthansa's turnaround was therefore a concerted attempt to more fully exploit hubbing opportunities at Frankfurt (Lehrer 1997b).

4. Strictly speaking, the constraints in the German telecommunications industry differ, in that until 1 January 1995 Deutsche Telekom was a public administration, rather than a joint stock company. However, the nature of the constraints mirror those in the private sector.

References

Batt, R. 1995. "Performance and Welfare Effects of Work Restructuring: Evidence from Telecommunications Services." Unpublished PhD Thesis, Massachusetts Institute of Technology.

Batt, R., and J. Keefe. 1997. United States. In: H. Katz (ed.), *Telecommunications: Worldwide Restructuring of Work and Employment Relations*, 31–88. Ithaca, New York: Cornell University Press.

Batt, R., and O. Darbishire. 1997. Institutional Determinants of Deregulation and Restructuring in Telecommunications: Britain, Germany and the United States Compared, *International Contributions to Labour Studies* 7: 59–80.

Carlsson, B. 1989. Flexibility and the theory of the firm, *International Journal of Industrial Organization* 7: 179–203.

Carter, C. F. 1977. Report of the Post Office Review Committee. Cmnd 6850. London: HMSO.

Darbishire, O. 1995. Switching Systems: Technological Change, Competition, and Privatisation, *Industrielle Beziehungen* 2(2): 156–179.

Darbishire, O. 1997a. Germany. In: H: Katz (ed.), *Telecommunications: Restructuring Work and Employment Relations Worldwide*, 189–227. Ithaca, New York: Cornell University Press.

Gerpott, T. J., and R. Pospischil. 1993. Internationale Effizienzvergleiche der DBP Telekom: Ergebnisse eines Benchmarking-Projektes zur Unterstützung von organisatorischem Wandel in einem staatlichen Telekommunikationsunternehmen, *Zeitschrift für betriebswirtschaftliche Forschung* 4: 366–389.

Hollingsworth, J. R., P. C. Schmitter, and W. Streeck. 1994. *Comparing Capitalist Economies: Performance and Control of Economic Sectors*. New York: Oxford University Press.

INSEAD. 1995. Lufthansa: The turnaround. Case Study, Fontainebleau: INSEAD.

Jürgens, U., T. Malsch, and K. Dohse. 1991. *Breaking from Taylorism: Changing Forms of Work in the Automobile Industry*. Cambridge: Cambridge University Press.

Katz, H., and C. Sabel. 1985. Industrial Relations and Industrial Adjustment in the Car Industry, *Industrial Relations* 24(3): 295–315.

Katzenstein, P. J. 1989. *Industry and Politics in West Germany: Toward the Third Republic*. Ithaca: Cornell University Press.

Klein, B. 1984. *Prices, wages, and business cycles*. New York: Pergamon.

Lane, C. 1989. *Management and Labor in Europe: The Industrial Enterprise in Germany, Britain and France*. Aldershot: Edward Elgar.

Lehrer, M. 1997a. German industrial strategy in turbulence: Corporate governance and managerial hierarchies in Lufthansa, *Industry and Innovation* 4(1): 115–40.

Lehrer, M. 1997b. Comparative Institutional Advantage in Corporate Governance and Managerial Hierarchies: The Case of European Airlines, Doctoral Dissertation, Fontainebleau: INSEAD.

North, D. C. 1990. *Institutions, institutional change and economic performance*. Cambridge, Cambridge University Press.

Pospischil, R. 1993. Reorganisation of European Telecommunications: The cases of British Telecom, France Télécom and Deutsche Telekom, *Telecommunications Policy*, November: 603–621.

Powell, W. W. 1990. Neither market nor hierarchy: Network forms of organization. In: B. Staw, and L. L. Cummings (eds.), *Research in Organizational Behavior*, 295–336. Greenwich, CT: JAI Press.

Sabel, C. F. 1994. Learning by Monitoring: The Institutions of Economic Development. In: N. J. Smelser, and R. Swedberg (eds.), *The Handbook of Economic Sociology*, 137–164. Princeton: Princeton University Press.

Soskice, D. 1994. Innovation Strategies of Companies: A Comparative Institutional Approach of some Cross-Country Differences. In: W. Zapf and M. Dierkes, *Institutionenvergleich und Institutionendynamik. WZB Jahrbuch 1994*, 271–289. Berlin: Sigma.

Streeck, W. 1988. Industrial Relations in West Germany, 1980–1987, *Labour* 2(3): 3–44.

Streeck, W. 1989. Successful Adjustment to Turbulent Markets: The Automobile Industry. In: P. J. Katzenstein, Katzenstein, P. J. 1989. *Industry and Politics in West Germany: Toward the Third Republic*, 113–156. Ithaka: Cornell University Press.

Streeck, W. 1997. German capitalism: Does it exist? Can it survive? In : C. Crouch and W. Streeck (eds.), *Economy of Modern Capitalism,* 33–54. London: Sage.

Whitley, R. 1996. The Social Construction of Economic Actors: Institutions and Types of Firm in Europe and Other Market Economies. In: R. Whitley, and P. H. Kristensen (eds.), *The Changing European Firm: Limits to Convergence*, 39–66. London: Routledge.

Williamson, O. E. 1975. *Markets and Hierarchies: Analysis and Antitrust Implications*. New York: The Free Press.

CHAPTER 5

Strategy, Structure and Performance in European Industry

Corporate and National Perspectives

Richard Whittington   Michael Mayer   Francesco Curto

1. Introduction

This chapter examines the performance consequences of strategic and structural change amongst large industrial firms in post-war Western Europe.[1] As such, it takes a very different perspective from other chapters in the volume, going above the sectoral level. To the extent that our firms are typically diversified, we are concerned with corporate performance, rather than the success of businesses within particular sectors. To the extent that these large firms together account for substantial proportions of domestic industrial output, we are also confronting issues of national rather than simply sectoral economic performance.

The theoretical starting point is different too. Corporate strategy and structure are, of course, the classic themes of business historian Alfred Chandler (1962, 1990). Like 'business systems' theorists (Whitley 1994), Chandler is concerned with the evolving balance between markets and hierarchies in the coordination of economic activity. He has also taken an ambitious international perspective in his work, comparing American, European and Asian economies within the same theoretical lens (Chandler 1990; Chandler et al. 1997). However, Chandler differs radically from 'business systems' theory in proposing universal relationships between corporate characteristics and economic performance, whether considered at the firm level or the national level. While Whitley (1994), for example, has argued that the efficiency of a particular form of economic organisation depends upon its context, and that different national patterns of organisation can be equally effective in international competition, Chandler (1962, 1990) prescribes quite strict strategic and structural rules for firm-level and national-level success. These rules originated in the experience of American business, but are applied across sectors and through all advanced industrial economies. If business systems theory sees history as laying a heavy guiding hand on the development of economies and sectors, from the Chandlerian perspective, history is merely the tale of gradual convergence on a single logic of corporate scope and organisation.

In international business history, Alfred Chandler's (1990) perspective has become 'the new orthodoxy' (Alford 1994). With his concern for change over time, for the organisation of economic activity between and within sectors, and for the patterns and performance of different nations, Chandler is contesting similar territory as comparative business systems theory. However, his focus on the corporate-level adds a further dimension. In today's advanced economies, the leading players in most sectors are increasingly likely to be members of large diversified corporations. The investment and divestment decisions, the managerial standards and practices, and the orientations towards quality and innovation that prevail at the corporate level can all have substantial impacts on the behaviour and performance of businesses competing at the sectoral level. Our purpose within this chapter, therefore, is to shift the focus upwards to examine the corporate framework in which a great deal of sectoral activity is located. In particular, we shall want to assess the robustness of Chandlerian themes within the diverse and changing context of contemporary Western Europe.

The chapter has five parts. We start by introducing the Chandlerian account of strategy, structure and performance, and current debates about its robustness in different times and different places. The next section documents our research approach, an extension of earlier research on the strategy and structure of large European corporations undertaken by Chandler's students at Harvard. The following two sections examine the performance consequences of the growing spread of diversified, multidivisional organisations throughout France, Germany and the United Kingdom in the post-war period. At both the level of national economic growth and corporate profitability, performance impacts are slight and ambiguous. We conclude by suggesting that the multi-sector corporation is an increasingly important phenomenon in Europe, but that its potential has not yet been fully realised at the sector level of economic activity. As European business begins to digest the wave of diversification and divisionalisation of the last three decades, managing the tension between sectoral and corporate levels is likely to be an important source of competitive advantage in future years.

2.   The Chandlerian Account of Strategy and Structure

Nearly thirty years ago, Bruce Scott and Alfred Chandler sent out five Harvard doctoral students — Channon, Dyas, Pavan, Rumelt and Thanheiser — to chart the evolving strategies and structures of large British, French, Italian, American and German industrial firms between 1950–1970. The students were all in search of the then new phenomenon, the diversified multidivisional corporation which

Chandler himself had characterised as the mark of modern and successful business around the world. In what was the first systematic international programme of comparative research on the modern corporation, the Harvard group concluded that America was in the lead, but that by 1970 European business too was fast adopting the model of diversification and divisionalisation pioneered on the other side of the Atlantic (Scott 1973).

This chapter follows in the tracks of the Harvard group, seeking to catch up with the progress of the diversified multidivisional corporation in Europe since the early 1970s. As we pursue this phenomenon we shall be exploring two important paths blazed by the Chandlerian tradition. The first takes us upwards, considering claims about relationships between national rates of diversification and divisionalisation and the industrial performance of whole economies; the second downwards, examining at the level of firms themselves the pay-offs from diversification and divisionalisation in terms of financial performance.

These dual levels of analysis — both country and corporate — reflect the development of Alfred Chandler's own thinking. In Chandler's (1962, 1977) early work, he posited an evolutionary model of individual corporate development that led from the centralised single business phase through to full diversification and adoption of the multidivisional structure. Diversification was driven by the need to optimise the usage of resources, in a quite Penrosian manner, and divisional-isation was to minimise coordination costs, in a logic akin to Williamson's (1975) regarding transaction costs. In the strategy field, this led to the hypothesis that, amongst large mature firms, the diversified would generally out-perform the undiversified, and, because of resource linkages, related diversifiers would out-perform unrelated or conglomerate diversifiers (Rumelt 1974). In terms of organisation, Williamson (1975) formalised (and slightly extended) the argument in his so-called 'M-form' hypothesis, that the multi-divisional form was superior financially to the centralised functional form for all large firms. By extension, the same was true for the superiority of divisionalised firms over holding company forms, which lacked the central controls necessary to minimise agency costs.

All this was at the level of the firm. However, in a move consonant with the institutional focus of the 'new growth theory' (Carlin 1996; Eichengreen 1996; Matthews 1986), Chandler and his followers have gone on to link corporate strategy and structure with national economic performance. For Chandler, the modern corporation is a central institution in the mobilisation, organisation and improvement of economic resources in contemporary economies. In the United States, for example, the largest 100 manufacturing firms accounted for 34.4 per cent of manufacturing value-added and 36.4 per cent of capital expenditure in 1987 (Chandler and Hikino 1997: 44). Chandler does not discount the importance of national culture or resource endowments, nor of other types of enterprises, nevertheless

"... the large industrial enterprise became an engine of modern economic growth in the century spanning the 1880s to the 1980s, an era of industrial capitalism when technological advance provided the most powerful dynamic for the sustained growth of nations and the global economy" (Chandler and Hikino 1997: 56).

National economic performance depends, therefore, considerably on the strategies and structures of big business. Comparing industrial performance in America, Germany and the United Kingdom from the late 19th Century to the middle of this century, Chandler (1990) attributes Britain's relative economic decline to a systematic failure on the part of business to invest in economies of scope and build managerial hierarchies. On the other hand, Germany and the United States owed their economic success in the first half of this century to the greater speed with which their corporations applied their resources in diversification and organised them in appropriate structures.

Thus the Chandlerian argument links diversification and divisionalisation to the performance of both firms and economies. At neither level, however, is the Chandlerian thesis uncontested. At the level of the firm, there have been changes in strategic and structural fashion in recent years. At the level of national economies, the American model of capitalism is less secure. In particular, we now give more recognition to the importance and sometimes equivalence of differences in institutional arrangements between countries (Hollingsworth and Boyer 1997; Whitley and Kristensen 1996).

To take business fashion first. Recent theoretical developments around 'core competencies' and the 'resource-based theory of the firm' advocate quite restricted patterns of diversification against the wide diversification advocated in the 1970s. Today, it is argued, rapid technological change, increasing international competition and a more ruthless market for corporate control are all working to force firms to concentrate on what they can do best. Indeed, studies in the United States have shown widespread 'down-scoping' since the 1980s and a return to the undiversified 'single business' strategy (Hoskisson and Hitt 1995; Markides 1996). At the level of the firm, therefore, the performance advantages of the diversified firm, and especially the widely-diversified conglomerate, are in doubt. Again, these firm-level phenomena are linked to national economic performance. The conglomerate emerged as a major component in the American pattern of diversification at about the same time as, from the 1970s, the United States first confronted the challenge from both Japan and a revivified Europe. Chandler (1990: 623–27) links the short-term financial orientation of the conglomerate to an increased inability on the part of contemporary American industry to make the long-term investments necessary for continued national economic competitiveness. Other commentators, looking back at the corporate restructuring achieved by the active capital markets of the United States during the 1980s, suggest that the new more focused enterprises may be at the root of the recent rejuvenation of American economic performance as a whole (Hatfield et al. 1996).

The multidivisional structure (or M-form) too has become increasingly criticised for its alleged excesses in planning, rationality and detachment (Mintzberg 1994). The modern managerial enterprise might be a victim of its own "excessive rationality" (Streeck 1997: 205). Influential theorists have proposed that business is now going 'beyond the M-form' towards a new 'N-form', whose flatter, hyper-decentralised network characteristics are more consistent with the fast-moving, focused strategies required today (Bartlett and Ghoshal 1993; Hedlund 1994). Several recent single-country studies have found that the loosely-structured holding company form is now enjoying something of a revival (Hill 1988; Markides 1996). This revival appears to be concentrated particularly in Europe (Mayer and Whittington 1996), and suggests an adaptiveness to European conditions on the part of the holding company that may have been neglected by the earlier universalist preconceptions of Harvard. However, it has also been noted that the loosely-structured holding company mimics in large part the fluid, fuzzy-boundaried decentralised characteristics of the new 'N-form' (Mowery 1992; Whittington and Mayer 1997). Thus, whether for local institutional reasons or for newly-discovered economic defects, the predominance and performance of the classic Harvard multidivisional are no longer to be taken for granted.

But beyond changes in business fashion, there has been a broader reappraisal of the kinds of universalistic intellectual endeavour characteristic of Harvard in the 1960s and early 1970s. The faltering economic performance of the United States, and increasing recognition of a multipolar world, have undermined confidence in universal prescriptions, especially those that propose American business as the model for the future (Locke 1996). Institutionalist studies of comparative 'business systems' suggest that different ways of organizing economic activity can be at least equally effective (Whitley 1994). American self-doubt has perhaps been most acutely triggered by the success of Japan, whose patterns of strategy and structure quite clearly contradicted the Chandlerian model (Fruin 1992). Empirical studies outside the United States, moreover, have not succeeded in finding stable relationships between strategy and performance over time (Grant and Jamine 1988) or any consistent superiority of the diversified multidivisional over other organisational strategies and structures (Ezzamel and Watson 1993; Hill 1988; Cable and Dirrheimer 1984). It seems that institutional and historical context may alter the relative local efficiency of different strategies and structures. The measures of economic performance might themselves be socially constructed (see the contributions by Morgan and Quack, and Salomon in this volume). Powerful societal actors such as banks, families and the state, may, moreover, seek to satisfy interests above and beyond pure economic efficiency (Fligstein 1985; Palmer et al. 1993). The adoption of particular strategies and structures might consequently be the result of 'societal choice' by these actors, not of economic determinism (Mayer and Whittington 1996).

In sum, Chandler has made strong and influential claims for the national and corporate benefits of a model of corporate strategy and structure that originated in the United States but which he and his students have generalised to Europe. The early Harvard studies in Europe had shown some initial progress towards American-style diversification and divisionalisation, but a great deal of time has passed since then. The passing decades have cast doubt upon the confident convergence thesis of the early 1970s. The flip-sides of diversification and divisionalisation have been revealed in the excesses of the conglomerate and the over-detached rationalism of the multidivisional. At the same time, the emergence of very different national models of business organisation, noted particularly in the literature of 'business systems', has challenged faith in universalist prescriptions, especially those simply 'made in America'. The large, multi-sector corporation clearly remains a significant actor in European economies, but the theory surrounding it is becoming increasingly insecure. Our purpose, then, is to test the durability of the original Chandlerian propositions in the conditions of contemporary Western Europe.

3.   Research Methods

The empirical objectives of this paper are twofold: first to examine trends in the strategies and structures of large French, German and British firms; second, to test the durability and transferability of established propositions about strategy, structure and performance. An essential principle of the research, therefore, has been to be as consistent as possible internally across countries and time and externally with the concepts and methods of the Harvard tradition that we are extending and testing. Recent approaches to diversification and organisation structure (Bartlett and Ghoshal 1993; Markides and Williamson 1996) have therefore been left aside. Except where we can make gains in accuracy, we have followed exactly the procedures of the original Harvard studies, both in their American and their European forms.

3.1 *Populations*

Following the practice of the original Harvard European studies (Channon 1973; Dyas and Thanheiser 1976), we have taken as our populations the domestically-owned firms drawn from each country's top 100 industrial enterprises by sales in 1983 and 1993 (foreign-owned firms are theoretically irrelevant as well as methodologically inconvenient). Our sources were the annual lists published in the *Times 1000*, *L'Expansion* and the *Schmacke Directory*. As for Harvard, we have compared countries at ten-year time intervals. In Britain, there were 75 domestically-owned firms in the 1983 Top 100 and 67 in 1993, the fall no doubt reflecting the internationalisation of British industry over this period (Channon (1973) had 84 British firms in 1970). The number of French domestically-owned top 100 firms in 1983 was 67 and 61 in 1993. In Germany, there were 60 domestically-owned firms in 1983, and 63 in 1993.[2]

3.2 *Diversification Strategy*

Diversification refers to bringing a range of activities, from various sectors, under the hierarchical control of a single corporate entity. Though diversification can be measured in many ways (Hall and St. John 1994), our concern with continuity leads us to focus on the categorical method of the Harvard studies.

Four basic categories of diversification strategy are distinguished — 'single business', 'dominant business', 'related business' and 'unrelated business' (Wrigley 1970; Channon 1973; Dyas and Thanheiser 1976). These four categories describe both degree and type of diversification (see Appendix 1 for precise definitions). Essentially the first two diversification categories are hardly diversified at all: 'single business' firms have more than 95 per cent of their turnover concentrated in one sort of business, as dairy products company Dairy Crest exemplifies, while 'dominant business' firms are slightly less focused, but still have more than 70 per cent of turnover from one kind of business, as for example hair-care company Wella. The two diversified strategies are differentiated according to type of diversification strategy. Although 'related business' companies derive less than 70 per cent of their turnover from a single type of business, the businesses they are in do possess market or technological relationships, as for example chemical company Rhône Poulenc. Unrelated companies may be no more diversified, the difference being in the absence of relationships, as in the case of Taittinger, involved in champagne, hotels and engineering. Companies following these two diversified strategies may unite quite a range of sectors, as Rhône Poulenc brings together heavy and fine chemicals with pharmaceuticals, or Taittinger activities from agriculture, manufacturing and services.

While the original European studies (Channon 1973; Dyas and Thanheiser 1976) used these four basic diversification categories, Rumelt (1974) in his American study sub-divided them into eight finer ones (see Appendix 1). As Rumelt's (1973) scheme has become influential in firm-level performance studies, we shall also use these in our discussion of European corporate performance.

As for Channon (1973) and Dyas and Thanheiser (1976), our diversification classifications have been based on annual reports and other public documentary sources, supplemented by our interview data (see below). The actual approach to classification differs slightly between the Wrigley and Rumeltian traditions, the first being more historically-sensitive and the second highlighting vertical integration. We have classified our firms according to both the Wrigley four categories and the Rumeltian four basic categories sub-divided into eight.[3]

3.3 *Organisational Structure*

The Chandlerian approach to organisational structure is concerned with the degrees to which responsibility for operating and strategic decisions are decentralised. Again, there are four basic categories (see Appendix 1). The classic 'functional' structure is centralised in both dimensions, with managers responsible for key functions such as sales and production represented in strategic as well as purely operational decisions. The 'holding company' is the reverse, with operating responsibility decentralised to subsidiaries, but also an absence of central control over the portfolio of activities at the level of the headquarters. The 'functional holding' is a hybrid, with peripheral activities organised loosely as a set of subsidiaries around a centralised core. In Chandlerian theory, none of these forms are compatible with large scale, diversified business. The preferred form for contemporary large-scale enterprise, therefore, is the multidivisional, with operating decisions decentralised to product-market divisions, while the corporate headquarters exerts strategic control over investment and performance through the portfolio as a whole. The business unit therefore is concerned with competitive strategy, the headquarters with the appropriation and application of resources amongst businesses and sectors.

All firms were classified according to these four structural categories. Data sources included the annual reports of comnpanies, published case studies, press articles, business histories and interviews. Interviews have been carried out with senior managers (including chief executives, but typically personnel directors, corporate planning directors or their direct reports) in seventy eight firms (against a total of seventy seven in the original three Harvard European studies; see Appendix 2 for list).

3.4 *National and Corporate Performance*

At the national level, Chandler (1990) and Chandler et al. (1997) use gross domestic product per head data as a measure of relative economic performance. As Hannah (1991) indicates, this measure is inappropriately broad, as Chandler's (1990) data in particular refer only to *industrial* firms. Accordingly, we have taken as our measure comparative growth rates in industrial production over the post-war period. This is a closer measure, but not perfect for at least two reasons. First, although indirect effects are likely to be large, the top 100 industrial firms in each economy account directly for only around 35–40 per cent of total industrial production, and the domestically-owned ones for less (Supple 1990). Second, our measure of industrial production includes construction, although we follow Harvard by excluding construction firms from our sample. Nevertheless, with these caveats, we believe that if the strong links between patterns of firm level strategy and structure and national economic performance claimed by Chandler (1990) are present, these should be reflected more directly by relative growth in industrial production than in GDP data.

At the level of the firm, Alford (1994) has noted how Chandler (1990) does not in fact use any profitability measures, something rather extraordinary in an account of the 'dynamics of industrial capitalism'. However, within the strategy literature there has grown since Rumelt (1973) a long and controversial tradition of strategy, structure and performance studies. As for Rumelt (1973), we shall measure performance at the level of the firm according to accounting measures of profitability. Accounting based measures are the most widely used measures of performance in research on diversification and organisational structure (Datta et al. 1991; Robins and Wiersema 1995) and have been used in studies on the United Kingdom (Grant and Jammine 1988), France (Belkaoui 1996) and Germany (Buehner 1991). Stock market measures have recently been deprecated for these kinds of studies in the United States (Markides 1996), but were especially inappropriate for this study because of the large number of companies that are either private or state-owned in Europe (Cable and Dirrheimer 1984). Accounting based measures have been shown to be related to a variety of other measures of financial performance and are assumed to "trigger long-run equilibrium adjustments" (Ezzamel and Watson 1993: 166).

Here we measure profitability just in terms of pre-tax return on total assets (ROA), following Toulan (1996). As was highlighted by Robins and Wiersema (1995: 286–287) "the use of ROA (…) helps to make the research replicable and cumulative", a central concern of the present study. ROA is additionally appropriate both because it allows for the differences in financing practices between European countries, and because European holding companies report profits and assets from their participations, but not their sales.[3] To smooth any irregularities, we averaged performance over three years, with 1983 and 1993 as mid-points (Hall and St. John 1994). Data were obtained from Datastream for the British companies, from the Bundesanzeiger for German companies and directly from annual reports for the French companies.

4. Strategy, Structure and National Performance

Chandler's (1990) original proposition was that during the first half of the century, British firms had lagged American and German ones in seeking out economies of scope through diversification and making appropriate organisational arrangements in terms of multidivisional structures. The result had been crippling for economic performance. More recently, however, we have seen that the experience of the 1970s and 1980s had prompted Chandler (1990) to increasing misgivings about the excesses of American conglomerate diversification, which he feared was damaging economic performance against more focused competition from Japan. For Europe in this more recent period, Chandler (1990) lacked systematic contemporary data, but again he saw Britain likely to be penalised, this time as over-involved in the conglomerate strategies facilitated by an active market for corporate control. By comparison, he thought Continental European economies would more easily correct any diversification excesses (Chandler 1990: 625–27). In short, Britain suffered first from having too little diversification, later by having, if not too much, at least the wrong sort.

As Figure 1 indicates, through most of the post-war period, Britain's relative industrial decline continued. Through the first three decades — roughly corresponding to Germany's *Wirtschaftswunder* and France's *trente glorieuses* — British industrial production lagged its European neighbours' severely. Only in the last 15 years has British industrial performance caught up; or, given the generally dismal performance of Europe, it might be better said that France and Germany have sunk to similar levels of mediocrity. How far do different patterns of strategy and structure account for these different growth rates?

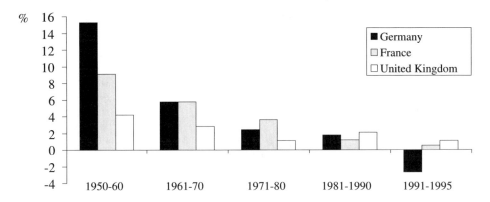

Figure 1. *Industrial Production: Annual Growth Rates*

Sources: Mitchell 1976;
         Handbook of International Economic Statistics.

Per cent of firms

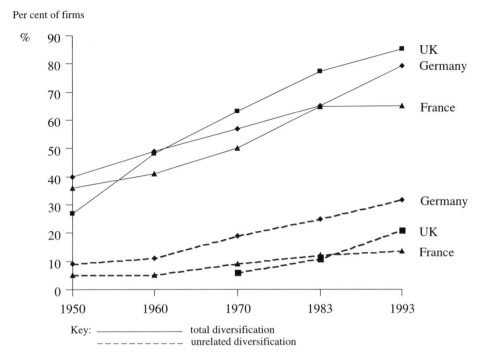

Figure 2. *Diversification Strategy in Post-War France, Germany and the United Kingdom*

Sources: 1950–1970: Dyas and Thanheiser (1976), Channon (1973) (no separate unrelated figures available for UK before 1970); 1983–1993: this study.

Figure 2 presents the trends in diversification strategy amongst domestically-owned top 100 industrial firms between 1950 and 1993 for France, Germany and the United Kingdom. For the period to 1970, the data are drawn from the earlier Harvard studies; for the more recent period, from our own work. For consistency, these data are on the Wrigley-basis used by the original Harvard European studies, rather than the pure Rumeltian used in most American studies. The top lines show the total proportions of firms using strategies of either related or unrelated diversification; the bottom lines distinguish those using just unrelated or conglomerate strategies of diversification.

The first thing to notice from Figure 2 is that French, German and British business has generally followed the pattern of increased diversification advocated by Harvard. Between 1950 and 1993, aggregate diversification (taking related and unrelated together) increased consistently in all three European countries on the Wrigley measure. There was a marked slow-down in diversification in France over the 1980s, but British and German aggregate diversification levels were still increasing rapidly. Making allowance for the different Rumeltian measure, with around 80 per cent of firms following diversified strategies by 1993, Britain and Germany had comfortably reached levels of diversification comparable to that achieved in the United States by 1969 (Rumelt 1973). In this sense, the early Harvard confidence in the catch-up of European business is broadly justified (Scott 1973). It may have been quite a long time coming, but European business is now increasingly organised within multi-sectoral corporations.

Yet there are some distinct oddities from a Chandlerian perspective. The earlier data in Figure 2, drawn from the Channon (1973) and Dyas and Thanheiser (1976) studies in which Chandler himself was involved, suggest that French and German firms even as far back as 1950 were much more likely to have stuck in the utterly undiversified category of 'single business' than British. Although the level of aggregate diversification was lower, it seems that by the end of the period for which Chandler (1990) had castigated British managers for undue conservatism, in fact more British firms had ventured out of their original core than their peers in France and Germany. Very soon, British firms exceeded French firms in terms of aggregate diversification (1960), and German ones for the approved strategy of related diversification (1970: no disaggregation available earlier for British firms). Yet growth in British industrial production remained well behind its Continental rivals until the 1980s. At the level of national performance, there seems no obvious pay-off to following the prescribed strategies of Harvard.

The reverse is also true: there are no evident penalties to ignoring Chandlerian prescriptions. Despite Chandler's (1990) anxiety about the British tendency to conglomeratisation, in fact the Germans show consistently higher levels of unrelated diversification, from 1970 at least. Until quite recently, the same is true of French business. Again, however, these tendencies find no clear reflection in the national performance data. German and French performance sink relative to British only in the last decade or so. Britain's relative growth improves through the 1980s and early 1990s against a background of steadily increasing conglomeratisation.

Another oddity is that in following American prescriptions, European business has actually begun to diverge from American practice. During the 1980s, American business turned away from diversification and back to its cores: by 1987, the 'single business' strategy accounted once more for nearly a third of Fortune 500 firms, equivalent to the level in 1949 (Markides 1996). European business, meanwhile, merrily continued on its diversification path, seeing general increases in unrelated, conglomerate diversification between 1983 and 1993. By the beginning of the 1980s, aggregate levels of diversification in all three European countries were already comparable to those in the United States, yet far from correcting what Americans perceived as excessive diversification, the Europeans continued to diversify still further. It is hard to know how to interpret this: is it another lamentable lag, equivalent to the mid-century slowness of European

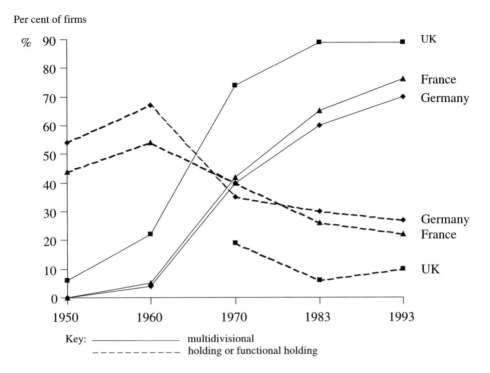

Figure 3. *Organisational Structure in Post-War France, Germany and the United Kingdom*

Sources: 1950–1970: Dyas and Thanheiser (1976), Channon (1973) (no separate holding figures available for UK before 1970); 1983–1993: this study.

business to diversify in the first place, or is it rather the establishment of a distinct and enduring pattern of European business organisation?

Further puzzles concerning the link between Chandlerian prescriptions and recent performance emerge in considering the progress of the multidivisional structure. Here British business emerges as the consistent leader, not the laggard of demonology. Figure 3 shows the proportions of domestically-owned top 100 industrial companies organised on either multidivisional or holding/function-holding lines (the pure functional company had more or less disappeared by the 1980s). Comparing the different national trends in divisionalisation, we see that in every decade, British firms were ahead of the French and German, even in 1950, the end-point of Chandler's (1990) own study. Indeed, by 1993, Britain was the only country to have surpassed the 77 per cent level of divisionalisation achieved by Rumelt's (1973) sample of American Fortune 500 firms as early as 1969. Sadly, this steady enthusiasm for the Harvard organisational model received no consistent return in terms of relative industrial growth.

Also worth remarking — besides the near complete collapse of the functional form in all three countries — is the persistence of the holding forms of organisation, which Chandler (1982) and Williamson (1975) had dismissed as utterly anachronistic: around a quarter of firms in France and Germany still had holding or functional-holding structures in 1993. Indeed, in the UK, where the holding and functional-holding had become nearly extinct by the early 1980s, there was even a slight revival. Amongst these holding companies, we find a mix of firms — some old-style personal holdings, some perhaps the flexible networks of contemporary fashion (Whittington and Mayer 1997). It is hard to generalise at this point. We shall return to the surprising vitality of the holding company as we consider findings on structure and performance at the level of the firm.

5.   Strategy, Structure and Corporate Performance

So far, we have considered the impact of national patterns of strategy, and structure on aggregate industrial growth. The picture at this high level has been disconcerting. Now we shall descend to the level of the firm to consider the relationships between strategy, structure and business performance. It is important to note here, though, that the metric has changed, from growth in production to financial profitability, something rather elided in the Chandlerian accounts.

Theory has established a quite clear hierarchy of performance expectations: diversifiers perform better than non-diversifiers; related diversifiers perform better than unrelated diversifiers; and the divisional form of organisation out-performs all (Rumelt 1973; Markides 1996). Although this hierarchy is expected to be stable across time and across countries, no single study has yet tested it both longitudinally and internationally. The data we present here, therefore, provide an opportunity to test the robustness of Harvard relationships with consistent data across three countries and two time periods.[4]

Table 1 reports the three year average returns on total assets (ROA) for the British, German and French firms classified in 1983 and 1993 according to the eight Rumeltian categories (Rumelt's categories, rather than Wrigley's, are typically used in performance analyses: the original Harvard European studies did not include any performance analysis). Because of some missing financial data — a number of the privately held companies in France and Germany do not publish the necessary data — the totals for each country and period are slightly smaller than in the earlier trend analyses. Allowing for this, it is interesting to note the distributions between finer categories: the more tightly-bundled strategy of related constrained diversification emerges as much more popular than the looser strategy of related linked. Also, reported returns are systematically higher in the United Kingdom than in the other two countries, around eight per cent ROA on average compared to four to six per cent in France and Germany: consequently,

Table 1: *Strategy and Performance in France, Germany and the United Kingdom, 1982–1994*

Strategy	United Kingdom				France				Germany			
	82–84		92–94		82–84		92–94		82–84		92–94	
	ROA	N	ROA	N	ROA	N	ROA	N	ROA	N	ROA	N
Single	-1.9	3	18.2	3	3.0	13	1.7	10	8.9	9	2.1	6
Dominant-vertical	8.7	7	5.8	5	5.4	7	0	5	1.4	3	-2.5	1
Dominant-constrained	7.5	2	10.6	2	1.3	3	4.4	5	6.9	3	6.2	4
Dominant-linked	–	–	7.7	2	–	–	–	–	1.4	1	-1.0	1
Dominant-unrelated	8.5	4	–	–	–	–	–	–	4.3	2	–	–
Related-constrained	8.9	22	9.1	26	6.0	18	5.7	22	7.5	18	6.0	17
Related-linked	7.7	16	8.1	12	2.8	5	3.5	4	4.2	6	0	–
Unrelated	7.5	13	8.4	17	5.1	8	3.5	8	5.1	9	3.2	15
F-Ratio	3.074[a]		2.639[a]		601		1.652		1.435[a]		5.978[a]	

[a] Significant at the 0.05 level

Source: Own data from a survey of each country's top 100 industrial enterprises.

we must guard against pooling data from different countries.

On the advantages of diversification in general, it is difficult to conclude. The differences in performance between strategic categories are statistically significant in the United Kingdom and Germany, but not in France. However, the undiversified (especially dominant) categories typically have small numbers, so that their averages are easily distorted by exceptions: for example, the wildly oscillating performance of single business companies in the United Kingdom is explicable by the category's dominance by poorly-performing nationalised companies in the early 1980s and by pharmaceutical companies in the early 1990s. Generally, the averages for the undiversified categories fluctuate too widely to allow safe judgement on the relative merits of diversification and non-diversification. As to the superiority of related over unrelated diversification, we have to discriminate. Related linked strategies do not consistently pay better than unrelated strategies. However, though the differences are not large, in every year and in all three countries, strategies of related constrained diversification do beat unrelated strategies; in all but one case, they also beat the less tightly focused related linked strategies. On this basis, the emerging American consensus against unfocused strategies may be generalizable across countries and time.

There is no clear support concerning the superiority of the divisional, however. On the performance of the functional structure, we can say little except to note its near complete disappearance. However, we have already remarked on the surprising resilience of holding company forms in Europe. Table 2 shows that the divisional form of organisation was out-performed by the pure holding in three out of the six comparisons; in one of the three remaining cases, France in the early 1980s, it was beaten by the hybrid functional-holding. This finding, consistent with others from Europe (Hill 1988; Cable and Dirrheimer 1984), rather qualifies the generalizability of the traditional Harvard claims for the superiority of the divisional structure in terms of economic performance. Either holding type forms are particularly well-adapted to the complex institutional conditions of Europe (Mayer and Whittington 1996) or their relative disadvantage to the multidivisional has evaporated over time with the new demands for flexibility and fluidity in today's fast-moving competitive environment (Whittington and Mayer 1997).

6.   Conclusions

Alfred Chandler offers a different and rival perspective on European economic organisation to many of the contributions in this volume. Taking a more macro view, he draws attention to the location of much sectoral activity within large diversified corporations. Taking a universalist perspective, he has prescribed common models of corporate strategy and structure across the industrial world. This strong challenge to the institutionally-sensitive and sectorally-embedded approach needs to be taken on.

Table 2: *Structure and Performance in France, Germany and the United Kingdom, 1982–1994*

	United Kingdom				France				Germany			
	82–84		92–94		82–84		92–94		82–84		92–94	
Structure	ROA	N	ROA	N	ROA	N	ROA	N	ROA	N	ROA	N
Functional	0.1	2	4.5	1	2.8	2	–	–	11.3	4	3.1	2
Functional-holding	11.0	1	–	–	6.1	5	3.8	5	5.8	13	1.5	6
Holding	8.4	3	10.1	6	2.6	9	2.9	8	4.5	5	4.3	6
Multi-divisional	7.9	61	8.8	60	4.8	38	4.0	41	6.2	29	3.8	40
F-Ratio	2.282[a]		.811		.444		.149		1.765		.837	

[a] significant at 0.10 level.

Source: Own data from a survey of each country's top 100 industrial enterprises.

In one important respect, Chandler (1962) and Scott (1973) have been right. Industrial activity in Europe is increasingly being organised in the diversified, divisionalised corporations that emerged for the first time in pre-war America. The post-war spread of diversification, in particular unrelated diversification, is bringing very different sectors of economic activity together under the control of common hierarchies of management. The broadly parallel nature of this trend across the three countries implies a considerable degree of institutional autonomy at the level of the corporation. The strategies and structures of corporate headquarters seem to be conforming to the kinds of universal logics prescribed by Harvard.

This dis-embedding at the level of the corporation may yet have important ramifications at the lower level of the sector. As Mueller and Loveridge (1997) have argued for the multinational corporation, but equally for the multi-business corporation, corporate structures are important transmission mechanisms for capital, personnel and management practices. The diversified corporation's widening embrace will bring more and more sectors closer together. As diversification spreads and divisional structures bite, distinct sectoral structures and practices may become increasingly overlayed by the blander logics of corporate best practice.

There are grounds for caution, however. Even at the corporate level, change has been slow and national idiosyncrasies remain. Since its first rush of adoption in the 1960s, it has taken three decades for the multidivisional to reach in Continental Europe levels equivalent to those of Rumelt's (1973) America. Holding forms of organisation persist and, if their recent revival in the United Kingdom is indicative, are not on a one-way ticket to extinction. Moreover, performance relationships are not as strong or universal as Harvard would expect. The absence of clear relationships between corporate strategies and structures and industrial growth rates at the national level suggests that headquarters' practices are not yet making much difference at the level of the business and sector, where work actually gets done. Just as the corporate level may be disembedded institutionally, it may be disarticulated sectorally. The same is true for firm-level performance, where relationships are weak and contradictory. While the related constrained pattern of diversification does, by a small margin, seem to outperform others fairly consistently across time and place, the multidivisional has no such firm advantage. The holding company, whether because well-adapted to the institutional complexities of Europe or anticipating the flexibility demanded by the new competition, emerges as a stronger performer than from earlier studies in the United States. The economics of diversification may tend towards universality, but the more sociologically-dependent phenomenon of organisation does not yet display the context-free advantages assumed by Harvard.

Our findings, then, suggest the importance of discriminating between levels and types of practices. Different sectors are slowly being brought in under common frameworks of ownership, becoming potentially subject to the standardising pressures of multinational and multi-business corporations. Sectoral approaches to economic organisation and performance need to take this into account. Nevertheless, it is likely that this corporate level is still relatively detached from the kind of institutional base in which a great deal of sectoral activity takes place. On the ground, corporate-driven practices have not yet begun to bite. However, as the catch-up phase of diversification and divisionalisation comes to completion, the tension between the institutionally-embedded sector and the more autonomous corporation will become an increasing one. The management of this tension, and the extraction from it of best practice from both levels, will be an important source of competitive advantage in the coming decade.

Notes

1. The research was funded by the Economic and Social Research Council and the Nuffield Foundation.

2. Three further Continental companies have not yet been analysed, awaiting completion of data.

3. The operationalization of the Wrigley measures varied slightly in the original European studies. To provide fully comparable data we followed the interpretations of the respective researchers in each of the countries.

4. Here we shall only be reporting univariate analyses, but we shall later conduct multivariate analyses controlling for industry, leverage and ownership effects.

Appendix 1

1.1   *Diversification Classifications*

Although studies differ in detail, diversification strategies in the Harvard tradition are basically defined by two ratios: the specialisation ratio, measuring the proportion of total turnover that is attributable to one kind of business; and the related ratio, the proportion of turnover attributable to different businesses that are related to each other (by technology or market). The definition of the various Wrigley and Rumeltian diversification categories in terms of these ratios is as follows:

Wrigley Classifications:

Single Business:	specialisation ratio (SR) > 95%
Dominant Business:	SR < 95%, > 70%
Related Business:	SR < 70%, related ratio (RR) > 70%
Unrelated Business	SR < 70%, RR < 70%

Rumelt Classifications:

Single Business:	SR > 95%
Dominant Vertical:	vertically-related sales > 70%
Dominant Constrained:	SR < 95%, > 70%, majority of other businesses related to one another through a core asset, market or skill
Dominant Linked:	SR < 95%, > 70%, majority of other businesses relate to just one other business
Dominant Unrelated:	SR < 95%, > 70%, other businesses unrelated
Related Constrained:	SR < 70%, RR > 70%, majority of businesses related to each other
Related Linked:	SR < 70%, RR > 70%, majority of businesses related to just one other business
Unrelated:	SR < 70%, RR < 70%

1.2   *Structure Classifications*

Harvard uses four basic structure classifications:

Functional:	centralised around core functions (marketing, manufacturing etc.)
Holding:	highly decentralised, with little control from the centre
Functional/Holding:	a centralised core, with highly decentralised periphery of subsidiaries
Multidivisional:	decentralised operations (product or geographical divisions), centralised strategy

Appendix 2

Interviewed firms (Britain, France and Germany)

ABF	FriedrichKrupp -Hoesch Krupp
Aérospatiale	Linde AG
Alcatel Alsthom	L'Oréal
Allied Domecq	Labinal
AMEC	Legrand
Arjo Wiggins Appleton	Lucas
BASF	LVMH
Bayernwerke AG	Matra-Hachette
Bertelsmann AG	Pernod Ricard
BICC	Preussag
Blue Circle Industries	PWA AG
BMW AG	Racal
BNFL	Reed
Bongrain	Renault
Bosch-Siemens	Rhône Poulenc
BP	RMC Group
BSN (Danone)	Rochling KG
Bull	Rolls Royce
British Steel	RTZ
Cadbury Schweppes	Ruhrkohle AG
CarnaudMetalbox	Ruhrgas AG
CEA-Industrie	Saint Gobain
Coats Viyella	Schering AG
Cookson	SEB
Elf-Aquitaine	Sextant Avionique
Essilor	Shell
Financière Agache	Siebe
Framatome	Siemens AG
Freudenberg and Co	SmithKline Beecham
GEA-AG	Strafor Facom
GKN plc	TI Group
Glynwed International	Usinor Sacilor
Groupe de la Cité	Valéo
Haindl GmbH	Vallourec
Hillsdown Holdings	Varta
Holzbrink	VIAG
IMI plc	Vorwerk
KolbenschmidtAG (Metalgesellschaft)	Wella AG
Klockner Werke AG	ZF-Friedrichshafen

References

Alford, B. W. E. 1994. Chandlerianism: the New Orthodoxy of US and European Corporate Development, *Journal of European Economic History* 23(3): 631–643.

Bartlett, C., and S. Ghoshal. 1993. Beyond the M-Form: Towards a Managerial Theory of the Firm, *Strategic Management Journal* 14: 23–46.

Belkaoui, A. R. 1996. Internationalization, Diversification Strategy and Ownership Structure: Implications for French MNE Performance, *International Business Review* 5(4): 367–376.

Buehner, R. 1991. The Success of Mergers in Germany, *Strategic Management Journal* 9: 513–532.

Cable, J., and M. J. Dirrheimer. 1983. Hierarchies and Markets: an Empirical Test of the Multidivisional Hypothesis in West Germany, *International Journal of Industrial Organization* 1: 43–62.

Carlin, W. 1996. West German Growth and Institutions, 1945–90. In: N. Crafts, and G. Toniolo (eds.), *Economic Growth in Europe since 1945*, 455–497. Cambridge: Cambridge University Press.

Chandler, A. D. 1962. *Strategy and Structure: Chapters in the History of American Industrial Enterprise.* Cambridge: MIT Press.

Chandler, A. D. 1977. *The Visible Hand: The Managerial Revolution in American Business.* Cambridge, Mass: Harvard University Press.

Chandler, A. D. 1982. The M-Form: Industrial Groups, American Style, *European Economic Review* 19: 3–23.

Chandler, A. D. 1990. *Scale and Scope: the Dynamics of Industrial Capitalism.* Cambridge, Mass: Harvard University Press.

Chandler, A. D., F. Amatori, and T. Hikino (eds.). 1997. *Big Business and the Wealth of Nations.* Cambridge: Cambridge University Press.

Chandler, A. D., and T. Hikino. 1997. The Large Industrial Enterprise and the Dynamics of Modern Economic Growth. In: A. D. Chandler, and F. Amatori and T. Hikino (eds.), *Big Business and the Wealth of Nations*, 24–57. Cambridge: Cambridge University Press.

Channon, D. 1973. *The Strategy and Structure of British Enterprise.* London: MacMillan.

Datta D., N. Rajagopolan, and A. Rajheed. 1991. Diversification and Performance: a Critical Review, *Journal of Management Studies* 25(5): 529–557.

Dyas G. P., and H. T. Thanheiser. 1976. *The Emerging European Enterprise.* London: MacMillan.

Eichengreen, B. 1996. Institutions and Economic Growth. In: N. Crafts, and G. Toniolo (eds.), *Economic Growth in Europe since 1945*, 38–72. Cambridge: Cambridge University Press.

Ezzamel M., and R. Watson. 1993. Organizational Form, Ownership Structure and Corporate Performance: a Contextual Empirical Analysis of UK Companies, *British Journal of Management* 4: 161–176.

Fligstein, N. 1985. The Spread of the Multi-Divisional Form among Large Firms, 1919–1979, *American Sociological Review* 50: 377–391.

Fruin, W.M,. 1992. *The Japanese Enterprise System.* Oxford: Clarendon Books.

Grant R., and A. P. Jammine,. 1988. Performance Differences between the Wrigley/Rumelt Strategic Categories, *Strategic Management Journal* 9: 333–346.

Hall, E. H., and C. H. St.John. 1994. A Methodological Note on Diversity Measurement, *Strategic Management Journal* 15: 153–168.

Handbook of International Economic Statistics, Central Intelligence Agency (different annual editions). Washington: CIA.

Hannah, L. 1991. Scale and Scope: Towards a European Visible Hand?, *Business History* 33(2): 297–309.

Hatfield, D. E., J. P. Liebeskind, and T. C. Opler. 1996. The Effects of Corporate Restructuring on Aggregate Industry Specialization, *Strategic Management Journal* 17: 55–72.

Hedlund G. 1994. A Model of Knowledge Management and the N-Form Corporation, *Strategic Management Journal* 15: 73–90.

Hill, C. W. L. 1988. Internal Capital Market Controls and Financial Performance in Multidivisional Firms, *Journal of Industrial Economics* 37(1): 67–83.

Hollingsworth, J. R., and R. Boyer (eds). 1997. *Contemporary Capitalism: The Embeddedness of Institutions*. Cambridge: Cambridge University Press.

Hoskisson, R. E., and M. A. Hitt. 1995. *Downscoping: Taming the Diversified Corporation*. Oxford: Oxford University Press.

Locke, R. R. 1996. *The Collapse of the American Management Mystique*. Oxford: Oxford University Press.

Markides, C. 1996. Causes and Consequences of Corporate Restructuring. In: H. Thomas, D. O'Neil, and J. Kelley (eds), *Strategic Renaissance and Business Transformation*, 415–436. Chichester: Wiley.

Markides, C., and P. J. Williamson. 1996. Corporate Diversification and Organizational Structure: a Resource-Based View', *Academy of Management Review* 39(2): 340–367.

Matthews, R. C. O. 1986. The Economics of Institutions and the Sources of Growth, *Economic Journal* 96: 903–910.

Mayer, M., and R. Whittington. 1996. The Survival of the European Holding Company: Institutional Choice and Contingency. In: R. Whitley, and P. H. Kristensen (eds.), *The Changing European Firm*, 87–109. London: Routledge.

Mintzberg, H. 1994. *The Rise and Fall of Strategic Planning*. Englewood Cliffs: Prentice Hall.

Mitchell, B. R. 1976. *European Historical Statistics*. London: Macmillan.

Mowery, D. 1992. Finance and Corporate Evolution in Five Industrial Economies, 1900–1950, *Industrial and Corporate Change* 1(1): 1–36.

Mueller, F. and Loveridge, R. 1997. Institutional, Sectoral and Corporate Dynamics in the Creation of Global Supply Chains. In: R. Whitley and P. H. Kristensen (eds.), *Governance at Work*, 120–36. Oxford: Oxford University Press.

Palmer, D. A., P. D. Jennings, and X. Zhou. 1993. Late Adoption of the Multidivisional Form by Large U. S. Corporations: Institutional, Political, and Economic Accounts, *Administrative Science Quarterly* 38: 100–131.

Robins, J., and M. F. Wiersema. 1995. A Resource Based Approach to the Multibusiness Firm: Empirical Analysis of Portfolio Interrelationships and Corporate Financial Performance, *Strategic Management Journal* 16: 227–299.

Rumelt, R. 1973. *Strategy, Structure and Economic Performance*. Boston: Harvard Business School.

Scott, B. 1973. The Industrial State: Old Myths and New Realities, *Harvard Business Review*, March-April: 135–148.

Streeck, W. 1997. Beneficial Constraints: On the Economic Limits of Rational Voluntarism. In: J. R. Hollingsworth, and R. Boyer (eds), *Contemporary Capitalism: The Embeddedness of Institutions*, 197–219. Cambridge: Cambridge University Press.

Supple, B. 1991. Scale and Scope: Alfred Chandler and the Dynamics of Industrial Capitalism, *Economic History Review* 44(3): 500–14.

Toulan, O. N. 1996. Non-Linearities in the Impact of Industry Structure, *Industrial and Corporate Change* 5(1): 175–202.

Whitley, R. 1994. Dominant Forms of Economic Organization in Market Economies, *Organization Studies* 15(2): 153–82.

Whitley, R., and P. H. Kristensen (eds.). 1996. *The Changing European Firm*. London: Routledge.

Whittington, R., and M. Mayer. 1997. Beyond or Behind the M-Form? The Structures of European Business, in D. O'Neal, and H. Thomas (eds), *Strategy Systems: Styles and Paradigms*, 241–258. London: Wiley.

Williamson, O. E. 1975. *Markets and Hierarchies: Analysis and Anti-Trust Implications*. New York: Free Press.

Wrigley, L. 1970. Divisional Autonomy and Diversification, unpublished PhD. Dissertation, Cambridge, Harvard Business School.

PART III

Societal Performance Standards and
Their Internationalisation

CHAPTER 6

Confidence and Confidentiality

The Social Construction of Performance Standards
in Banking

Glenn Morgan   Sigrid Quack

1.   Introduction

Performance standards refer to the way in which the activities and outcomes of
organisations are judged. In economic orthodoxy, the hidden hand of the market
is the final judge of organisational performance. Failure to meet the performance
standards which dominate a particular market and are the function of supply and
demand leads the organisation to go out of existence. However, some economists
recognise the difficulty of reconciling what can actually be observed in particular
markets and what the theory predicts. The result is a rather uneasy appeal to 'the
long run' or some other concept to allow for this gap. For example, Williamson refers
to 'weak-form selection — according to which the fitter, but not necessarily the
fittest, in some absolute sense, are selected' (Williamson 1994: 87). He states that:

> "Transaction cost economising does not always operate smoothly or quickly. Thus
> we should 'expect [transaction cost economising] to be most clearly exhibited in
> industries where entry is [easy] and where the struggle for survival is [keen]'
> (Koopmans). Transaction cost economics nevertheless maintains that later, if not
> sooner, inefficiency in the commercial sector invites its own demise — all the more
> so as international competition has become more vigorous. Politically imposed
> impediments (tariffs, quotas, subsidies, rules) can, however, delay the reckoning;
> and disadvantaged parties …may also be able to delay changes unless compensated
> by buyouts." (Williamson 1994: 87)

Williamson describes these exceptions and qualifications as "tosh", a "source of
interesting variety" that "adds spice to life" but does not get to the "essentials"
of economic ordering (Williamson 1994: 97–8). In this chapter, we take a different
view. Performance and selection can be studied in a systematic way without
appealing to long-run, invisible processes or becoming lost in 'tosh'. What needs
to be understood is how in particular social contexts, performance standards are

constructed and with what effect. There are many different ways of measuring, monitoring and judging the performance of organisations in market societies. Different standards of performance emerge within nations (and sectors) as a result of historical institutional features of industrial development. Standards of performance have to be implemented and enforced by particular social actors, whether those be shareholders, regulators, the government or other categories of stakeholder. Thus when we refer to a social structure of performance standards we are referring to both the mechanisms and processes which shape the way in which organisations are judged *and* the agents who play a central role in this.

The construction of a social structure of performance standards is particularly significant in the banking industry. It is impossible to understand banking systems and the performance of individual banks simply by reference to processes of market selection for the simple reason that the fate of banks and the banking system has implications for everybody in a particular social context. Banks need to be understood from two perspectives — as organisations in their own right and as part of a wider system of the provision of credit and money transmission. As organisations in their own right, banks have to meet their own performance goals in relation to the expectations of owners (these might be shareholders or depositors or the government), customers and managers. However, they are also essential parts of a monetised economy with a central role to play in the overall security of the financial system as a whole. The financial sector is essential to the management of credit as well as the allocation of finance for investment, the security and stability of deposits and savings and the maintenance of the money transmission system. All national financial systems generate rules of action and institutional mechanisms which attempt to balance the interests of the individual banks with the complex requirements which arise from the role of the financial system within the social and economic order as a whole. Individual financial institutions are not free to do what they want irrespective of the consequences for the soundness of the system as a whole. The actions of any particular bank may have system-wide consequences because of the way in which financial institutions are linked together; therefore, there inevitably develops a structure of regulation and control which places limits on what any individual bank is allowed to do.

From this perspective, the social structure of performance standards in any financial organisation and system has two elements. On the one hand, as a firm, a bank has a set of obligations to its immediate stakeholders (shareholders, depositors etc.) concerned with the successful management of its own business; on the other hand, as a participant in the wider financial system it has obligations to act in ways which maintain order and stability. Central to this process is the nature of risk and how it is managed. Banking is essentially a process of managing risk. The social structure of performance standards refers to what risks banks can take, how they can protect themselves against risk, what rewards they can claim from bearing risks and how governments will help them bear risks.

In any national system, we can identify a number of ways in which risks in the financial system can be controlled:

- *Compartmentalisation:* Activities may be compartmentalised in order to ensure that failure in one area does not risk contaminating other areas of the business.
- *Prohibition:* Certain activities, which are deemed 'too risky' may be prohibited (this may include prohibiting competition by setting agreed prices and margins or it may simply involve prohibiting certain sorts of dealing). It is also the case that certain individuals or organisations are prohibited from undertaking banking activity as they are deemed untrustworthy, whilst others are formally or informally licensed to act in this capacity.
- *Insurance:* Other activities may be allowed but only where the organisation can demonstrate that it has 'insured' itself against loss (e.g. by depositing liquidity reserves with the central bank or by complying to internal capital ratio requirements).
- *Monitoring:* Activities may be allowed so long as the banking authorities are given access to detailed information which can assure them that the bank is not at risk.

But what about the rewards to taking on risks? In a simple economistic model, high risks would generate high rewards whilst low risks would generate low rewards. Within a social structure of performance standards model, however, other alternatives can be envisaged. Most obviously, cartelisation of the banking sector can mean that those within the cartel earn high rewards by fixing prices even where risks are low. This also has the consequence that high risk business will either not be funded or will gravitate to banks which are outside the cartel. Thus the financial system bifurcates between the inner core which is stable, highly profitable and low risk and the outsiders where business is unstable and high risk. This bifurcation may be reinforced if banks in the inner core believe that the state or the regulators will help them if they get into difficulty and therefore become tempted to move either directly or indirectly into the risky business taken on by the outsiders. Podolny has described a further variation of this process which he labels the 'Matthew effect'. In this context, organisations are willing to pay a premium to be linked to a particular inner core bank because the reputational effect of the bank will have positive consequences for other areas of the organisation's business (Podolny 1993, 1994). Therefore, business which is low risk brings higher rewards to the high status bank than it would do to the low status bank. Within the inner circle, rewards are generally standardised not so much according to the level of risk involved but according to the prices agreed within this group.

For those outside the cartel, taking higher risks, there is greater variability in reward. In general terms, as the power to price fix declines (either directly or indirectly), there emerges greater variation in performance.

In the following section, we compare Britain and Germany using this framework (for an application to France, see Salomon in this volume). Previous research has highlighted the different nature of the British capital-market based and the German bank-finance based financial system (Zysman 1983; Lane 1989; Vitols 1997), the impact of these two different financial systems on the nature of the firm and work systems in other economic sectors (Whitley and Kristensen 1996, 1997) as well as the well known distinction between short- and long-termism in business goals of investors in the financial sector (Hutton 1995; Coleman 1996). Lane and Quack (2000), in particular, have investigated how the institutional environment in both countries impacts on banks' perception and handling of risk with regard to financing small- and medium sized enterprises. In this paper, however, it is our aim to explain why the performance standards which were considered as appropriate for banking in one country were very different from those in the other country. Based on this analysis, we will furthermore show that the two banking systems evolved in very distinctive ways when confronted with the increasing internationalisation of financial markets.

2.   Financial Systems in Britain and Germany in the Post-War Period

2.1 *Compartmentalisation*

Compartmentalisation is a process which ensures that one part of the financial system is protected from failure in another part because the firms in the two sectors are separate legal entities. Compartmentalisation therefore generates specialist institutions dependent for their survival on their ability to be successful in particular, defined markets. It may emerge for historical reasons, as it did in Britain, or it may be legislated into existence as was the case in the USA following the Wall Street crash. Compartmentalisation, however, runs contrary to three broad trends which favour the exact opposite, i.e. the creation of universal banking institutions. The first trend is for financial organisations to diversify in order to reduce risk, i.e. to ensure that if there is failure in one area, the organisation has other areas of business which are being successful and can therefore compensate. Secondly, since financial markets carry very varying levels of risk and reward, there is an ever-present temptation for those in markets with relatively low level of returns to extend into more profitable sectors. Thirdly, business and personal customers may want all of their banking services to be supplied by one institution, or even if this is not demonstrably the case, management can use this as a justification for universal banking.

The British financial system up into the post war period was highly compartmentalised with divisions between the Clearing Banks (mainly concerned with money transmission and the provision of credit through overdraft and other short-term lending facilities), the merchant banks (who organised the provision of both long and short-term credit for companies and the government as well as acting as investment managers and advisers), the Stock Exchange and the savings sector (based mainly on the life insurance companies). Each group of institutions was overseen by the Bank of England which allowed the different sectors to regulate their own conditions of competition in return for cooperating with the Bank in overall control of the economy. Within each sphere, firms cooperated informally to set the basic rules of the game (often including prices) which ensured that all were able to survive comfortably so long as they played the same sort of game and were not tempted to over-extend themselves. In return, all these institutions had to perform as the Bank asked at crucial times — whether this was moving interest rates, supporting new government issues or rallying around a failing institution (Ingham 1984). The performance criteria along which these institutions were measured and measured themselves were derived primarily from the internal dynamics of the financial system as set up in the 18th century when managing the government finances and the secondary markets which built upon this was central (Carruthers 1996; Neal 1990). Performance with regard to financing manufacturing industry was of only minor importance and rarely entered into the deliberations of the City (except when occasionally outside events forced it on to the political agenda as with the Macmillan Committee in the inter-war years) (Ingham 1984; Weiss and Hobson 1995). For the Bank of England, compartmentalisation meant that it could keep a close (but informal) eye over the different sectors and institutions. As cross-contamination was unlikely, the task for the Bank was not as difficult as it might have been had the institutions been balancing different types of risk.

In Germany, on the other hand, universal banking had emerged in the 19th century as a way of coordinating the collection and distribution of funds from the hands of individuals to investment in emerging industries. Banks had played a central role in lending long-term to industry and as part of that process, issuing and owning shares (Deeg 1992). In the German system, therefore, the performance of banks — as perceived by key stakeholders — has never been assessed solely within the financial system (or in relation to state financing) but also with regard to their role in the financing of other economic sectors. The German commercial banks were universal financial institutions capable of providing their corporate customers with a full range of services. In the other sectors of German banking, the savings bank system and the cooperative bank system, a similar though less developed model of universal banking existed. Although in these two sectors the primary customer base consisted of individuals and small to medium sized companies (compared to the commercial banks which concentrated on the large company sector) and their range of products was more limited, within this framework, they also operated a range of lending and financing services that made them universal banking institutions. Because the basis of the German system was universal banking (even though it was segmented into the three groupings of commercial banks, savings banks and cooperative banks), the possibility of cross-contamination and meltdown of the system was always high as the inflation of the 1920s and the crises of the early 1930s demonstrated. Rather than abandoning the universal banking system (as, for example, happened in the USA in the 1930s) the German system moved from the 1930s onwards to find other ways in which risks could be controlled.

2.2 *Prohibition*

In the British system, there was very little direct control exercised over what financial institutions could or could not do within their particular specialist area. New products such as unit trusts (in the inter-war years) and Eurobond issues (in the post-war period) could be developed with only informal reference in the first instance to the Bank or the Treasury. The compartmentalisation of the system meant that potential risks from such innovations could be restricted to the single company or sector within which the new product had been launched. This is not to say that no control was exercised but this was generally very informal, based on the approval or disapproval of the Governor of the Bank of England. The Governor's displeasure, however, tended to be directed at the degree to which financial institutions were cooperating with the Bank in the money markets to control credit rather than with reference to new products. This was reflected in the way in which the Bank prohibited who was considered worthy of running a financial institution. The Bank did not operate a formal licensing system, preferring instead to use informal nods and winks based on social networks. Access to the inner circle of those who received the Bank's protection was confined to those who were deemed socially acceptable (Cassis 1994; Kynaston 1994, 1995; Michie 1992).

Within each of the main business areas, there tended to be price fixing agreements amongst the main companies. For example, in the Stock Exchange, there were fixed commissions which were not varied according to the size of the sale or purchase. The clearing banks operated an interest rate cartel for their personal customer business. These agreements were generally justified on the grounds that they reduced risk by ensuring that a price war did not lead to companies taking on business at a rate which was not viable in the long term.

The Bank and the Treasury colluded in this in return for cooperation from the various financial institutions in the management of monetary and fiscal policy. Competition between institutions was consequently limited, if not entirely prohibited. Failure to abide by these rules would lead to the Governor's disapproval which could in turn result in the withdrawal of access to the Bank's financial support in times of crisis. In so far as prohibitions existed in the British system, they arose from the informal power exercised by the Bank of England as the intermediary between the state and the financial institutions. The state itself played little direct role in the process (see Kynaston 1994, 1995; Cassis 1994 for detailed historical accounts of these processes in the period up to 1914).

In Germany, there was a much wider range of direct prohibitions on types of financial activity up to the 1970s. Some of these prohibitions applied to all banking groups, such as the ban on advertising and the limitation of the number of retail bank branches (once this restriction had been removed in 1958, the figure shot up from 13,000 to 26,000 by 1967). These bans had been put in place by the state after the 1931 banking crisis in order to reduce the degree of risk in the financial system. A framework agreement which had been negotiated by the commercial banks in 1932 was also declared universally and legally binding by the Banking Commissioner. Until the 1960s, this accord set the basis for agreed interest rates for deposits and lending between the state and all the banking institutions, as well as fixed fees for other financial services. The system also involved a formal system of licensing whereby only those who met certain business criteria were able to operate as banks. Other prohibitions were directed more specifically at certain types of financial intermediaries. Savings and cooperative banks were restricted up into the 1970s to simple and safe savings and investment products for the personal market and 'low-risk' lending to certain customer groups on the grounds that risky business was inconsistent with their public mission (Deeg 1992: 120; Oellerking and Holzgrabe 1990). In contrast to Anglo-Saxon countries, life insurance companies in Germany had to direct most of their investment into real estate, long-term deposits and bank bonds and could only invest a very small proportion of their assets directly in the stock market which was dominated by the banks (Vitols 1996).

The German system differed from the British in two main respects. Firstly, it involved more prohibition on activities than the British system. Whereas in Britain, companies felt free to develop new products without first having to seek permission from the authorities, in Germany, the system tended to work the other way. Even after general prohibitions were removed in the 1950s and 1960s, and group specific restrictions relaxed in the 1970s, the Bundesbank and Federal Banking Supervisory Authority (FBSA) would make use of their authority to issue informal letters of recommendation declaring newly emerging products or developments as 'undesirable' if they were considered as harmful for the stability of the overall banking system. Among financial institutions there remained an implicit agreement that they would not venture into new areas unless they had been sanctioned through the authorities, or a 'Gentlemen's agreement' had been negotiated between regulatory bodies, the banking associations and/or the leading banks. Secondly, the system of prohibitions and controls was more formal and strictly regulated by the corporate partners (i.e. the collective agreements of employers, the various state authorities and the employees) in the German context than in Britain.

2.3 *Insurance*

The nature of formal regulation of the German system underwent a transformation when prohibitions were gradually dismantled during the 1950s and 1960s, and subsequently replaced by various banking acts which were concerned with prudential control. As Vitols points out (1997), Germany was one of the first countries to introduce in its 1961 Banking Act quantitative standards for bank capital ratios which were binding for all three banking groups. Germany was also at the forefront in its use of explicit liquidity requirements for long-term lending. The capital adequacy regulations acted as a form of insurance against 'excessive' lending and disproportionate maturity risk transformation which were considered as one of the reasons for the financial crisis in the 1930s. Violations of the ratios could lead to the withdrawal of a bank's license. Further discipline on banks to keep the rules and avoid high risk ventures was exerted by the rediscount policy of the Bundesbank. The central bank could not be expected to offer significant or long-term credit for banks that were in danger of collapse (Pozdena and Alexander 1992). Banks knew that little ex post support was to be expected and that they either had to secure a sufficient and adequate capital basis if they wanted to engage in risky lending acitivities, or that they had to refrain from such activities. In cases where banks went under, depositors' losses would be at least partially covered by the deposit insurance systems which were run by the different banking associations (Hein 1996). In Germany, thus, from the 1960s onward formal regulation aimed at 'ex ante risk reduction' (see Lane and Quack, 2000) through prudential control and 'insurance'. Those, however, who were tempted to violate the rules of the game knew that they would be left to the workings of the market without major support from the Bundesbank.

In Britain, on the other hand, the system operated in a much more informal way. No specific quantitative standards were set for prudential purposes though the Bank did set informal qualitative and quantitative ceilings on what banks could lend. It did this through requiring them to maintain a certain proportion of their assets in liquid form. The Bank altered these levels according to its perceptions of the need to boost or restrain credit expansion rather than through any concern with liquidity ratios per se. As far as these were concerned, the Bank maintained a 'watchful' eye over the institutions with which it dealt, expecting to be kept informed if problems were arising. The Bank was the 'lender of last resort' within the system. So long as a financial institution had kept on good terms with the Bank, operating as a proper 'member' of the City club and carrying out its obligations as decreed by the Bank, it could expect that in times of crisis, the Bank would come to its rescue. Moran notes that "in the 1960s the Bank supported about a dozen institutions without any publicity and controversy and in the 1970s organised the much larger secondary banking rescue with only a little public argument" (Moran 1986: 19). In all these cases, the banking institutions were not constrained by formal regulations and controls in the way that would have been the case in Germany. Acceptance of the informal constraints and the indefinite duties set within the City club was rewarded by the Bank of England acting as 'lender of last resort', in effect, organising privately and secretly ex post support for institutions when they were in financial danger. This also meant that the British system lacked a formal system for protecting depositors; it was expected that the Bank in its role as 'lender of last resort' would act to ensure this was not a problem.

Both systems shared for a time one specific mechanism of insurance. This was that banks, unlike other public companies, were allowed to maintain undisclosed hidden reserves. Hidden reserves were again justified by reference to risk. Hidden reserves meant that banks could smooth out their publicly declared earnings year on year. Crisis years which might weaken confidence in the managerial ability of the bank, thus provoking a downward spiral of reduced and riskier business, could be avoided as the bank could transfer money out of its hidden reserves to conceal the seriousness of any losses. In times of high profit, funds could be placed into the hidden reserves to cover these contingencies rather than being distributed in dividends to shareholders. In Britain, this privilege came under attack during the 1960s and was eventually abandoned whereas in Germany it remained a crucial part of the system up into the 1990s.

2.4 *Monitoring*

In Britain, there was no significant legislation on banking supervision and licensing until 1979. The system of monitoring was extremely informal. The Bank of England expected to be kept informed of what was going on but had no systematic reporting system, relying on rumours and networks within the limited social and geographical space of the Square Mile, as the financial district of the City of London was known. Up until 1974, banking supervision had been in the control of the Discount Office of the Bank which had a staff of only 15, most of whom were concerned with the discount markets rather than monitoring banks' assets. This attitude came from the belief of the Bank that it was able to control the risk in the financial system in two ways. Firstly, it was able to control who became parts of the system; only those who showed that they were willing to follow the Bank's lead could expect to gain access to the key markets. Secondly, it was able to provide lender of last resort facilities on a secret basis if there was a risk of collapse. In both cases, it was the Bank's informal power and influence over the government and other actors in the system which was crucial. It was basically an informal system in which judgements about the suitability of the individuals controlling the institutions and the reputation of the institutions themselves were reinforced through shared social and business networks.

In Germany the Federal Banking Supervisory Authority (FBSA) has a formal responsibility for monitoring the banks' liquidity and capital standards on a regular basis. Although the FBSA tends to act secretively, reflected in the fact that before 1995, the agency did not even publish a report for the wider public, it has been active in ensuring that the quantitative standards for bank capital and liquidity are revised in order to keep up to date with banking trends. It has also issued additional regulations to those in the Banking Act to prevent dangers for individual banks or instabilities emerging in the banking system. The German system has been highly formalised with clear standards for liquidity and capital reserves.

In summary, we can describe the differences between the two systems in Table 1 below.

2.5 *Implications for Performance Standards*

How did these mechanisms contribute to performance standards in the two banking systems? In broad terms, the German system was based on a series of explicit and clear standards to which financial institutions were expected to conform. These standards were meant to ensure that the universal banks did not take risks which would weaken and contaminate the whole system. Certain types of activity that were deemed risky or capable of producing risk were prohibited, whilst other types of activity were only allowed subject to adequate capital reserves. Banks were therefore reluctant to go into new areas of business and even in existing areas were highly risk averse. They knew that if they did get into difficulties the Bundesbank would refuse to come to their rescue and the FBSA might suspend their licence. Therefore, they had no alternative but to produce highly effective systems of internal control that met the external requirements.

In Britain, on the other hand, financial institutions were given a high level of freedom to develop new products and markets as they wanted. There were few formal constraints on their activities and no effective demands for quantitative targets. Instead a system of informal control operated, built around the Bank of England. In return for cooperating with the Bank's aims in credit and monetary

Table 1: *A Comparison of the Use of Different Mechanisms of Managing Risk in the British and German Financial Systems in the Period up to the 1970s*

	Britain	Germany
Compartmentalisation	High: specialist institutions	Low: universal banking Segmentation between commercial, savings and co-operative banks
Prohibitions		
– On activities	Low	Commercial banks: Medium Savings/co-operative banks: High
– On who can act as a bank	High within inner circle: informal. Low outside inner circle	High: Formal
– On competition	High	High
'Insurance'		
– Capital adequacy	Informal: variable	Formal: high
– Hidden reserves	Important	Important
– Central Bank as 'lender of last resort'	Important	Rarely used
– Central Bank liquidity requirements	No formal requirements	Highly formal requirements
– Deposit insurance	No	Yes
Monitoring	Informal: based on social networks: low on quantitative indicators	Formal: use of key quantitative indicators

policy, the financial institutions were given freedom to run their own affairs with the knowledge that if there was a major problem the Bank would stabilise the system by acting as lender of last resort. The Bank maintained an oversight of this process through regular social and business interactions within and outside the Square Mile of the City of London. British institutions were likely to take on more risks, partly because there was no formal system forcing them to allocate reserves against particular types of business, but also because there was the safety net of the Bank available to them. For most of the period, the safety net was sparingly used and avoided as much as possible but at the end of the day, it was there and everybody knew it was there. Thus the British system tempted the institutions towards the cliff edge whilst the German system resolutely kept all institutions at a distance.

There was, however, one further aspect of difference which needs to be emphasised. In the German system, the formalisation of control and the comprehensive nature of prudential regulation spread throughout the financial structure. As in other parts of the German system, the integrated relationship between industry associations, systems of regulation and the state meant that all the key actors played by the same framework rules (even though savings and cooperative banks had to follow a more narrowly defined set of additional rules). This does not mean that within the German system there existed no status differences between and within banking groups (until the late 1970s, for example, an inner circle of major commercial banks maintained its exclusive access to new stock issues and syndicated loans (Deeg 1992: 141)). But there was no room outside the system where different games could be played for higher risks and higher rewards. What could be risked, and how, was strictly controlled. Outsiders such as foreign banks were not allowed to disrupt the system by bringing in new products or methods of working. Nor were insiders able to step outside the tight bounds of what the associations and the state had agreed for their role. The imposition of capital adequacy ratios made high-risk strategies more 'expensive' and first mover advantages into highly risky business less attractive for German than for British banks. As a consequence, German banks were more homogeneous in their risk-taking and their strategies focused primarily on their long-term market positioning in the national market.

In Britain, on the other hand, the system was built on a recognition that there were insiders and outsiders. The insiders were the institutions close to the Bank of England both for historic and social reasons and because over time, they had proved themselves necessary and trustworthy in the maintenance of the Bank's monetary and credit policies. These institutions were offered the protection of the Bank as the 'lender of last resort'. In return, they had to keep close to the Bank and watch out for its signs of favour and disfavour. However, because all of this was informal, not written down anywhere and, even less, legislated about by the state, there was nothing to stop others trying to get into the system. Business went to the insiders simply because they were known and had the reputation of being part of the City's inner circle and therefore 'as safe as the Bank of England', their protector. Mostly, this group could afford to turn away risky business because they were assured a steady and profitable business from their position in the centre of the financial system. The business that was turned away attracted the outsiders, those who were not under the Bank's protection. The outsiders took on the risky business that the insiders rejected. However, precisely because they were outsiders, in the British system there were no effective controls over them, no system of capital adequacy or liquidity ratios. The Bank of England controlled the financial system but it was only willing to take responsibility for those at the centre. The rest were left to operate on the periphery without any real rules or supervision. This group developed the freedom of the system further and faster, becoming the most innovative sector of the industry. In the 1950s, this was the sector that developed Eurobonds and put these to work in extending credit to UK consumers and firms out of the reach of the credit controls which the Bank was placing on its insider institutions. The result was that the British system as a whole was more risk taking than the German, not because the core institutions were taking any greater risks than their German counterparts (though it was true that the risks they were taking and the way they were protecting against them was different). What was distinctive was that there was a sector of the British system which was essentially without rules or supervision and it was this very sector that was left to feed on the riskiest business which had been rejected by the core institutions, forcing it to become the most innovative and responsive if it was to survive (as well as the most susceptible to fraud and crime). However, it was not until the 1960s that this really became an issue for the Bank of England for three main reasons. Firstly, until the 1960s, this sector was relatively small. Secondly, there was no connection between the insiders and the outsiders; they remained socially and economically distinct. Nevertheless, thirdly, many of those in the outsider group were actually trying to move to the inside and were therefore looking to demonstrate 'respectability' in the hope that it could get them into the City club. Once these conditions disappeared (as they did in the late 1960s and 1970s), the inter-relationship between the unregulated outsiders and the protected insiders became crucial to the way in which the British system changed.

In conclusion, the two systems operated in fundamentally different ways. In the German system, there were clear rules laid down about how banks could act. These rules were enforced by the industry associations and the regulators. Within this framework, each banking group would be guided in their approach to risk and rewards by the interests and influence of their particular key stake-holders (e.g. *Länder* and municipalities giving particular emphasis to the safety and local orientation of the investments of savings banks; members of cooperative banks emphasising that they should have priority in access to the funds accumulated by their banks; or managers prioritising lending to and shareholding of large companies as the most profitable activities of commercial banks). Although competition could lead to some differences in performance between the institutions, they basically operated in a standardised way, achieving similar levels of profit by operating risk averse policies within the structure of price fixing that was agreed. In so far as performance was an issue at all, comparisons within and across groups would thus refer to volume and market share oriented criteria such as size of deposits, volume of lending, etc. In Britain, the rules were informal, dependent on cooperation between the Bank and the inner core of City organisations. The specialised institutions together with the Bank of England set up their own standards, including price fixing. The inner core operated an internal, financial system set of collectively organised and maintained performance criteria which were oriented towards their key stakeholder, the Bank of England. Good performance was mainly a matter of maintaining social position and standing with one's peers and the Bank; if this was sustained, market decisions that brought a firm to bankruptcy and beyond could be dealt with because colleagues and the Bank would rally round to provide support in times of crisis. For the periphery, risks were more real but this led to rapid innovation and experimentation as the outsiders took advantage of the lack of restrictions. The result of these differences was that Germany grew universal banking institutions which were strong on formalised, sector encompassing risk control, whilst in Britain, specialised institutions developed with informal systems of risk control.

3.   Crisis and Change in the 1970s

The dangers for the two systems as change began to be enforced arose from different sources. In Germany, the danger was that the conservative banking system would begin to hamper the industrial sector by poor and expensive service. In Britain, the danger was that the Bank of England would be unable to maintain its informal system of control, leading to increasing competition and instability in the financial sector as a whole as insiders and outsiders competed for business with few controls in place on either their activities or their structures. During the 1970s and 1980s, whilst the British system underwent a period of crisis which led to a new set of relationships between the Bank and the constituent parts of the sector, Germany moved more slowly and more cautiously. In both systems, the growing internationalisation of finance was the major factor for change.

In Britain, the lack of formal regulations and the potential for new entrants outside of the Bank of England's control was realised with the growth of the Eurodollar market and what was termed as the 'secondary banking sector'. These secondary banks combined borrowing on the Eurodollar market with offering higher interest rates to depositors. The result was that they accumulated large amounts of funds which they in turn lend to personal customers and companies. Up to 1,200 finance houses came into existence in the period up to 1959 using depositors' funds as well as their own borrowings to lend. As the Eurocurrency markets expanded, more funds became available for this 'fringe' or 'secondary' banking sector as it became known. As Moran states: "The consequence was that big companies who voluntarily exercised restraint found their business nibbled away." (Moran 1986: 21). The 1960s and early 1970s were characterised by two contradictory processes. On the one hand, the lack of regulation enabled new entrants into the system with new types of products. These new entrants were outside the Bank of England framework. They took higher risks in order to gain business and they ignored the Bank's attempts to restrain credit. On the other hand, some of the core institutions (such as the Clearing Banks) which surrounded the Bank found that they were losing business to the new entrants. They therefore pressurised the Bank to allow them similar freedoms. Others such as the merchant banks found that they were gaining business directing the new credit within the system into syndicated loans, stock market investment and merger bids. They also were therefore keen to extend the new openness in the system.

In 1970, the new Conservative government introduced a system of Competition and Credit Control (CCC). For the first time, all banks (i.e. the secondary, fringe banks as well as the Clearing Banks) were placed under the same obligation to maintain 12.5 per cent of eligible liabilities in specified reserve assets. For the Clearing Banks, this changed their relationship to the Bank of England. Whilst the 'fringe' banks had not had to make any formal provision for reserves, the clearing banks had had to cooperate with the Bank's qualitative and quantitative lending ceilings. Speigelberg notes that this meant that

> "a large proportion of their funds had to be set aside and could not be lent in the ordinary way. It also represented a sizable loss of earnings — the money could have been put to better use. At the same time, the banks were subject to official requests for restraint and selectivity in lending." (Speigelberg 1973: 109).

The replacement of these informal controls (which fell primarily on one sector of the industry — the clearing banks) with formal quantitative controls which, in theory, affected all was welcomed by the Clearers as enabling them to compete better with the fringe banks. In return, however, the Clearers had to abandon many of their long standing cartel agreements. In September, 1971, their interest rate cartel was discontinued. In the months which followed, a series of other inter-bank agreements were wound up in areas such as charges for encashment of cheques by customers of non-clearing banks, commissions on traveller's cheques, etc. The result was a heightening of competition between the Clearing Banks and the secondary banks in all areas of their businesses and a massive expansion of credit, particularly in the property sector (Clarke 1986; Saunders 1990). When property prices crashed, this affected predominantly the fringe banks though some Clearing Banks had been lending to property developers and the secondary sector and there was therefore the potential for contaminating the whole banking system. In 1974, according to Clarke, even "the NatWest was forced to issue a statement denying that it was receiving Bank of England assistance" (Clarke 1986: 40).

In late 1973, the Bank of England tried to do what it had done in the past, i.e. to act as 'lender of the last resort' and provide what was termed a 'lifeboat' for the ailing institutions. It therefore summoned the Chairmen of the Clearing

Banks to help provide funds to those on the brink of bankruptcy. The Clearers put up 90 per cent of this sum and the Bank itself 10 per cent. These sums were lent at between 0.5 and 2 per cent above the prevailing money market rate but it was not clear how long it would take the rescued firms to repay the loan. By September 1974, £900 million had been lent. In March 1975, the sum had reached £1,200 million which represented 40 per cent of the total capital and reserves of the Clearers. At this point, the Clearers refused to lend any more and the Bank had to assume sole responsibility for any further rescues. Fortunately, by this time, the crisis had almost run its course.

The secondary banking crisis marked the beginning of the end of the old system. The informality of the Bank's supervisory role was clearly no longer adequate to monitor and control the risks inherent in an increasingly complex financial system. The Bank began slowly to create a more formal regulatory structure. Following the 1973–4 crisis, it was agreed to set up a new department of banking and money market supervision which had 7 principals and 30 other staff. Within three years, this had grown to 70 and the department was seeking more and more information to provide a risk-asset ratio to bank borrowing. However, these changes were still enveloped in the Bank's belief that personal contact was crucial and that there were certain institutions that were too prestigious to be subjected to the indignity of detailed supervision. Therefore, the system worked not on the basis solely of the statistical returns but three-monthly meetings between the supervisors and the senior management of banks, in which the latter were given the opportunity to explain and justify their returns. For the top tier of banks, including the Clearers, the main merchant banks and others deemed by City insiders to be trustworthy, only a 12 monthly interview was thought necessary and they were also allowed to make less detailed returns. Aspects of this system were formalised in the 1979 Banking Act which had been made necessary in part by the requirement of the European Community that all member states have legislation on the authorisation and supervision of credit institutions. Only Britain and the Netherlands lacked such legislation. The failure of JMB (a small secondary bank which through its connection to the established bullion merchants, Johnson Matthey, was treated as part of the City insider group) in 1984 raised new questions about the effectiveness of the system and further banking legislation took place in 1987. This established a Board for Banking Supervision which was to have six independent members and report directly to the Chancellor. The banking supervision department within the Bank was further strengthened to over 200 by the end of 1988. Each individual supervisor concentrated on fewer banks and accountants and auditors were expected to report any problems to the Bank. Under this system, banking regulation increasingly focused on the details of what was occurring within any particular firm. The old method based on informal networks and contacts was replaced by a system dependent on monitoring and information collected in an impersonal manner.

These changes were part of a broader dismantling of the old bifurcated structure in which a core of inner institutions were protected by the Bank whilst an outer ring of firms involved themselves in more risky ventures. Instead, a standardised and formalised platform was being constructed for all those institutions in the financial sector. This meant that for particular lines of business there were quantitative reserve requirements that all had to meet. However, instead of restricting access to those business areas to specialist institutions which met certain indefinable characteristics of 'reputation and standing', access was becoming increasingly open to those with the capital available. In the new situation, there was no expectation that the Bank would be able to offer protection. Risks were increasingly real risks that firms had to protect themselves against. Similarly, rewards and profits were shifting away from reflecting standardised price fixing agreements towards reflecting the skill of the individual firms in managing their business. Banks now had to compete directly against each other (as well as others) in areas where they had previously 'administered' the market. Their orientation gradually changed from placing the Bank's desires at the top of their list of priorities to considering more directly their shareholders. Thus they switched from an internal financial system set of collectively organised and maintained performance indicators to a set of external, firm specific and shareholder defined performance criteria. A new set of performance measures emerged which was related much more directly to performance in financial markets.

This led to three associated changes in the British financial system from the 1970s onwards. The first was a gradual increase in the size and amounts of capital employed. This was necessary in order to achieve the scale of business necessary given increasing reserve requirements and the requirements arising from the perceived need to deal in a range of international markets. Thus by the mid 1980s, the old Stock Exchange, based on a partnership structure, was being replaced by a series of takeovers and mergers which created massive integrated market making groups capable of dealing world-wide.

Secondly, this was associated with a shift towards the creation of universal banking. Mainly these moves were led by the Clearing Banks who acquired control of members of the Stock Market when it was opened up and supplemented this with the acquisition of merchant banks. Clearing banks like the Midland, Barclays and NatWest sought to establish themselves as universal institutions, operating in all fields of financial services both in the UK and in the main overseas markets. A number of other 'quasi-universal' institutions were established under the leadership of the larger merchant banks, such as Morgan Grenfell and Barings. In all these cases, management struggled to bring order and cohesion to businesses which were used to a high degree of autonomy and freedom. British bankers found that it was easy enough to create universal banking institutions but much more difficult to make them work successfully. Whereas German universal banks had long had a system which enforced conformity and standardisation with low levels of risk and uncertainty, the British attempts at universal banking were continually undermined by the clash between the risk taking investment banking culture (which could sometimes tip into blatant disregard of formal regulations) and the caution of the retail bankers. Even in those efforts led by former merchant bankers, the difficulties of meeting new regulatory requirements at the same time as matching the capital strength of overseas competitors created great problems. The attempts by British bankers to create universal banking have not therefore been successful. Either the bank has withdrawn from some of the more difficult markets, as was the case in the late 1990s with Barclays and NatWest or the bank has been the subject of a takeover or merger usually with a more dominant partner from overseas, such as Midland with the Hong Kong and Shanghai Bank, Morgan Grenfell with Deutsche Bank and Barings (though in rather different circumstances) with ING. The result is a gradual overseas takeover of many British financial institutions, in the process turning them into parts of a universal banking system domiciled elsewhere. Those which remain British owned are increasingly turning back to their national market as their primary base and constructing a larger, more integrated institution based primarily on service to UK based personal and corporate customers (e.g. Lloyds Bank).

Thirdly, these processes were associated with an increasing differentiation of performance as individual firms found new ways to make (and lose) money in the diverse financial markets in which they were now operating. Before the 1970s, each category of institution knew that it shared a common fate with other members of its 'club'. From the 1970s onwards, there were diverse paths open to each institution. Some have survived as small independent players, many more have become parts of larger conglomerates either British or overseas owned. These conglomerates have also met different fates. Some have been swallowed up by other firms whilst others still survive. The British financial scene reflects a complex mixture of banking structures, shaped partially by the distinctive history of the City of London, but also increasingly by the integration of British financial institutions into universal banks domiciled elsewhere. The features of the transition process of British financial institutions are summarised in Table 2.

In Germany, there were essentially two phases in the process of transition. In the first phase from the late 1960s to the early 1980s, the Bundesbank began to open up the system but in response to the instabilities this caused, there was a process of partial retrenchment back towards stricter regulation and standardisation. In the second phase, from the mid to late 1980s onwards, there has been an opening up of the system which has brought greater differentiation and diversity.

The years 1967 and 1968 represent important changes in the banking sector and German economy as a whole. Economic policy took a shift towards Keynesianism,

Table 2: *Transition in British Financial Institutions: Risk, Regulation and Performance*

	Pre-1970s	Post 1970s
Industry structure	Specialist, segmented and bifurcated	Diverse
Regulation	Informal, personal	Formal, quantitative
Firms and risk	Bank of England as protector	Size of capital base and internal controls to protect the firm
Performance criteria for core firms	Conformity to informal rules and expectations; driven by internal, financial system set of collectively organised criteria; social reputation	External, firm-specific share-holder set of criteria; financial performance
Performance outcomes	Standardised within segments	Differentiated

and part of this policy was to fully deregulate interest rates — against the opposition of the banks. The government believed that competition in the banking sector would lead to a market-induced reduction of interest rates and thereby assist its growth-oriented economic policy to overcome the recession. It therefore sought to dismantle some of the controls it had operated in the financial sector, e.g. allowing banks to individually determine fees and to attract customers through advertising and reforming the savings bank and cooperative bank sectors by enlarging their areas of business in exchange for the loss of their tax-privileges. In this environment of increasing competition and the relaxation of interest rate controls, some of the German banks began to look to the Euromarkets for new funds. However, the Bundesbank tried to keep control over this through issuing temporary bans on capital imports and raising reserve requirements (Kloten and Bofinger 1991: 131) as well as increasing interest rates. In turn, the banks responded by setting up offices in Luxembourg to access the Euromarket funds.

In the early 1970s, thus, there was a shift of parts of the German banking sector towards more profitable, but also more risky business. The adverse effects of this business policy for the overall financial system soon became visible. In 1974, economic recession, major losses of several Landesbanken and the collapse of Herstatt, one of West Germany's largest private banking houses, which had been preceded by the bankruptcy of another banking partnership in Munich a year before, gave a severe blow to the public's trust in the banking sector. Many of these difficulties arose from the new business conduct of parts of the banking sector. Some institutions, and particularly those aiming at entering new markets, were competing for the most profitable business. In order to achieve rapid growth they left behind old prudential rules, either by escaping to less or non-regulated types of business (e.g. Euromarkets in Luxembourg, currency exchange business) or sometimes even by violating existing regulation. The less successful of them were directly punished, either by market failure or moral persuasion of their stakeholders to restrict themselves to safer business.

The Bundesbank and FBSA, however, feared that these cases were only the tip of the iceberg and that banks' chase for more risky business could threaten the overall performance of the financial system in Germany. At the same time, the Bundesbank was very concerned about maintaining and defending its control of the domestic monetary system against destabilising influences of financial innovations and international capital markets. The 1974 crisis seemed to confirm the scepticism of the Bundesbank and, during the following decade, gave rise to what one could call a coordinated effort to shelter the German financial system from negative international influences. This was achieved through various means: regulators, in consultation with the banking associations, reinforced prudential controls of banks and continued to issue informal regulations which relied on the consent of banking associations and individual banks (Hein 1996; Andreas 1991). In return, the latter were allowed to operate corporatist arrangements which protected them to a large extent from foreign competition. Only a selected choice of financial innovations was admitted in Germany. In exchange, however, the Bundesbank silently accepted that German banks would use their Luxembourg base to operate in Euromarkets as long as they followed a prudential approach and kept the Bundesbank informed about their activities (Kolbeck 1987). Thus, despite their increasing presence in international financial centres, German banks remained risk averse in their activities, an attitude reinforced by the way in which low inflation and fixed interest rates in the German context reduced the need for the sort of financial innovations which were sweeping the Anglo-Saxon economies in the 1970s.

In sum, during the 1970s the rules of the game became more similar for the three competing banking groups and their activities more alike in so far as they all converged towards universal banking. This was partly the result of the liberalisation of special regulations which had limited saving and cooperative banks in the past in exchange for taxation privileges. The comprehensive Banking Law set incentives for all banking groups to engage in a wide spectrum of activities. As a result, all groups diversified their products and services — a strategy that proved very profitable as long as there was still unsatisfied domestic demand for deposits, investment and lending up to the mid-1980s. By then, commercial, saving and cooperative banks had all developed into complex financial groups which covered the whole range of financial services and were competing for market shares particularly amongst personal and small business customers. Within the given constraints that were reinforced in the 1970s, banks continued to follow relatively risk-averse strategies as long as domestic markets provided enough potential for growth and international activities were still considered as a 'free leg'. The actual value of a bank was still impossible to determine because, in contrast to Britain, banks in Germany did not disclose their hidden reserves. There was also a wide consensus among bank managers, regulators, and other key stakeholders that medium-term stability in the growth of profits and dividends was an important factor in order to maintain public trust in the performance of individual financial institutions as well as the banking industry as a whole.

During the 1980s, however, international developments began to impact more strongly on the German system. With the strength of the German economy and its currency, there was a significant inflow of foreign capital whilst Germans were also more interested in buying foreign securities. A few large German companies started to raise some of their new capital on international capital markets and therefore sought quotation at the New York, London or Tokyo stock exchange. In addition, the same companies directed increasing amounts of their direct investments abroad and thereby reinforced the links between national and international capital markets (though see Thompson, this volume, for a discussion of the size and significance of these processes). Faced with this evolution, the Bundesbank had to reconsider its former restrictive policy towards financial innovations if it did not want to hamper the competitiveness of German capital markets. The growing consolidation of Franco-German cooperation over exchange rates and the enhanced expectation of a trend towards monetary union also encouraged the Bundesbank to remove a whole series of formal and informal regulations that in the past had sheltered the German capital market. This included easier access of foreign investors (removal of dividend coupon taxation in 1984) and foreign financial institutions to German capital markets (access to consortia issuing foreign DM bonds in 1985, reduction of liquidity reserves in 1986) and admission of variable interest rate instruments in Germany (floating rate notes and zero bonds in 1985, security-based investment funds, commercial papers and money market funds in 1990s). As a consequence, the power of German banks to regulate domestic capital markets became weakened and they were exposed to more foreign competition. In return, however, new market opportunities both at home and abroad were opened up.

The increasing importance of the international context was reinforced by the Basle agreements on capital adequacy which were raising the standards and transparency of rules on measuring capital. In Germany, this meant the counting of capital against risks had to be substantially tightened. The consequence was that German banks had to raise more capital if they wanted to expand. For the commercial banks, this was a further encouragement to internationalise since funds could be raised more cheaply by issuing new shares in London, New York and Tokyo rather than confining themselves to Frankfurt, a process which has led to increasing foreign ownership of these institutions (Büschgen 1995: 637). Thus the commercial banks consolidated themselves by developing a twin strategy of reorganising and rationalising their domestic banking operations (D'Alessio and Oberbeck 1997) whilst also expanding their international activities with new financial products such as futures, options and swaps. This expansion has been accompanied by the acquisition of foreign operations, particularly in London.

Saving and cooperative banks, in contrast, can neither generate new capital abroad nor extend their business to global markets nor can they directly follow their customers abroad. Even allowing for the bridgehead functions of Landes-banken and DG-Bank in international markets, savings and cooperative banks experience disadvantages vis-à-vis commercial banks particularly in business with exporting companies. In most regional states, they also continue to be prohibited from undertaking speculative business such as financial futures and real estate transactions which are so important to commercial banks now. Saving and cooperative banks are still quite weak in new lucrative areas such as securities and foreign trade and under-represented among the more wealthy customer groups. However, if they follow too closely the example of profit-maximising commercial banks they might face opposition from their stakeholders who are predominantly interested in safe investments. The result has been growing differences within the savings bank and cooperative bank sectors as some (mainly in the large urban areas) have sought to match the commercial banks whilst others (usually small and rural) have kept to their traditional patterns. Table 3 provides a synopsis of the transition of German financial institutions.

The next decade, thus, might see a renewed differentiation of strategies and performance standards between and within the different banking groups (Deeg 1996). If large commercial banks (and possibly also merged Landesbanken and an enlarged DG-Bank) continue their current strategy of internationalisation they will have to operate increasingly under the rules of international financial centres, and the City of London in particular (Krumnow 1996). This means highly profitable, but also highly risky business which gives rise to a greater volatility of business results and income than they were used in the past. Domestic activities might come under increasing scrutiny with regard to their profitability, but will be an important fall-back position to cover losses from the more risky markets. Whereas commercial banks will be exposed to a larger extent than before to the world of short-term shareholder value, some cooperative and saving banks might even reinforce their identity as local players operating a mixture of performance standards which are related to both their financial performance and their 'social' function for regional economies.

4. Conclusions

Our argument has been that performance standards are set in specific social and economic contexts. As these contexts change, performance standards themselves begin to also change. However, the nature of these changes is not to discard entirely the previous system but rather to evolve into a new structure. In both societies, there was an attempt to balance the interests of individual firms against

Table 3: *Transition in German Financial Institutions: Risk, Regulation and Performance*

	Pre- 1970s	1970s–1980s	1990s
Industry structure	Universal: segmentation between bank types according to predominant customer	Universal conglomerates: decreased differentiation between bank types; all banks chasing similar customers	Universal conglomerates; Increased differentiation between international and national banks
Regulation	Formal, quantitative: prohibition of activities	Formal, quantitative: prudential control; barriers to foreign entry	Formal, quantitative: tighter control of capital
Firms and risk	Risk averse within given set of prohibitions	Size of capital base acts as an *additional* restraint on the amount of risk undertaken	Size of capital base and internal controls differentiate the attitudes of the different banking segments to risk
Firm strategy	Conformity to prohibitive rules and expectations	Conformity to (national) prudential rules plus some searching for high-risk/high-reward business	Largest commercial and Landesbanken search out international business which requires conformity to international prudential rules
Performance criteria	Volume oriented criteria linked to distinct purposes of different bank segments	Market share and medium-term growth of income; growing standardisation across different bank segments	Increasing differentiation of bank types; commercial banks increasingly driven by shareholder expectations
Performance outcomes	Standardised within bank types	Standardisation across bank types	Differentiation within and between bank types

the systemic goals evolved informally in the British case through the interaction of the core institutions with the Bank of England and formally in the German case through the corporatist associations, the regulators and the Central bank.

In Britain, in return for cooperation with the Bank of England, the core financial institutions were given relative freedom from interference to the extent that cartels were encouraged and supported. In this context, the specialist firms were used to running their business with a very loose influence from regulators; their major performance requirement was to maintain their reputation and standing with the Bank of England through cooperating when called upon to help in propping up the system or any of its component parts. This in turn guaranteed that the institution would be able to make money in a relatively risk-free environment. This social structure of performance standards lasted until the 1960s when both sides of the relationship — the firms and the Bank — found it impossible to continue to shore the system up and maintain the exclusive privileges and responsibilities that had been the bedrock of the system for the previous hundred years. During the 1970s and 1980s, a new system began to evolve influenced by the changed international environment for finance and its regulation. The breakdown of the cartels, one after the other in banking and the Stock Exchange, spelled the end for the small independent specialist firms. They were rapidly swallowed up within universal banking institutions that were now subjected to formal regulation. However, within these universal banks, they retained much of their independence to make business and develop new products. Each bank was now competing strongly against the others and in order to create a distinctive position for itself it looked to each specialist division to succeed. The result was a growing differentiation of performance between financial institutions in particular years and their own performances over the years. The old normative structure which limited and constrained competition by placing barriers around specialist institutions and encouraging informal cooperation was gone. In its place was a universal banking system but one which remained distinctive from the German because the degree and nature of regulation and control over the different parts of the universal institution were much looser, allowing higher levels of risk to be undertaken and thus increasing the differentiation and variation of performance between firms.

The German system on the other hand remained for a much longer period of time within a formal regulatory structure that placed strong controls on the amount of risk that could be undertaken. In spite of their different histories, the three sectors of German banking evolved first a system of cooperation and later as competition was introduced, moved towards a similar universal banking structure. Whilst the cooperative and the savings bank sectors were seen to have a specific social function, they were also expected to provide as full a range of services as the commercial banks and in this they were helped by local and national state support for institutions such as the Landesbanken. Thus there was a convergence in their standards of performance both as a result of being subjected to similar formal regulatory procedures and in terms of what was expected of them by the government and their customers.

Over the last decade, the opening up of the German system has begun to create a differentiation once more between the commercial banks and the others. Because of their capital structure, the commercial banks have been able to take advantage of the opportunities to move abroad and develop subsidiaries in Luxembourg and the UK. The result has been heightened competition between the different banking groups inside Germany through a growing separation of the commercial banks from the savings and cooperative banking systems. This separation is further reinforced by the interest of the commercial banks in establishing themselves as international banks quoted on the international stock exchanges and subject to the auditing and regulatory requirements of these other jurisdictions. In turn, the commercial banks are entering into new areas of risk, protected only by their capital base, their internal controls and the level of managerial skill embedded in them.

The world financial system is currently undergoing a complex set of transformations. Barely thirty years ago, financial systems were primarily nationally based. Within national boundaries, there were clear expectations about what sort of performance was required from banks. These requirements developed from a complex balance of the interests of the individual firm with the interests of the system as a whole. The negotiation of this balance was historically constructed and gave a particular social structure of performance standards to the industry in each country. As international financial markets developed, these systems have been unable to maintain their isolation (Morgan 1997). In trying to come to terms with this new environment, the old structures have had to change. New balances are being created partly by action at the international level to create standards of regulation that can guard against systemic disorder at this level and partly by the action of regulators and firms at national level. There is a growing predominance of performance standards based on capital markets but firms have different ways of responding to these standards.

References

Andreas, K. 1991. Kapitalmarkt. In: N. Kloten, and J. H. von Stein (eds), *Obst/Hintner. Geld-, Bank- und Börsenwesen,* 955–997. Stuttgart: Poeschel.

Büschgen, H. E. 1995. Die Deutsche Bank von 1957 bis zur Gegenwart. Aufstieg zum internationalen Finanzdienstleistungskonzern. In: L. Gall et al., *Die Deutsche Bank 1870–1995,* 579–880. München: Beck.

Carruthers, B. G. 1996. *City of Capital: Politics and Markets in the English Financial Revolution*. Princeton, NJ: Princeton University Press.

Cassis, Y. 1994. *City Bankers, 1890–1914*. Cambridge: Cambridge University Press.

Clarke, M. 1986. *Regulating the City*. Milton Keynes: Open University Press.

Coleman, W. D. 1996. *Financial services, globalization and domestic policy change*. New York: St. Martin's Press.

D'Alessio, N. and, H. Oberbeck. 1997. The End of the German Model? Developmental Tendencies in the German Banking Industry. In: G. Morgan, and D. Knights (eds), *Regulation and Deregulation in European Financial Services*, 86–104. London: Macmillan.

Deeg, R. 1992. Banks and the State in Germany: The Critical Role of Subnational Institutions in Economic Governance. P.h.D.-Thesis, Mimeo. Cambridge MA: MIT.

Deeg, R. 1996. German Banks and Industrial Finance in the 1990s, WZB-Discussion Paper FS I 96–323, Berlin.

Hein, M. 1996. *Die Banken. Eine Einführung*. Mannheim: B. I.-Taschenbuchverlag.

Hutton, W. 1995. *The state we're in*. London: Jonathan Cape.

Ingham, G. 1984. *Capitalism Divided? The City and Industry in British Social Development*. London: Macmillan.

Kolbeck, R. 1987. Geschäftspolitische Auswirkungen der Konsolidierungsvorschrift des Kreditwesengesetzes. In: J. Krumnow, and M. Metz (eds.), *Rechnungswesen im Dienste der Bankpolitik*, 297–315. Stuttgart: Poeschel.

Kloten, N., and P. Bofinger. 1991. Geldpolitik in der offenen Volkswirtschaft. In: N. Kloten, and J. H. von Stein (eds), *Obst/Hintner. Geld-, Bank- und Börsenwesen*, 127–147. Stuttgart: Poeschel.

Krumnow, J. 1996. IAS-Rechnungslegung für Banken. In: *Die Bank* 7: 396–403.

Kynaston, D. 1994. *The City of London: Volume I: A World of its Own 1815–1890*. London: Chatto and Windus.

Kynaston, D. 1995, *The City of London: Volume II: Golden Years 1890–1914*. London: Chatto and Windus

Lane, C. 1989. *Management and labour in Europe. The industrial enterprise in Germany, Britain and France*. Aldershot: Edward Elgar.

Lane, C., and S. Quack. 2000. Provision of Loan Finance to SMEs in Britain and Germany: An Examination of Risk Handling from the Perspective of New Institutionalism in Organisational Theory. *Organisation Studies* 21, 1.

Michie, R. C. 1992. *The City of London: Contiuity and Change 1850–1990*. London: Macmillan.

Moran, M. 1986. *The Politics of Banking*. 2 ed. London : Macmillan.

Morgan, G. 1997. The Global Context of Financial Services: National Systems and the International Political Economy. In: G. Morgan, and D. Knights (eds): *Regulation and Deregulation in European Financial Services*, 14–41. London: Macmillan.

Neal, L. 1990. *The Rise of Financial Capitalism: International Capital Markets in the Age of Reason*. Cambridge: Cambridge University Press.

Oellerking, C., and M. Holzgrabe. 1990. *Sparkassen und Genossenschaftsbanken im Spannungsverhältnis zwischen Moral und Ökonomie: Strukturelemente, Organisationsgrundsätze und Geschäftspolitik*. Frankfurt am Main: Verlag Peter Lang.

Podolny, J. M. 1993. A Status-based Model of Market Competition, *American Journal of Sociology* 98: 829–872.

Podolny, J. M. 1994. Market Uncertainty and the Social Character of Economic Exchange, *Administrative Science Quarterly* 39: 458–483.

Pozdena, R. J., and V. Alexander. 1992. Bank Structure in West Germany. In: G. Kaufmann (ed.): *Banking Structure in Major Countries,* 555–594. Boston, Dordrecht, London: Kluwer.

Saunders, P. 1990. *A Nation of Homeowners.* London: Allen Unwin.

Speigelberg, R. 1973. *The City: Power without Accountability.* London: Quartet Books.

Vitols, S. 1996. Modernizing Capital: Banks and the Regulation of Long-term Finance in Postwar Germany and the U.S, P.h.D.-Thesis, Mimeo. University of Wisconsin-Madison.

Vitols, S. 1997. Financial Systems and Industrial Policy in Germany and Great Britain: The Limits of Convergence, pp. 221–55 in D. Forsyth and T. Notermans (eds): *Regime Changes: Macroeconomic Policy and Financial Regulation in Europe from the 1930s to the 1990s.* Providence, R. I.: Berghahn Books.

Weiss, L., and J. Hobson. 1995. *States and Economic Development.* Cambridge: Polity.

Whitley, R., and P. H. Kristensen (eds.). 1996. *The Changing European Firm. Limits to Convergence.* London: Routledge.

Whitley, R., and P. H. Kristensen (eds.). 1997. *Governance at Work: The Social Regulation of Economic Relations.* Oxford: Oxford University Press.

Williamson, O. 1994. Transaction Cost Economics and Organisation Theory. In: N. J. Smelser and R. Swedberg (eds.), *The Handbook of Economic Sociology,* 77–107. Princeton, NJ: Princeton University Press.

Zysman, J. 1983. *Governments, Markets and Growth.* London: Cornell University Press.

CHAPTER 7

Changing Performance Standards in the French Banking System

Danielle Salomon

1. Introduction

The issues of economic performance and how it is measured do not obviously belong to traditional sociology. However, the globalisation of trade and financial markets and the growing importance of multinational firms in the activity of national economies and the world economy has brought the issue of performance back onto the agenda. Increasing cross-border economic activity and exchange means also that the resources on which companies from different countries compete and the measures along which their performance is assessed are no longer only a matter of the decisions taken by national actors within the borders of their home country. On the contrary, performance and performance measures — and particularly financial ratios — can be regarded as part of the pressures for standardisation to which managers and policy-makers within local and national contexts are exposed. But such tendencies for standardisation go often hand in hand with the reinforcement of existing and the emergence of new specificities of social embeddedness and a persistent divergence between different local and national contexts (Boyer 1993; Crouch and Streeck 1996; Cohen 1996). Therefore, it is not only likely that different performance standards co-exist in distinct social environments but also that identical performance standards, such as financial ratios of profitability, are used with various meanings and therefore cannot be extracted from the social context in which they are calculated and evaluated (Whitley 1994). In this chapter, the tensions between international standardisation and national embeddedness of performance standards will be analysed with regard to developments in the French banking sector.

In France, the opening of borders and of competition has started a dramatic change. France was characterised from 1945 by a centralised policy of *dirigisme* which put into the control of the state, all the key elements of economic planning and coordination. The banking system was central to this process. In this system, the role and structure of the main actors was determined by the state, especially the Direction du Trésor (belonging to the Ministry of Economy and Finance) and the Banque de France. These institutions managed a system in which the banks were protected from competition. Different banking organisations operated within defined spheres often as monopoly providers. In return for these privileges they were expected to conform to the policies of the Ministry and the Banque both in terms of setting the rates for savings and lending to various groups as well as allocating funds in accordance with the priorities of the state.

Within this system, the key performance standards for the actors within the various banking sectors was first of all conformity to the planning objectives of the state. Without such conformity access to funds and profits could not be achieved (cf. the discussion of Germany and the UK in Morgan and Quack, this volume).

Since the gradual extension of attempts to create a Single European market beginning in the mid-1980s and the growing internationalisation of financial markets, this highly regulated system has begun to be transformed. This process has been articulated in terms of deregulating the sector and thereby unleashing competitive forces from both inside and outside France, which would improve the efficiency of the allocative processes of the financial sector. The initial policy that depended on the withdrawal of the state from direct control of the financial sector has, however, been affected by the recession of late 1980s and early 1990s. This recession brought renewed demands for the state to play a direct role in its resolution at the very time when it was seeking, at least in part, to divest itself of such responsibility. The result has been that competing priorities have emerged from different actors following their own interests and logics, often in contradiction with one another, without the state being able to assert a single dominant policy. This impacted differentially on the various banking institutions. For the very largest the slow down and delay in the transition reduced their ability to play the European game of mergers and acquisitions, although on the other hand, it also protected them from hostile raids by making them less attractive to acquire.

In this context of uncertainty the French financial institutions and especially the major banks have suffered significant losses, with average profit levels lower than those in other countries. Average return on assets from 1991–1995 were just 0.2 per cent in the French banking sector, compared to 0.9 per cent in the USA and 0.6 per cent in the UK. Average return on equity between 1991 to 1994 was 17.7 per cent in the US banking sector, compared to just 5.3 per cent in France. These figures reflect the underlying uncertainties in the transformation of French banking. On the one hand, the shift towards deregulation is meant to free up the banking system and encourage higher levels of efficiency, competition and profitability. On the other hand, the question of performance and how the banks act remains of central concern to the authorities. Thus the shift towards financial performance outcomes as paramount (which is implicit in the deregulated model) runs counter to the state's unwillingness to entirely give up its capacity to control and direct the financial system. Tendencies towards standardising performance measures around financial criteria are supported and reinforced by international capital markets as well as the international regulatory regime. However, the local specificities of the French system mean that there are multiple other performance criteria which continue to influence the banking sector. Studying the performance of French banking institutions and their evolution calls for the study of deregulation as a dynamic process of transformation managed by the state. The analysis of performance in the banking sector is thus not separable from the public policy on which it depends.

2.   The State Regulated System

On the eve of deregulation, the French banking system was the result of a long period of centralisation and administration by the state that had produced sedimentation and inertia. The main goal of state policy was to make the banking sector an obedient tool in the hands of the government. The directive role of the state emerged firstly from the perceived failure of the banks in the inter-war years (Andrieu 1990) and secondly from the post-1945 commitment to rebuild the French economy (see Zysman 1983 for a detailed account). State policies towards banking were developed in line with this ambition. The policies gained further coherence through the fact that all these instruments were concentrated in the hands of a small number of like-minded individuals within particular public institutions. In fact, the main decisions were of a regulatory nature, not requiring legislative decisions and almost no matters were submitted to public deliberation.

The state used a variety of means to ensure the banking sector performed its designated role in the reconstruction of France. The major banking policies were quantitative and coercive measures and strict control of competition. They mixed together issues of various types: monetary policy, financial integrity, allocation of resources to the economic sectors. Credit ceilings and exchange controls were used to control inflation and currency balances (monetary policy), to limit the expansion of the banks (integrity) and to allocate resources according to the choices of the government when allowing some sectors to operate outside the general credit limits (economic policy). Credit ceilings, exchange controls, the fact that large institutions belonged to the public sector (e.g. the main commercial banks, La Poste, Banque de France, Caisse des Dépôts et Consignations, etc.), the public missions given to financial institutions (e.g. Crédit Foncier de France, saving instruments destined to public programs such as social housing, etc.), gave the state major powers to shape the financial system. The state was also able to shape the sector through its control of the number of players and their legal statuses and privileges as well as influencing access to capital.

This structure forged an obedient tool in the hands of government, since financial intermediation was a monopoly of banks who served the state by allocating resources to chosen clients, activities or sectors, at administered prices. Moreover, the public institutions were managed by civil servants from the Inspection des Finances and the administration of Treasury, all of whom tended to share an educational background in the most prestigious of the grandes écoles, the Ecole National d'Administrative (ENA) (see Thoenig 1987; Kessler 1968; Bauer and Bertin-Mourot 1991). The banking sector was highly focused on the domestic allocation of resources, with strict exchange control and little internationalisation. This meant that the key resources for banking activity were funds derived from savings within France. Publicly-owned institutions such as Credit Agricole, La Poste, and the mutual savings banks were crucial to collecting these savings which the state then redirected according to its policy requirements. The major collectors were publicly owned, and Banque de France, as lender of last resort, financed the banks in accordance with its overall policies.

Such a centralised system was extremely coherent. The state through the government, the Ministry of Economy and Finance, the Treasury administration and Banque de France was able to control the flow of funds from savers into the productive economy. Charges for personal banking services were kept low to encourage savings whilst bank profits were guaranteed by regulations which inhibited competition.

In such a context, the banking institutions had two main concerns: keeping their privileges or privileged access to the state and growing through gaining market shares. This led them to satisfy the main demands of the state, as far as allocation of resources was concerned, by providing credits at administered prices. The banks also participated in the industrial rescues of the 1970s and the state supported part of their losses (Cohen 1992). Their second aim was to gain new clients and deposits. With high interest rates on lending but low rates on savings, the costs of deposit collection were covered. It was a euphoric time for banks, not propitious for innovation, organisational change, transparency or fine tuned risk system. Banks, in this context, became more than organisations: they were 'two-faced institutions' (Meyer and Rowan 1991) which both served and used the state for their interests.

3. The Origins of Deregulation

As recently as the beginning of the 1980s, the regulated system remained stable. However, the actions of Mitterand's first government under Mauroy with its attempts to increase state control of the economy led to a flight of capital from

France. This in turn triggered three successive devaluations (October 1981, June 1982 and March 1983) as well as increases in interest rates, resulting in an increasing cost of debt. This crisis prompted what Cohen termed a 'burst of reality' (Cohen 1992) and the political turning point of 1982–3. Neo-liberal ideas favouring deregulation of the financial sector gained increasing prominence amongst managers, civil servants and politicians (Jobert 1994) and led to the emergence of a pro-European discourse among these groups of social actors (Cohen 1996).

The deregulation-reregulation process was conceived as an incremental process, which had to anticipate and incorporate events occurring both within the domestic and the European scenes. The idea was to open the borders progressively, i.e. on one side to introduce the principles of free competition and on the other side to give time to the banking institutions and the various actors to adapt to these new rules. Competition and market regulations were seen as mechanisms that could be used in tandem to enable the actors to change and adapt.

In France, the main acts were to revise the main banking law (1984), then to remove state control of credit ceilings and exchange control (1985 to 1989) and to abolish the banking monopoly by creating financial capital markets (1985) and finally authorising other operators to offer financial services. Supervision and control were switched from quantitative *a priori* measures to *a posteriori* ones, introducing the prudential ratios required by European directives (1988 to 1992) according to which the banking institutions are directly responsible for their choices and growth but limited in their actions by prescribed ratios of risks and solvency. The right-wing parties who won the 1986 legislative elections started in addition a progressive privatisation program of the main public banking institutions (1986–1988), a policy continued from 1993 on by all the governments, whatever their political colour.

However, the state was slower to abolish the various elements of distinction and privileges attached to the banking institutions. For example, even in 1998, Crédit Agricole, although privatised, still benefited from the shared monopoly of solicitors' deposits; Caisses d'Epargne still had popular savings passbooks and no shareholder to pay off; Crédit Mutuel also had a tax-free saving products, etc. The Banking Act of 1984, despite concentrating all the financial institutions under the single name of 'banking institutions' (établissements de crédit), maintained their differences through distinct statuses and separate professional representatives, (although they are all members of the single Association Française des Etablissements de Crédit et des Entreprises d'Investissement (AFECEI)). The ownership conditions of the various institutions remain distinct. The private sector bank entities have shareholders requiring market level return. The mutual banks are cooperatives with social shareholders whose rights to returns are in practice limited. The saving and provident institutions own their own capital, whilst the nationalised banks negotiate between Paris and Brussels their conditions of existence.

If the allocation of resources, i.e. of credits at administered prices to various clients, activities and sectors according to government priorities, is not any more the key feature of the banking activity, this does not mean that compartmentalisation has disappeared or that open competition has been established. Some allocative decisions remain in the control of the state, for example: agriculture still receives supported loans, innovation and risk and joint venture capital are still supported by public institutions or funds. The state maintains its central role because it controls the allocation of many of the key aspects of transformation, e.g. the number of players, the choice between market or centralised regulation when a banking institution faces heavy losses, the timing of particular aspects of the transformation and the overall 'rules of the game'.

4.   Unanticipated Changes to the Deregulation Process

Under deregulation, monetary policy and the financial integrity of the banks and the system as a whole become the concern of the central bank and a range of associated bodies: Conseil National du Crédit, in charge of the knowledge of the sector, Comité des Etablissements de Crédit, in charge of banking licences, Comité de la Réglementation Bancaire, which elaborates the rules of the banking sector and Commission Bancaire which is in charge of control and sanctions. These four organisations are dominated by Banque de France personnel but they work hand in hand with the Treasury administration for rules and control, and their management is shared between Banque de France and Ministry of Economy and Finance, represented by the administration of Treasury. Responsibility for directing funds is now shared between various actors and is the locus of the main change of modes of governance within the deregulated system (Kooiman 1993).

This process of transformation was made more complex by the recession which France experienced in the late 1980s. Among the first signs of the recession were the growing number of overindebted people that were unable to pay back their loans. A lot of mortgage credits had been signed on progressive monthly instalments to benefit from inflation. Once inflation was curbed, the real cost for these households turned out to be intolerable. In addition, banking institutions, after the release of credit controls, had rushed into lending money. Consumer credit had been seen as highly profitable. French households had low rates of debt compared to the US or UK rates. Failure to repay debt was exacerbated by growing unemployment and loss of salaries. This situation became visible in local social and political institutions as early as 1987 and 1988, when people came to complain about their financial problems and ask for help. It also became visible in the losses of the credit institutions from 1989 on as more people failed to repay debt. The crisis spread to the property sector from 1992 costing hundreds of millions of francs to banks, many of which had to be recapitalised by the state, e.g. Credit Lyonnais. Small and medium size enterprises were also sources of losses for the banks. From 1991 to 1996, banking institutions continued to declare losses or low levels of profit.

From 1986 on, deregulation meant that the managers of public entities or recently privatised banking institutions were left free to pursue their own strategies. The only demand from the state was that they were to achieve a positive return on investment, even if this was lower than the market average. For example, Credit Lyonnais, led by the powerful Jean-Yves Habere, a former Director of the Treasury, followed a strategy that brought profits until 1992 but then led to huge losses. The state's emphasis on the strategic autonomy of banking organisations led it to refrain from intervention until the crisis was so great that rescue was inevitable.

Deregulation was not accompanied within the banks by the development of adequate mechanisms of internal risk management (Salomon 1999). The regulatory authorities were supposed to monitor risk, whilst the organisations themselves concentrated on growth. Nationalised banks were not facing any uncertainty and grew into heavy bureaucratic 'machines'. Risk analysis was substituted by internal professional norms and clan relationships between the actors involved. Subjective decisions were taken where, in a complex and uncertain environment, procedural rationality should prevail. When internal risk management systems are weak, this means that the probability of taking the wrong decision and defaults may increase. This has two consequences: the first is that banking institutions and their clients both lose. Clients, who should not be lent to, are given loans, which they cannot repay, leading to bankruptcy. The bank, in turn, suffers losses from these defaults. The second consequence is that once the problems in the risk system are diagnosed, the rational position is to withdraw, at least temporarily, from lending. This explains why one sees the succession of the same sequence of boom, followed by losses, succeeded by a credit crunch in various banking segments (Pastré 1993). In a system where universal banking institutions represent one third of the activity, their withdrawal from lending leads to a break down of the whole market.

However, not all institutions are affected in the same way. For instance, specialist financial institutions had developed fine-tuned risk systems simply in order to survive. When recession occurred, if their risk system was in fact efficient and resilient, they benefited from a competitive advantage: they were better able to eliminate the worst clients and drive them towards their competitors with weaker risk management systems. Consumer credit is a perfect illustration of this. Almost ten years after the crisis, most of the commercial banks have given up managing the lending process themselves, instead contracting it out to specialist institutions with tighter risk management systems through the creation of joint ventures.

Banking and financial deregulation was initiated in a context where the
European Union was restarting under the political impulse of François Mitterrand.
The Ministers of Economy and Finance, Jacques Delors and Pierre Bérégovoy
both showed strong European convictions and were helped by advisers and a
growing group of civil servants more and more willing to break with the 'dirigiste'
tradition and to take on a more free market position. Deregulation has been
implemented through certain key symbolic events: for example, the ending of
exchange and credit controls, the introduction of deregulated financial markets,
etc. No real public and political debate took place around these changes and the
main actors of the transformation belonged to the small public policy community
of Treasury, Banque de France and the minister of Economy and Finance adviser's
team. If the idea was clear to these actors, they failed to appreciate the difficulties
of creating institutional change.

Many factors were not satisfactorily anticipated:

– the strength of the economic recession,
– the extent of the organisational incapacity and failure of the risk systems of
  the large banking institutions,
– the intensity of the claims which would be made on the state to intervene
  in the allocation of resources (credits, discounted interests rates, etc.),

The success of the transition from an *a priori* control system to an *a posteriori*
one in a context of globalisation, rested on the efficiency of the internal risk and
control systems of the banking institutions, as well as upon the external control
systems operated by banking supervisors and regulators. These combined elements
were in theory the corner stones of the transformation, yet neither were firmly
in place. The internal risk systems for banks were particularly crucial to this
process yet the large banks were not keen on initiating the organisational changes
necessary to achieve this. Instead they concentrated on their specific resources,
that is to say their clients and eventually their deposits. The fierce competition,
which followed, led to a cut-throat war, in which the margins decreased dramatically, and the quality of loans (and clients) declined.

The failures that resulted from these problems had systemic and collective
consequences. On a systemic basis, understanding that the major institutions were
not able to cope with their risks was raising a thorny problem to the supervising
authorities, as far as on the one hand they were still in charge of systemic risk
and the reputation of Paris as a financial centre, and on the other hand, they had
lost their former coercive powers. This situation led particularly the Banque de
France to take any opportunity to persuade banks to change.

On a collective basis, the consequences were triple: first, the failure of the
risk management system became a disaster as the extent of losses in some
institutions, such as Credit Lyonnais was concerned. Secondly, the losses were

so huge that it was not possible to hide the problem and it was propelled into the public arena. Furthermore since finance has to do with reputation and confidence, this meant that both the problem and the proposed solution were revealed simultaneously, though the extent of the difficulties was not immediately clear due to the complexities of bank balance sheets. The losses were interpreted as a deficiency of the state and its reputation, both as a major shareholder and as supervisor was called into question. The accountability of the managers was also raised. Finally, the withdrawal of banks from the lending markets did not help the economic recovery that the government was striving for.

The recession created tensions between the various aims of public authorities and made them contradictory. France was a strong partisan of European integration, pushing in favour of the incorporation of open competition rules, but the dramatic losses that occurred led to opposite objectives: on one side, it was clear that one of the priorities was to clean up the situation, whilst preserving the reputation of the French financial markets and on the other side, there was a need to maintain social peace, which meant not causing excessive defaults and bankruptcies. These contradictions led to the symbolic choice of supporting public banks such as Crédit Lyonnais, and not letting the market rule. This situation had the advantage, from the government point of view, of allowing it to continue to administer the financial system. However, it also had the disadvantage of encouraging organisations not to reform in the belief that the state would rescue them as it had done before deregulation (Salomon 1997).

These uncertainties increased the already confused situation in which both managers and the state were caught amidst negotiations with Brussels, emergency bailouts, claims from local elected officials for debt relief, and strikes from threatened workers in the banks. The state encouraged banks to restore their profitability, without giving them clear guidelines about how to achieve this. It sought to withdraw further from control of the financial sector in order to protect itself from further demands for intervention. After the right wing party's victory in 1993, the state concentrated on privatisations after cleaning up the losses of the sector. It did not help the dialogue between the various actors or attempt to institute a settlement that could benefit the whole sector. On the contrary, it encouraged the stronger actors (mainly the large and private banking institutions and their representatives) to intensify their claims for help in restructuring from both Paris and Brussels.

The larger banking institutions were not ready to face strong international competition, nor were the state and the supervision and control authorities. The more competitive operators were also happy to gain time against their outside competitors and benefit from national protection factors. From January 1 1993, any banking institution established in the European Union could offer financial services in any other country of the Union according to the regulations in its home base. France has very protective laws, for instance in consumer credit activity, as well as rules and practices that increase the cost of the financial services and therefore weaken the capacity of the French banks to compete with banking institutions of other countries benefiting from a more flexible context.

The political arguments that arose emphasised existing tensions between the logics defended by the government and administration of the Treasury, sensitive to the demands of the corporate sector for lower lending rates and more flexibility from banks in lending, and the central bank's views, supported by the international and European regulators keen at avoiding any systemic problems and wishing to help the banking institutions recover and develop better risk management systems.

Banking, because of its visibility on the public scene, has become part of the wider political cleavages in France, for example the clash between the liberal and 'dirigiste' points of view, the clash between local and national politicians, the debates on the use of banks as instruments of social and economic policy, the clash between those in favour of more rapid European integration and those wishing to delay the process. By becoming embroiled in these processes, the financial sector became an additional bargaining issue in the growing fragmentation of French society. In this game, two sets of resources structured the actors' behaviours: firstly the protection that the state was able to give certain actors, and secondly the capacities of those actors to play the game of free competition without the state's help. In the French situation it was rational for all actors to preserve or gain additional protection through creating special relationships with key stakeholders such as the state. Commercial banks felt comfortable in protecting their interests by adopting conservative views on lending, and concentrating on good markets, segments or clients. This period was also used to undertake internal changes in the large banks. Between 1992 and 1996 the level of profits was related to the degree of autonomy from the state that an institution could have and to the degree of protection against competition rules, that is to say dependent clients and shareholders satisfying themselves from low level returns.

5.   Conclusion

The dirigiste system was not a favourable resource for the French banking system, as it faced the necessary transformation consequent on the opening of borders. The problems, bargaining and delays that stemmed from the first phase of the transition created confusion and conflicts. It did not allow innovation, resilience, adaptation of skills, internal changes, etc., but on the contrary encouraged conservatism, segmentation, and protection. As far as the principle of deregulation was concerned, that is to say to change the general posture of the French state and its public authorities, that aim is not yet accomplished either. The state still holds some of the main resources determining competition, e.g. control over the number of actors, the status of banking institutions, the pace of privatisation, public services products, administered rates, etc. as well as the laws governing working conditions, public access and, ultimately, interest rates. As far as banking institutions are concerned, if on one side they are not as advanced or competitive as those in US, UK or other European systems, on the other side they have been protected from bankruptcy (except for a few little ones), and from hostile and foreign raids. If they did not provide good returns to their shareholders, they also did not institute mass redundancies, although thousands of people quit their jobs voluntarily. The size of some banks such as Société Générale or BNP allowed them to expand internationally and achieve good profits out of this expansion. The specialisation and organisational capacities of some of the medium size banking institutions, such as CCF or Cetelem, also led some of them to become profitable companies and significant competitors in other European markets within their particular markets. In 1996 and more so in 1997 banks, the French banking system showed that it had recovered from the deep crisis of the 1991–1995 period.

Although there is still a lot to achieve, especially since now the international competition is starting to become real with the aggressive entry of US companies, it is clear that the various actors used the delay given by the time of confusion with profit. It also seems clear that it was a learning period for everyone. Not only did the banks transform their organisational skills and systems, but also the actors learnt about the rules of the new game as well as the new hierarchies. Even the state has become less ambiguous and has asserted more firmly and publicly its choices to maintain some social and public services within banking activities as well as to encourage some new segments such as risk capital, etc.

In this context, various actors struggle to define the new rules of the game in a complex process of conflict and bargaining. In the old 'dirigiste' system, French banking institutions were constrained to act according to the performance criteria set by the state élite. In return, they were protected from competition. The pressure to open up the French financial markets from 1983 left the institutions free to pursue new objectives. However, few of the banks had the internal risk management systems in place that were necessary. The result was an expansion of credit to risky borrowers. Once the economic conditions changed with the recession of the late 1980s, defaults and bankruptcies increased, severely weakening the banks' capital base. The state was torn between a return to 'dirigisme' or further weakening direct control. It chose to seek compromise by allowing the banks time to restructure through providing them with a protective shelter. By the mid-1990s, most banks had restructured. In terms of financial performance, their situation had improved thanks to the help of the state. In broader terms, however, there remained uncertainties. What were the key performance criteria for the banks? Were they to be driven entirely by market efficiency? Would the

French state allow any banks to fail? Or would the state continue to support them in return for the banks' cooperation in its wider social and economic goals for France? It is unlikely that these long-standing performance objectives will be entirely jettisoned. The phenomenon of path dependency leads us to expect that the French state will face any new problems in the financial sector with a continued preference for smooth change in spite of its adherence to strict deregulation. Similarly, the major banks know that one key performance criteria remains their ability to meet the state's objectives, no matter what the preferences of their other key stakeholders.

References

Boyer, R. 1993. Nouveaux regards sur la théorie de la convergence: un processus de globalisation mais encore la siècle des nations, *Problèmes économiques* 2: 415–416.

Andrieu, C. 1990. *La banque sous l'Occupation. Paradoxes de l'histoire d'une profession.* Paris: Presses de la FNSP.

Bauer, M., and B. Bertin-Mourot. 1991. *„Les 200" en France et en Allemagne. Deux modèles contrastés de détection-sélection-formation de dirigeants de grandes entreprises.* Paris: CNRS et Heidrick and Struggles.

Cohen, E. 1992. Représentation de l'adversaire et politique économique (Nationalisation, Politique industrielle et engagement européen), IVè Congrès de l'AFSP, *Les représentations de l'adversaire dans la gauche française : le cas du parti socialiste.* Table Ronde n°5, Paris.

Cohen, E. 1996. *La tentation hexagonale. La souveraineté à l'épreuve de la mondialisation.* Paris: Fayard.

Crouch, C. and Streeck, W. 1996. L'avenir du capitalisme diversifié. In: Crouch, C. and Streeck, W. (eds.), *Les capitalismes en Europe*, 11–25. Paris: La Découverte.

Meyer, J. W., and B. Rowan. 1991. Institutionalized Organizations: Formal Structure as Myth and Ceremony. In: Powell, W. W. and DiMaggio, P. (eds.), *The New Institutionalism in Organizational Analysis*, 41–62. Chicago: The University of Chicago Press.

Kessler, M. C. 1968. *Le Conseil d'Etat.* Paris: A. Colin.

Kooiman, J. (ed.). 1993. *Modern Governance*, London: Sage.

Pastré, O. 1993. Le système bancaire français, bilan et perspectives, *Revue d'Economie Financière* 27, Hiver: 233–272.

Salomon, D. 1997. Quand une politique publique en cache une autre … La loi Neiertz comme réponse politique et acte opportuniste des organes de tutelle. In: M. Gardaz (ed.), *Le surendettement des particuliers*, 13–37. Paris: Anthropos/Economica.

Salomon, D. (1999), Deregulation and Embeddedness: The Case of the French Banking System. In: Morgan, G. and Engwall, L. (eds.), *Regulation and organizations. International perspectives*, 69–81. London: Routledge.

Thoenig, J. C. 1987. *L'Ere des Technocrates.* Paris: L'Harmattan.

Whitley, R. 1994. Dominant Forms of Economic Organization in Market Economies, *Organization Studies*, 15(2): 153–182.

Zysman, J. 1983. *Governments, Markets and Growth. Financial Systems and the politics of Industrial Choice*. London: Cornell University Press.

CHAPTER 8

Reproducing Diversity
ISO 9000 and Work Organisation in the French and German Car Industry

Bob Hancké   Steven Casper

1. Introduction

The liberalisation of trade and increased international competition in important manufacturing sectors have revived an old debate in the social sciences. Will the production systems of different countries begin to resemble one another as a result of competitive pressures? The argument in favour of convergence relies on a simple yet powerful idea: international competition, especially in relatively saturated markets — i.e. most engineering sectors producing mass-consumption goods — forces firms to be efficient in order to retain market share. Open world markets therefore select the most efficient production system from among the main candidates. Transmission mechanisms such as business consulting, which frequently transfer organisational arrangements existing elsewhere, make the adoption of such best practice solutions relatively easy. International competition and organisational re-engineering combined therefore push for convergence of production systems.

This chapter examines ISO 9000, a widely applied quality management system, in the French and German car industries. The car sector is a prime example of an internationalised, technologically mature sector: roughly half of the US trade deficit with Japan in 1991 was attributable to cars, and international car trade has been a major topic of negotiation in the GATT and WTO talks and was, until recently, a highly protected sector. The car industry is also a laboratory for new management techniques and organisational principles. More than in any other sector do market pressures, organisational learning, and the active transfer of best practice models push firms to converge around a single system (Womack et al. 1991; Kenney and Florida 1993). Finally, in the reorganisation of the industry over the last decade, quality considerations played a central role. Managing the new, considerably more fragile production systems conceived around lean production and just-in-time (JIT) delivery systems, required more attention to quality. For almost a decade, therefore, ISO 9000 norms have been actively used by the car firms for their own final assembly operations and for their links with suppliers.

The disproportionate international openness of the sector, the near-universal acceptance of lean production as the most efficient production system (Streeck 1996) and the universal adoption of standardised norms that deal with the organisation of quality make the car industry a critical case for the argument on convergence. Has the widespread adoption of ISO 9000 and similar quality norms in the reorganisation of the car industry contributed to a convergence in the way companies produce cars in different countries?

It is important to note an important difference between ISO 9000 and the transfer of 'lean production' concepts. Lean production is, in essence, a set of general principles that need to be fitted to the specifics of the existing production system, and it is therefore somewhat unsurprising that these principles have very different translations in different contexts. What makes ISO 9000 interesting in this regard, is that it presents itself as a much *harder*, universal instrument with relatively detailed guidelines for tasks and work organisation. Furthermore, the French and German versions of ISO 9000 manuals are simple translations of the English one. Finally, ISO 9000 is also considerably narrower than lean production: it deals only with quality and was often a supporting element in the introduction of lean production. When tasks were redesigned and teams installed to meet more stringent quality demands, a performance measurement system became necessary to guide and monitor these reorganisations.

This chapter, which is based on a detailed analysis of the interaction between ISO 9000 and regimes of work organisation in the French and German automobile industry, argues that the expected convergence in production systems is not taking place. In France, the introduction of the quality standards reproduced, while modernising, the underlying Taylorist company organisation. In Germany, in contrast, ISO 9000 norms were embedded within new production concepts, where they ended up reinforcing the autonomy of skilled workers. While contributing to a profound modernisation of the industry in the two countries, ISO 9000 thus also in subtle ways reproduced the previously existing differences between the organisation of production.

The explanation for this is that the ISO 9000 norms were not really imported from outside into the systems, but that they were truly redefined and re-con- structed by the crucial actors within each of the countries to fit their own views of what they could contribute to their industries and production systems. They were, in contrast to their commonly accepted image, only partly given, and the account that follows raises doubts about which part of them really is sufficiently *unnegotiable* and *hard* to be able to impose a universal logic overriding the existing institutional constructions. We suggest, in fact, that this hard part — assuming that it exists — is extremely small. Without the active re-interpretation and, hence, the contextualisation of the ISO 9000 norms, they would simply be rejected by the system.[1]

These divergent interpretations of the norms, in turn, are possible because the quality standards are in fact sufficiently flexible for such multiple uses. ISO 9000 norms are, in other words, not the same things in different countries. Through the remoulding, they become something else for the relevant actors — workers, firms, and industry. They are solutions for very different problems, with very different issues at stake, and intersect with very different practices and identities.

The chapter is organised as follows. The next section locates ISO 9000 standards in the current processes of industrial reorganisation. Section 3 then examines the argument why ISO 9000 would lead to convergence, while Section 4 details our point about the role of institutions governing ISO 9000 implementation. Section 5 provides the empirical treatment of ISO 9000 and work organisation in the French and German car industries. Section 6 concludes.

2. ISO 9000 in Industry

Since the invention of interchangeable parts, technical norms have become an essential condition for mass production. Beside product norms, which describe what is made, increasingly attention is devoted to how products are made. A growing number of process norms are being developed to help companies design management systems for quality control, environmental impact assessment, product testing, and other areas of company organisation.

National-level quality management norms were first used in the 1950s by the US Department of Defence to assess the ability of contractors of complex weapons system to consistently produce defect-free products (Hutchins 1994: 49). However, their transfer and wide application to commercial products occurred primarily in the United Kingdom during the 1980s, with the publication of BS 5750 in 1979 (Hutchins 1994: 70). The British Institute for Standards (BIS) was the first national standards setting body to actively push quality certification as an important component of firm competitiveness, developing an assortment of consulting and certification services to aid companies using BS 5750 (Tate 1997). BS 5750 is loosely based on the NATO version of the US MIL-Q 9858A norms, and became the prototype for the ISO 9000 series, first published in 1987 (Hutchins 1994: 70–71).

ISO 9000 is currently the overwhelmingly dominant management system used for quality control throughout the OECD. The series has supplanted BS 5750 in the UK and been widely adopted by national standard setting bodies throughout the advanced capitalist economies. By definition, ISO 9000 norms do not follow national practice in their construction, and are themselves sufficiently standardised and unequivocal so that they can be used in a variety of commercial settings. ISO 9000 comprises three series of prescriptive technical norms. The most comprehensive series is ISO 9001, which contains twenty quality assurance elements covering production, installation, servicing, and design. The ISO 9002 series is identical to the 9001 series, minus the two elements dealing with design processes. Most traditional suppliers without product development competencies aim for this series. The ISO 9003 series is less comprehensive, designed for companies involved in packaging and distribution only; it contains only 12 of the 20 elements in ISO 9001 and is rarely used by manufacturing firms (for an overview, see Paradis et al. 1996: Chapter 2).

In contrast to quality designations such as the Malcolm Baldridge Award and other quality awards in the US and Europe, ISO 9000 certification does not assure that a company produces zero-defect products or has a world-class quality management system. Yet because it mandates documented process controls throughout the firm that help employees find and eliminate faults more quickly, the ISO 9000 system increases product consistency and thus reduces the risk of systematic failures. Though mistakes can still occur, the use of a quality management system radically improves the probability that each product will be manufactured correctly.

Third party auditing and certification assures that the various tasks are being performed properly. Members of the auditing team usually have experience in the firm's sector (Hutchins 1994: 174). This helps ensure that the firm is creating a quality management system that reflects the particular demands of each sector. For example, a key element of ISO 9001 and 9002 is the norm specifying statistical techniques. The norm reads that "your organisation shall identify and use appropriate statistical techniques as necessary to verify the acceptability of process capability, product characteristics, and service" (Paradis et al. 1996: 67). Within the automobile industry and other serial production sectors, this requirement entails the introduction of statistical process controls (SPC), procedures that would not be necessary in batch production industries, such as parts of the machine tools sector.

ISO 9000 certification is an on-going process. After a firm passes an initial audit, certification agencies are required to conduct conformity inspections at six month intervals and have the right to conduct surprise inspections if third parties complain that particular firms are lapsing on agreed quality control norms (Hutchins 1994: 175). Most certification agencies mandate a new comprehensive audit every three years.

Since their inception, the spread of ISO 9000 standards in different forms has been extremely rapid. Why have firms, who paid attention to quality before, adopted the relatively unknown and novel ISO 9000 system? The answer lies in the transparency associated with these quality standards. This is perhaps best illustrated by recent developments in the car industry. In response to fluctuating market demands, final assemblers have fundamentally reorganised their links with suppliers, first by eliminating their own inventories of parts and demanding from suppliers that they deliver products directly to the assembly line when needed, and secondly by outsourcing the design and manufacturing of complex sub-assemblies such as seats, brake and heating systems (Clark and Fujimoto 1991). These decentralised structures create a series of new risks for the final assemblers, since they are no longer able to check every part for defects. Such defects, especially when they are of a serial nature, can shut down the entire production line.

Since final assemblers must find new ways to assure that their suppliers are delivering parts with few if any defects, quality monitoring has become a key problem. The existence of a certified quality management system allows final assemblers to verify that the supplier can achieve quality control at a minimal level without detailed, and costly, supervision by the final assembler. It is this external monitoring ability that is the driving force behind the rapid push by final assemblers to require ISO 9000 certification by suppliers (Tuckman 1994: 740). Evidence from our case studies indicates that profoundly different rules have developed to support ISO 9000 norms within French and German firms. Nevertheless, in both countries ISO 9000 has been a key element in lowering the monitoring costs resulting from the new supplier network strategies.

Their international nature makes the ISO 9000 norms particularly useful in an evaluation of foreign suppliers. Because of the quasi-official nature of the norms and the implicit sanctioning capacity of the certifying agencies, a foreign buyer can rely on the value of the ISO norms. At the same time, because they are reasonably well understood, the buyers can assume that they have sufficient inside knowledge about the suppliers to be able to enter a transaction without the usual profound information asymmetries. Conversely, ISO 9000 has advantages for domestic supplier firms as well. They allow the supplier to position itself favourably on international markets, which leads to economies of scale and potential learning externalities; these in turn, feed back into the domestic buyer's operations through higher quality and, in some cases, reduced prices.

Having identified the key function of the ISO 9000 norms does not explain how the norms were successfully introduced into the two countries. We must also examine the problem of implementation. How was the ISO 9000 quality system introduced in the French and German car industries, and why did they lead to different outcomes in these countries, despite their purported standardised nature, which has the potential to lead to more similar patterns of work organisation? The next sections treat these issues.

3.   ISO 9000, Convergence and Institutions

Why would ISO 9000 further a convergence in patterns of work organisation? Critics of ISO 9000 and other quality-related company improvement programs have pointed out that the standards parallel the prescriptive character of work found in Taylorist work organisation, this time using the brains of workers as well as their bodies (Tuckman 1994). ISO 9000 norms directly influence the organisation of important parts of production: they specify how a firm should measure quality, take corrective action when quality drops, and most importantly, implement preventive quality control. Companies implement quality management procedures throughout the organisation and then keep detailed records assuring that the procedures are being met over time.

As part of this process, work procedures have to be spelt out and the quality-related requirements of each task documented in detail. In this sense, ISO 9000 is a management information system hidden underneath a quality program, and thus it complements and completes the Taylorist logic of transferring knowledge over the labour process to management (Tuckman 1994: 740). The implicit neo-Taylorist logic is related to the origins of ISO 9000, which emerged first in the US and the UK, countries with a profound Taylorist industrial tradition (Braverman 1974; Sabel 1982; Piore and Sabel 1984). Moreover, analyses of ISO 9000 in French companies (Duval 1998) suggest indeed that the norms express an underlying neo-Taylorist logic. In short, ISO 9000 pushes firms to converge around a neo-Taylorist company model, found in different forms in the Anglo-Saxon economies and France.

This argument ignores an important set of factors related to firm governance. France and the US share, in fact, many institutions that influence company behaviour and organisation. These include weak and fragmented labour relations systems, weak unions who pay little attention to such issues as work organisation, skills and training, and weak or absent institutions for workplace representation. Because of this institutional environment of firms, the introduction of technological and organisational innovations in these countries frequently takes place on management's terms.

In a setting with other, more powerful institutions for firm governance, however, the implementation of ISO 9000 may well have substantially different effects. Imagine an institutional environment, which includes a strong, relatively centralised labour relations system, strong unions with an interest in work organisation, training and skill formation more generally. In short, imagine the introduction of ISO 9000 and similar quality management systems in companies in a country like Germany. What would happen?

Answering this question requires a further dissection of ISO 9000, but this time from *within* the firm. As said, ISO 9000 does not deal with product quality, but provides rules for a management system that *produces* quality, i.e. goods and services made right the first time according to correct specifications. The quality standards therefore deal with the organisation of tasks. They prescribe a series of control points in the tasks that have to be passed.

Precisely this emphasis on tasks makes ISO 9000 extremely malleable. Even within rigid Taylorist production systems or in the new Toyotism, workers retain and create degrees of freedom in how exactly each task is done and many authors have, correctly in our view, seen this as the expression of struggles over the organisation of work and the social identities this embodies (Sabel 1982; Streeck 1996). These struggles are profoundly influenced by the institutional context within which they take place, such as the organisation and power basis of labour unions, co-determination systems, and training systems.

4.   Workplace Governance in France and Germany

ISO 9000 standards are process norms dealing with tasks and the actual contents and organisation of tasks are subject to struggles that are heavily influenced by the power resources that workers and managers can bring to bear on their implementation. We can thus expect, instead of a convergence toward a neo-Taylorist organisation model, ISO 9000 to have substantially different effects in different institutional settings of firm governance. Industrial organisation in Germany and France is governed by very different institutions, and in large measure as a result of these differences in the institutional framework, the organisation of work has followed very different trajectories in the two countries. This section briefly outlines how differences in the German and French industrial relations and vocational training systems lead to different processes of firm representation and worker competencies.

In Germany works councils are the critical actors in the struggles over workplace organisation. They police collective bargaining agreements, dealing with wages and job classifications, negotiated at the branch level. Works councils also police training practices inside the companies and have a legal right to intervene in work reorganisation. Despite the strength of unions and works councils, workplace reorganisation is a relatively co-operative process, typically with management stating its wishes in broad terms, and negotiating the details with the works councils, who represent the targeted workers. Works council strength is the reason why such reorganisations are relatively co-operative: because of the power vested in them — inside the company by the workers, outside by the unions — workers trust their policing capacity and allow job negotiations on job redesign without fear for exploitation.

The role of the outside unions is at least as important. They provide the local unions and the works councils with external expertise on many issues regarding company and work organisation, directly through the national and regional offices with a dense network of internal experts on these issues, and indirectly through technology expertise and a nation-wide network of academics providing the unions with topical expertise (Széll et al. 1989).[2] IG Metall, for example, has been a major player in the debates over work organisation in the Germany engineering industry in the 1980s (Turner 1991).

This complex system of institutions of firm governance is the stage where new ideas regarding work are implemented. For example, when lean production was introduced in the German car industry in response to the crisis of the early 1990s, these institutional resources were mobilised by workers and unions to shape it according to their occupational identities and class interests. Teams, for example, became autonomous teams, where many administrative tasks were decentralised, and jobs were enlarged to include many low-level management tasks, much in line with proposals that IG Metall floated in the debate. Rather than a blind transfer, therefore, the introduction of lean production in the German car industry became a process whereby many of the existing rules regarding work were modernised and re-affirmed (Streeck 1996).

A comparison with France sheds light on the importance of this institutional set-up for work reorganisation. First of all, workplace union organisations are extremely weak in France: until 1968, there was no legal protection for local union work, and the subsequent increase in the number of workplace unions did not erase the organisational heritage of exclusion. In large measure, this is related to the lack of support by the external union: doubting the capacity of the company sections to negotiate, the industry federations have kept a highly centralised grip on collective bargaining and on resources. The effects of this centralised structure were clear when the famous Auroux laws on workplace organisation were introduced in 1982. Because the local unions lacked the resources for creatively engaging the new bodies of workplace participation created by the laws, the latter not only failed miserably in their initially set goals, but in fact contributed to the decline of labour unions in France (Eyraud and Tchobanian 1985; Howell 1992).

French works councils are not necessarily better placed: since they are consultative bodies who lack hard rights, and include management as well as worker representatives, they do not have an independent power basis. Furthermore, since the mid-1980s roughly half of the works councillors in France are elected on non-union slates and therefore have no access whatsoever to the expertise provided by the labour unions — an expertise system which is topical, i.e. not permanent, and provided by external union-affiliated offices, not by in-house staff (Daley 1996).

Finally, the French training system is notoriously weak. There is no link between school education and workplace training for the young, and although formally the unions play a role in determining the contents of training curricula, they are marginal actors, as are most employers' associations. Most of the training system is, in fact, colonised by the large firms, either directly or indirectly through their technological pilot role which becomes the key reference for the education ministry (Möbus and Verdier 1997). Thus, whereas the German system relies on a flexible system of skill acquisition, which produces portable skills, French workers typically receive a broad general education in school, and a highly specialised training inside the company.

Because of this institutional setting, work organisation in French companies has been modernised while retaining much of its Taylorist character: semi-skilled workers, trained in multiple jobs, receive detailed instructions from engineers and are subject to extensive off-line checks on effort, productivity and quality. New ideas on work organisation — and, again, lean production in the car industry is a case in point — have, because of how they are translated by the institutional setting, had effects on French workplaces that are considerably different from Germany. Teams in France are mainly organised along geography on the assembly line, not functionally, and have little autonomy in terms of work organisation and pacing. In these teams, workers are, in principle, able to perform a large variety of the tasks. Individual jobs are subject to improvement only after approval by process engineers.

5.   ISO 9000 and Work Organisation in the French and German Car Industry

These variations in the institutions governing industrial organisation help us to understand, in the following sections, why ISO 9000 norm implementation has proceeded along different trajectories in French and German manufacturing firms.

Before the introduction of ISO 9000, quality control routines were well developed in most German firms. Even though many of the production processes, especially in mass production industries, were Fordist in character, highly skilled workers retained substantial autonomy. They were responsible for checking their product quality, and while this may have been a highly idiosyncratic process, involving much tacit occupational knowledge, the general skill level and decentralised authority systems in German companies assured high and constant quality. Importantly, primary quality control was in principle on-line: monitoring product quality was an integral part of the workers' tasks.

The problem with the system was its idiosyncratic nature. Since so much of the process was embedded in the routines and knowledge of the workers, it was very hard for outsiders, ranging from engineers and managers to parties outside the company, to understand how quality was actually achieved. Moreover, as the production systems in the car industry and its main suppliers became more complex as a result of new models of supplier organisation, the division of labour upon which this quality monitoring system was based, was upset.

In this context of rapid organisational change, ISO 9000 and similar quality standards were introduced in the German car industry, first for suppliers and immediately thereafter for final assemblers as well. The main benefit of the ISO 9000 system in its various versions was that it made transparent to outsiders how quality was achieved. This had become a necessity, not just for reasons having to do with retaining market share in the face of increased competition in the industry, but primarily because of the shift in liability risks that was introduced following the innovations in the supplier strategies of the large firms (Casper 1995). Whereas traditionally, the large car firms were, according to German commercial law, responsible for entry inspections of the supplied products, the designation of the main system suppliers as just-in-time suppliers shifted the liability onto the latter. Insurance premiums, which had been relatively low under the old regime as a result of the size of the car manufacturers, shot up because the suppliers were exposed to more risks and, because of their size, less able to bear those costs. ISO 9000 solved this problem by introducing a standardised, relatively well understood, state of the art 'neutral' instrument for quality monitoring. It thus secured the autonomy of small firms vis-à-vis their larger clients.

In contrast to Germany, in French companies quality control was typically the responsibility of a separate quality control department, staffed with technicians and engineers. The work was performed by semi-skilled workers according to detailed instructions, and as a result, quality control was, in fact, kept as much as possible beyond the reach of the workers.

Quality control programs became a necessity in the French car industry in a parallel but slightly different way than in Germany. When the car companies in France entered a profound financial crisis in the first half of the 1980s, they sought to off-load as much as possible of their costs onto their suppliers, through outsourcing and just-in-time delivery. Yet once they engaged in this restructuring, they rapidly discovered that their suppliers were incapable of making the technological jump associated with such an organisational innovation. Quality monitoring programs such as ISO 9000 then entered the stage as a way of measuring the performance improvements among the suppliers, and helping them locate sources of adjustment problems.

The generalised introduction of ISO 9000 therefore certainly furthered a rapid modernisation of the French car industry. However, it also contributed to a reproduction of the previously existing hierarchical relationship between final assemblers and their suppliers. Their primary role was to legitimise the emphasis on quality in inter-firm relationships, thereby opening up the possibility of broader audits, which involved finance, training schemes, marketing, technological capabilities, etc. In short, the emphasis on quality forced the suppliers to open up their entire internal operations to the final assemblers. If before the introduction of ISO 9000 the car manufacturers dominated their suppliers by treating them as cheap executors of their orders, afterwards they were able to do so through the total transparency that the quality standards imposed.

Against this background of a substantial modernisation of the links with suppliers in both Germany and France, ISO 9000 standards were also introduced in the final assembly plants. As a result of this innovation, a new interface for the organisation of quality control had to be developed. The next sections examine these.

5.1 Germany: Product Quality as a Safeguard of Autonomy

The German institutional context on relations between small and large firms is set up in such a way that it ultimately protects the weaker small firms against abuse by the large firms, and ISO 9000 became an instrument to reaffirm that. Workplace institutions provide, in a parallel way, a set of rules that protect workers and workers skills (Streeck 1989, 1991) and, again, ISO 9000 became embedded in this system of rules.

In German workplaces, ISO 9000 was incorporated in the job designs of workers. They replaced the previously existing occupational knowledge-based system with a more formalised, transparent system, but left the actual implementation to the (primarily skilled) workers themselves. Additionally, works councils provided a forum for workers to protect these rights. Since they assure that the flexible deployment of skills in general takes place in an equitable way, workers trust their authority and competencies in the introduction of ISO 9000 as well. Works councils and local unions also rely on the expertise provided by union experts on work organisation and the union-affiliated expertise offices. For the introduction of ISO 9000 in the workplaces, workers have extensive checklists at their disposal, which help them in evaluating and steering the implementation of ISO 9000 in the workplaces. As a result of this institutional set-up, the introduction of a quality management system such as ISO 9000 is a negotiated affair in Germany, but without involving extensive conflict. Workers usually incorporate most quality control duties into their work and have a large voice in negotiations with industrial engineers and the quality control manager over how this is to be done.

An illustrative example is provided by one firm that we visited which made sophisticated car axles. Before the incorporation of ISO 9000 quality management procedures, this company had already organised its shop into a number of production cells, each of which contained about eight skilled workers who collectively created their own division of labour according to group work principles. When this firm accepted a JIT delivery contract it underwent a thorough reorganisation of quality control in order to meet ISO 9001 certification requirements for

Germany. As a result, one of these cells had incorporated statistical process control checks into its work process. Workers took control of detailed tolerance measurement on selected parts and recorded the results according to procedures satisfying ISO 9000 norms. Within the German context, quality control, even of a more formalised nature, has thus remained under the control of skilled workers.

In sum, the new production systems that car producers world-wide have introduced in recent years required profound changes in work organisation, and quality management systems such as ISO 9000 played a critical part in this reorganisation. However, ISO 9000 did not push work organisation and supplier relations down a neo-taylorist, hierarchical path. Instead, through the institutions governing work organisation, the ISO 9000 standards created a new framework in Germany, which protected the autonomy of both workers and small firms.

This picture contrasts sharply with the situation in France, where precisely the absence of such institutions provided management and workers (as well as large firms and small firms) with very different resources that could be mobilised in the implementation of ISO 9000.

5.2 *France: Control through Quality*

French workplaces have undergone many changes since the early 1980s, the most important of which is, perhaps, the reorganisation of tasks and job classifications: instead of employing narrowly trained specialised workers (*ouvriers specialisés*, OS), companies have tried to integrate several such descriptions into the position of the so-called *opérateur*. Typically, an *opérateur* is able to perform different tasks of the former OS; its true novelty, however, resides in the amount of peripheral tasks. Currently, the car firms expect their line workers to be able to manage their own workplace; do basic on-line quality control; check, discuss and improve parts quality with suppliers; and participate in team-like structures where they discuss potential improvements in work organisation, machinery and process design. Moreover, in its latest model, the Mégane, Renault called in assembly workers in product and process design.

Alongside legal changes in the structure of the firm, new management concepts and changing demands from workers, ISO 9000 was part of this workplace revolution. The successful implementation of the standards require workers' skills to be broader, the organisation of work more transparent, while new workplace institutions are necessary that assure a smooth information flow between workers and their supervisors. The introduction of ISO 9000 standards thus crowned a series of organisational innovations that had been underway in French industry since the mid-1980s.

However, in their implementation, the quality standards also reinforced elements in the French workplaces that reduced worker autonomy. In France, the

ISO 9000 standards are being interpreted as elements to help recreate the traditional Taylorist workplaces in a new shape (Linhart 1991). First, all the basic elements of classical Taylorism are still there: workers still have very detailed task descriptions (there are just more of them), work pace is still imposed by machines, and the division between conception and execution remains strong (Duval 1996). Between 1984 and 1991, the period that is frequently treated as the time when post-Taylorism became the norm in French industry (Linhart 1993), the numbers of workers in the French car industry who said they performed repetitive work on an assembly line, increased by almost a third, and those who claimed to be working under machine-imposed rhythms by almost 40 per cent (Duval 1996: 36–37). Secondly, while teams are formally responsible for on-line quality control as prescribed by the ISO 9000 system, a separate quality control team checks the products that come off the line.

In French car companies, ISO 9000 norms reinforced the neo-Taylorist nature of the workplace by removing uncontrollable risks and other worker-related contingencies from the workplace. In order to assure quality, according to the dominant translation of ISO 9000 norms in the French context, work processes have to be standardised as much as possible. This is exactly what the car industry had been offering all along, and which it refined in the second half of the 1980s with the introduction of lean manufacturing concepts (Berggren 1990; Womack et al. 1991). ISO 9000 quality control and the neo-Taylorist workplaces thus entered into a happy marriage, where both worked in the same direction: reducing variability in processes by reducing workers' autonomy in decision-making (Campinos-Dubernet 1994).

This is perhaps best illustrated by the example of the new assembly lines in French car plants. Despite the increased sophistication and complexity of the products made on them, they are, in fact, extremely conventional in layout, and have adopted only little of the new assembly techniques found in other European countries. In the assembly plant in Flins, for example, where the new Renault Clio is made, the assembly line has important small ergonomic improvements, but its basic organisation is the same as the one used for previous models: a standard moving assembly line. A major problem in the organisation of this line was its balancing, since there was one bottleneck, the place where the doors are reattached to the car, which was unable to keep up with the cycle times of the rest of the plant. Engineers looked for a solution in a further division of the work in smaller parts in order to balance the line. (Information based on a plant visit in February 1998.)

Quality control is largely integrated into the work process in the Flins plant: every worker checks his or her own work after finishing the job; every team (an administrative unit rather than a self-administered group of workers) does the same for the next section of the line. However, between line sections a central quality control service inspects every car.

The quality standards system had very different results in France as compared to Germany because of the total absence of precisely those institutions that underpinned the worker-oriented implementation in Germany. Works councils played little or no role in the introduction of ISO 9000, and unions generally left quality as well as general issues related to workplace organisation to management. Their relative indifference to such workplace issues also explains why outside union-affiliated expertise agencies have played no role in the introduction of ISO 9000. The introduction of ISO 9000 was a relatively unproblematic management affair in France, because the institutions that would have provided the resources for workers and their representatives to negotiate their implementation, were simply too weak.

6. Conclusion

ISO 9000, which is purported to be a universal quality management system, was implemented in very different ways, with very different effects, in France and Germany. Understanding why this was the case requires an analysis of how ISO 9000 was engaged by the relevant actors in both countries. ISO 9000 neither imposed a neo-Taylorist logic nor did it simply reproduce the old system. In both cases, management introduced such a quality system to meet new organisational demands. However, as a result of the different institutional resources that could be mobilised by workers, this introduction resulted in very different scenarios.

Quality management in general, and ISO 9000 in particular, speaks directly to a field in German companies where competencies were traditionally well-defined and where institutions existed that protected those: work organisation and job design. In Germany, the array of organisational innovations since the mid-1980s such as teams and lean production and the way they interacted with conceptions of occupational identity, have shaped the setting within which ISO 9000 was introduced. The skilled workers took over quality control tasks and re-appropriated them as part of their new job descriptions. Since quality control always was primarily on-line in Germany, its modernisation along ISO 9000 lines easily fitted with the existing work organisation in Germany where quality control was also always performed by the workers themselves. Consequently, there never was a struggle over ISO in Germany: while it was implemented, it was also changed.

In France, on the other hand, ISO 9000 in fact crowned a workplace revolution. Quality control had always been a matter of technicians, not the workers, and the introduction of ISO 9000 shifted that balance, since part of the off-line quality control was now moved to the line workers. However, the introduction of on-line quality control took place against the background of modernised but still hierarchical workplaces, and the result was therefore not the widening of tasks through a re-appropriation of the ISO 9000 system by workers that we found in Germany, but an articulation of those elements in ISO 9000 which fitted and reinforced the hierarchical organisation of the workplaces. ISO 9000's logic was alien to the French production system, and it had therefore to be changed and moulded as well, but the result was a different division of labour between workers and technicians than in Germany.

The introduction and implementation of ISO 9000 led to different outcomes in France and Germany because the quality management system had to be reinterpreted and reorganised to fit the reorganisation of the production system. It became, as it were, a part of that, but thus also changed in character, as a result of how the relevant economic actors were able to mobilise resources in their institutional environment to shape the outcomes of the innovation process. It incorporated, in other words, these two very different scenarios, and which one prevailed, resulted from these struggles, not from an intrinsic neo-Taylorist logic embedded in ISO 9000 or from a blind reproduction of previously existing patterns.

Notes

1. One might even wonder if ISO 9000 standards can be anything else than relatively *soft*, since if they were not, they might simply be rejected by the system. Teubner (1998) argues along the same lines that good faith, a common principle in much of continental civil law, is impossible to apply in the British case, where it has been imported as a result EU-harmonisation, and rejected by the British legal system. Instead of a contribution to British law, changed in meaning, perhaps, it becomes an irritant.

2. The DGB has set up a series of local technology consulting offices (*Technologieberatungsstelle*), who publish checklists and similar guides for union delegates on quality management systems, ISO 9000 and the introduction of SAP process controls so that the works councillors and unionists can evaluate the impact of these new systems on the workplaces in their jurisdiction.

References

Berggren, C. 1990. *Det Nya Bilarbetet*. Lund: Arkiv.

Braverman, H. 1974. *Labor and Monopoly Capital*. New York: Monthly Review Press.

Campinos-Dubernet, M. 1994. Le client-cible ou le client-acteur des politiques de qualité: quels problèmes de coordination? In: P. Charpentier, R. Foot and P.-E. Tixier (eds.), *Mutations de l'entreprise et performance. Coopérer, oui mais comment?* Actes du Colloque, Paris, 30 novembre, Cahier de Recherche no 70, 45–53. Paris: GIP Mutations Industrielles.

Casper, S. 1995. How Public Law Influences Decentralized Supplier Network Organization in Germany: The cases of BMW and Audi. WZB-Discussion Paper FS I 95–314, Berlin.

Clark, K., and T. Fujimoto. 1991. *Product Development Performance: Strategy, Organization and Management of the World Auto Industry*. Boston: Harvard Business School Press.

Daley, A. 1996. The Travail of Sisyphus: French Unions after 1981, mimeo.

Duval, G. 1996. Les habits neufs du taylorisme, *Alternatives Economiques* 137: 30–39.

Duval, G. 1998. *L'entreprise efficace à l'heure de Swatch et Mc Donalds. La seconde vie du taylorisme.* Paris: Syros.

Eyraud, F., and R. Tchobanian. 1985. The Auroux Reforms and Company Level Industrial Relations in France, *British Journal of Industrial Relations* 23(2): 241–259.

Howell, C. 1992. *Regulating Labour. The State and Industrial Relations in France.* Princeton: Princeton University Press.

Hutchins, G. 1994. *ISO 9000: A Comprehensive Guide to Registration, Audit Guidelines, and Successful Certification.* Essex Junction: Omneo.

Kenney, M., and R. Florida. 1993. *Beyond mass production. The Japanese system and its transfer to the U.S.* New York, NY: Oxford University Press.

Linhart, D. 1991. *Le torticolis de l'autruche. L'éternelle modernisation des entreprises françaises.* Paris: Le Seuil.

Linhart, D. 1993. À propos du post-taylorisme, *Sociologie du travail* 35(1): 63–74.

Möbus, M., and E. Verdier, (eds). 1997. *Les diplômes professionnels en Allemagne et en France. Conception et jeux d'acteurs.* Paris: l'Harmattan.

Paradis, G. W. and F. Small. 1996. *Demystifying ISO 9000.* Reading MA: Addison-Wesley.

Piore, M. J., and C. F. Sabel. 1984. *The Second Industrial Divide. Possibilities for Prosperity.* New York: Basic Books.

Sabel, C. F. 1982. *Work and Politics.* Cambridge: Cambridge University Press.

Streeck, W. 1989. Successful Adjustment to Turbulent Markets. In: P. Katzenstein (ed.), *Toward the Third Republic. Industry and Politics in West Germany*, 113–156. Ithaca NY: Cornell University Press.

Streeck, W. 1991. On the Institutional Conditions of Diversified Quality Production. In: E. Matzner and W. Streeck (eds.), *Beyond Keynesianism. The Socio-Economics of Full Employment*, 21–61. Brookfield VT: Elgar.

Streeck, W. 1996. Lean Production in the German Automobile Industry? A Test Case for Convergence Theory. In: S. Berger, and R. Dore (eds.), *National Diversity and Global Capitalism*, 138–170. Ithaca NY: Cornell University Press.

Széll, G., P. Blyton, and C. Cornforth, (eds.). 1989. *The State, Trade Unions and Self-Management.* Berlin: De Gruyter.

Tate, J. 1997. National Institutions and Industrial Standardization, Paper presented at the conference on Varieties of Capitalism, 6–8 June 1997, WZB Berlin.

Teubner, G. 1998. Legal Irritants: Good Faith in British Law Or How Unifying Law Ends Up in New Divergences, *The Modern Law Review* 61(1): 11–32.

Tuckman, A. 1994. The Yellow Brick Road: Total quality management and the restructuring of organisational culture, *Organization Studies* 15(5): 727–751.

Turner, L. 1991. *Democracy at Work. Changing World Markets and the Future of Labor Unions.* Ithaca NY: Cornell University Press.

Womack, J., D. Roos, and D. Jones. 1991. *The Machine that Changed the World.* New York: Harper and Row.

PART IV

National Business Systems and Corporate Performance in Globalising Markets

CHAPTER 9

Where Do Multinational Corporations Conduct Their Business Activity and What are the Consequences for National Systems?

Grahame F. Thompson

1. Introduction

With the advent of 'globalisation', and the dramatic advance of the multinational firm, the conception of the central importance of various 'national systems' (of business, of innovation, of labour relations, of finance, of production, etc.) is now often thought to be under siege as business practices rapidly internationalise. Firms now roam the globe in search of cheap but efficient production locations that offer them the largest and most secure and profitable return on competitive success. The precise impact of these internationalising processes on the nature of the socially and economically embedded national (or regional) business systems has become the subject of much analysis and speculation (Chesnais 1991; Dicken et al. 1994; Hollingsworth and Boyer 1996; Lazonick and O'Sullivan 1996; Mueller 1994; Soskice 1991; Tiberi-Vipraio 1996; Whitley 1992; Whitley and Kristensen 1996, 1997).

This chapter is concerned to do a number of things. The first is to analyse whether the advance of multinational corporations' (MNC) activity has been quite so rapid and widespread as is often assumed by the strong globalisation thesis, and particularly so fast as to seriously undermine the continuation of a national or local business system. This will involve the examination of a range of measures of the internationalisation of economic activity, not just the expansion of foreign direct investment (FDI) which is the measure most often used to bolster the strong globalisation thesis. This part of the chapter is quantitative in character. Until we know the true extent of such internationalisation, and whether it is increasing as rapidly and dramatically as is often argued, there is little point in speculating about its precise impact on the embeddedness of national systems.

One problem here is that there is no unambiguous evidence available or single statistical indicator that can reveal the true position. Thus the chapter is designed to present a range of indicators and to assess the strengths and weaknesses of each. Secondly, the chapter looks at the possible forms of the internationalisation of business activity identified in the context of the review of these different measures. This is done in relation to the debate about the continued relevance of national systems of business and innovation. Thirdly, the implication of these trends for economic performance and the nature of the international economy are briefly examined.

2.   The Advance of the MNC: Traditional Measures

The data plotted in Figure 1 represents a typical illustration of why the idea of a globalised production system is now so advanced that it is thought to be transforming the business landscape. In the mid-1980s there was a dramatic increase in the flows of FDI going to the advanced countries, followed nearly a decade later by a similar upsurge in FDI flows to the developing economies. Although the flows to the advanced countries fell away significantly in the recession years of the early 1990s, the pattern established for these countries in the early eighties re-emerged again after 1992.

The reasons for this upsurge are many. In the most recent period it probably represents a response to the significant liberalisation of foreign investment as the barriers to FDI continue to fall in both the advanced and developing countries.

FDI has been a feature of the international economy for more than a hundred years. There is thus an accumulated stock inherited from the past. This is shown for the years 1980 to 1995 in Table 1, expressed as a percentage of GDP. As might be expected there has been a growth in its importance relative to gross domestic product (GDP) since 1980–at the world level it has more than doubled from 4.6 per cent to 10.1 per cent. But the absolute levels in 1995 still remain modest for most countries and groupings. The UK is a conspicuous exception amongst the larger advanced countries. At the other end of the spectrum Japan remains largely untouched by inward FDI (and even its outward stock, at 6 per cent of GDP in 1995, was modest). It is surely debatable whether a stock of foreign owned productive activity of around 10 per cent or less of GDP for most of the advanced countries is sufficient to as yet dislodge any indigenously embedded national business system. It could be argued to have been more important for a small number of rapidly developing countries that have relied upon FDI as the main stimulant to their development strategies, but even this can be challenged (see the discussion around Table 7 below).

Many quite reasonable adjustments to these FDI flow and stock figures could be undertaken to make them more representative of the 'true' position that they

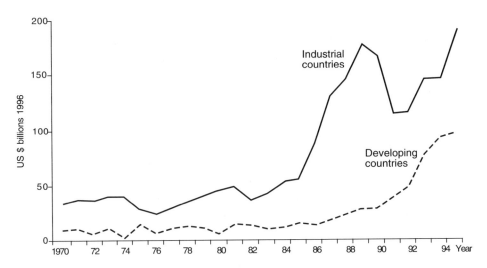

Figure 1. *Real FDI Flows to Industrial and Developing Countries, 1970–1995 (1996 US$ billions)*

International Finance Corporation, *Foreign Direct Investment,* Washington DC, 1997, Figure 2.4, p.16.

Table 1: *Inward FDI Stock as a Percentage of GDP (1980, 1985, 1990, 1995)*

	1980	1985	1990	1995
World	4.6	6.5	8.3	10.1
Developed Economies	4.8	6.0	8.3	9.1
of which: EU	5.5	8.2	10.9	13.4
(UK)	11.7	14.0	22.3	28.5
(Germany)	4.5	6.0	7.4	6.9
USA	3.1	4.6	7.2	7.7
Japan	0.3	0.4	0.3	0.3
Developing Economies	4.3	8.1	8.7	15.4
of which: LA & Caribbean	6.4	10.8	11.6	18.4
(Brazil)	6.9	11.3	8.1	17.8
Asia	3.5	7.3	7.3	14.2
South, East & SE Asia	3.8	6.5	8.7	15.1
Central & Eastern Europe	–	0.1	1.3	4.9

Compiled from UN (1997: Annex, Table B.6)

are designed to measure. For instance, the stock figures are calculated in terms of historic costs whereas they should perhaps be re-adjusted to current values which would no doubt increase their significance somewhat (Graham 1996: 10–13).

But there is a range of other problems with taking FDI flows or stocks as the single most useful measure of the internationalisation of productive activity. FDI has become the premier indicator because it is the most standardised international measure available. But we need to look at different and more appropriate indicators, which present a somewhat different picture of the extent of internationalised business activity.

Contrary to common claims FDI is not a measure of the assets held in affiliated firms. Rather it measures what is going on on the liabilities side of company's balance sheets. FDI flows are made up of changes in the shares, loans and retained earnings of affiliate companies that are operating abroad, though in a number of countries the reporting of FDI does not even include retained earnings. These have become an important element in the amount of activity conducted abroad (so in this sense, FDI might underestimate the extent of this activity in some countries). But in general the FDI measure is likely to overestimate this activity. Companies not only massage their liabilities for tax purposes — which has nothing necessarily to do with their ability to produce from their assets — but a major form of FDI liability management, namely the purchase of existing company shares and bonds, also need have no direct relationship to changes in the productive capacity of the assets so acquired. If a foreign company acquires an already existing domestic company's liabilities through an acquisition or merger (A&M), but does not alter the asset structure of the acquired company, there is no necessary increase in the productive potential in the country in which it has invested. This would appear as an inward flow of FDI however. There has been a dramatic growth in the extent of A&M activity internationally, particularly as stimulated by the privatisation programmes embarked upon by both the advanced and latterly the developing countries. In 1996 nearly 50 per cent of global FDI flows were made up of cross-border mergers and acquisitions and this is expected to increase as a proportion in the future (UN 1997: 9, 36).

Thus what is needed are new measures of internationalisation that capture more of what is going on on the asset side of companies balance sheets, or which look directly at productive activity accounted for by foreign affiliates as registered in a country's national accounts. But here there are major problems of access to relevant and appropriate information.

3.   Alternative Company Based Measures

In any scrutiny of company accounts, for instance, it is important to recognise what companies are doing on their 'home' territory at the same time as they are investing and operating abroad. FDI flows only capture what companies are 'lending' to their affiliates abroad not what they are at the same time investing in their home country or territory. Even where there is some assessment of the extent of foreign owned assets by MNCs, the companies included are usually those already classified by the extent of their foreign owned assets, thereby prematurely skewing the analysis in favour of the overseas orientation of company activity (UN 1997: 29–31, Table 1.7).

In work reported in detail elsewhere I have developed three large scale cross-sectional data sets designed to circumvent some of these problems (see Hirst and Thompson 1996; Allen and Thompson 1997). The first of these contains information for 1987 on the sales, assets, profits, and subsidiaries and affiliates of over five hundred MNCs from five countries: Canada, Germany, Japan, UK and USA. The second set contains information for 1990 on these aspects for manufacturing multinationals. The third set gives data for sales and assets for 1993 of over five thousand MNCs from six countries: France, Germany, Japan, Netherlands, UK and USA.[1] The fact that these data are classified for home territory activity as well as for that conducted overseas by companies from these countries allows us to more accurately judge the extent of the internationalisation of their activity. Note that these data do not indicate flows across borders but the results of such flows as expressed in terms of the ex-post economic activity they have engendered.

A way of integrating the analysis of the data sets for different years can be seen in Table 2 which reports the distribution of manufacturing subsidiaries and affiliates (S&As) for 1987 and 1990. Some interesting differences between the countries emerge. First, just 41 per cent of Japanese S&As were home-country based in 1990, while 78 per cent of German S&As were located in Europe. Other than this difference, home country based S&As were again evident, though for US and Canadian firms Europe was a particularly important site for S&As. Clearly, the USA and Canada operate much like a single integrated North American economy for US and Canadian international firms. Perhaps surprisingly the UK was not as well represented in the USA as might have been expected. But Latin America figured as a relatively important destination for all the countries in the case of S&As.

These data are summarised in Table 3 in terms of the proportions allocated to the home-nation/region. Canada is the least 'home centred' economy, followed by the USA and Japan. Germany remains highly concentrated in Europe. Indeed, its concentration on this area seems to have increased a little between 1987 and 1990.

Tables 4 and 5 provide added comparable results for sales and assets, integrating the 1993 analysis into the picture and also looking at the service sector position. Table 4 provides the relevant figures for sales activity. It compares the percentage distribution of MNC sales to the home-region for the country company-sets, for which there was data in 1987, 1990 and 1993 (the 'home region' is common for all these data, which includes the home country).[2] Clearly, although these data should be treated with some caution, they provide a reasonable guide to the magnitudes involved. The importance of the home base for manufacturing

Table 2: *Distribution of Subsidiaries and Affiliates of Manufacturing MNC's: 1987 and 1990 (%)*

	Europe		USA		Canada		Africa		SE Asia		Japan		Middle East		Caribbean		Latin America		Pacific Rim		Other	
	1987	1990	1987	1990	1987	1990	1987	1990	1987	1990	1987	1990	1987	1990	1987	1990	1987	1990	1987	1990	1987	1990
Canada	27	31	22	23	34	24	1	2	3	4	2	1	0	0	2	3	5	6	4	4	1	1
Germany	76	78	7	8	3	2	2	2	3	3	2	1	0	0	0	0	5	4	2	1	0	0
Japan	15	17	13	14	2	2	1	1	13	17	49	41	1	1	0	0	5	4	2	3	0	0
UK	64	60	13	11	2	3	7	7	5	7	1	1	1	1	0	1	3	3	4	5	0	0
USA	27	29	44	38	5	5	2	2	5	7	2	3	1	1	2	2	9	10	3	3	1	0

Source: Own 1987 and 1990 data files.

Table 3: *Percentage Distribution of Manufacturing Subsidiaries & Affiliates to Home Country/Region 1987 and 1990*

Country	1987	1990
Canada	56	47
Germany	76	78
Japan	62	58
UK	64	60
USA	58	53

Note: Home country/region defined as:
Canada   = Canada and USA
Germany = Germany and rest of Europe
Japan   = Japan and S.E. Asia
UK   = UK and rest of Europe
USA   = USA, Canada and Latin America

Source: Own 1987 and 1990 data files

Table 4: *Percentage Distribution of MNC's Sales to Home Country/Region 1987, 1990 and 1993*

Country	Manufacturing			Services	
	1987	1990	1993	1987	1993
Canada	n.a.	77	n.a.	n.a.	n.a.
Germany	72	75	75	n.a.	n.a.
Japan	64	65	75	89	77
UK	66	59	65	74	77
USA	70	63	67	93	79

Note: n.a. = not available

Source: Own 1987, 1990 and 1993 data files.

sales remained about the same for Germany, the UK and the USA between 1987 and 1993, whereas it increased for Japan. For services there was a decrease for Japan and the USA, and a slight increase for the UK.

As far as asset data is concerned, the results of a similar exercise are presented in Table 5.[3] Overall these display a slightly less home country/regional bias than do the sales figures (which is perhaps surprising — we might have expected MNCs sales to be more internationalised than their assets). In as much as one can draw any generalisations from these figures it seems that manufacturing asset distributions became more home-country/regionally biased between the late-1980s and early-1990s, while for services USA companies became less concentrated (I am less happy about drawing any strong conclusions from Japanese data, however, particularly as far as services are concerned).

Finally we can turn to profit data. This is the least satisfactory from the point of view of data availability, and only the results shown in Figure 2 could be

Table 5: *Percentage Distribution of MNC's Assets to Home Country/Region 1987, 1990 and 1993*

Country	Manufacturing			Services	
	1987	1990	1993	1987	1993
Canada	n.a.	74	n.a.	n.a.	n.a.
Japan	n.a.	n.a.	97	77	92
UK	52	48	62	n.a.	69
USA	67	66	73	81	77

Note: n.a. = not available

Source: Own 1987, 1990 and 1993 data files.

generated. It provides gross profit distributions for four sets of country manufacturing companies for 1990. Profit distribution follows the pattern established by other indicators: the centrality of 'home country/region' as the site of profit declaration (if not generation — these data do not allow us to distinguish between where profits were generated and where they were declared). Clearly the UK, and to a lesser extent US, manufacturing companies are the ones most open to profit declaration in other than the home region/country.

These data are clearly not ideal since for the most part the way the data is recorded in company accounts only allows for the allocation of their activities as between their 'home region' as defined in endnote 2. However, for some of the data and countries, and for some years, it was possible to disaggregate this into a home country allocation (as shown to a large extent in Table 2, and for 1993 data on the other measures), which confirmed the basic home centredness of the data as presented in these tables and the figure (see Allen and Thompson 1997 in particular).

The main conclusion to be drawn from this analysis is an obvious one. The 'home orientated' nature of MNC activity along all the dimensions looked at remains significant, even if this could be a regionally centred one. Thus MNCs still rely upon their 'home base' as the centre for their economic activities, despite all the speculation about globalisation. From these results we should be reasonably confident that, in the aggregate, international companies are still predominantly MNCs (with a clear home base to their operations) and not transnational corporations (TNCs) (which represent footloose stateless companies). As indicated above there are two aspects to this home-centredness. One is the role of the 'home country' and the other that of the 'home region'. As far as the data can be disaggregated, in 1993 home country biases were as significant as the home region biases found in 1987. Given that it is only possible to specify an aggregated regional breakdown for 1987 and 1990, then strictly speaking the three cross-sectional analyses can only be compared on this basis. But these confirm that as

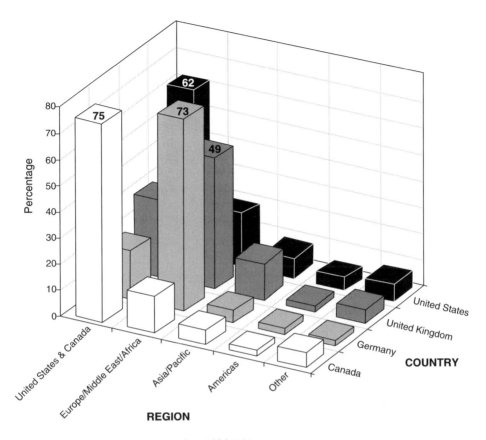

Figure 2. *The distribution of Profits, 1990 (%)*

Source: Data Files.

much as between two thirds and three-quarters of MNC aggregate business activity remains centred on the home region in this sense.

However, it is worth raising a possible caveat to this conclusion, which will be additionally explored below. A strong features of the globalisation thesis is that joint-ventures, partnerships, strategic alliances and liaisons are drawing firms into increasingly interdependent international networks of business activity. The relatively 'open' dispersion of S&As as demonstrated by Tables 1 and 2 could indicate this. A potential problem, then, with the quantitative data presented in this chapter so far is that it does not capture this qualitative change in company business strategies. The fact that only 25 per cent to 30 per cent of company activity is conducted abroad does not of itself tell us anything about the strategic importance of that 25 per cent to 30 per cent to the overall business activity of firms. It might represent the key to their performative success both internationally and domestically. The fact that we have seen a wider international dispersion of S&As could be taken as an indicator of this 'networking' trend in operation. We address this further below.

4.   Measures of Internationalisation from National Accounts Data

The adjustments to measures of internationalisation made up to now do not exhaust those needed to properly assess the popular belief that MNCs are now so footloose that they are undermining the continued viability of national economies or national systems of business. They need supplementing by examining the extent of internationalisation in relation to overall national output, and then with that derived directly from national account statistics. This gives some added insights into the true extent of internationalisation.

The data in Table 6 shows the estimated gross product that foreign affiliates were responsible for producing compared to the GDP of various country groupings and the world total. Note that for the developed countries this only increased from 5.1 per cent in 1982 to 5.4 per cent in 1994 (despite the massive increase in FDI flows over this period); from 6 per cent to 9.1 per cent (i.e. an admittedly 50 per cent increase) for the developing countries; and from 5.2 per cent to 6.0 per cent for the world total overall. But these hardly seem dramatic levels or major growth rates for the crucial developed countries where fears of the end of national business systems are most pronounced.

In addition, the data in Table 7 reveals the importance of FDI inflows as a contribution to the gross fixed domestic capital formation (GDFCF) in a range of country groupings. Again, what is significant here is the relative unimportance of FDI flows in their contribution to domestic investment (even accepting the criticisms of this measure as outlined above). In a number of cases the contribution

Table 6: *Gross Product of Foreign Affiliates as a % of GDP (1982, 1990 and 1994)*

Region	1982	1990	1994
World	5.2	6.7	6.0
Developed Countries	5.1	6.7	5.4
European Union	5.7	8.6	7.7
North America	5.1	6.7	5.2
Developing Countries	6.0	7.0	9.1
Latin America & the Caribbean	7.6	9.3	10.3
Asia	5.6	5.9	8.6
South East Asia	5.0	7.0	9.0
Central & Eastern Europe	0.1	1.1	2.3

Source: Adapted from UN (1997: 267, Table A4)

of FDI to GDFCF actually fell in the mid-1990s from that averaged over the late-1980s. It is clear from these figures that economies cannot borrow their way to prosperity via a reliance on FDI. What remains crucial to domestic development strategies is domestic savings, which still remain the main source of financial resources for domestic investment in all advanced and developing economies. It is still the nature of domestic financial systems that are crucial to the long-run developmental success of different economies.

Finally, it is worth considering various other detailed attempts to assess the extent of internationalised production as derived directly from national accounts and measures of national output. For 1990, for instance, Lipsey et al. (1995) calculated that foreign based output amounted to only about 7 per cent of overall world output (see also Table 6 above), up from 4.5 per cent in 1970 (Lipsey 1997: 2). Although the share was higher in industry (including manufacturing, trade, construction and public utilities) at about 15 per cent in 1990 (up from 11 per cent in 1977), it was negligible in services, which amounted to 60 per cent of total world output in 1990. By 1995 foreign based output was estimated to have increased to 7.5 per cent of total world output, hardly a dramatic and earth shattering change.

The story of US international firms is interesting in its own right. Their overseas output peaked in 1977 at about 8 per cent of US GDP, and has been declining ever since to about 5.5 per cent in 1995. In manufacturing the production

Table 7: *Share of Inward FDI flows in Gross Fixed Capital Formation (1985–1995 %)*

Region	Average 1985–90	1991	1992	1993	1994	1995
World	5.1	3.1	3.3	4.4	4.5	5.2
Developed Economies	5.5	3.2	3.2	3.7	3.5	4.4
of which: EU	9.1	5.4	5.5	5.9	5.0	6.8
(UK)	13.7	9.4	9.8	11.0	6.8	13.2
(Germany)	1.6	1.0	0.6	0.4	0.2	1.7
USA	5.3	3.1	2.4	4.9	4.8	5.9
Japan	0.2	0.2	0.2	–	0.1	–
Developing Economies	8.0	4.4	5.1	6.6	8.0	8.2
of which: LA & Caribbean	11.3	7.8	8.1	7.2	10.3	11.0
(Brazil)	3.1	1.4	3.0	1.3	3.0	4.7
Asia	7.6	3.4	4.2	6.5	7.2	7.5
South, East & SE Asia	9.7	3.8	4.7	7.5	8.3	9.0
Central & Eastern Europe	1.0	0.4	0.8	7.9	5.0	5.2

Source: Compiled from UN (1997, Annex: Table B.5).

by majority-owned US foreign affiliates was 15.5 per cent of US manufacturing output in 1977, reaching over 17 per cent in 1990, but settling back to 16 per cent in 1995, i.e. it has remained almost stable over the past twenty years. In terms of employment the trends have been similar. There was a rapid increase in US firms' employment overseas relative to that at home from 1957 to 1977, but since then the trend has been a decreasing one. In 1994 the foreign manufacturing affiliate employment of US firms remained well below its 1977 level. Most of these decreases in the overseas proportion of US firms' production and employment can be accounted for by the relative decline in the importance of the manufacturing sector in the US economy as a whole. In fact, the story of the internationalisation of the US manufacturing sector has really been one confined to the inward side. MNC production in the USA as a proportion of GDP rose from almost zero in 1970 to just over 8 per cent in 1995, and in the manufacturing sector from 4 per cent in 1977 to 13 per cent in 1994 (Ramstetter 1998: 195, Figure 8.3).

The story of the Japanese economy is almost the reverse of the one for the USA. There has been virtually no growth in the importance of overseas production to GDP in Japan, indeed in terms of directly measured output indicators the trend has been a declining one (Ramstetter 1998: 194, Figure 8.2). On the other hand, Japanese multinationals have been expanding their activities abroad relative to their production at home. For all Japanese manufacturing companies the overseas production ratio doubled from 5 per cent in 1985 to nearly 10 per cent in 1996 (for only those companies with overseas affiliates this ratio also doubled, from about 13.5 per cent to 27.5 per cent over the same period; MITI 1997). Given Japanese overall output growth rates, however, absolute levels of these ratios relative to GDP are low and changes have been modest.

Similar calculations as these for the other advanced countries are not readily available. The broad picture is indicated by the data contained in Table 6. But for the Asia-Pacific region as a whole Ramstetter (1998: 208) has produced a comprehensive survey along these lines, in particular comparing FDI based indicators with those derived directly from national accounting data, the results of which are worth quoting:

> "[The finding that] FDI-based indicators and foreign MNC shares of production often display very different trends, strongly suggests that FDI-related indicators are rather poor indicators of foreign MNC presence. More specifically, since foreign MNC shares of production are clearly more accurate measures of foreign MNC presence, focussing on FDI-related measures apparently leads to significant over-estimation of the extent to which MNC presence has grown in the Asia Pacific region since the 1970s."

This remains a salutary warning for all those approaches that stress the simple growth of FDI flows and stocks as indicating the necessary growth of a global business environment. And it is in respect of these business based approaches towards globalisation and its supposed consequences that this chapter now turns.

5.   Business Stategy and the Future of National Systems

It is the Bartlett and Ghoshal (1989) typology of different forms of international company that has struck a chord with those researchers concentrating upon company-form and the analysis of company-strategy. Building upon their suggestions it is possible to draw a conceptual distinction between four organisational types of global business; labelled multinational, global, international and transnational respectively. The outline characteristics of these types of companies are:

- those that build upon a strong local presence through sensitivity and responsiveness to national differences (their 'multinational companies');
- those that build cost advantages through centralised global-scaled operations (their 'global companies');
- those that exploit parent company knowledge and capabilities through worldwide diffusion and adaptation (their 'international companies');
- those that disperse their activities to relatively independent and specialised units seeking to be globally competitive through multinational flexibility and world-wide knowledge development and learning capabilities (their 'transnational companies').

Thus broadly speaking these forms proceed from a more national focus to a greater transnational one. An attempt to empirically test for these organisational types found that the most common remained the multinational type whilst the least common was the transnational type (Leong and Tan 1993). This finding set the trend for further empirical work that cast a doubt on the full development of the global economy and the transnational type of corporate form; the majority of 'international' firms still remain tethered to a definite national country base, confirming the analysis above.

5.1 Technology

The issue of innovation and the role of technology is another dimension along which the process of company internationalisation is often thought to be rapidly proceeding, and which is used to bolster the argument about the globalisation of company activity. Again, there is little systematic company based evidence about how much of this remains parent country focused rather than overseas focussed, but what evidence is available broadly supports the conlcusion that this type of activity remains far from fully globalized. For instance, in their analysis of the international distribution of R&D laboratories of 500 major firms, Casson, Pearce, and Singh (1992) found some degree of interdependency, but it varied greatly between two parent country firms. Firms from the Netherlands, Switzerland, West-Germany and the UK showed significant foreign orientation (the international to home ratio of laboratories for companies from these countries were all over 60 per cent), while the other nine countries or groupings showed considerably lower ratios (the average ratio was 39 per cent). The dominant country in terms of number of companies and total laboratories, the USA, had a ratio of only 31 per cent, confirming it as a relatively 'closed' country on this measure. Countries like Japan and Sweden also remain very closed. In addition, papers by Patel and Pavitt (1991) and Patel (1995) indicate that on other measures of technological activity, such as patent registration, no more than 10 per cent of patents granted to international firms by the US patent office originated from foreign subsidiaries, and that the share of patents coming from foreign subsidiaries did not substantially increase between 1969 and 1986, nor between 1986 and 1990 (based upon the analysis of 686 of the worlds largest manufacturing companies). The home territory remained the dominant site for the location of this form of R&D activity, reinforcing the local innovation system.

But patent registration represents an intermediate 'output' end of innovative activity. When it is supplemented by direct 'input' data associated with R&D expenditures, there is also little evidence of any systematic change in the location or composition of this type of investment as between the advanced countries over the period from 1970 to 1990 (Archibugie and Michie 1997). Thus these national and company-based studies conclude that at most only between 10 per cent and 30 per cent of the technological activity of multinationals is likely to be located in foreign subsidiaries. As Patel (1995: 151) comments: "The main conclusion of this paper is that there is no systematic evidence to suggest that widespread globalisation of the production of technology has occured in the 1980s."

5.2 *Behavioural Characteristics*

These findings about technology are reinforced by the detailed empirical analysis of Pauly and Reich (1997) into the characteristic features of US, German and Japanese MNCs. They argue that there are systematic differences between the strategies adopted by MNCs originating from each of these three countries in the areas of research and development, corporate governance and finance, and investment and intra-firm trade, which arise from deeply entrenched socio-economic institutional characteristics and cultures of the three countries. The broad but complex nature of the US, the German and the Japanese business systems are still intact, they argue, and these have heavily marked the MNCs origination

Table 8: *Multinational Corporate Structures and Strategies*

	United States	Germany	Japan
Direct investment	Extensive inward and outward	Selective/outward orientation	Extensive outward; limited competition from inward
Intrafirm trade	Moderate	Higher	Very high
Research and development	Fluctuating; diversified; innovation oriented	Narrow base/process, diffusion orientation	High, steady growth; high-technology and process orientation
Corporate governance	Short-term shareholding; managers highly constrained by capital markets; risk-seeking, financial-centred strategies	Managerial autonomy except during crises; no take-over risk; conservative, long-term strategies	Stable shareholders; networked-constrained managers; take-over risk only within network/aggressive market share-centred strategies
Corporate financing	Diversified, global funding; highly price sensitive	Concentrated, regional funding; limited price sensitivity	Concentrated, national funding; low price sensitivity

Source: Pauly and Reich (1997: 23, Table 4).

from these countries as their own activities have internationalised. In terms of R&D, Japanese firms conduct remarkably little R&D abroad and German firms have made significant R&D commitments in the USA but little elsewhere. For the companies from these two counties the vast bulk of their R&D effort is directed either to the customisation of products for local markets or the gathering of knowledge for transfer back home. The companies from these two countries thus organise their overseas R&D to either bolster their domestic innovation systems, or to enhance their capacity to export from their domestic economies — 'trade creating' activity (this conclusion for Japan is strongly confirmed by the analysis of Fransman 1997 and Yoshitomi 1996). US companies, by contrast, conform closely to their 'national type' in conducting much more of their R&D abroad, and using this to provide substitute overseas production sites for 'trade displacing' activity. These different investment, R&D and trade strategies are reinforced, it is argued, by the domestic corporate governance systems in which the parent companies are located. The well known nature of the links between banks and commercial enterprises, the complex cross holding of shares in some of the countries, the differential role of the stock-exchanges in each country, and the type of behaviour this engenders, were not being undermined but being reinforced, according to this analysis. Recognizably different behavioural patterns persist in the leading MNCs' strategic orientation towards the internationalisation of their activities. Table 8 sums up the conclusions of Pauly and Reich's analysis.

5.3 *The Reorganisation of Production?*

The analysis of Pauly and Reich (1997) provides a bridge between the formal quantitative analysis of MNC activity and the more qualitative approach to the organisation of the business of innovative product development and competitive success. Often this approach is based upon case studies, something relatively ignored by this chapter up to now. In addition, their approach essentially stresses the effects of particular national business systems on the companies that operate internationally from them. Another way of approaching this issue is to look at what effects the introduction of a MNC from abroad might have upon an already established business system. It is now time to bring these elements into the picture.

The classic way economics tackles the analysis of technology and innovation is via the production function approach. Production is conceived in a 'linear' form where a series of inputs are marshalled and combined together to produce an output. Innovation is introduced into these models via the addition of another input measured by some variable associated with technological advance; the number of patents registered, number of scientists and engineers, number and location of R&D laboratories, R&D expenditures, etc. The linear model also describes the innovation process as a sequence of stages; from research to development, then to production, and finally to marketing, where there is little communication or connection between these stages.

In contrast to this linear model, however, it has become increasingly clear that there is a lot more to innovation than just the application of another 'resource input' or the organisation of a sequence of separated stages. Non-linear, looped and feedback models recognise the existence of many 'intangible' assets in the innovation process; those associated with incremental learning, tacit knowledge, with the locational 'milieu' in which companies operate, with the habits, conventions and routines that serve to 'socially organise' the production process, etc. One significant way of expressing these aspects is as 'untraded interdependencies' (Storper 1995). They represent an 'asset' that cannot be easily identified as a measurable input into the production process. Rather they exist as locationally specific 'externalities' which firms can only access by actually setting up operations within the location in question. This can account for the significant development of 'innovation without R&D' that is usually associated with local and regional economic districts. In part this 'innovation without R&D' has to do with process innovation but also with incremental product innovations based upon how the innovation process is differentially spatially organised.

These issues, then, bring back into the picture the spatially and locationally specific business systems as a central element for firms' innovative activity and competitive performance (see also the contributions of Deakin et al. and Lehrer and Darbishire to this volume).

Drawing on these considerations enables us to make sense of the way international firms look for particular comparative and competitive strengths in locational advantages associated with national or regional production, innovation and business systems. MNCs thus seek to tap into the advantages offered by particular locations so as to strengthen their overall competitive performance and success. They often look for quite small advantages associated with a specific part of their overall production process — creating complex international divisions of labour based upon locational specialisation. Take the Jæren district of Norway as an example (Asheim and Isaksen 1997: 317–18). This has specialised in the production of advanced industrial robots. A leading local firm (Trallfa Robot) was taken over by the Swiss-Swedish MNC ABB in the late 1980s (creating ABB Flexible Automation). ABB produced most of its robots for the European car makers in Västerås in Sweden, but instead of restructuring by closing down the Jæren plant and moving production to Sweden, ABB increased capacity and employment in its Norwegian subsidiary in order to capture the specialist externalities available in the local area. It this way the presence of ABB has strengthened the local innovative and business system, rather than undermined it.

Another example of a similar process can be seen by the way that German bank multinationals have tapped into the comparative advantages of the City of London's financial system, without necessarily undermining either that systems operation or their own domestic activities (Soskice 1997: 76–77; Morgan and Quack in this volume). Deutsche Bank, Dresdner Bank, the Norddeutsche Landesbank and Commerzbank have all moved — or are in the process of moving — their international operations away from Frankfurt to London. But they have maintained their domestic operations — those that support the high skill competence and long-term relationship associated with local manufacturing — within Germany. Similarly, German chemical firms like BASF, Bayer and Hoechst have run down their biotechnology operations in Germany and concentrated them in the USA where there is a technical and organisational advantage. Meanwhile their mainstream high value-added chemical research and production is still concentrated in Germany.

These changes in the conduct of international business can be characterised in terms of the introduction of sophisticated networks of specialisation and value-added. In some sectors these may not even involve any direct investment overseas. The development of cross-border production networks that assemble diverse points of innovation do so by drawing in independent indigenous suppliers who link into the commodity chain, or chains of system assembly and standard setting (Borrus and Zysman 1997), without this requiring an explicit physical investment strategy on the part of the lead MNC firm. The MNC only acts as the 'organiser' of the independent, part-contractors and sub-system assemblers that occupy the strategic positions in the network. Thus here we have the internationalisation of production without any necessary overseas investment. Borrus and Zysman probably exaggerate the extent of this as a new paradigm for global competition that all sectors will follow (which they call 'Wintelism' — combining Windows and Intel type production technologies), but it captures elements of a number of well recognised developments in international business (for an analysis of similar trends in the telecommunications sector, see Loveridge and Mueller in this volume).

An example of this is the way Singapore has developed a comparative advantage in hard disk drive (HDD) production and assembly, based upon the technological and organisational innovativeness of its local firms (but also supplemented initially by MNC investment (Wong 1997)). Subsequent spin-off developments and new local investment have served to strengthen the production and innovation system. Nor is this based upon any labour cost advantage, since direct and indirect labour costs only amount to 6 per cent of the total cost of a HDD (Wong: 199, Table 7). The Singapore element in several complex transnational production networks for computer equipment is now well established. The key point to recognise from these examples is summed up by Borrus and Zysman (1997: 143):

> "This era is [...] one in which an increasingly global market coexists with enduring national foundations of distinctive economic growth trajectories and corporate strategies. Globalisation has not led to the elimination of national systems of production. National systems endure; but they are evolving together in a world economy that increasingly has a regional structure."[4]

6.   Conclusion

The argument of this chapter has involved a number of points. The first is that the extent of the internationalisation of business activity is often exaggerated in both popular and academic accounts. Nor is it increasing at a particularly dramatic rate. From the quantitative analysis reported in the first part of the paper it is reasonable to suggest that between 65–70 per cent of MNC value-added continues to be produced on the home territory. This conclusion coincides with the arguments of Tyson (1991), Kapstein (1991) and Lazonick (1993) in their debate with Reich (1990, 1991) about the nature of international business (see also Hu 1992, 1995). The former authors challenged Reich on his assumption that American business had gone 'transnational', and that this did not matter. Tyson (1991: 38) pointed out that: "Within manufacturing, US parent operations account for 78 percent of total assets, 70 percent of total sales, and 70 percent of total employment of US multinational in 1988". The analysis reported here confirms this finding for a wider range of countries.

But there has obviously been some internationalisation of business activity. Thus a second issue was to assess the strategies of companies that originated from different business systems. Despite the home centredness of the main findings, the remaining activity of the country groupings is quite diverse. That is, the different country MNCs operate in different areas to different extents. The MNCs are not all the same in terms of the geographical spread of their extra-home territorial activity, nor in the way they have gone about internationalising their activities. Here it was argued that the production and business systems of the originating countries still marked the MNCs with a particular approach and attitude.

Connected to this is the question of what effects the limited internationalisation of business activity is having on national systems of business, of production and innovation. Here the argument is that this has yet to develop to such an extent that national systems are being radically undermined, transformed or rendered redundant. Indeed, in many ways these systems are being reinforced and strengthened by the internationalisation of business. Firms are locking themselves into the advantages offered by particular locational production configurations, which are enhancing their ability to compete. In addition, the continuation of a clear home centredness for most MNCs also needs to be recognised as providing them with advantages that they will not easily give up.

Finally, it is worth raising the issue of the 'governance' consequences of this analysis. These are twofold. In the first place, if national systems of production, business and technology still remain firmly embedded, then there is still scope for the management of these in the interests of the stability and productivity of the national economy. Secondly, given that MNCs remain tethered to their home economies, whether this is nationally specified or regionally so, this provides the opportunity for national or regional bodies to more effectively monitor, regulate and govern them than if they were genuinely 'footloose capital'.

Thus the overall conclusion of the chapter is that the extent of internationalisation and its potential detrimental consequences for the regulation of MNC activity and for national economies is severely exaggerated. International businesses are still largely confined to their home territory in terms of their overall activity; they remain heavily 'nationally embedded'.

Notes

1. In 1993 the six most important country investors abroad were: USA ($50,244m), UK ($25,332m), Japan ($13,600m), France ($12,166m), Germany ($11,673m), and Netherlands ($10,404m) (OECD 1993: 16). Thus this analysis covers the main externally investing countries in the late 1980s and early 1990s.

2. Thus the 'home region' for German companies in all years comprises Germany itself, the rest of Europe, the Middle East and Africa (although these latter two areas account for very little overall sales); 'home region' for Japanese companies comprises Japan and S. E. Asia; for the UK it comprises the UK itself, the rest of Europe, the Middle East and Africa (again, where the latter two areas were not very important); and for US companies it includes the US and Canada. These aggregations are dictated by the way it was possible to code the 1987 data.

3. Assets are measured as total assets for these calculations (total assets includes financial assets and inventories as well as fixed assets). A better indicator would be either net fixed assets or operating assets, which indicate more closely to the real capital stock. These were not extractable from the company accounts. Thus these data probably overestimate the value of real capital assets involved. These problems become more acute for some of the financial institutions included in the 'service' category of companies.

4. The analysis conducted here mainly refers to manufacturing, banking and new IT technologies. But the traditional service sectors are also internationalising, as indicated by the quantitative analysis reported above. In fact, the case of accounting and law firms largely confirms the points already made about the way strategic management of these firms, and the way they 'fit' into the business systems where they are newly locating, is proceeding (see Barrett et al. 1997, and Spar 1997).

References

Allen, J., and G. F. Thompson. 1997. Think Global, and Then Think Again — Economic Globalisation in Context, *Area* 29(3): 213–27.

Archibugi, D., and J. Michie. 1997. The Globalisation of Technology: a New Taxonomy. In: D. Archibugie and J. Michie (eds.), *Technology, Globalisation and Economic Performance*, 172–197. Cambridge: Cambridge University Press.

Asheim, B. T., and A. Isaksen. 1997. Location, Agglomeration and Innovation: Towards Regional Innovation Systems in Norway?, *European Planning Studies* 5(3): 299- 330.

Barrett, M., D. J. Cooper, and K. Jamal. 1997. "That's Pretty Close" and the "Friction of Space": Managing a Global Audit. In: H. K. Rasmussen (ed.), *Accounting Time and Space, Proceedings 1*, 217–295. Copenhagen: Copenhagen Business School.

Bartlett, C. A., and S. Ghoshal. 1989. *Managing Across Borders — The Transnational Solution.* Boston: Harvard Business School Press.

Borrus, M., and J. Zysman. 1997. Globalization with Borders: The Rise of Wintelism as the Future of Global Competition, *Industry and Innovation* 4(2): 141–66.

Casson, M., R. D. Pearce, and S. Singh. 1992. Global Integration through the Decentralisation of R&D. In: M. Casson (ed.), *International Business and Global Integration.* Basingstoke: Macmillan.

Chesnais, F. 1991. National Systems of Innovation, Foreign Direct Investment and the Operations of Multinational Enterprises. In: B.-A. Ludvall (ed.), *National Systems of Innovation: Towards a Theory of Innovations and Interactive Learning*, 265–295. London: Pinter Publishers.

Dicken, P., M. Forsgren, and A. Malmberg. 1994. The Local Embeddedness of Transnational Corporations. In: A. Amin, and N. Thrift (eds.), *Globalization, Institutions, and Regional Development in Europe*, 23–45. Oxford: Oxford University Press.

Fransman, M. 1997. Is National Technology Policy Obsolete in a Globalised World? The Japanese Response. In: D. Archibugi, and J. Michie (eds.), *Technology, Globalisation and Economic Performance*, 50–82. Cambridge: Cambridge University Press.

Graham, E. M. 1996. *Global Corporations and National Governments*. Washington, DC: Institute for International Economics.

Hirst, P. Q., and G. F. Thompson. 1996. *Globalization in Question: The International Economy and the Possibilities of Governance*. Cambridge: Polity Press.

Hollingsworth, J. R., and R. Boyer (eds.). 1996. *Contemporary Capitalism: The Embeddedness of Institutions*. Cambridge: Cambridge University Press.

Hu, Y.-S. 1992. Global or Stateless Firms are National Corporations with International Operations, *California Management Review* 34(2) Winter: 107–126.

Hu, Y.-S. 1995. The International Transferability of the Firm's Advantage, *California Management Review* 37(4) Summer: 73–88.

International Finance Corporation. 1997. *Foreign Direct Investment*, Washington, DC: International Finance Corporation.

Kapstein, E. B. 1991. We are us: the myth of the multi-national, *The National Interest,*. Winter 1991/92: 55–62.

Lazonick, W. 1993. Industry Clusters versus Global Webs: Organizational Capabilities in the American Economy, *Industrial and Corporate Change* 2(2): 1–21.

Lazonick, W., and M. O'Sullivan. 1996. Organization, Finance and International Competition, *Industrial and Corporate Change* 5(1): 1–49.

Leong, S. M., and C. T. Tan. 1993. Managing Across Borders: An Empirical Test of the Bartlett and Ghoshal [1989] Organizational Typology, *Journal of International Business Studies* 24(3): 449–64.

Lipsey, R. E. 1997. Global Production Systems and Local Labour Conditions, Conference on International Solidarity and Globalisation, 27–28 October, Stockholm.

Lipsey, R. E., M. Blomström, and E. Ramstetter. 1995. Internationalized Production in World Output, *NBER Working Paper 5385*, December, Cambridge, Mass.

MITI. 1997. *The 6th Basic Survey of Overseas Business Activities*. Tokyo: MITI (http://www.jef.or.jp/news/970508.html).

Mueller, F. 1994. Societal Effect, Organizational Effect and Globalization, *Organization Studies* 15(3): 407–28.

OECD. 1993. *Financial Market Trends*, Issue No. 58. Paris: OECD.

Patel, P. 1995. Localised Production of Technology for Global Markets, *Cambridge Journal of Economics* 19: 141–153.

Patel, P., and K. Pavitt. 1991. Large Firms in the Production of the World's Technology: An Important Case of "Non-Globalisation", *Journal of International Business Studies* 22(1): 1–21.

Pauly, L. W., and S. Reich. 1997. National Structures and Multinational Behaviour: Enduring
    Differences in the Age of Globalization, *International Organizations* 51(1): 1–30.
Ramstetter, E. 1998. Measuring the Size of Foreign Multinationals in the Asia Pacific.
    In: G. F. Thompson (ed.), *Economic Dynamism in the Asia-Pacific: The Growth of
    Integration and Competitiveness*. London: Routledge.
Reich, R. B. 1990. Who Is Us?, *Harvard Business Review,* January-February: 53–64.
Reich, R. B. 1991. *The Work of Nations*. New York: Alfred Knopf.
Soskice, D. 1991. The Institutional Infrastructure for International Competitiveness: A
    Comparative Analysis of the UK and Germany. In: A. B. Atkinson, and R. Brunetta
    (eds.), *Economics of the New Europe*, 45–66. New York: University Press.
Soskice, D. 1997. German Technology Policy, Innovation, and National Institutional
    Frameworks, *Industry and Innovation* 4(1): 75–96.
Spar, D. L. 1997. Lawyers Abroad: The Internationalization of Legal Practice, *California
    Management Review* 37(3), Spring: 8–28.
Storper, M. 1995. The Resurgence of Regional Economies, Ten Years Later: The Region
    as a Nexus of Untraded Interdependencies, *European Urban and Regional Studies*
    2(3): 191–221.
Tiberi-Vipraio, P. 1996. From Local to Global Networking: The Restructuring of Italian
    Industrial Districts, *Journal of Industry Studies* 3(2): 135–51.
Tyson, L. 1991. They are not us: why American ownership still matters, *The American
    Prospect,* Winter: 37–49.
United Nations. 1997. *World Investment Report 1997: Transnational Corporations, Market
    Structure and Competition Policy.* United Nations Conference on Trade and Develop-
    ment, United Nations, New York and Geneva.
Whitley, R. (ed.). 1992. *European Business Systems. Firms and Markets in their National
    Contexts.* London: Sage.
Whitley, R., and P. H. Kristensen (eds.). 1996. *The Changing European Firm. Limits to
    Convergence.* London: Routledge.
Whitley, R., and P. H. Kristensen (eds.). 1997. *Governance at Work: The Social Regulation
    of Economic Relations.* Oxford: Oxford University Press.
Wong, P.-K. 1997. Creation of a Regional Hub for Flexible Production: The Case of the
    Hard Disk Drive Industry in Singapore, *Industry and Innovation* 4(2): 183–206.
Yoshitomi, M. 1996. On the Changing International Competitiveness of Japanese
    Manufacturing Since 1985, *Oxford Review of Economic Policy* 12(3), Autumn: 61–73.

CHAPTER 10

Flagships, Flotillas and Corvettes
Corporate Actors, National Business Systems and Sectoral Dynamics in Telecommunications[*]

Ray Loveridge   Frank Mueller

1. Introduction

In this paper we propose to examine the recent history of sectoral boundary changes with specific reference to the telecommunications sector. We will demonstrate shifts between different levels of a global system over time, and the effect that this has had on nationally-based capabilities. In the case of telecommunications international regulation has been in existence for over a century but national suppliers were generally publicly owned and met international standards in relatively idiosyncratic ways. Over the past twenty years the technological convergence of computing, satellite, cable transmission and telecommunications services has brought about major changes in products, and in the firms supplying the various industrial markets on a now global basis.

In this global arena old sectoral boundaries are no longer distinct. Instead flagship firms provide important coordinating nodes in networks of suppliers, often on a concurrent or simultaneously tiered basis. In such alliances functions such as software provision or revenue sharing constitute common dependencies. The nationally specific path by which a former national provider assumes the role of an international 'flagship' might be assumed to provide significant competitive advantages. However these advantages seem to be capable of dissipation in the face of competition from more agile 'corvettes' who have been more successful in providing solutions for the complex technological problems presented by interfaces within the global network. As a result there appears to be a widening, rather than narrowing, of strategic options, whilst national actors

* We are grateful to Glenn Morgan, David Parker and Sigrid Quack for valuable comments. All remaining errors are the sole responsibility of the authors.

appear to be under pressure to move outside of institutionalised constraints upon their power to choose.

2. The Telecommunications Sector

During the early 19th century most Western governments established state-run postal services, often reviving or bureaucratising earlier and more fragmented modes of communication. These, in turn, were conjoined by international business agreements that spread from Europe and USA up to the establishment of the International Postal Union (IPU), one of the first truly global organisations. Thus when telephony spread from the USA to Europe it did so through the medium of publicly established postal monopolies in most of the latter countries. These became transformed into service providers in the new telephonic market under the new label of post, telegraph and telephone administrations (PTTs). Towards the end of the last century the IPU spawned the body now known as the International Telecommunication Union (ITU) designed to mediate and monitor standards of communication across member countries world-wide.

Economically and institutionally, therefore, the industry is relatively unique in two important respects. The first is the degree of government sponsorship given to early service providers and in the creation of a nation-wide infrastructure. The second unusual feature of the industry is in the extent to which it was, from its origins, an international activity in which the price mechanism, of itself, would not bring about the necessary level of standardisation in mode and quality required for effective communication. The requirement for coordination in standards across national boundaries had already been recognised in the maritime sector, and was to be discovered in air transport and traffic control. But from the start telecommunications was more closely wedded to the setting of standards in technology than former attempts at permanent international alliances. Communication evidently depends upon both effective transmission, travel and reception and, whilst confined to cable and unmediated radio, there was a strong incentive for members of participating nations to ensure that each stage of the process took place effectively. But this requirement had to be set against the desire of each government in industrialised states to ensure that its economy developed a manufacturing sector associated with the new technology. Vertical or quasi-vertical integration within national boundaries became commonplace. Thus the practice of establishing a ring of 'preferred suppliers' — usually no more than two original equipment manufacturers — was the normal manner of supplying and developing the technological needs of publicly owned or regulated PTTs in each country.

In this way the global telecommunications sector represented a relatively stable inter-organisational network with its vertically ordered roots in the supply of equipment within each national economy. However it became evident by the middle of this century that large suppliers of electrical and electronic equipment were also supplying a telecommunications market that stretched beyond that of their parent country. These companies included GE in the USA, Siemens in Germany, Philips in the Netherlands, Ericsson in Sweden, Thomson and Alcatel in France and Plessey in Britain. Across a range of markets, but principally in telephonic equipment, these companies both *collaborated* (initially only through licensing and price-fixing) and *competed*.

3. The 'Information Super-Highway'

Until well into the 1980s it was possible to portray the structure of the cross-national telecommunications industry in terms not unlike those used by Chandler (1990) to describe the German business system i.e. as 'co-operative capitalism'. In each country the public telecommunications operators (PTOs) worked closely with their owner/regulator in national government and with their suppliers. Beyond their national boundaries they managed a communications system that was largely concentrated on the cable and wireless infrastructure of the developed countries and operated according to a 'web of rules' shaped by a common technology. Within each country the PTT provided an internal labour market in which long training and formal qualification provided entry to stable careers with relatively high occupationally related pensions and social benefits. Whilst equipment suppliers did not usually match the life-time benefits of these, largely publicly controlled service providers, they generally offered rewards and conditions that were among the best in their respective manufacturing sectors. Trade unions were generally strong in these heavily bureaucratised work contexts (Bain 1970); their officials figured highly in their national movements and gained easy access to government.

The effects of technological change were first felt in the contest to introduce digital exchanges beginning in the 1950s but not successfully achieved until the 1970s and only diffused in the 1980s. Originally conceived as a step towards improving the quality of service it became the means by which, so-called, generic intelligent network architecture was pioneered by Bell Communications Research in 1985 (Mansell 1993). This term subsumes a number of different ways in which computers can be positioned vis à vis the PTTs' switch board and the scope of the services they provide and the tasks they perform in such provisions. The supply of these computers need not be left to the PTTs and, indeed, the role of orchestrating the service output and demand input to such computers need not be left solely to the PTT. The concurrent development of satellite radio and television mediation, together with the networking capabilities of personal computers (both resulting from US Defense research and development expenditures), had greatly extended the range of contributing equipment suppliers, as well as an ever expanding scope of, so-called, value-adding service providers.

In many respects there has been a drastic change in the attitude of government towards the status of the telecommunications industry. From being a closely regulated or state owned monopoly it is now seen by most national governments as a sector in which only private capital can provide the massive amount of investment required in order to provide an appropriate range of technological options in a rapidly changing field. Since the early 1990s part or full privatisations through stock market flotations have taken place in Portugal, Italy, Australia, France, Spain, the Netherlands and Denmark (*Financial Times*, 19 November 1997). Consequently the development of new 'value-adding' services has been opened to competition among private providers in many countries. The former PTTs have taken on a new role as public telecommunication operators (PTOs) with a duty to provide exchange services and broad-band cable capacity for a variety of such service providers.

The development of satellite radio and television mediation has removed much of the technical uncertainty from global oral and visual communication. The monthly average US dollar revenues per cellular telephone subscriber have fallen consistently, from 200 in 1985 to around 65 in 1992 and further thereafter (*Economist*, Survey, 23rd October 1993). To the growing range of technical options has to be added pluralism in the forms of corporate ownership. Hence a single international telephone call can not only involve several media (high frequency radio, satellite, undersea cable etc), but also a variety of private service providers, each with their separate tariff of charges.

The sheer variety of media and modes of telecommunications provision make for a new complexity in managerial control and coordination. Some such as Mansell (1993) doubt the political capability of prevailing supra-national agencies to cope with these problems. One evident market-driven solution is that of allowing the emergence of greater integration in the provision of services and equipment through corporate alliances or direct mergers — a process encompassing markets, hierarchies and networks all in one. This is a process that might be expected to occur as the sector life-cycle moves from the entrepreneurial or architectural stage into one of shake-out and consolidation across new global markets (Abernathy et al. 1984). However the role of PTOs in the provision of open network architecture within each nation state remains pivotal both to the extension of the market for value-adding services and for the exercise of the national governments' ability to regulate that market.

The European Commission has been influential in opening access to markets for both equipment suppliers to national PTOs within the European Union and to providing access for so-called value-adding service providers to the public

Table 1: *Company Shares of the European Telecommunications Equipment Market (Community and EFTA Countries) 1987*

	Market share (%)
Alcatel (CGE/ITT)	31
Siemens	19
GEC/Plessey	15
Ericsson	9
Philips	5
IBM	5
GTE	3
Italtel	3
Other companies	12
Total	100

Source: Ungerer (1988: 129).

Table 2: *European Telecommunications Companies: Suppliers in the World Market 1987*

	Sales to: (in %)			
	Europe	N. America	Asia	Other
Alcatel (CGE/ITT)	70	10	13	7
Siemens	71	10	8	11
Ericsson	56	12	13	19
GEC	66	15	10	9
Philips	54	2	31	13
Plessey	74	13	3	10
Italtel	81	0	5	14

Source: Ungerer (1988: 94).

networks controlled by PTOs. Open Network Provision (ONP) was defined in a Green Paper published by the Commission in 1987 and translated into a series of Directives in 1990. These covered both standards for equipment testing certification, rules of procurement, terms of service and conditions of access to public network. The background to this was the disproportionate capture of the European telecommunications equipment market by European firms in the mid eighties (see Tables 1 and 2).

Ultimately, the objective was seen to be that of creating a level playing field for competition. The existent European Telecommunications Standards Institute (ETSI) was charged with implementing these directives and created the Strategic Coordination Group in order to involve existing PTOs in the process. The model taken was that already implemented by the Federal agencies in the USA, the so-called Open Network Architecture (ONA), but the sovereignty enjoyed by the latter was not present in the European context. Furthermore, the emergent nature of the technology made detailed specification problematic. By late 1991 only Germany, the Netherlands, Denmark and the UK had taken significant moves to implement ONA, and nationally divergent trajectories in regulating the use of satellites and the design of interfacing equipment and value-adding systems still exist in the late 1990s.

Collaboration between national PTOs on innovatory projects such as the Broadband Interconnection Trial and the Managed Transmission Network has until recently, been erratic and unenthusiastic. The costing of both remains opaque and the pricing of local services appears to vary greatly in spite of subsequent inquiries by the Commission. Nevertheless, by January 1998 the EC decreed that all national networks of member states must provide open access to all service providers meeting EC standards. New competition is still often described as 'creaming' off the most easily accessible niches, leaving the enormous level of investment required to maintain the technology fluid infrastructure to no more than a handful of PTOs; the most significant of these niches being, of course, that of the mobile telephone networks.

At a global level the attempt to create a 'level playing field' has also defied the governance structures of GATT. This body passed the task of coordinating national strategies to the newly created World Trade Organisation but working parties failed to agree in April 1996 after the UK and France withdrew. Most ASEAN countries prevent foreign ownership of their PTOs; the Japanese government permits only 20 per cent of the NTT (privatised in 1985) to be owned by foreigners and retains power to appoint executives and to block new flotations. As in other fields of international trade the US government feels that its markets are relatively open, while those of other nations are closed to US competition. In particular it views the 60 per cent of the world population that constitutes the Asian market serviced by only 15 per cent of the world's telephone connections, as the next major available market for US service providers, given the saturation of their own domestic market. In any case, this point demonstrates the intricate inter-linking between national and inter-national structures of governance, which is far from following a simple direction of replacing the former by the latter.

4. The Market as a Passage to the Super-Highway

While there has been a general acceptance of the market mechanism in transforming national telecom infrastructures, national responses to this Schumpeterian 'gale of creative destruction' have varied enormously. In the USA the AT&T's monopoly of service provision was challenged both through the regulatory machinery (the Federal Communications Commission) and the courts by would-be new entrants, MCI and Sprint. As a result in 1984 seven new regional companies

Table 3: *The World's Top 10 International Telecommunications Carriers*

Rank	Company	Country	1994
1	AT&T	United States	7947
2	Deutsche Telekom	Germany	5147
3	MCI	United States	3517
4	France Télécom	France	2603
5	BT[a]	United Kingdom	2489
6	Telecom Italia[b]	Italy	1708
7	Swiss PTT	Switzerland	1649
8	Stentor[c]	Canada	n.a.
9	Hong Kong[a,d]	Hong Kong	1578
10	Sprint	United States	1471

Figures show outgoing or carrier-billed international telephone traffic, in millions of minutes.

[a] Data for the fiscal year, ending March 31, 1995. HKT and Mercury are majority-owned by Cable & Wireless (UK)

[b] Combined totals for Iritel and Italcabale. Prior to 1994, Iritel (formerly ASST) handled intra-continental traffic only, and Itacable carried overseas traffic.

[c] Stentor was formerly Telecom Canada; Stentor traffic is for US only, of which approximately 70 per cent is originated by Bell Canada.

[d] Includes Hong Kong-China traffic.

Source: adapted from Financial Times 3.10.95.

or Regional Bell Operating Companies were formed while, initially, AT&T retained virtual control over international calls. By the mid 1990s, however, the opening of the market for long-distance calls has visibly contributed to the creation of new telecom giants, namely Sprint and MCI (for the ranking of these and other companies among the top ten international carriers, see Table 3). Indeed, during the 1980s the US government pursued a consistent policy of trying to establish a 'level playing field' in the global telecommunications market (Cawson et al. 1990: 80). Deregulation in the US not only had a very important demonstration effect on other market liberal governments but also stimulated European corporate users into embracing the agenda of de-regulation and choice of equipment suppliers and service providers.

In the UK, in 1978 the Carter Committee of enquiry into the Post Office (including telecommunications) identified major weaknesses in management, and suggested that telecommunications provision should be separated from the Post Office. Physical separation occurred in 1981 when the Telecommunications Act established a separate public corporation of British Telecom (BT). The Telecommunications Act of 1984 privatised BT and established OFTEL. Liberalisation extended unevenly to all three major segments of the UK telecommunications market: retail customers for equipment, corporate customers and network services. The first network license issued by the Department of Industry went to Mercury. The market thus created was regulated according to the criteria set out in the 1984 Act in which prices were to be determined largely in relation to long-term costs. Subsequently, BT has retained 89–90 per cent of the domestic market[1] whilst acquiring or entering into alliances with a number of US service providers.

In France, the policy agenda was different: the influential Nora/Minc Report (1980), that had been commissioned by the French government of Giscard d'Estaing, called for a national strategy to meet the US challenge to the 'strategic' telecommunications industry. Consequently, the responsible ministry (DGT) was given the task of leading the whole electronics *filiere* to greater international competitiveness (Humphreys 1991: 115). Both France and Germany pursued an approach that differed from Britain's neo-liberal agenda and discovered the virtues of a 'middle way':

> "gradually relaxing monopoly control and partially opening up their markets to competition, while at the same time retaining institutional structures that were well suited to maintenance of the options of PTT-led R & D, industrial and protectionist procurement and certification policies" (Humphreys 1991: 129).

France Télécom (FT) retains a key position in a much wider group of companies (CDGECOM) brought together under the Ministére des Postes and Télécommunications to provide a complete range of CIT services. In other words there has been an emergent strategy, which is represented by a statutory hierarchy of permitted access to the network owned by FT. However the establishment of the Minitel network for the telephone subscribers in 1979 was part of a strategy that provided 5.5 million subscribers to the public data network in 1991 compared with the UK's 3,500 customers.

The position of the Deutsche Bundespost (DBP) was embedded in statutory authority, requiring a two thirds vote in the Bundestag in order to modify the monopoly it held over the provision of telecommunications services. Over much of the 1980s proposals for liberalisation were discussed and in 1989 concessions to private service providers were made. In the following year the post and telephonic organisations were separated and the strategy of the new organisation was declared to be that of becoming 'the European hub for network operation'. In November 1996 the public sale of shares in the new organisation was attempted in all the major world stock exchanges. The recent privatisation of Deutsche Telekom (DT) has shown how much has changed between 1986 and 1996: in 1989 Morgan suggested that among the major advanced capitalist states, the FRG stood out as an island of stability (meaning 'no-change') in terms of its telecommunications regime (Morgan 1989).

Japan's main provider of domestic routes, the former PTO, Nippon Telephone and Telegraph (NTT) also remains relatively intact with only weak competition from the newly emergent competitor, MPT, since privatisation in 1984. Competition in long-distance provision is provided by four major new common carriers (NCCs), working as a consortium along certain routes. Foreign ownership is, however, restricted to 20 per cent in both markets.

5.   'Paths to Freedom'

In a comparative study of government-industry relations within telecommunications across European states, Hulsink (1996) reports what he observes to be a persistence of divergent modes of deregulation based on national context. He explains this in terms of "the critical processes of problem formulation, agenda setting, formation, enforcement and actual implementation of an appropriate policy response (that) are still largely shaped by domestic stakeholders and ruling coalitions". In the development of global markets for telecom services there is, Hulsink suggests, "still substantial manoeuvrability left for national governments and private stakeholders" (Hulsink 1996: 23).

In this regard the market-led or liberal response of the British government, the negotiated corporatist response of the Dutch government and that of the state-orchestration and sponsorship role played by the French government are to be seen as reflecting widely disparate national styles. In a very crude sense they can be portrayed as representing points on a continuum of *demarche* as Evans (1994) describes the extent to which the state enters into a role as mid-wife in the birth of a new sector. The stylistic differentiation between national systems has, according to Hulsink (1996), to be explained within the context of wider societal-governmental-industrial relationships in the manner explored by Shonfield (1965) as long ago as 1965 and more recently by Zysman (1994) and others.

In the analysis of widely differing but distinctive patterns of adaptation to the 'exogenous' effects of radical changes in market and technological structures experienced globally over the last decades, it has become common to seek explanation in national culture. Extra-economic factors such as national ideology (Lodge and Vogel 1987) and nationally distinctive configurations of societal institutions (Best 1990) are seen as contributing to relative levels of success in long-term economic development and short-term performance in the face of rapid environmental changes. The first has tended to typify developmental or collectively entrepreneurial attitudes with a communitarian belief system while short-term opportunism has been associated with liberal individualism. The 'new institutionalist' school lays emphasis on the shaping of recursive patterns of corporate or inter-firm behaviour by national institutions both in functionally significant areas of business such as education and training, finance, etc. as well as upon underlying familial patterns of socialisation.

Important in the self-confirming nature of national business systems (NBS's) is, according to Whitley (1992), the level of communal commitment to

- business dependence on strong cohesive government;
- state commitment to industrial development and risk sharing;
- capital market or credit-based financial system;
- unitary or dual education and training system;
- strength of skill-based trade unions;
- the significance of publicly certified skills and professional expertise.

Given the importance of these institutionalised routes to both financial resources and to resources represented in humanly embodied skills, unsurprisingly, their institutionalised closure is seen to result in self-reinforcing trajectories in the economic development of nations.

The divergence of these trajectories illustrated in Hulsink's (1996) analysis of the paths to deregulation of the telecommunications industry would appear to support this view. Levy and Spiller (1997) also argue that national institutions have contributed to the development of a credible PTO and the effectiveness of regulation within the industry. Based on five national case studies they agree that without such a pre-existing social infrastructure a privatised telecom sector in these countries will remain undeveloped. Further evidence of persistent divergence in national approaches to privatisation may be found in the manner in which capital ownership is allocated before, during and after the process is undertaken. Both the French and Italian governments are notable in their establishment of *noyeaux durs* or a core of long term stakeholders (Parker 1998). The former government has maintained a 51 per cent state holding but most European governments retain a 'golden share' in their former PTT. Generally national banks are large stakeholders in PTOs within mainland Europe, Credit Suisse being somewhat unique in holding shares in several European PTOs including Telecom Italia.

For the most part only a minority of the equity has been sold on the open market, employees often have a formal collective stake, with other PTO partners in strategic alliances, usually formed before privatisation, also possessing mutual holdings. The most extensive of these is Unisource originally formed between the Swedish and Dutch PTTs but now including Italy, Belgium, Switzerland, Ireland and Austria. These small PTOs have acquired a powerful partner in the world's largest long distance carrier AT&T through the World Source alliance (AT&T having acquired a holding in each constituent PTO). The two largest European carriers DT and FT are also joined in a strategic alliance which again extends to the US, through an agreement with Swift, then, third largest long distance carrier in the American market.

By contrast the major PTOs in USA, AT&T and in Britain, BT and C & W, appear to have a more global spread of interests being dependent on minority equity stakes in local NCCs throughout the world but more particularly in the Americas (BT) and the Pacific Rim (C & W). The latter company recently (1997) sold a 49 per cent stake in Hong Kong Telecom to the government of mainland China, supposedly in exchange for access to this much larger potential market whilst relinquishing its monopoly over the regionally important Hong Kong exchange (January 1998). In 1996 it was the joint venture between BT and MCI, second largest long distance carrier in the USA, that appeared to provide the former company with its platform for growth outside the United Kingdom. The unravelling of this venture (Concert) in the following year appeared to be triggered by the renegotiation of the deal demanded by BT as a result of the marking down of its (BT's) shares on the London Stock Exchange after the announcement of MCI's annual trading results in the USA. Seizing the opportunity a much smaller US carrier, World Com, was able to raise the necessary paper to buy the devalued stock of MCI and thereafter to withdraw from the Concert joint-venture. Other minority partners such as TELEFÓNICA, who had actually withdrawn from the Unisource partnership in order to join Concert, were left with little basis for development outside of their home market and with an eroded reputation among other possible collaborators. Perhaps more significantly, the role of strategic alliances based solely on equity holding and aimed at obtaining license to serve another country's domestic market appears to be increasingly questioned (*European Telecommunications* November 1997: 50–51). This is especially so when such alliances are so exposed to immediate reactions of stock exchange investors, and more particularly, to those of their financial agents and analysts, as is likely to be the case in alliances that include Anglo-American partners.

6. Flagships, Flotillas and Corvettes

What emerges from the preceding description of the development of the telecommunications sector is that the last quarter century of its development consisted of the emergence of an ever expanding series of concentric but interdependent markets. These have spread like ripples from the earlier technological development of transistors in the Bell Laboratory of AT&T in 1948 to the first uses of digitalised telephonic hubs and then of satellite mediators in the late 1970s. One might, in the manner of Freeman et al. (1982) see these developments as themselves relating to a 'carrier wave' of 'generic' innovation in operational paradigms. Crudely speaking, near the centre of this outward movement of markets is a global contest between nationally based PTOs or service providers. Their primary equipment suppliers have been conjoined in this technology-driven contest between these major players, and their strategies are currently shaped by the emergent alliances between service providers. Over the last decade or so a proliferation of so-called 'value-added' service providers has taken place, most notably in the provision of integrated business and manufacturing information systems. (Within this group of providers are many corporations from other sectors who begin by serving their own internal needs before diversifying into selling their systems to others.) Again this market has its own equipment suppliers. Beyond these markets are a multiplicity of consumer markets in which telecommunications are combined with personal computers as part of the 'self service' society that Gershuny and Miles (1983) and others, see as emerging from the diffusion of access to global networks.

In the course of the struggle to appropriate market position and technological advantage the old hierarchical ordering of the sectoral supply chain disintegrates and boundaries disappear. The contest becomes 'architectural' in nature as old participants compete with new entrants to reconstruct relations of dominance or dependency. More recently Kim and Kogut (1996) have described such pivotal technological inventions as providing 'platforms' from which firms that are successful in acquiring an early and cumulative capability can follow the development of the technology into a range of diversified applications. Decisions as to the 'relatedness' and 'directionality' in their applications of the new technology are critical to their ability to 'stretch' what they perceive to be core capabilities.

Within this open-ended struggle observers such as Stopford and Strange (1991) suggest that the sovereignty of the nation state has become eroded. Indeed Reich (1991) has portrayed the role of the nation state as that of servicing a global web of business transactions on which major multinational corporations (MNCs) occupy nodal positions. Successful national governments are those which anticipate the needs of these nation-less new sovereign bodies, especially in shaping their needs for educated labour and for the development of new knowledge. In the contest for technology and innovation the MNC has, according to the early observations of Buckley and Casson (1976), developed a distinctive 'ownership' advantage over domestic firms, in the 'frictionless' transfer of knowledge and information across frontiers. Thus successful national systems will be those that act as the generator and locus of discourse or design of such knowledge for use by incumbent MNCs. Some observers, including Reich himself, believe that national business systems possess variable strengths in the production of this capacity. (This is indeed the underlying proposition of so-called national innovation systems (NIS)analysis — see for example Lundvall 1992). Others see the ability of MNCs to occupy a nodal or 'flagship' position on global networks to be a product of the parent national business system. It is suggested by Hollingsworth et al. (1994: 279) that:

"The persistence of national traits in multi-national enterprises thus tends to confirm the idea that purely economically driven economic behaviour is under-determined, leaving fundamental gaps in the orientations of actors that must be filled by rules generated and enforced by more-than-economic social institutions."

More directly the rootedness of nodal service providers in vertical supply chains and competitor consortia located within their home or parent country has been seen by some authors to be of significance in encouraging innovation and flexible responsiveness to 'external' market demand. D'Cruz and Rugman (1994) use the example of France Télécom as a successful 'flagship' around which the national government has arraigned a flotilla of key suppliers and customers. From this domestic base it has extended its European influence through an alliance with the equally nationally embedded Deutsche Telekom. Such influences can extend downwards in attempts to bring about collaboration between major equipment suppliers such as Alcatel and Siemens. It can also extend upwards to representations to the umbrella of cross-national and regional (EU) regulatory and standardising agencies who fix boundaries for future markets. Equally the influence of FT/DT in EU initiated research and development (R & D) and educational projects is seen by these authors to have been important in setting directions for their European competitors.

NTT, the former Japanese PTT, represents an even more extreme example of 'competitive closure' to use the terminology of Cawson et al. (1990). Over the 1980s NTT held the position of fifth in R & D expenditures across all of Japanese manufacturing. Its leading suppliers NEC and Fujitsu were in fact, third and sixth respectively. They have been labelled by Kodama (1991) as 'knowledge creating companies' rather than manufacturers, that is to say that the level of the annual R & D expenditure has grown to be higher than that of their annual capital expenditures; in the first case by 1.30 times and in the second by 1.44 times. The stimuli for the great surge in R & D expenditures appear to have derived from the development of the integrated digital exchange by a number of leading Western suppliers among whom was the relatively small Canadian supplier Northern Telecommunications (now Nortel). This advance was of course accompanied by the emergence of new technologies such as fibre optic and satellite communication developments in US military programmes. The then publicly owned NTT initiated a series of alliances with suppliers over the 1980s, using the tax incentives offered under the 1961 Engineering Research Association Act to encourage suppliers to embark on large scale pre-production collaborative research (NTT was, and is, legally prevented from manufacturing its own equipment). Its most successful alliances proved to be with single specialist suppliers: in 1986 NTT registered 655 patents jointly with one or more suppliers. However Kodama (1991: 199) attributes much of the success of this collaboration to the fusion of specialist know-how contained within the Sumitomo group which owns NEC (electronic devices), SEI (cables) and NSG (glass).

However the success of relatively small countries in producing world-class equipment suppliers such as Nokia (Finland), Ericsson (Sweden) and Nortel (Northern Telecommunications Corporation of Canada) can be explained, at least in part, by other characteristics of the flagship/flotilla model of relational transacting. As has been pointed out elsewhere (Loveridge 1997) social closure in the form of inter-organizational alliances are historically at least as likely to have been undertaken for defensive purposes (e.g. cartels) as developmental and to have resulted in greater, rather than reduced, rigidity in response to innovation. The recent under performance of DT remains a threat to its future and is, according to Lehrer and Darbishire (this volume) largely due to the 'functional silos' of its internal work specialisation and institutionalised management practices. Another example of recent poor performance can be found in AT&T's central laboratories. These produced the revolutionary applications of semi-conducting materials to electronic engineering that began the creation of a new sector. Over the 1980's according to Filoche (1997) AT&T lost the confidence of its customers in the so-called 'Baby Bells' created after the 1984 break-up of the company into autonomous regionally based local providers. The problems solved in equipment design by the central R & D facility were those of its parent AT&T, a long distance operation, not those appropriate to the domestic carriers that were its customers. Nortel, the Canadian digital equipment manufacturer was the major beneficiary of their disappointments, standing ready to match their needs in a customised and innovative way.

Going back even further to the evolution of analogue based exchanges the technical capabilities of Ericsson were partly responsible for bringing it into partnership with French supplier Matra in the 1970s. But, according to Mansell (1993), the diplomatic marginality of the Swedish company allowed the French government to escape from an embarrassing choice of Philips over its prevailing German collaborator, Siemens, on technical grounds. Thus the 'outsider' status of these corvette suppliers has enabled them, both technologically, organizationally and politically, to remain outside of the nationally specific paradigm that dominates each of the more integrated supply chains of the former large PTTs.

7.   The Scattering of Flotillas?

As suggested earlier, the global telecommunications network is made up of a vast variety of carrier technologies and even greater variety in user software. The problems of inter-face marketing and of equipment integration and operational coordination are of an order hitherto not encountered in any area of socio-economic activity. While relational contracting within flagship-flotilla configurations of MNCs offer one framework within which to produce answers to these problems, by their very nature such alliances also prescribe boundaries. The mutual appropriation of technological knowledge within alliances usually complements a mutual exchange of licenses to operate across national territories as well as other elements of exclusivity. At the same time the centrifugal nature of technological development allows access to markets for an ever growing swarm of Schumpeterian entrepreneurial companies like Nortel. These become established (or not) on the basis of providing new solutions to existing problems or new applications or extensions to network capabilities.

These suppliers resemble corvettes darting in and out between the arraigned formations of flotillas. They provide customised solutions to local problems. For the most part they remain small, being more likely to be software designers or assemblers of unique configurations of hard and software manufactured by others. They are the epitome of Bell's (1973) and Reich's (1990) notion of knowledge workers. A few like Ericsson and Nortel create integrating technological platforms for future new product development and, in doing so, develop vertical links with customers and suppliers that establish them as new flagships. In this way the nation state or region in which they first established can become increasingly dependent on their success as has Canada on the R & D expenditure of Nortel and Bombardier (a regional aircraft and vehicle manufacturer). Ericsson has grown within a remarkably short period to being the 57th largest publicly quoted corporation in the world (*Financial Times*, 22.1.98). Much of its equipment assembly is located in South East Asia, even R & D and Design & Development is likely to become increasingly footloose in its location outside Sweden.

A second newcomer to the world league of largest corporations is Lucent Technologies, the US equipment supplier spun-off by AT&T in 1996. Now 45th largest firm in the world in terms of market capitalisation, like Ericsson, it is larger than most of its customers and is now winning back most of the BabyBell local carriers in the domestic market of the USA (*Financial Times*, 21.1.98: 28). As a portent of future trends the success of Lucent is taken as significant by many analysts. The erosion of national monopolies over equipment supply began in the 1970s with the introduction of computerized exchanges. The inability of local suppliers to develop, first analogue, then digital, equipment brought about a series of cross-country alliances, joint-ventures and licensing which penetrated even closed systems such as that of France and — but not to any significant extent — that of Japan. Companies outside of the telecommunications sector such as IBM became attractive partners in the attempt by century-old monopoly suppliers to gain the new technological expertise. Most national governments, as ultimate customer/owners of these PTTs, attempted to orchestrate this movement towards the internationalisation of supply.

Clearly the two positions are not antithetical and a willingness to accept the appearance of partners as competitors in different regional or product markets would ensure the continuance of such alliances containing widely differing national perspectives on the design and marketing of their products. Undeniably the potential market for whole systems designers as partners in government sponsored projects in developing countries will continue to expand, into the foreseeable future. But in such markets the equipment supplier can even be a rival to its own national carrier in competing for the design partnership sought by the client government. The choice of partners in such projects can also be seen as involving issues of national sovereignty for the host government in the retention of control of the pace and direction of systems development. Hence it is no longer usual for governments of developing states to choose a single national systems supplier but rather to select an international consortium over which greater control can be exercised by virtue of the plurality of interests involved. In this respect it is interesting to observe that the Japanese government's policy of prohibiting its major internal carrier NTT from acquiring overseas interests, whilst serving as a main customer for a domestic R & D consortium, has aided in the creation of several of the strongest Japanese partners in the supply of equipment to other Asian countries.

8.   Discussion

The former uniformity of government-sector relations within the telecommunications sector across most national business systems might seem to belie a belief in their holistic and uniquely various nature. Clearly sectorally specific conditions can overcome nationally specific modes of institutional closure (Sorge 1996). A variety of potential reasons can be given by government for directly intervening in the creation and operation of communications systems. For example national security and international diplomacy might legitimate the control and monitoring of information carried by the system or for attempting control over its design. This tension is especially present in the transfer of military design to commercial applications. However it is evident that the French and Japanese governments have been consciously motivated by a desire to emulate American commercial success in the electronics sector. Telecommunications has a pivotal role in the creation of a market for this broader national objective, a goal sustained through a succession of governments of different political persuasions. Clearly the extent of this government commitment to national or, now, regional champions during a transformative stage of sectoral development can be an assurance to customers, suppliers, and for potential collaboration in cross-national strategic alliances.

However it is difficult to imagine the transformation in technology, and in global technological capabilities that has taken place within the industry without the massive allocation of US public resources to military R & D in the associated fields of electronics, computerization, satellite design and launch, internet etc. since World War Two (Freeman et al. 1992). Without the existence of these relatively 'free-goods' it seems unlikely that even the technically advanced and communitarian national business systems of Germany and Japan (Lodge and Vogel

1987; Best 1990) could have reached the present state of design development. To that extent it can be suggested that the manner in which the US government chose to transfer this technological knowledge into the market place (generally through those US private corporations in which it had been developed) afforded considerable external benefits to its allies in the Cold War — and even to its foes in an indirect manner! The market that subsequently developed has been shaped by pre-existing and ongoing national and commercial interests.

The question that this chapter has sought to address is that of the enduring nature of these interests in so far as this can be discovered to be shaped and sustained within nationally distinctive institutions and ideologies. That such distinctions exist at both the level of government strategies and policies *and at corporate level* can hardly be denied on the basis of available evidence (for evidence from other sectors, see also Thompson in this volume). The paths taken to the privatization of former PTTs have left varying amounts of public control with national governments, who have to combine this proprietorial role with that of regulating entrance to and management of their domestic market place. Small wonder, then, that international agreement on setting operating standards for the use of new combinative technologies have been difficult to arrive at and that the emergence of cross-national European carriers and suppliers, was so long delayed.

There is clear evidence that national governments have become increasingly aware of the fusion of adjacent industrial markets for the emergent technologies. Among liberal democracies only in France has this awareness taken the form of explicit government intervention to bring about a systemic restructuring around the application of micro electronics to a range of industries; most particularly in the creation of a market for telecommunications/information technology. But, at the same time, in the more 'integrated' or 'social democratic' systems of Continental European nations (Amable et al. 1997) the costs of change have tended to be absorbed internally within the corporate over-staffing of new task structures brought about by changes in technologies. In some cases this was as much as eight times that of PTOs in market-based systems such as BT or Australian Telecom. Furthermore the managed introduction of design changes has not always been efficacious in preserving the national capabilities of equipment suppliers as is shown by the serial restructuring of the French industry taken together with the demise of domestic computer suppliers in most European countries. This history might be taken as indicative of the problems involved in making choices between technologies whose emergent characteristics give rise to ever more costly complex and open-ended options. Only on the grounds of national survival, such as those provided by 'defence' in the Cold War, can such choices be openly justified to democratic electorates with impunity.

Yet it would be folly to suggest that the dichotomy between those governments seen to be more 'developmental' towards sponsorship of their national carriers and suppliers and those that are more 'regulatory' in promoting a 'level playing field' for their consumer-citizens will disappear in the short run. However there appears to be an emergent awareness among the corporate players themselves that 'lock-in' to nationally based recipes in the design, marketing and operating of their products is potentially crippling in a global arena. In many cases the attitudes of corporate executives in telecommunications cannot help but be influenced by changes elsewhere in their national business systems. Thus the increasing internationalisation of German banks may itself influence decisions by DT, Siemens and others to float on major world bourses. Also the erosion of so-called corporatist structures of joint-regulation between employers, labour unions and the government in Scandinavian countries have contributed to, as well as being shaped by, market pressures.

Yet in spite of this new climate the PTOs of the major industrial states remain in a dominant position within their domestic market. Not only is their position pivotal to the development and access to new value-added IT services, but they all figure among the world's largest corporations with a capability to orchestrate the design of their own equipment. The separate attempts by European PTOs to gain access to the huge American market, and to a lesser extent, the Japanese market, through alliances with domestic PTOs, have complicated the path to the emergence of a consolidated European industry or, even, of European agreed standards of equipment. However, it may be that in the opening-up of markets in developing Asian countries the shape of the global sector will be decided. In this region fast growing corvettes among European equipment suppliers have obtained a lead role in shaping new infrastructural forms and combining different media in a creative manner. In the developed countries the retro-fitting of older exchanges and enlarging their capabilities for value-adding services is also an intensely competitive market enveloping a variety of niche specialists. In both markets the creativity and agility required of what we have described as corvette firms is at a premium, but so, also, is reliability of delivery and implementation.

It remains to be seen whether these characteristics can be successfully combined within the organizational structures and processes of major integrated suppliers such as Siemens and Alcatel; the record of Nortel, Ericsson and Nokia seems to suggest that it can be found in what Amable et al. (1997) describe as the 'social-democracies'. The latter analysts locate the ability of such business systems to innovate to institutional structures that derive from an ideological commitment to partnership between labour and capital which is translated into flatter and more organic structures of authority within firms. Such national ideal types are confirmed in the research of Kristensen et al. (1996). However it might seem that these micro structures are also under severe threat from market pressures, not least because of the internal problems associated with the control and coordination of globally separated business units.

9. Conclusion

The telecommunications sector has been described as having the unique characteristics of all providers of international communications. It is both heavily regulated by *national* governments, concerned with issues of sovereignty and boundary protection, whilst also being the subject of *global* coordination and control from its infancy. In this respect many of the issues discussed in this chapter reflect similar concerns to those confronted in the regulation of the air and maritime transportation. It can, perhaps, be argued that the regulation of telecommunications represents a higher order of complexity to those of the latter sectors both in terms of the speed of change, its technical content and the sheer volume of traffic and variety of media. For all of these reasons the testing of the long established national relationships within the sector has been severe. Yet the evidence examined in this chapter suggests that actors were heavily influenced by nationally specific institutional modes, styles and ideologies in the *path* chosen towards modifying organizational and technological forms. As against the evidence of cross-national variety we have to set the universal adoption of privatisation as the model of adaptation, a model set by the USA and Britain. There may be many explanations for this latter phenomenon from the economistic one of there being a ceiling to public revenue raising to that of mimetic social pressures upon government strategy processes. In itself this global movement demands much more detailed analysis than can be attempted here. Certainly the partial abandonment of the wholly domestically oriented approach to development of the electronics and telecommunications sectors by the French government in the 1970s indicated a realization of limits to the capabilities of wholly or near closed national systems of innovations.

What the evidence suggests, however, is that in the telecom sector market regulation has yet to be restored to its former stability under the old IPU/ITU administration. The former model of sectoral 'best practice' has given way to a variety of shifting niche markets. In this context the long term ability of national governments to determine the direction and configuration of national servers and equipment manufacturers, even as majority owners of the latter, becomes increasingly diminished. While authority can be exercised within domestically dominant PTOs in which the government has a stake, the operational efficacy of those servers is still heavily reliant on its systemic position within a global transmission network, a position that can now be challenged through a variety of media. In this situation national servers wish to join alliances, not simply to enjoy access to the others' markets, but also to provide collectivities with control over significant areas of the global network.

Again governmental diplomacy has played a significant role in shaping such alliances, as in the creation of the Siemens-Alcatel alliance and in subsequent adoption of suppliers from the 'marginal' social democracies. But increasing tensions are evident within corporate management as a result of senior executives wishing to pursue a course of action independent of national consideration. The latest of these to be made public was in the case of the resignation of the president of Telecom Italia in 1997. Similarly tensions appear within alliances and joint ventures such as GEC-Siemens when one party wishes to constrain the other for reasons of domestically oriented priorities. In what Amable et al. (1997) describe as the 'integrated' societies of Continental Europe the view taken by governments on the corporate absorption of welfare 'externalities' has, hitherto, been very different from that in 'marchand' societies (i.e. Anglo Saxon countries). However there is plentiful evidence of the existence of growing differences in the stance taken by corporate actors in the former type of society and, indeed, differences *within* corporate decision making about where the balance of costs and benefits should lie. The recent history of competitive performance within the telecommunications sector suggests an inevitable movement toward the objectives of corporate survival at the expense of wider communitarian goals. We would argue that in a situation in which normative boundaries are being increasingly eroded at a multiplicity of levels from that of the firm upwards to sectoral set, national, and even, regional regulation, the role of the corporate actor as creator of new identities is becoming increasingly important. The nodal position occupied by both large PTOs, and their successful suppliers, along global networks is, evidently, tending to bring about a re-orientation towards the orchestration of inter-dependent collaborators far beyond their parent country. The capabilities required for this managerial role may be very different from those displayed hitherto within nationally bounded systems — or even within the flitting corvettes produced by 'social democracies'.

In two previous papers (Mueller and Loveridge 1995, 1997) we explored the contesting forces shaping the developing relationship between MNCs and the institutions that underpin national business systems — and industrial districts — by using the example of the automotive sector. We argued that in spite of the particular characteristics of this sector it provided an example of the manner in which sectoral contingencies perceived by the negotiating agents, both national and corporate, can shape the arena in which their transactions take place as well as the sanctions available to them. Furthermore, we showed that the *political* significance of this debate has been signalled in the fears expressed over many years by political economists over the strategic dependence of the nation on the foreign-based MNC. Whilst this argument has already been discussed with regard to government's role in the restructuring of the UK's automobile and microelectronics industries (Dyerson and Mueller 1993), it is at least equally potent in a 'strategic industry' like telecommunications. We suggested in the previous papers and re-assert in this paper that the notion of the MNC as a *wholly* exploitative force has clearly been rejected by most national governments who, over the last fifteen years, have increasingly competed for foreign direct investment as the basis for economic development or national regeneration, but also to benefit from technology transfer from globally competitive MNCs. The approach suggested here means that there is an interactive relationship between national institutions, national ideologies and national policy regimes on the one hand, and corporate agendas on the other hand (Mueller and Loveridge 1995, 1997). Therefore, insofar as they mutually constitute each other, one needs to analyse systems and agents at the same time. Opportunities or threats can be created by governments but they need to be grasped by existing or new corporate agents. Thus, whether and in what form these responses take place depends upon the strengths and weaknesses of the organisations in question.

Notes

1. As of 1997. Its shares of the business market and business international calls are much lower, namely around 70 per cent and 50 per cent respectively.

References

Abernathy W. J., K. B. Clark, and A. M. Kantow. 1983. *Industrial Renaissance*. New York: Basic Books.

Amable, B., R. Barré, and R. Boyer. 1997. *Les Systèmes d'Innovation à L'Ère de la Globalisation*. Paris: Economica.

Bell, D. 1973. *The Coming of the Post Industrial Society*. New York: Basic Books.

Best, M. H. 1990. *The New Competition*. Oxford: Polity.

Buckley, P., and M. Casson. 1976. *The Future of the Multinational Corporation*. London: Macmillan.

Cawson, A., K. Morgan, D.Webber, P. Holmes, and A. Stevens. 1990. *Hostile Brothers*. Oxford: Clarendon Press.

Chandler, A. 1990. *Scale and Scope*. Cambridge MA: Belknap Press.

D'Cruz, J., and A. M. Rugman. 1994. The Five Partners Model: France Telecom, Alcatel and the Global Telecommunications Industry, *European Management Review* 12(1): 59–66.

Dyerson, R., and F. Mueller. 1993. Intervention by Outsiders: A Strategic Management Perspective on Government Industrial Policy, *Journal of Public Policy* 13(1): 69–88.

Evans, P. 1995. *Embedded Autonomy*. Princeton NJ: Princeton University Press.

Filoche, C. 1997. Regulating Change, Dynamics of Organizational Forms and Technological Innovation: the case of the US Telecommunications Industry, ASEAT Workshop, University of Manchester Institute of Science and Technology, September.

Freeman, C., J. Clark, and L. Soete. 1982. *Unemployment and Technical Innovation*. London: Pinter.

Gershuny, J. I., and I. D. Miles. 1983. *The Service Economy*. London: Pinter.

Hollingsworth, J.R, P. C. Schmitter, and W. Streek (eds.). 1994. *Governing Capitalist Economies, Performance and Control of Economic Sectors*. Oxford: Oxford University Press.

Hulsink, W. 1996. Persistent Divergence in a Converging European Industry: a Comparison of Telecommunications Restructuring in France, the Netherlands, and the United Kingdom. Science Policy Research Unit Centre for Information and Communication Technology, Falmer: Sussex.

Humphreys, P. 1991. The State and Telecommunications Modernization in Britain, France and West Germany. In: U. Hilpert (ed.), *State policies and techno-industrial innovation*, 109–32. London: Routledge.

Kim, D. J., and B. Kogut. 1996. Technological Platforms and Diversification, *Organisation Science* 7(3), May-June: 283–301.

Kodama, F. 1991. *Emerging Patterns of Innovation*. Cambridge MA: Harvard Business School Press.

Kristensen, P. H., K. Lilja, and R. Tainio. 1996. Comparing typical firms in Denmark and Finland. In: R. Whitley, and P. H. Kristensen (eds.), *The Changing European Firm*, 113–117. London: Routledge.

Levy, B., and P. T. Spiller (eds.). 1997. *Regulations, Institutions and Commitment: Comparative Studies of Telecommunications*. Cambridge UK: Cambridge University Press.

Lodge, G. C., and G. F. Vogel. 1987. *Ideology and National Competitiveness*. Boston MA: Harvard Business School Press.

Loveridge, R. 1997. Putting Nationalism back into National Business Systems. In: A. Bugra, and B. Usdiken (eds.), *State, Market and Organizational Form*, 289–318. Berlin: De Gruyter.

Lundvall, B.-Å. (ed.). 1992. *National Systems of Innovation — towards a theory of innovation and interactive learning*. London: Pinter.

Mansell, R. 1993. *The New Telecommunications*. London: Sage.

Morgan, K. 1989. Telecom strategies in Britain and France. In: M. Sharp, and P. Holmes (eds.), *Strategies for New Technology*, Seitenangabe. London: Philip Allan.

Mueller, F., and R. Loveridge. 1997. Institutional, Sectoral and Corporate Dynamics in the Creation of Global Supply Chains. In: R. Whitley, and P. H. Kristensen (eds.), *Governance at Work*, 120–36. Oxford: Oxford University Press.

Mueller, F., and R. Loveridge. 1995. The 'Second Industrial Divide'? — The Role of the Large Firm in the Baden-Württemberg Model, *Industrial and Corporate Change* 4(3), Autumn: 499–526.

Parker, D. 1998. 'Privatisation in the EU: an overview. In: D. Parker (ed.), *Privatisation in the European Union: Theory and Policy*, Seitenangaben. London: Routledge.

Prahalad, C. K., and G. Hamel. 1990. The Core Competence of the Corporation, *Harvard Business Review* 68(3): 79–91.

Reich, R. B. 1991. *The Work of Nations*. New York: Alfred Knopf.

Shonfield, A. 1965. *Modern Capitalism*. Oxford: Oxford University Press.

Sorge, A. 1996. Societal effects in cross-national organization studies: conceptualizing diversity in actors and systems. In: R. Whitley, and P. H. Kristensen (eds.), *The Changing European Firm*, 67–86. London: Routledge.

Stopford, J., and S. Strange with J. Henley. 1991. *Rival States, Rival Firms*. Cambridge, UK: Cambridge University Press.

Ungerer, H. (with the collaboration of N. P. Costello). 1988. *Telecommunications in Europe*. Luxembourg: Office for Official Publications of the European Communities.

Whitley, R. 1992. The Comparative Study of Business Systems in Europe: Issues and Choices. In: R. Whitley (ed.), *European Business Systems: Firms and Markets in their National Contexts*, 267–84. London: Sage.

Zysman, J. 1994. Can Japanese Direct Investment Sustain European Development in Electronics?. In: M. Mason, and D. Encarnation (eds.), *Does Ownership Matter? Japanese Multinationals in Europe*, 331–362. Oxford: Clarendon Press.

CHAPTER 11

Economic Performance and National Business Systems

France and the United Kingdom in the International Construction Sector

Elisabeth Campagnac   Yuh-Jye Lin   Graham M. Winch

1. Introduction

Our aim in this paper is to investigate the link between the sector specific business system for construction in France and Great Britain, and performance in international construction markets. We intend to show how these results relate to different social models of organisation for the resolution of the problem of coordination and integration in the production process. We will show that these differences

- are the result of social models of organisation at the level of the sector, and embody different representations of efficiency;
- produce different levels of performance in the global market by generating distinctively national competitive advantages.

Our approach to posing the problem of coordination and integration will combine the analysis of the governance of transactions developed by Williamson, and the value chain/value system approach of Porter. For, it is only by identifying what has to be coordinated and integrated that national business systems as distinctive configurations of market/hierarchy relations can be linked to value systems, and hence performance. We will make this link through the concept of model of organisation. Our argument will be that differences in performance between national business systems can be analysed most incisively through analysing differences in modes of coordination and integration within specific value systems. These differences in modes of coordination and integration take the form of different models of organisation, and these models of organisation, we will show, have different potential for performance in global markets.

After a presentation of the key features of the international construction market, identifying the differences in performance by the British and French industries, we will pose the problem of coordination and integration in construction projects in terms of the governance of transactions in the construction value system, before presenting the two different models of organisation which have developed within the British and French business systems to solve these — the professional and the industrial respectively. Our paper will conclude with some reflections upon how differences in performance are generated within models of organisation, and propose a broader distinction between loose and tight business systems.

2.   The International Construction Industry

The international construction industry is supplier in the globally traded market for construction services. The vast bulk of construction services in the world economy is traded domestically in that supply is met entirely from within the country where demand is generated and the built product is located. Our focus here is upon the relatively small proportion of global construction demand that is met by supply across national borders. The site-specific nature of the constructed product means that demand, even if financed through global markets and expressed by internationally mobile clients, is inherently local — the issue is whether that demand has been met by construction firms located outside the country where the site is located.

On the demand side, the international construction industry builds products as varied as dams, power stations, mass transit systems, housing, and petroleum refineries. On the supply side, the industry is divided into two major blocs — the supply of architectural and engineering design services, and the supply of site-related construction services. These may be supplied together as 'turnkey' packages, but are more typically supplied separately to the client. The supplier of the services may offer them as part of a consortium or joint venture, and/or may subcontract many of the services in turn to specialists who may also operate internationally, or be restricted to the domestic market where the site is located.

The history of the international construction industry prior to the period under consideration here is well told by Linder (1994). The analysis here will focus upon the period after 1980, when the international market witnessed considerable changes (Campagnac 1992). The demand coming from former colonies and other developing countries, often funded by international aid organisations, together with the oil-rich Middle East was replaced by an increasing interpenetration of the markets of the advanced countries, and growing demand from newly industrialising countries, especially in south-east Asia, and most recently, China.

As Campagnac (1992) argues, these developments did not simply mean a shift in the geographical location of demand, but also a profound recomposition of the nature of demand, and the terms of competition. Demand increasingly shifted towards more sophisticated built products, and competition became more orientated towards a range of services rather than the realisation of the works on site alone. For success in the international market, increasing emphasis was required in the financial and engineering aspects of the project, and in the management and coordination of the production process. The management of the project, and the effective coordination and integration of the entire value system are only some of the elements of competitive advantage, but it is upon these that we will concentrate here, while not forgetting that competitive advantage also depends upon the capacity to generate strategic alliances, obtain finance, and to mobilise networks of sub-contract firms in the country of production.

An important recent development in the international market has been the rapid diffusion of what is most widely known as build 'own operate transfer' (BOOT) contracting, deploying project finance techniques where the loans are secured on the facility being constructed, and reimbursed from the revenues generated from charging for the use of the facility. This is what is known as the Private Finance Initiative in the UK, and has long been used in France where it is known as *concession* (Martinand 1993). As most of the facilities procured through this approach are public goods, the skills required for success in this market include managing relations with state authorities, raising finance, and operating the facility efficiently, as well as designing and constructing the facility.

Our data on performance in the international construction market are taken from the annual surveys published in *Engineering News Record* (ENR) of the largest 225 (formerly 250) suppliers of construction services, and the largest 200 suppliers of architectural and engineering design services — Lin (1999) and Strassman and Wells (1988) provide reviews of the strengths and weaknesses of this data set. Definitions within the data set change periodically, but consistent data are available for the periods 1980 to 1993 for construction services, and 1982 to 1996 for design services, and it is upon these periods that we will rely[1]. The construction services figures are based on the US dollar value of new contracts awarded outside the home country of the responding firm, while those for architecture and engineering services are based on 'billings' for work undertaken outside the home country. Typically, architectural and engineering design services account for around 5 per cent of the total market, but this is almost pure value added, while the figures for construction contain a large amount of work which is often sub-contracted to local firms or firms from third countries. It is also in the design phase that the key choices of construction technologies are made, often favouring specialist technology suppliers from the same country (Soubra 1993).

The data set is focused principally on the supply-side — the unit of analysis is the construction firm, and there is limited information on the nature of demand. While an understanding of the demand side is important for any complete analysis of competitiveness, a supply side data set is adequate for exploring the links between performance in international markets and national business systems. In particular, what these data allow us to do is analyse performance in terms of share of the market in internationally traded design and construction services over time. Measuring performance in terms of market share is, of course not the only measure — many would prefer other allocative measures such as profitability or value, while others would insist upon attention to distributional measures such as incomes, employment generation, or wealth distribution. However, the criterion of share of the global market is a widely used and accepted criterion of comparative performance in the global economy.

The market is increasingly dominated by the leading industrialised countries, led by the United States. This is not a market where economies of scale are important. Globally, the largest firms in terms of total turnover tend to be Japanese — but this is due to high levels of concentration in the large domestic market, not predominance in the international market. The relative performance in terms of market share of British and French firms over the period for the supply of construction, and architectural and engineering services is presented in Figures 1 and 2 respectively, together with the performance of their major competitors. Figure 1 shows that, in broad terms, the British and French shares of the global market for construction services are close over the period as a whole, although this overall picture does hide important regional differences.[2] However, Figure 2 shows that the British share in architectural and engineering design is typically more than double that of the French. Our analysis here will focus on the overall international picture, and it is these differences in performance that this paper will attempt to explain.

3.   National Business Systems and the Problem of Coordination and Integration

Whitley (1992: 10) has defined national business systems as "particular arrangements of hierarchy-market relations which become institutionalised and relatively successful in particular contexts". The question that this section will pose, is what have the relations been arranged for? In other words, we will introduce a process dimension to the essentially structural concept of national business system, allowing a more tectonic (Winch 1994) approach. Thus the analysis is action-orientated in terms of how networks of actors have ordered their social and economic relations to achieve their joint and several objectives. Our analysis will be derived from a combination of Porter's value chain and value system analysis and Williamson's institutional economics. Williamson is used here simply to respond to the question unanswered by Porter regarding the mode of coordination

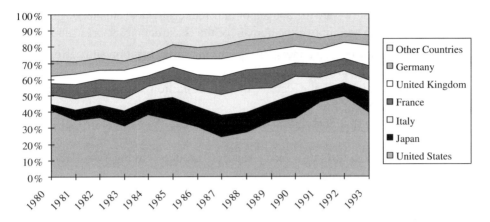

Figure 1. *National Shares of International Market for Construction Services (%)*

Source: Engineering News Record (various years)

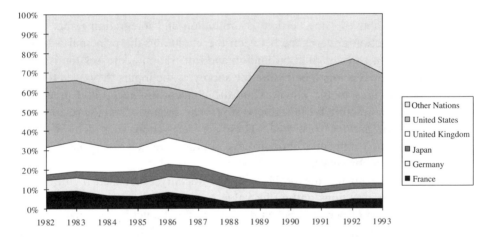

Figure 2. *National Shares of International Design Services Market*

Source: Engineering News Record (various years)

and integration between the different value chains in the overall value system for the production of a good or service — a full analysis in the framework of institutional economics is not appropriate here.

Following Porter (1985), we have divided the value system into four main value chains in a simplified version of the process model presented in Winch (1996a) in the manner illustrated in Figure 3. This series of value chains in the value system of construction is distinctively characterised by a determinate life cycle and the progressive reduction of uncertainty through that life cycle (Winch et al. 1998). The first two are the domain of the architectural and engineering services sub-market, and the second two the domain of the construction services sub-market:

– Articulating the overall concept by specifying form, function and performance in complete *definition* of the built product;
– Working through all the details of that definition to provide a complete *description* of the built product;
– Implementing that description on site to achieve the overall *structure* of the built product;
– Completing that structure ready for use through making *installations and finishes* of equipment and surfaces.

In order to give a full analysis of modes of coordination and integration in the value system, it is necessary to distinguish, as shown in Figure 3, between what can be defined as vertical coordination and integration and horizontal coordination and integration. Vertical coordination is focused upon the relationship of the client (i.e. the source of capital and articulator of demand for the built facility and hence the project) to the various principal actors responsible for the chains of the value system defined above. Thus vertical coordination and integration refers to the nature of transaction governance between the client and the principal actors in the value system. Horizontal coordination and integration addresses the issue of how those principal actors then assure the supply of the inputs they need to meet their responsibilities to the client. Thus the concept embraces both questions related to sub-contracting for the supply of services required, and the relationship between the firm and its workforce.[3] These are transactions of which the client, in formal terms, is innocent, but can have profound effects for project or firm performance in global markets.

Thus we are posing the problem of the socially embedded nature of the governance of transactions within the value system as what has to be explained in the construction of performance at the international level by national business systems. Our concept of governance is distinguished from those developed elsewhere (e.g. Kristensen 1997) which focus upon governance within labour processes — the classic problem of transforming labour power into work done. As Lazonick (1991) emphasises, value is only created within specific labour processes, but value is also accumulated through sequences of labour processes. The problem we are addressing here is the problem of coordination and integration between labour processes — in other words, how is an entire system of value generation governed? Outside a *Kombinat* delivering goods and services to the state in a total command economy, the governance of any value system consists of a mixture of internal, market, and collaborative forms of coordination and integration.

Winch (1996a) provided an initial analysis of these issues, but mainly addressed the horizontal dimension. We wish to focus here upon the vertical

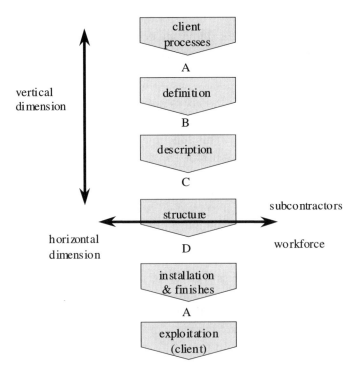

Figure 3. *The Construction Value System and Its Principal Transactions*

dimension, where problems of very high uncertainty and low transaction frequency in the upstream transactions phases combine with asset specificities generated through the fundamental transformation and low transaction frequency in the downstream transactions. Williamson himself (1985) tantalisingly offers one solution to the vertical problem — trilateral governance — but leaves the concept largely undeveloped. Stinchcombe (1990, chap. 6), analysed in detail one aspect of trilateral governance — the use of complex forms of contract which turn market into hierarchy. These are typically standardised and finely adapted to the legal system of the country concerned forming an important part of the regulatory aspect of the national contracting system in both France and Great Britain, and are deployed principally to govern transactions B and C respectively. In the international market, standard forms of contract are also available from the Swiss-based Fédération Internationale des Ingénieurs Conseils (FIDIC). A second aspect of trilateral governance is the development of control actors (Winch 1996b) — typified by the quantity surveyor and *bureau de contrôle* in the British and French systems. The principal contractor for the definition/description stage is also often retained to act as a control actor and coordinator during the structure, and installation and finishes stages; again this is principally deployed to govern transactions B and C.[4] Our analysis here, for the sake of clarity, will develop the analysis around the internal and external modes of coordination and integration (for a more detailed historical analysis see Campagnac (1996b) and Winch (1996b)).

In France, the long tradition of the state with its own technical capacity, linked to the political imperative to impose the will of the centre upon the national space, and the resulting emphasis given to the *aménagement du territoire* (Picon 1992) means that transaction A is typically integrated into the state as client, particularly in civil engineering. This function is performed by the members of the *corps des ponts* and their assistants in the *Directions Départementales de l'Equipement* (Thoenig 1987). On many building projects, while the state still retains a strong policy interest, transaction A is governed typically externally through the distinctively French system of architectural *concours*, where the market is in ideas, and prices are regulated through fee scales. The extensive role of the state in France, together with the way in which the state structures the market means that these policies are widespread throughout the French industry.

The traditional British process is governed rather differently. The British state as client has no technical competence in respect of the construction process,[5] and transaction A is coordinated externally in a manner that is highly distinctive to the British system — professional governance. The profound difference between the *corps* and the profession as institutional arrangements for the regulation of technical expertise were developed by Campagnac and Winch (1997); the principal point to be made here is that British civil engineering and architectural consultants are members of self-governing networks overseen by the professional institutions. They are typically appointed on a non-competitive basis on the basis of reputation and performance on earlier projects for the same client, governed by terms of appointment drawn up by the professional institutions themselves. Although the state has recently tried to introduce a price-competitive element into the selection of suppliers, the non-competitive appointment of architects and engineers remains the norm. Thus while the French system governs transaction A internally through the integration of engineering expertise into the state, or through the distinctive market for ideas which is the *concours*, governed through state codes, the British system relies upon an external governance system which can be called professional, depending upon self-regulation by the professionals themselves.

Turning to transaction B, this is governed internally in Britain, in the sense that the professional practice which is commissioned at A to do the definition typically does the description work as well. In France, it is at this point that coordination and integration are externalised through the market in both building and civil engineering. However, what is formally a competitive tendering process is deeply embedded in the social networks that exist between client and contractor. Sharing the same educational and technical culture through formation in the Grandes Ecoles d'Ingénieurs and pantouflage between the corps and the Senior cadres of the construction corporations means that the corps forms a strong social network developing a much higher trust relationship between client and contractor than is possible within the British system. Thus the formal governance from the *Code des Marchés Publics*, and enabled by the *bureau de contrôle* is complemented by a strong informal network that overcomes the information-thin nature of external market governance. Thus the French system demonstrates a considerable ability to negotiate and renegotiate the contract that governs this transaction in the search for savings for the client and profits for the contractor — the process of *variante*.

Transaction C is governed internally in France in the strong relationship between the contractors' *bureau d'etudes* carrying out description work, and their site operations engaged in structural work. In the horizontal dimension, integration is usually achieved internally through the direct and continuing employment of *operatives*. Transaction D is typically coordinated externally through a series of individual contracts with trade contractors held by the client, and managed on the client's behalf by the *pilote* who may be either the architect or the contractor for the structural works. These installation and finishes firms are often local and artisanal in character, although for the technologically more demanding trades, large national firms are also mobilised.

It is transaction C that is externally governed through the market within the British system — competitive tendering on the basis of price alone is the norm, subject to complex contract forms established largely by the professionals and the third party attention of the quantity surveyor. Typically, transactions C and D are bundled together in a general contract in Britain. Thus the transaction between structural works and installation and finishes — D — is usually governed internally in the British system in the vertical mode, but externally in the horizontal mode as the trade contractors carrying out the works are in sub-contract to the general contractor. The human resource dimension is also handled very differently in the UK, with the external mobilisation of self-employed gangs of operatives leading to very low levels of integration with the firm. The mode of governance at C is widely criticised within the UK for its inflexibility, and tendency to generate adversarial relationships between the actors, and the debilitating effects of self-employment (Winch 1998).

4.   From the Problem of Coordination and Integration to Models of Organisation

Braudel and Labrousse close their monumental social and economic history of France by returning to one of their central concerns — the comparison with Great Britain — arguing that the two countries represent two very different models of capitalism (1982: 1736). The previous section defined the problem that the business system is trying to solve in terms of the coordination and integration of a network of diverse actors. However, we need to go further than this simple representation of the problem. As Lazonick (1991) has argued, Williamson's formulation, from the starting-point of efficiency, is static and a-historical, and the same argument could be applied to the work of Porter. Our aim, having posed the problem of what is to be coordinated, is to develop a socially contextualised analysis of how effective coordination is achieved in two very different ways in France and Great Britain by developing the concept of the model of organisation as the interface between the national business system and the industrial sector — as the resultant of the societal and sectoral effects.

Airaudi (1995) has argued that there is a double-competition in globalising; as well as the competition between particular products, technologies, services, and capital, there is a latent competition between models of organisation themselves. The stakes are not only to obtain a modification of competitive forces, but also a change in the rules of the game. By model of organisation, Airaudi aims to articulate two modes: a mode specifically management and organisational, and a social mode in articulation with the influence of social groups. This definition is close to that of Veltz and Zarifian (1992: 53), for whom a model of organisation is "un ensemble de schémas-types de répresentations et d'actions, où s'imbriquent étroitement les formes sociales et les formes technico-économique d'identification et de résolution des problèmes d'efficience économique". Thus we can define a model of organisation as an ideal type which exists in a particular sector at a particular period through which actors solve the problems of coordination and integration. We propose here that the sector-specific modes of coordination and integration in British and French construction are embedded in two nationally distinctive models of organisation — the professional and industrial.

4.1 The Industrial Model of Coordination and Integration

The model of organisation that we have characterised as industrial, corresponding broadly to the French case, has two major characteristics:

- engineering design capability is integrated into either the client or the contractor (i.e. supplier of construction services);
- it is deeply embedded in the long-standing French tradition of the public/ private partnership in public services (Martinand 1993).

The French contractor typically internalises both the problem of vertical coordination across transaction C with its *bureau d'études*, and the horizontal coordination problem by directly employing its workforce on a continuous basis. Thus the integration of French contractor's engineering design capability is aimed at increasing its capacity to win tenders through the optimisation of site productivity, not to sell engineering design as a separate service. This strategy means that the focus is upon the efficiency and effectiveness of performance on site. For example, engineering calculations are aimed at reducing the consumption of materials, and innovations in both process and product are oriented towards this end. Engineering effort is also deployed to optimise the methods of construction, particularly the effective deployment of labour and plant. This growing integration is the result of a strategic initiative by the construction corporations implementing the *stratégie ensemblière* (Campagnac 1996b) of moving up the value system towards the client.

Thus in the French model, contractors are focused upon the search for efficiency by managing design and construction as an integrated whole (Campagnac et al. 1991), and the search for productivity through the effective combination of labour, materials and plant in a manner adapted to the constraints of variability in demand and in the construction process. For this reason, the integration of the workforce and human resource management plays an important role in the firm, focused on individualised negotiations with the workforce regarding performance, and a neo-Taylorist strategy. The aim is to reduce uncertainty, and to manage variability and productivity through this integration. The largely immigrant workforce was formed, during the seventies, in a Taylorist industrial manner without much training, but during the eighties, the trend was more towards the recruitment of young people to meet new needs for autonomy, initiative and individual competencies. The counterpart of this was a large reduction in employment.

In order to understand this strategy by the construction corporations — and this is the second aspect of the model — it is vital to understand the central role of the state in this *étatique* system (Boyer 1996a). This rests on the Colbertian tradition of a mutuality of relations between actors from the public and private sectors, as well as a legitimation through the notion of the general interest. The state's strategies towards the sector include the strong promotion of innovation in order to reduce costs on publicly funded projects. This aimed first at generating economies of scale, but more recently at economies of scope and speed. In order to support these innovations, the state developed new funding arrangements around deploying public, para-public and mixed forms as well as private initiative, generating a mass demand for the built product. As part of the same Colbertian tradition, the state retains strong engineering design capabilities itself, particularly for the upstream definition phases of the project.

In sum, the industrial model rests fundamentally upon a combination of coordination internally by hierarchy, and through action by the state, mediated by the *grands corps* and the common system of education. However, this articulation cannot be analysed simply in terms of social networks, but also in terms of the distinctively productivist representation of efficiency analysed above. Even where there appear to be exceptions to the model, such as the case of Technip which is an independent design services firm and the leading French firm in the international market, closer examination reveals that they conform to the model. Technip is owned by four leading French clients, two of which are from the public sector.

4.2 *The Professional Model of Coordination and Integration*

In our discussion of Figure 3, we emphasised the role of professionals in governing the upstream transactions in the British process. The essence of this professional governance is captured in the memorandum for the foundation of the Association of Consulting Engineers, the trade association for engineering consultancy firms, in 1913:

> "[An engineering consultancy devotes itself] to advising the public on engineering matters or to the designing or supervising the construction of engineering works, and for such purposes occupies and employs [its] own office and staff, and is not directly or indirectly concerned or interested in commercial or manufacturing interests such as would tend to influence [its] exercise of independent professional judgement in the matters upon which [it] advises." (Rimmer 1988: 761)

Our argument is that for transactions under very high uncertainty at A and B which Williamson (1975) would predict as internalised and governed hierarchically, an alternative is available where hierarchy is not possible either due to low transaction frequency nor desirable due to policy considerations — professional governance which has the following features:

– Purchasing design services separately from construction services greatly reduces the possibility of opportunism due to asset specificity after the fundamental transformation. The contracts for the remaining 95 per cent of the value can be let once uncertainty has been considerably reduced.
– Professional firms offer standardised intangibility (Larson 1977) of the service offered — clients do not know what they will get, but they know how it will be achieved due to formal work plans established independently.
– Redress in the case of poor performance is available to the client through the professional institution (e.g. Institution of Civil Engineers) which takes responsibility for regulating the formation and practice of its members.
– Liability is unlimited and personal — it is the *personne physique*, not the *personne morale* who is liable.
– It offers a form of high-trust relation between parties who do not know each other — reputational effects are paramount and generated collectively by the professional institution, supported by the universities which form the professionals.

Independent engineering consultancies are by no means a uniquely British phenomenon, but it can be argued that Great Britain, together with the United States and Canada, have developed the profession to its most sophisticated form. As Campagnac and Winch (1997) emphasised, there is more than one way of organising engineering expertise, and we would contend, there are important differing properties of this different forms of organisation with regard to transaction governance.

In the construction phases of the project, this distinctively professional governance of the design phases leaves a deep mark. British contractors typically have no engineering design capability — they have very little opportunity to optimise the project from a production point of view, the product being described in complete detail before they tender for it. Thus, their competitive efforts go into buying more cheaply the pre-defined inputs, and so the competitive tender on price at transactions C is replicated in the horizontal mode by competitive tendering on price for all the subcontractors as well. Even where British firms such as Trafalgar House Engineering and Construction,[6] which is a global market leader in both the design and the construction services sub-markets, appear to break with the model, in fact they support it. Trafalgar House is more of a holding company than an integrated supplier of design and construction services (Lorrain and Stocker 1994), typically selling engineering and construction services separately.

This strategy extends to the supply of labour inputs as well. Work remains organised on a craft basis, mirroring the professional organisation of engineering, with little attempt to rationalise the production process itself to improve productivity, and to provide adequate training. Payment is typically made on a gang rather than individual basis to self-employed workers on a lump-sum basis. Self-employment means that the workforce is externalised from the firm, and the relationship is one of a pure cash nexus. The paradox of productivity and flexibility (Winch 1994) is resolved very much in favour of flexibility, compared to the French emphasis upon productivity.

4.3 Two Models in Competition

We have attempted to formalise our argument in Table 1. At the techno-economic level, there are two distinct aspects of the analysis. Firstly, the differing approaches to the management of risk; secondly the mode of coordination of the process. So far as the management of risk is concerned, the professional model locates the conditions of efficiency essentially at the level of an economy of exchange and contracts, regulated by the intervention of professionalised actors and project managers. The industrial model locates efficiency at the level of a more integrated management of the production process, integrating the offer of the product and the service. In this model, the engineer working directly for the contractor or as member of a subsidiary specialist engineering firm is dominant. So far as the coordination of the process is concerned, the emphasis of the professional model is upon externalisation and coordination through the market, and a competence in how to buy the skills required for the project. In the industrial model, on the other hand, coordination is more internalised and hierarchical, with the emphasis upon how to make the built facility.

An important aspect of these differences is the representation of efficiency that each model favours. The professional model prefers a representation that favours financial measures of productivity and efficiency — measuring in monetary terms inputs and outputs to the process. The industrial model favours what can be called a productive representation of efficiency, orientated more towards the integrated design and management of the project as a whole, and the optimisation of the factors of production in a post-Tayloristic manner which is better adapted to the current market situation (Campagnac 1984), an approach which is closer to a technical logic. These differences are well captured by a respondent to the Channel Tunnel survey who reported "l'impression que les français faisaient 'le Tunnel' et les anglais de 'l'argent'" (Campagnac and Winch 1998: 192).

At the social level, there are two aspects to explore — the character of the key actors, and the nature of human resources. In the professional model, the key actors

Table 1: *The Professional and Industrial Modes of Organisation Compared*

Element of comparison	Professional model	Industrial model
Technico-economic level		
Management of risk	externalise risk; manage through contract; risk shedding	internalise risk; manage in process; risk sharing
Mode of coordination	market/collaborative; how to buy	hierarchy/collaborative; how to make
Representations of efficiency	financial: allocative efficiency	productive: organisational efficiency
Social level		
Key actors	professionals; project managers.	*corps d'état* enterprises.
Human resources	elaborated division of labour; craft trade unionism and responsible autonomy; team-working;	integrated hierarchy Taylorism and neo-Taylorism; competitive individualism

Source: Developed from Campagnac and Winch (1998).

are the different professionals involved in the process, coordinated by the project manager. In the industrial model, the key actors are, rather, the engineers working for the major construction groups, legitimated and coordinated through social networks such as the *corps des ponts* with engineers working for the state. A notable feature of the professional model is the considerable elaboration of different professions — each particular technical competence aims to develop its own professional association, clearly defining itself from the others (Abbott 1988). Within the *corps*, on the other hand, engineers have more general training and a greater overlap in expertise, combining *esprit de corps* with interpersonal rivalry.

These differences in the key actors are associated with differences in human resource management (Winch et al. 1997; Winch et al. 2000). At the managerial level, the more elaborated division of labour leads to a greater emphasis upon teamworking, while French managers are able to be more individualistic. The British worked through multiple hierarchies where legitimacy was attained through demonstrated performance, while the French had more integrated hierarchies, with legitimacy ascribed through position within the hierarchies of engineering schools and the associated *corps*.

At the operative level, similar differences exist (Campagnac 1996a). The British workforce also manifests a high level of specialisation, but this is not a detailed division of labour in the Taylorist sense, but the effect of a strongly trade-based specialisation. The trade is the basis for the allocation of tasks and qualifications, and this approach has been taken to its ultimate conclusion in the development of labour only subcontracting which is now the predominance of self-employment in labour-only sub-contract gangs (Winch 1998). One can contrast this situation with the more Taylorist one in France where productivity is achieved through greater standardisation of tasks and the calculation of standard times. French workers also enjoy higher basic rates and bonuses related to individual efforts.

Broadly speaking the French model can be characterised as one in which suppliers of construction services — contractors — have made strategic choices to integrate engineering design capabilities so that site operations for structure in particular, but also installation and finishes can be optimised in an approximation to the manufacturing model. This can be seen most clearly in the intensive internal integration of transaction C, with growing emphasis being given to simultaneous engineering, and the training of an industrial workforce to implement the optimised processes. In the British model, the strategic decision has been made to separate engineering design and construction services, so as to strengthen the relationship of suppliers of design services — usually architectural and engineering practices — in relation to the client, emphasising the setting of product specifications and the performance of the product in use in response to client requirements, rather than the optimisation of the production process.

5.   From Models of Organisation to Competitive Advantage

Our analysis of the two different models of organisation in the British and French construction industries indicates some of the ways in which differences in performance in the international construction market are attained. In construction services, the broadly similar levels of performance are attained in two very different ways. Interview data with senior managers of British international construction services companies shows that they see their principal competitive advantage in project management skills — knowing where to buy the specialist trades required, and how to effectively integrate them into the production process. Access to technologies in this perspective is a market entry, not order-winning criterion. Many construction technologies are not proprietary, and where they are they can be licensed or incorporated through joint venture partners or trade subcontractors. What is much more important is prior experience in managing similar projects enabling learning over time. "There was unanimous agreement that skills in coordinating construction projects formed the major competitive advantage available to contractors" (Enderwick 1989: 142). This flexibility, and knowledge of how to buy, rather than how to make serves British firms well in markets where other actors in the value system make the key technological choices, and the problem is the integration of diverse technologies.

Turning to the design services sub-market, the source of the British competitive advantage appears clear. Seymour reports (1987: 160) British consultants as arguing that their international success rests upon their independence, and that, in particular, to favour British contractors would compromise their own competitive advantage. The ability to package a set of engineering and architectural competencies independently of production concerns allows British firms to offer support and advice to clients in their relations with the suppliers of construction services. Thus, British firms clearly disintegrate the supply of design services and construction services, allowing the client to buy the former, which are high value added but a small (around 5 per cent) proportion of the total project cost, separately, and then to reduce uncertainty before entering into the main investment phase of the project. This decoupling has been much criticised within the British industry domestically, leading to adversarial relations and high production costs, but it offers clients important risk management benefits, in particular allowing clients to make technological choices independently of suppliers of construction services in order to maximise life-cycle rather than production cost criteria. By stressing this aspect, British and other Anglo-Saxon design services suppliers have been able to influence both the technical standards governing technological choices and the complex contracts used to procure suppliers of construction services through FIDIC.

French construction executives emphasise the integrated nature of their offer to the client. For those particular product types where production cost and technical complexity are paramount, and clients are prepared to allow suppliers to make technological choices — water and sewage systems is one — French firms have a major competitive advantage over their British counterparts. The growth of the BOOT market has, in particular, allowed French firms to strongly articulate the triangular relationship between governments, clients, and technological requirements, giving French firms competitive advantage in the construction and exploitation of autoroutes and a whole range of urban services such as tramways and cable systems. This competitive advantage is derived from the long experience of concession in the French domestic market, which in turn, is deeply embedded in the *étatique* character of the French system.

French engineering capabilities are either integrated into clients, which are usually state-owned, or into the suppliers of construction services which orientate them towards effectiveness in site operations, not towards designing to meet client requirements. Engineering capabilities integrated into the state are inherently difficult to export, except in the context of bilateral trade agreements which have generally been on the decline. The competitive strengths deriving from the integration of engineering capabilities into construction services are mixed. Although it clearly enhances efficiency and effectiveness in site operations, it poses important risk management problems for clients. Firstly, the cost of construction is overshadowed in the life-cycle of the product by its cost-in-use. Designs aimed at optimising the construction process may jeopardise the long-term value of the constructed product. Secondly, it pushes the problem of coordination and integration to a higher uncertainty transaction (C → B → A), posing more acute problems of governance. While these can be well managed in the French national context through the social networks and public/private partnerships mediated by the *grands corps* and similar, this is not so easily the case in the international market. In sum, our argument is that the French business system has generated a strongly integrated model of organisation in construction which is very effective domestically, but which has certain features which are difficult to export.

Thus we are arguing that the French model of organisation in construction is more tightly coupled than the British. While creating a domestic industry which is generally considered to be more efficient than the British, this tighter coupling generates a distinctive set of competitive advantages in the international market, but also a clear set of competitive disadvantages in the design services sub-market. This is most clear in the problems that the French model has with competition in design services. The British model of organisation, on the other hand, is more loosely coupled, which generates notably problems in the domestic industry, but provides a distinctive set of competitive advantages in international markets, which, in their nature are more loosely coupled. Porter (1990) has clearly demonstrated the link between national business systems and competitive advantage in international competition; we are arguing that the differences in the British and French models of organisation confer nationally distinctive sources of competitive advantage on engineering and construction firms from those countries which produce similar levels of performance overall, but built up from very different levels of performance in particular market sub-sectors. As a result, the geographical distribution of demand for the two industries is very different. Further research needs to focus on the demand side to identify the sub-markets and geographic regions which favour each of these two models of organisation, and on the supply side to identify other national models of organisation in construction.

One of the most important questions that needs to be addressed in such research is the nature of demand. Research needs to identify the ways in which the relationship with the client is constituted in different parts of the world and for different product types, by identifying the different economic and institutional mechanisms through which this relationship is generated. Is there a strong relationship between the influence of international institutions, negotiations between states, and common knowledge regarding engineering principles shared between clients and their suppliers of design and construction services in the manner suggested by the theory of conventions in order to achieve agreement about what constitutes good quality (Eymard-Duvernay 1985)?

6.   Some Concluding Thoughts

The issues addressed in this chapter are those of uncertainty, information and trust in international markets. Transactions under high uncertainty require trust for effective governance (Nooteboom et al. 1997). Trust is typically seen as being generated in specific social contexts (Fukuyama 1995), but in their very nature, these locally specific contexts do not scale easily to the international level. Other mechanisms for establishing trust may need to be generated. One conclusion from our argument, as can been seen from our data on the design services sub-market, is that the professional governance of high uncertainty transactions seems to offer one way of generating trust in the global market. This is a weak trust mechanism, but at the international level, it can be a major source of competitive advantage. The problem is particularly acute in the service sector, where production often has to move to the point of consumption. Most manufactured goods can be exported finished from a business system — the product embodies all the social relations inherent in the model of organisation that produced it. Most services have to be produced at their point of consumption by the consumer,[7] which means that it is difficult for firms to draw competitive advantage from locally specific networks of production — the model of organisation itself has to be exported. Another conclusion is that, as shown by our construction services sub-market data, very different models of organisation with distinctive competitive advantages can achieve similar levels of performance in international markets, and these models of organisation embody very different representations of efficiency. Globalisation is not, therefore, an homogenising process, but a dynamic interplay of distinctive competitive advantages, derived from different national models of organisation. A third is that the concept of national business system needs to be complemented by that of the model of organisation which is both sectorally specific, and also includes cognitive aspects such as the representation of efficiency. National business systems, we would propose, consist not only of sets of institutions, but also culturally specific ways of thinking about economic problems — an issue addressed in more detail in part II of this volume. While in Anglo-Saxon countries such as the UK, the market tends to be perceived by decision-makers as non-embedded, in countries such as France, decision-makers are more clearly aware of the embedded nature of economic activity.

Moving from the level of the model of organisation to that of the national business system, a fourth conclusion is that we can possibly distinguish between loose and tight national business systems. Tight systems are those with extensive state coordination of and cooperation with the private sector; where the elements of the system are finely honed to relate to each other, be it through negotiation and compromise between social partners or state action; and where trust is developed through social networks span different types of actors in the business system. Uncertainty and risk tend to be managed by internalising transactions, and flexibility is achieved through integration and polyvalence. Tight systems find it relatively easy to achieve the type of diversified quality production that characterises the German and Japanese business systems (Hollingsworth 1997). Loose systems are those where the state takes a regulatory rather than proactive role; where social partners are seen as opponents, and where relations between the actors are cast in terms of contract rather than social terms. Uncertainty and risk tend to be managed through externalising transactions, flexibility is achieved through specialisation, and trust is generated through social networks restricted to single types of actors such as professions. Loose systems either achieve inflexible forms of integration such as mass production through strong hierarchies, such as in the US, or fail to achieve the necessary integration due to social fragmentation as in Great Britain (Lazonick 1991).

This distinction between loose and tight business systems may help to explain the much greater variability in performance of firms in particular sectors found in British companies compared to other European countries. Although leading British firms perform as well as those from anywhere else, they are followed by a long tail which drags down average performance (Hanson et al. 1993). This is also noted by Deakin and his colleagues elsewhere in this volume. Tight systems might be expected to diffuse best practice more rapidly than loose ones so that average performance is closer to the best in the former. This distinction might also explain the relative strengths of Great Britain in the world trade in services (Porter 1990), in contrast to its relatively weak position in manufacturing. Of particular interest here is the role of the professions in loose systems — Strange (1996: 98) identifies them as a major force in globalisation, most obviously in accountancy and its offspring management consultancy.

If this distinction is robust, then the question begged is what are the criteria for this differentiation of markets and the associated competencies required for competitive performance? Are they linked to our distinction between world trade in markets for finished goods and services such as the provision and operation of urban services, where tight systems could have the advantage, and other service and intermediate goods sectors where loose systems could have more of an advantage? This may be because the principal features of the tight system — state coordination, social partners sharing a common geographic space, and social networks are more difficult to establish at the international level. Thus the skills learned in performing in loose systems where information-thin market governance prevails may be more appropriate than those learned in tight systems which rely more on information-thick non-market governance when operating internationally in certain sectors (see Lehrer and Darbishire, in this volume, for a similar argument relating to other network industries). In an important sense, international trade is founded on differences and reproduces new differences between national business systems and their internationally competitive models of organisation, and this requires a renewal of our theoretical approaches to globalisation and international comparative research.

Notes

1. From 1994 on, the construction services data are based on 'revenues'. This has a major negative impact on the share of the American firms, mainly in favour of Japan, but does not appear to significantly alter the relative shares of France and the United Kingdom.

2. For instance, in 1993, the French share of the European international construction services sub-market was 16.9 per cent against the British share of 9 per cent, while the British share of the US international sub-market was 37.8 per cent against 5.7 per cent for the French.

3. We have, in effect, reversed the distinction of Boyer (1996b) between a *rapport horizontal* between firms, and a *rapport vertical* integrating capital and labour. This is in order to be consistent with the traditional notion of vertical integration along the value system.

4. Williamson (1985: 75) notes the role of the architect in trilateral governance transaction between the client and structural contractor, but is silent on how the transaction between the architect itself and the client is governed.

5. The British state is unusual in possessing no corps of engineers such as the US Army Corps of Engineers who have played such an important role in gaining access for US firms to overseas markets (Rimmer 1988) — the rebuilding of Kuwait after the Gulf War is a classic example.

6. The Trafalgar House group was taken over by Kvaerner of Norway in 1995.

7. This is not always the case — tourism is notable for moving the customer to the point of production which is usually strongly related to a particular local context.

References

Abbott, A. 1988. *The System of Professions.* Chicago: University of Chicago Press.

Airaudi, S. 1995. Pour une Théorie des Modèles d'Organisation, *Revue Française de Gestion,* Nov/Déc: 5–10.

Boyer, R. 1996a. Le Capitalisme Etatique Française à la Croisée des Chemins. In: C. Crouch, and W. Streek (eds.), *Les Capitalismes en Europe,* 97–138. Paris: La Découverte.

Boyer, R. 1996b. Les Capitalismes à la Croisée des Chemins, *Sciences Humaines,* Sept/ Oct.: 44–47.

Braudel, F., and E. Labrousse. 1982. *Histoire Economique et Social de la France.* Vol. 4. Paris: Presses Universitaire de France.

Campagnac, E. 1984. *Construction et architecture: métiers en mutation?* Paris: Ed. L'Equerre.

Campagnac, E. (ed.). 1992. *Les Grands Groupes de la Construction: de Nouveaux Acteurs Urbains?* Paris: L'Harmattan.

Campagnac, E. 1996a. La Maîtrise du Risque entre Différences et Cooperation: le Cas du Severn Bridge, Working Paper no. 12, Le Groupe Bagnolet, London.

Campagnac, E. 1996b. Les Stratégies Ensemblières à l'Epreuve de la Réglementation des Marchés Publics en France, Working Paper no. 7, Le Groupe Bagnolet, London.

Campagnac, E., J. Bobroff, and C. Caro. 1991. *Nouvelles approches de la productivité et méthodes d'organisation d'entreprises.* Paris: Plan Construction et Architecture.

Campagnac, E., and G. M. Winch. 1997. The Social Regulation of Technical Expertise: The Corps and Profession in Great Britain and France. In: R. Whitley, and P. H. Kristensen (eds.), *Governance at Work: the Social Regulation of Economic Relations,* 86–103. Oxford: OUP.

Campagnac, E., and G. M. Winch. 1998. Civil Engineering Joint Ventures: The British And French Models Of Organisation In Confrontation. In: R. Lundin, and C. Midler (eds.), *Projects as Arenas for Renewal and Learning Processes,* 191–206. Dordrecht: Kluwer.

Colombard-Prout, M. 1988. France. In: W. P. Strassman, and J. Wells (eds.),*The Global Construction Industry, strategies for entry, growth and survival,* 104–119. London: Unwin Hyman.

Enderwick, P. 1989. Multinational Contracting. In: P. Enderwick (ed.), *Multinational Service Firms,* 132–151. London: Routledge.

Engineering News Record (different annual editions), New York: McGraw-Hill.

Eymard-Duvernay, F. 1985. Conventions et Qualité des Biens. In: R. Salis, and L. Thevenot (eds.), *Le Travail: marchées, règles et conventions,* 239–248. Paris: Economica.

Fukuyama, F. 1995. *Trust: The Social Virtues and the Creation of Prosperity.* London: Hamish Hamilton.

Hanson, P., C. Voss, K. Blackmon, and B. Oak. 1993. *Made in Europe — A Four Nations Best Practice Study.* Warwick: IBM Consulting Group.

Hollingsworth, J. R. 1997. Continuities and Changes in Social Systems of Production: The Cases of Japan, Germany and the United States. In: J. R. Hollingsworth, and R. Boyer (eds.), *Contemporary Capitalism : the Embeddedness of Institutions,* 265–310. Cambridge: Cambridge University Press.

Kristensen, P. H. 1997. National Systems of Governance and Managerial Prerogatives in the Evolution of Work Systems. In: R. Whitley, and P. H. Kristensen (eds.), *Governance at Work: the Social Regulation of Economic Relations,* 3–48. Oxford: OUP.

Larson, M. S. 1977. *The Rise of Professionalism.* Berkeley: University of California Press.

Lazonick, W. 1991. *Business Organization and the Myth of the Market Economy.* Cambridge: Cambridge University Press.

Lin, Y.-J. 1999. Competitive Advantage of Nations and Segmented International Construction Markets: study of international construction contracting from 1981 to 1990, Ph.D. Thesis. London: University College London.

Linder, M. 1994. *Projecting Capitalism.* Westport: Greenwood Press.

Lorrain, D., and G. Stocker. 1994. *La Privatisation des Services Urbains en Europe.* Paris: La Découverte.

Martinand, C. (ed.). 1993. *Le financement privé des équipements publics: l'expérience française.* Paris: Economica.

Nooteboom, B., H. Berger, and N. G. Noorderhaven. 1997. Effects of Trust and Governance on Relational Risk, *Academy of Management Journal* 40: 308–338.

Picon, A. 1992. *L'Invention de L'Ingénieur Moderne: L'Ecole des Ponts et Chaussées 1747–1851.* Paris: Presses Pont et Chaussées.

Porter, M. 1985. *Competitive Advantage.* New York: Free Press.

Porter, M. 1990. *The Competitive Advantage of Nations.* New York: Macmillan.

Rimmer, P. J. 1988. The Internationalization of Engineering Consultancies: the Problems of Breaking into the Club, *Environment and Planning A* 20: 761–788.

Seymour, H. 1987. *The Multinational Construction Industry.* London: Croon Helm.

Soubra, Y. 1993. International Competitiveness and Corporate Strategies in the Construction Services Sector. In: Y. Aharoni (ed.), *Coalitions and Competition,* 193–210. London: Routledge.

Stinchcombe, A. L. 1990. *Information and Organizations.* Berkeley: University of California Press.

Strange, S. 1996. *The Retreat of the State: The Diffusion of Power in the World Economy.* Cambridge: CUP.

Strassmann, W. P., and J. Wells (eds.). 1988. *The Global Construction Industry, strategies for entry, growth and survival.* London: Unwin Hyman.

Thoenig, J.-C. 1987. *L'Ere des Technocrats.*(2nd ed.) Paris: L'Harmattan.

Veltz, P., and P. Zarifian. 1992. Modèle systémique et flexibilité. In: G. Terssac, and P. Dubois (eds.), *Les nouvelles rationalisations de la production,* 43–61. Toulouse: CEPADUES.

Whitley, R. 1992. *Business Systems in East Asia.* London: Sage.

Whitley, R., and P. H. Kristensen (eds.). 1997. *Governance at Work: the Social Regulation of Economic Relations.* Oxford: OUP.

Williamson, O. E. 1975. *Markets and Hierarchies: Analysis and Anti-Trust Implications.* New York: Free Press.

Williamson, O. E. 1985. *The Economic Institutions of Capitalism.* New York: The Free Press.

Winch, G. M. 1994. *Managing Production: Engineering Change and Stability.* Oxford: Clarendon Press.

Winch, G. M. 1996a. Contracting Systems in the European Construction Industry: A Sectoral Approach to the Dynamics of Business Systems. In: R. Whitley, and P. H. Kristensen (eds.), *The Changing European Firm,* 241–270. London: Routledge.

Winch, G. M. 1996b. The Contracting System in the British Construction Industry: The Rigidities of Flexibility, Working Paper No. 6. Le Groupe Bagnolet, London.

Winch, G. M. 1998. The Growth of Self-employment in British Construction, *Construction Management and Economics* 16: 531–542.

Winch, G. M., C. C. J. M. Millar, and N. Clifton. 1997. Culture and Organization: The Case of Transmanche-Link, *British Journal of Management* 8: 237–249.

Winch, G. M., A. Usmani, and A. Edkins. 1998. Towards Total Project Quality: A Gap Analysis Approach, *Construction Management and Economics* 16: 193–207.

Winch, G. M., N. Clifton and C. C. J. M. Millar. 2000. Organization and Management in an Anglo-French Consortium: The Case of Transmanche-Link, *Journal of Management Studies* 37.

PART V

Institutional Legacies and Performance Outcomes in National Business Systems

CHAPTER 12

Sector Specialisation and Performance in the Netherlands

Ad van Iterson

1. Introduction

This chapter explores the legacy of sector specialisation in the Dutch business system. To what extent is the international performance of different sectors in the Netherlands influenced by the historical particularities of Dutch business and institutions? Elaborating on earlier work on the Dutch business system (van Iterson and Olie 1992; Sorge and van Iterson 1995; van Iterson 1997), we will examine why certain sectors — e.g. agriculture, transport and transshipment, financial services, foods and drinks, and mineral fuels and chemicals — have prospered in their social-institutional context and why other sectors have not done so. Likewise, we will consider the extent to which competition for social and economic space between different groups or classes (Kristensen 1996) can account for this sector specialisation which led to an idiosyncratic route to industrialisation compared to other European societies. In the second part of this contribution, the 20th century corporatist industrial system (in the Netherlands known as pillarisation), will be discussed. This centralised institutional setting of coalition building between élites representing the 'social partners' (employers, employees and government) began to disappear in the 1970s. In the 'liberal order' which emerged from this point the 'pre-industrial' principles of consensus and peer control, operating at both the workplace level and in the board rooms, remain viable. These rules of action, it is concluded, are much more crucial in the adaptation process to increasing scale and globalising markets than the formal corporatist system ever was. This hypothesis may shed a somewhat different light on the often made observation that the Dutch business system has become a high performing blend of the Anglo-Saxon and the Germanic systems.

2.   The Route to Sector Specialisation and Dominance in the Netherlands

Nowadays, the Netherlands are celebrated for their artificiality. The surface of this most densely populated country in Europe (457 inhabitant per square kilometre) is extensively and intensively cultivated, and generally 'man-made' to an extent which is singular in the world. In the Middle Ages, however, the lower parts of the Netherlands consisted largely of marshes and peat bogs (Lambert 1985). It was a territory difficult to get at and therefore quite unsuitable for the formation of a society in which semi-autarkic farmers lived in dependence on a warrior class (i.e. the classic model of Western European Feudalism). In the maritime provinces of Holland and Zeeland, peasant farmers were free from feudal ties and obligations already from the 12th century onwards. In the ensuing ages, reclaimed land was parcelled out for small farmers (Israel 1995). By the 16th century, increasing intensification and specialisation has rendered Dutch agriculture an unparalleled productivity (De Vries 1974; Mokyr 1976; Israel 1995).

The quasi-absence of feudalism offered the town-dwellers the chance to specialise in commercial activities (De Vries 1973). The many outlets to the open sea and inland waterways explains why economic expansion was sought in fishing, overseas carrying and river traffic. The seagoing ships which ensured dominance over the North Sea herring grounds for centuries and which took care of the bulk-carrying traffic between the Baltic (grain and timber) and the Bay of Biscay (wine and salt), were technically ahead of their time. As the peasant farmers were included in nascent urban trading networks, chances did increase for both groups. Also profiting were the related small-scale, diversified manufacturing industries in the cities, which tended to be energy-intensive because fuel was available at low costs as the abundant peat could be transported by canal (De Zeeuw 1978). Some of these industries were supportive (e.g. shipbuilding, rope- and sailmaking), whilst the majority further processed trading goods. Especially in the sugar refineries, soap works, bleach- and dye-works for wool and linen, tobacco processors etc., expert knowledge of both domestic and colonial commodities was accelerated. The productive cooperation between peasantry, commerce and industry, free from feudal command and guild restrictions, offered the opportunity to vary output patterns (Maddison 1991: 33). It also brought about a strong population growth, which again contributed to the on-going process of urbanisation and cultivation of old and new land.

To understand the later corporatist character of the Dutch agricultural sector, the organisation of collective effort of drainage and land reclamation is vital. To fund, construct and maintain dykes, dams and drainage channels, local polder and drainage boards developed. These *heemraadschappen* were mobilised by volunteering farmers and citizens, with some help from the local government (Israel 1995: 10). Upon these initiatives, regional organisations or *hoogheemraadschappen* emerged, providing for jurisdiction. These formal agencies, too, were "founded on the traditional Germanic cooperative principles of quasi-government through peer control" (Sorge and van Iterson 1995: 191). They consisted also of representatives of towns, rural localities, and the nobility. Moreover these regional boards were limited in reach, and, because of their character of proportionality, not contradictory to the associations on which they were superimposed. Both these local and regional water district boards can be regarded as a cradle of the Dutch governance principle of consensus building via peer control of representation of local interests (van Iterson 1997). But they also constituted a basis for the ensuing corporatist organisation of the agricultural sector. The social structure of the polders induced the independent farmers to enter upon horizontal collaboration. Through associations at the service of agriculture and its marketing, the small farmers have been able to reap economies of scale and market access. Indeed, capital intensity and the level of technology in agriculture have been traditionally very high (de Vries 1974). In later centuries, the cooperative principle and company networking were reinforced by corporatist associations *(productschappen)* which go on to play an important role in the self-government of the agricultural sector and the related food supply sector. The strength of these *productschappen,* or commodity boards, is precisely that companies all along the value chain share resources.

In the larger cities, above all Amsterdam, the merchant élites further developed the fishing and trading activities which had brought them wealth and engaged in initially supporting activities — banking, insurance, warehousing — which soon were to evolve in crucial sectors as well. This implied, firstly, the emergence of large-scale trade organisations active in the expanding world market (Boxer 1973; Blussé and Gaastra 1981). The most famous is the Dutch East India Company, one of the world's first public limited companies and the largest multinational trading firm in the 17th century (Gaastra 1981; Steensgaard 1982), with supportive factories all over Asia, where natural and human resources were unscrupulously utilised. Alongside that, Amsterdam developed into the single most important financial centre in Europe through the establishment of the Bank of Amsterdam and a considerable number of merchant-banking houses active in foreign lending.

Here, the role of governmental agencies is more influential than in the rural sector. In fact, the East and West India Companies combined the pursuit of commercial and military interests (Furber 1976). Although officially independent, they were hybrids: "neither a simple partnership for trade nor a state agency" (Steensgaard 1982: 251). The proportionality of their governance (the highest managerial functionaries represented provincial boards of directors) reflected the national character of these enterprises. At the same time, and this is considered a typically 'modern' aspect, managerial discretion from owners was high as shares were widely dispersed (Gaastra 1981).

The Bank of Amsterdam was founded in 1609 by the city government. It was one of the first public banks in Western Europe (Kindleberger 1993). Its initial purpose is well known: to put an end to the confusion from foreign coin by providing valid money (Smith 1982). But already in its first century one witnesses a strong diversification of activities (Barbour 1966). The Bank of Amsterdam contributed greatly to the Dutch international trade in coin: silver from Mexico was minted into various coins for export to the Baltic, the Levant and the Far East. Sophisticated techniques such as trading in options were also first developed in Amsterdam. In the 17th and 18th centuries, Holland dominated the international capital markets of Europe. The Dutch merchant-banking houses invested heavily in securities and operations in the German Empire, Britain, France and the United States, respectively (Riley 1980). Only the French occupation in 1793 of the Netherlands put an end to this foreign lending of Dutch savings.

Important to notice, at the end of this section, is that successful Dutch merchants did not strive to purchase offices, honours or landed estates (Riley 1980: 62), as was the usual way to advance into the nobility in countries such as France and England where the higher aristocracy was included in courtly circles (Elias 1983). Dutch merchants stayed in commerce, as did their offspring (Barbour 1966: 141). This feature might contribute to explain the ongoing strength of commercial sectors in the Netherlands.

3.   Sector Dominance in the Industrialised Era

The rise of the Dutch Republic to world leadership in agricultural productivity, in overseas trade, in transshipment and in finance in the early modern epoch was nothing less than a divergent path to industrialisation (van Iterson 1997). Dutch industrialisation can only be qualified as 'retarded' when compared with the English Industrial Revolution based on the large-scale application of steam-driven technology in the factory system. What contributed to the Republic's early prosperity, were technological innovations of a less radical nature. In fact, it was above all improvements of traditional devices. Drainage, farming and manufacturing profited greatly from the advanced windmill technology; fishing and bulk freightage from the introduction of the fast 'fluit' ship which doubled the speed. In addition, one can refer to fodder crops, methods of soil replenishment, improved sluices, harbour cranes, timber-saws, and textile looms (Davids 1993). Also the sophistication achieved in finance, accounting, warfare, discipline and punishment was a rationalisation of existing techniques rather than revolutionary break-throughs. Finally, the same applies to advances in classifying, testing, storing, transporting, processing and marketing trade commodities.

The agrarian-commercial character of the Dutch economy did not change substantially until the 1880s (van Zanden 1993: 142–156), when the Netherlands started to close the 'industrial gap' by catching up remarkably fast with the second spurt in mechanisation which accompanied the birth of the chemical and electrical industries. Even then, the fundamentally 'pre-industrial' character of the Dutch business system is anything but wiped out. In fact, the structure of the emerging concentrated sectors between 1880 and 1920 reflects largely the above-sketched two historical main streams: the agricultural/processing sector and the trade/transport/financial sector. Both sectors were able to profit from a rapid increase in demand for products such as petrol, detergents, branded articles — typically the first frontier in purchasing when the standard of living of the lower and middle classes rises.

The vast majority of the largest multinational corporations in present Dutch business have found their genesis in these decades. The Dutch part of Unilever (foods, drinks, detergents) was founded in 1870; the Dutch part of the Royal Dutch Shell Group (oil and petroleum products) in 1890, AKZO Nobel (chemicals, synthetic fibres, varnishes, pharmaceuticals) in 1910 (margarine), 1918 (salt) and in 1923 (pharmaceuticals). Unilever, Shell and AKZO Nobel, together with Heineken (beer, founded in 1863) and DSM (chemicals, energy, fertilisers; evolved from the coal-mining industry which gained momentum between 1900 and 1914), form the backbone of the Dutch processing industries sector. As to the other mainstream, the trade, transport and financial sector, one sees that supermarket chain AHOLD was established in 1887, retail trader Vendex International in 1888, wholesaler and retail trader SHV in 1896, trading company Hagemeyer in 1900, and the Royal Dutch Airlines KLM in 1919. The history of the three large banks which emerged from the 1990s merger wave — ABN Amro, ING Group and Rabobank — is too complicated to summarise here, but most of the commercial banks from which the big three developed originate from the same decades. The same observation can be made with regard to insurance and investment companies, such as Fortis Amev, Aegon and the Achmea group.

All above-mentioned companies — except SHV and Rabobank which are not quoted — are in the 1996/7 top twenty of the largest listed corporations in the Netherlands in terms of turnover and all but two are in the 1996/7 top twenty in terms of profit (Jaarboek van Nederlandse Ondernemingen 1997). The remaining six companies in the top twenty turnover involve a publisher (Elsevier), a paper producer (KNP BT), a steel and aluminium producer (Hoogovens), a music company (Polygram), a post and telecommunication company (KPN) and one of the world leaders in consumer electronics and industrial electronic equipment: Philips, founded in 1891. Together with aircraft constructor Fokker, founded in 1919, Philips attests to the fact that, despite the above-sketched continuities between the early-modern and modern Dutch business structure, a concentrated industrial sector based on large batch production of composite consumer goods and machineries *did* evolve in the Netherlands. Nevertheless, post-war history has shown that above all this end of the Dutch industrial spectre is vulnerable. The liquidation of the shipbuilding industry in the 1970s may be largely due to competition by low-wage countries, but that argument is only of limited import- ance with regard to Fokker and Philips. Both firms enjoyed considerable financial support from the national government, in the case of Fokker even huge support. Nonetheless, the aircraft builder was disssolved in 1996.

A sizeable number of Dutch top twenty companies can also be found in the European top 300 firms in terms of turnover, as indicated in Table 1. Of these, three are in the top twenty: the Royal Dutch Shell Group (nr. 2 on the list), Unilever (11) and Philips (16) (see Table 1).

If one looks again at the domestic situation, but then at the aggregate level of industries, the same pattern of strong sectors emerges. For instance, the processing sectors — food and drinks together with the chemical and mineral oil/ coal processing — make up no less than 40.7 per cent of the total industrial turnover (see Table 2).

In numbers of firms, the agricultural, trade and services sectors make up 85 per cent of Dutch business. The percentage of firms in the processing industries is included in the remaining 15 per cent (manufacturing etc.). A very careful

Table 1: *Dutch Companies in the European Top 300 in Terms of Sales, 1997*

Mark	Company	Sales (in USD)
2	Royal Dutch Oil	74,244,093
11	Unilever	50,352,719
16	Philips electronics	39,685,134
24	ING Group	34,109,314
41	ABN AMRO Holding	26,593,829
58	Royal AHOLD	20,955,494
75	SHV Holdings	17,184,561
107	Rabobank	13,573,641
109	AEGON	13,507,685
114	AKZO Nobel	12,868,777
128	ROYAL PTT Nederland	11,760,151
138	NEDERLANDSE GASUNIE	10,750,746
184	KONINKLIJKE KNP BT	7,821,175
221	VENDEX INTERNATIONAL	6,618,889
243	Heineken	6,061,023
249	DSM	5,886,098
267	KLM	5,479,843
299	Hagemeyer	4,712,199

Source: Worldscope GLOBAL.

Table 2: *Turnover of Some Industrial Sectors in the Netherlands (per ultimo 1996)*

Sector	Turn-over (in millions of guilders)	Turn-over (in %)
Food and drinks	72,717	21.7
Chemical industry	47,892	14.3
Mineral oil and coal processing	16,006	4.7
Total	334,702	100

Source: Statistics Netherlands (1997).

Table 3: *Sectoral Distribution in the Netherlands (per 1.1.1997)*

Sector	% number of firms
Agriculture, fishery, forestry, hunting	17
Manufacturing, winning of minerals, construction	15
Trade	25
Services	43
Total	100

Source: Statistics Netherlands (1997).

estimation, then, would be that 90 per cent of the Dutch economic units is active in the strong sectors (see Table 3).

In an earlier publication (van Iterson and Olie 1992), a discussion has been presented of the 'waisted' structure of Dutch business, with on the one hand some twenty large corporations with world-wide operations, employing between 20,000 and 300,000 people, and on the other hand half a million registered companies employing less than 10 people, making up 91 per cent of the Dutch firms, and with only a small number of medium-sized firms in between. Above, the performance of the largest multinational companies (MNCs) has been briefly considered. However, a relatively high number of firms below the waist too are active and successful in the global arena — for one reason that they export directly, but also because they have sub-contracting relations with firms above the waist.

In the late 1990s, the high performing Dutch business system — with above EU-average annual growth rate in gross domestic product (GDP) (2.8 against 2.4 per cent over 1983–1997) and almost total industrial peace — has gained broad acknowledgement as the 'Polder model', the success of which is held to be above all owing to moderate wages demands by the trade unions or — as many put it — to the Dutch corporatist industrial system. This chapter hopefully makes clear that there is more to the system's viability than union cooperativeness alone. Indeed, it is very debatable whether the formal corporatist system still exists and moreover whether it was ever beneficial to the competitiveness of Dutch business and its strong sectors.

Let us return to the decades when the Netherlands caught up with industrial mass production capitalism in their dominant sectors. Between 1880 and 1920 one sees not only a strong continuation of the early modern Dutch business system on a larger scale and in larger units, but also the dissemination of the cooperative and corporatist principles from the agricultural sector to all other sectors. First, one discerns this latter trend in farm credit banks, such as the present Rabobank, which financed purchasing, processing and sales cooperative associations. More important, however, was the application of the corporatist principle via different employers' organisations and trade unions. But here something peculiar happened. The self-organisation of employers, craftsmen and workers came to be incorporated in a larger societal phenomenon which evolved in the late nineteenth century Netherlands: the strong vertical ideological segmentation of collective actors, known as pillarisation. This included a pattern of segregation of groups at the bottom and coalitions of élites at the top between the traditionally fragmented protestant denominations, the liberals, the Roman-Catholics and the socialists, which latter two had just fought their way to the public arena (Lijphart 1968). Hence, political parties, trade unions, schools, mutual health and social insurance and professional organisations were established along these confessional and political lines. Compromises and coalitions between the pillarised institutions was only achieved at the highest possible centralised levels. In this respect, the pillarised system was a far cry from the traditional corporatist principle in agriculture of which the decentralised character has been elucidated above. So, although the new system was inspired by the older one, it took a different course — especially after World War Two when the Foundation of Labour and the Social Economic Council were established. In these very powerful advisory boards to the government, representatives of central organisations of employers and employees, later on together with Crown-appointed independent experts, bargained over the development of wages and labour conditions. Their advice led to binding wage guidelines at sector level (Windmuller 1969). In the 1960s, when economic growth and internationalisation gained momentum in the Netherlands, the rigidity of the corporatist guided wage policy was more and more denounced as a hindrance to flexibility and led to the total abolition of the system in 1983 (van Veen 1997).

4.   The Dutch Business System as a Blend of the Anglo-Saxon and the Germanic Systems

The fact that the Dutch pattern of corporatists industrial organisation largely gave way to a more 'liberal-capitalist' order in the last three decades (Visser 1992), can be to a large extent attributed to the capital intensive multinationals 'above the waist'. In the process of concentration of the 1970s-1990s they became powerful enough to operate more and more independently, e.g. through forcing unions to accept single-firm collective agreements (Visser 1992). The shifting power balance in favour of these global economic actors, in combination with the processes of secularisation and a reduction in ideological conflict in the wider society, finally made official corporatism obsolete, except for the agricultural sector and the marketing of foodstuffs, where traditional corporatism of the *productschappen* is still strong.

However, the dissolution of the corporatist structure did not imply that the same fate befell the 'pre-industrial' regulatory principles of consensus and proportionality. The willingness to find consensus within the collectivity and with external relations contributed to the commonly held notion of the Dutch firm as a 'nexus of stakeholders' (van Iterson and Olie 1992) where neither of the parties dominates. Despite their large managerial discretion (as a result of dispersed share ownership, effective protection against unfriendly take-overs, the permanent tenure of executives and the arm's length relations with governmental and financial institutions), executive boards in the larger enterprises of the concentrated sectors tend to pursue the public interest of the company and not the partial interests of shareholders, management itself or any other collective actor. This commitment to the firm's interest is also by and large accepted by the lower echelons. Their cooperativeness has facilitated the operation of the co-determination system on the shop floor in which the works councils enjoy an accepted role.

Despite high job fragmentation and strong managerial coordination of complementary processes as a consequence of the size and technology of operations (process and mass production), worker and workers' teams in large Dutch companies are still granted relatively high discretion (van Iterson 1997) — not because Dutch employers are such convinced democrats, but because it has proven to pay off (Lammers 1973). Following Whitley's terminology (1997), Dutch work systems can be qualified as 'negotiated' rather than 'Taylorist'. As a result, peer control in (semi-)autonomous work teams has been retained in the Netherlands and, so it can be hypothesised, developed into a strong asset as Dutch business came to be more and more included in globalising markets.

A more or less comparable 'clever use' of national idiosyncratic governance principles for the benefit of high performance in globalising markets may be discernible in the decision-making at higher echelons in larger Dutch firms. At this level, again, the twin features of the pressures of the international market and the dominant perception of the firm as a nexus of stakeholders, expressed in consensus-seeking behaviour, seem to reinforce one another. It might have the effect that management, in spite of its high autonomy from supervisors, shareholders, government, banks and institutional investors, does not become too self-involved and arrogant. This, again, might have the effect that external perspectives will be embraced, which can contribute to the effectiveness of top management, especially in the strong sectors.

Concluding this section, we can agree with the often made observation that the Dutch business system is a high performing blend of the Anglo-Saxon and the Germanic systems (Calori and de Woot 1995; Scott, 1997; Hollingsworth and Boyer 1997) as long as 'Germanic' refers to the traditional cooperative principles of quasi-government through peer control and *not* to the formal institutions of corporatism.

5. Conclusion

Dutch business caught up remarkably fast with large-scale industrial capitalism in the decades between 1880 and 1920. This is the more surprising since both the state and the banks — often so elementary in continental industrialisation — played a limited role in the Netherlands.

In contrast to the days of the East and West Indies Companies and the colonisation of sundry coastal areas, the Dutch government in the nineteenth century was no longer able to organise such a concerted effort. With some exceptions, the central government was not able to support the development of specific sectors. The commitment of banks to industrial development was also almost absent (Scott 1997: 153). From the post-Napoleonic decades onwards, Dutch banks invested almost exclusively in foreign public loans, which was in line with the general sentiment that the Netherlands was a trading nation and should not strive for an industrial future (Stokman et al. 1985). Instead, Dutch banks have specialised in short-term credit provision and trade finance. In contrast to most other European countries in which bank lending has been crucial, firms in the Netherlands were reliant on a well-developed capital market. The limited role of governmental and financial institutions, combined with a poorly developed vocational training system, may underline the significant role that the traditional rules of action and governance principles have played in the development of a modern business system, just as it did in some East Asian countries (Whitley 1992).

Following the surprising emergence of Japanese business, it has been a fad in the 1980s to attribute business success (or failure) to 'culture' — corporate or national culture or, ideally, a synergy between both levels. This culturalist approach has been rightfully scorned for being reductionist. However, if one thinks of the ossifying Dutch corporatist system, the near absence of both state support and a credit based financial system, one is tempted to look for a 'cultural' explanation for the successful Dutch model. Here, this means that we attach great value to rules of action and governance principles stimulating specific sectoral capabilities, e.g. in certain modes of production such as processing raw materials, and, in the end, flexibility in global competition — leading to a seventh position in the world in terms of competitiveness (World competitiveness report 1996).

Research on the influence of the socially constituted evolution in sector specialisation on performance outcomes is also in the Netherlands still in its infancy. For want of systematic studies, the aid of various measures for performance has been called in here: turnover, profit, net added value, number of firms, number of employees — depending on what seemed to be available. Nonetheless, it is hopefully clear that performance differences in the Netherlands do reflect to a significant degree certain rules of action, governance principles and sectoral specialisation, which emerged in the late-medieval and early-modern era. The following quote from Kristensen (1997: 13) also applies to the Republic of the United Provinces' venture:

> "it is through this experimental historical process that the fundamental principles of national governance systems are established or socially constructed to structure the game among strategic actors during the following maturing industrial period".

It is precisely this continuity between the early-modern and the present era that helps to account for the seeming paradox that the Dutch business system has "come to be focused on activities which are elementary and yet highly modernised and capital intensive, simultaneously pre- and post-industrial" (Sorge and van Iterson 1995: 191).

It might look like too large a leap: from medieval geographical conditions, limiting the possibilities for feudalisation, leading to consensual rules of action, peer control and specialisation in the agricultural, commercial and processing sectors, which finally prove to be an asset for flexible adaptation to globalising markets in the twentieth century. However, it must be emphasised that the consensual rules of action and the stakeholders' concept of business grow along and change along with the social groups which express themselves in it. As a consequence of this relative autonomy of long-term changes in economic relations and the perceptions of these relations (Elias 1978), business systems change in directions nobody has intended or even foreseen, but which nevertheless are to be understood from earlier configurations. They change form and content, they also fuse with globalising processes, but remain identifiable. Therefore, one can recognise rules of action, modes of production and market access strategies, developed in the polders and the commercial towns of the Dutch Republic — the cradles of the two main streams of Dutch business — in the offices and on the shopfloor of Dutch firms. The resulting differences in performance outcomes, then, will also reflect the historical legacy of sector specialisation and dominance. The prominent national and international position of enterprises in these dominant sectors might serve as a strong indication for the plausibility of this assumption.

References

1997. *Jaarboek van Nederlandse Ondernemingen*. Amsterdam: Amsterdam Exchanges

1996. *World competitiveness report*. Lausanne: IMD.

Barbour, V. 1966. *Capitalism and Amsterdam in the 17th Century*. Ann Arbor, Michigan: University of Michigan Press.

Blussé, L., and F. Gaastra (eds.). 1981. *Companies and Trade. Essays on Overseas Trading Companies during the Ancien Régime*. Leiden: Leiden University Press.

Boxer, C. R. 1973. *The Dutch Seaborne Empire, 1600–1800*. Harmondsworth: Penguin.

Burke, P. 1974. *Venice and Amsterdam: A Study of Seventeenth-century Elites*. London: Temple Smith.

Calori, R., and P. de Woot. 1995. *A European Management Model*. Englewood Cliffs: Prentice Hall.

Davids, C. A. 1993. Technological Change and the Economic Expansion of the Dutch Republic, 1580–1680. In: C. A. Davids, and L. Noordegraaf (eds.), *The Dutch Economy in the Golden Age: Nine Studies*, 79–104. Amsterdam: NEHA.

Elias, N. 1978. *What is sociology?* London: Hutchinson.

Elias, N. 1983. *The Court Society*. Oxford: Basic Blackwell.

Furber, H. 1976. *Rival Empires of Trade in the Orient 1600–1800*. Minneapolis: University of Minneapolis Press.

Gaastra, F. 1981. The Shifting Balance of Trade of the Dutch East India Company. In: L. Blussé, and F. Gaastra (eds.), *Companies and Trade. Essays on Overseas Trading Companies during the Ancien Régime*, 47–70. Leiden: Leiden University Press.

Hollingsworth, J. R., and R. Boyer (eds.). 1997. *Contemporary Capitalism. The Embeddedness of Institutions*. Cambridge: Cambridge UP.

Israel, J. 1995. *The Dutch Republic. Its Rise, Greatness, and Fall 1477–1806*. Oxford: Clarendon Press.

Iterson, A. van, and R. Olie. 1992. European Business Systems: The Dutch Case. In: R. Whitley (ed.), *European Business Systems*, 98–116. London: Sage.

Iterson, A. van. 1997. The Development of National Governance Principles in the Netherlands. In: R. Whitley, and P. H. Kristensen, *Governance at Work: The Social Regulation of Economic Relations in Europe*, 49–61. Oxford: Oxford University Press.

Kindleberger, C. P. 1993. *A financial history of Western Europe.*(2nd ed.) Oxford: Oxford University Press.

Kristensen, P. H. 1996. Variations in the Nature of the Firm in Europe. In: R. Whitley, and P. H. Kristensen, *The Changing European Firm. Limits to Convergence*, 1–36. London: Routledge.

Kristensen, P. H. 1997. National Systems of Governance and Managerial Prerogatives in the Evolution of Work Systems. England, Germany, and Denmark Compared. In: R. Whitley, and P. H. Kristensen, *Governance at Work: The Social Regulation of Economic Relations in Europe*, 3–46. Oxford: Oxford University Press.

Lambert, A. 1985. *The Making of the Dutch Landscape*. London: Academic Press.

Lammers, C. 1973. Self-Management and Participation: Two Conceptions of Democratisation in Organisations, *Organisation and Administrative Sciences* 5(4): 17–33.

Lijphart, A. 1968. *The Politics of Accommodation: Pluralism and Democracy in the Netherlands*. Berkeley, LA: University of Calfornia Press.

Maddison, A. 1991. *Dynamic Forces in Capitalist Development*. Oxford: Oxford University Press.

Mokyr, J. 1976. *Industrialization in the Low Countries 1795–1850*. New Haven: Yale University Press.

Riley, J. C. 1980. *International Government Finance and the Amsterdam Capital Market, 1740–1815*. Cambridge: Cambridge University Press.

Scott, John. 1997. *Corporate Business and Capitalist Classes*. Oxford: Oxford University Press.

Smith, A. 1982 [1776]), *An Inquiry into the Nature and Causes of the Wealth of Nations*. Harmondsworth: Penguin Books.

Sorge, A., and A. van Iterson. 1995. Human Resource Management in the Netherlands. In: I. Brunstein (ed.), *Human Resource Management in Western Europe*, 191–209. Berlin, New York: De Gruyter.

Statistics Netherlands. 1997, *Industriemonitor, Divisie Landbouw, Nijverheid en Milieu, Sector Industrie(1)*. January. Voorburg: Statistics Netherlands.

Steensgaard, N. 1982. The Dutch East India Company as an Institutional Innovation. In: M. Aymard (ed.), *Dutch Capitalism and World Capitalism*, 235–257. Cambridge: Cambridge University Press.

Stokman, F. N., F. W. Wasseur, and D. Elsas. 1985. The Dutch Network: Types of Interlocks and Network Structure. In: F. N. Stokman, R. Ziegler, and J. Scott, *Networks of Corporate Power*, 112–130. Cambridge: Cambridge University Press.

Veen, Tom van. 1997. *Studies in Wage Bargaining. The influence of taxes and social security contributions on wages*. Maastricht: Maastricht University Press.

Visser, J. 1992. The Netherlands: The End of an Era and the End of a System. In: A. Ferner, and R. Hyman (eds.), *Industrial Relations in the New Europe*, 323–356. Oxford: Basic Blackwell.

Vries, J. de. 1973. On the Modernity of the Dutch Republic, *Journal of Economic History* 23: 191–202.

Vries, J. de. 1974. *The Dutch Rural Economy in the Golden Age, 1500–1700*. New Haven: Yale University Press.

Whitley, R. 1992. *Business Systems in East Asia*. London: Sage.

Whitley, R. 1997. The Social Regulation of Work Systems. Institutions, Interest Groups and Varieties of Work Organisation in Capitalist Societies. In: R. Whitley, and P. H. Kristensen, *Governance at Work: The Social Regulation of Economic Relations in Europe*, 227–260. Oxford: Oxford University Press.

Windmuller, J. 1969. *Labour relations in the Netherlands*. Ithaca: Cornell University Press.

Worldscope GLOBAL, DC-ROM, Worldscope/Disclosure Partners: Bethesda, Maryland.

Zanden, J. L. van. 1993. *The Rise and Decline of Holland's Economy. Merchant Capitalism and the Labour Market*. Manchester: Manchester University Press.

Zeeuw, J. W. de. 1978. Peat and the Dutch Golden Age, *AAG Bijdragen* 21: 3–32.

CHAPTER 13

Economic Performance of Finland
After the Second World War

From Success to Failure

Risto Tainio   Matti Pohjola   Kari Lilja

1. Introduction

The economic performance of nations has long been one of the central themes
and debates among governments, industries and companies all over the world.
This stems from the increased global competition and indisputable differences
in the level of competitiveness and patterns of performance between various
countries. It is not, however, evident how these performance differences in and
between nations are identified and compared. An even more complex question
is how observed performance at a national level is to be explained and understood.

A starting point to describe the economic performance of a nation is productivity. It describes the volume of the output produced by a unit of labour or
capital. Productivity is one of the major causes of national per capita income
(Porter 1990; Pohjola 1996). The productivity of capital affects the returns to
shareholders, and the productivity of labour affects the returns to employees
through wages. This influence, however, varies in different national contexts, and
therefore we also need sectoral analysis in order to assess the level of national
performance from a comparative perspective.

A nation's economic performance depends on various factors and processes.
These include explanations based on factors of production (land, labour, and
natural resources), macro-economic phenomena (interest rates, government deficits,
exchange rates etc.) and government policies (protection, import promotion, and
subsidies). While each of them provide some truth in shaping and gaining
comparative advantage for specific nations, none of them is sufficient by itself
to provide a universal explanation for the performance of a nation. More complex
and broader processes seem to be at work in specific historical periods and
institutional contexts. Especially national institutions, related structures, and the
modes of governance have been found to have a persistent, and even increasing,

impact on the performance of nations. There seem to exist a number of context-specific ways of organising and coordinating economic activities successfully, or unsuccessfully, in a market economy (Porter 1990; Whitley 1992).

In the European context Finland has often been used as an example of an exceptionally successful national economy, where backward starting conditions for industrialisation and raw-material-based exports did not lead to a monocultural enclave economy (Senghaas 1985). Instead, Finland was able to create dynamic growth and forest-based industrial progress originating mainly from natural conditions and resources. In the late 1980s Finland was widely labelled 'Japan of the North' based mainly on gross domestic product (GDP) per capita growth. In the beginning of the 1990s the Finnish economy, however, experienced a dramatic dive into a deep economic crisis and long lasting recession.

In this paper we explore how the unique features of the Finnish business system enabled successful economic growth under a specific world-wide institutional constellation. But when this overall constellation broke down the Finnish economy encountered severe structural problems. The institutional setting and the related capacities, which originated from the post-war period turned from catalysts to constraints on a successful economic development.

The economic crisis of Finland in the 1990s has been explained mainly from external factors like the slow-down of the world, especially European, economy and the collapse of the Soviet Union, which, at its height, accounted for about 25 per cent of Finnish exports, and from the internal mistakes in exchange and monetary policies, for example the overvalued mark, and uncontrolled deregulation of the Finnish financial markets during the 1980s.

In this paper we adopt a more historical and institutional view. We argue that after World War II the desire for national independence and unity led to a foreign policy driven economic system, which was based on state-led long-term investments in heavy industries, protection from foreign competition, and wide reliance on planned demand markets in the Soviet Union. Under these conditions the success of Finland was accomplished mainly through a forest sector specialisation, large industrial investments to capital intensive 'raw material processors' (Lilja and Tainio 1996), and abundance of labour — without a distinct pressure for efficient utilisation of capital. The economic development of Finland was based on an extensive rather than intensive growth strategy.

In the following we pay a special attention to the ways in which the Soviet linkage has influenced the development of the Finnish economy after the Second World War. Finland's special geopolitical location between Eastern and Western power blocks made the Soviet influence on the Finnish economy and politics stronger than on other western countries. The linkage also created its own special institutions through which it structured the development of the Finnish business system and the governance of its firms and organisations.

In this view, Finland, which has always been regarded as a particular variant of western market economies, can also be seen as a special case among East European countries

2. Economic Performance of Finland in a Comparative Perspective

Before national independence in 1917 Finland had been a part of the Swedish Kingdom for several hundred years and an autonomous Grand Duchy of the Russian Empire between 1809–1917. During the latter period a well-functioning forest sector economy and state machinery were established in Finland.

After the First World War Finland, among other newly independent states which emerged from the Russian and Austria-Hungarian empires, was forced to rearrange its political and economic relations.

Finland sought safety from the Soviet Union and bolshevism by leaning both politically and economically to the West. Finland's weak international position, the constant threat posed by Soviet Russia, and a spirit of nationalism fostered structures reflecting national self-preservation and defensiveness (Kuisma 1993).

The Finnish paper industry lost its former Russian markets, but succeeded rapidly in penetrating western markets through existing market channels (Ahvenainen 1974; see also Lilja and Tainio 1996). This was due to multiple factors, of which the most important was the centralisation of marketing efforts by Finnish paper and pulp producers. These firms eliminated their mutual rivalry by building distribution channels in export cartels which unified the entire industry and all producers into a strong, organic entity (Kuisma 1993). It was these cooperative networks and cartellisation that became the success strategy of relatively small Finnish firms in the competition against western big business.

After the First World War Finland was successful compared to other small, agrarian, raw-material suppliers of Eastern Europe. Through forest industrialisation

Table 1: *GNP per Capita in Selected European Countries, 1913 and 1938*

Country	1913	1938
Baltic countries	–	501
Bulgaria	263	420
Finland	520	913
Greece	322	590
Hungary	372	451
Poland	–	372
Rumania	–	343
Yugoslavia	284	329

Source: Bairoch (1976: 297).

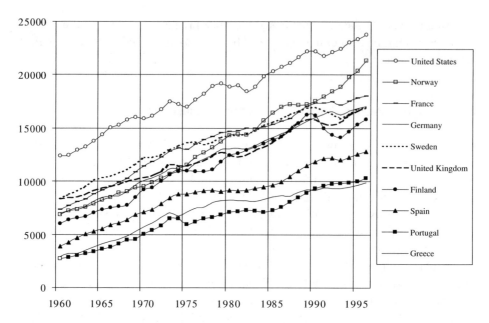

Figure 1. *GDP per capita in Finland and in selected other countries 1960–1996 (US$, 1990 purchasing power parities)*

Source: OECD National Accounts (different annual editions).

and strong government interventions it was able to lift itself closer to the relatively prosperous West European countries (Kuisma 1996) (see Table 1).

Prosperous development was ended by the Second World War, which hit Finland hard as it did most European countries. Recovery from the war, especially the war indemnities to the Soviet Union, became a national 'project' in which government and industry worked together to achieve economic success. The companies specialised in building and expanding production capacity and solving production problems. The government bore the risks by providing low-interest funding, guaranteeing raw material supplies, and devaluing the Finnish mark twice in 1949.

The goals of national economic policy which were set in the early 1950s were: economic growth, low interest rates and large-scale investments. The results of this policy are seen in Figure 1, where Finland's GDP per capita is presented in comparison with some selected countries.

Figure 1 illustrates stable growth until 1989, with the exception of a few recessions. The dive from 1989 on was deepest and fastest in Finland among all the other countries considered. By 1991 Finland's relative standard of living, measured by the ratio of GDP per capita, had returned to the level of the early 1980s.

Pohjola (1996) has compared the development of GDP per capita and the productivity of labour in the major OECD-countries during 1960–1992. In Table 2

Table 2: *Standard of Living and Productivity of Labour in some OECD-Countries, 1960–1992*

Country	Standard of living (GNP/population)					Productivity of labour		
	Relative to the USA (%)			Average annual growth (%)		Relative to the USA (%)		Average annual growth (%)
	1960	1990	1992	1960–1990	1990–1992	1960	1990	1960–1990
Australia	79	80	81	2.1	2.1	79	82	1.5
Belgium	56	73	75	2.9	3.0	59	86	2.7
Spain	32	53	55	3.7	3.8	34	72	3.9
Netherlands	61	72	74	2.5	2.6	70	85	2.0
Ireland	33	51	54	3.4	3.6	34	65	3.5
Great Britain	69	73	71	2.2	2.1	60	73	2.0
Italy	46	69	71	3.4	3.4	45	84	3.4
Austria	52	70	72	3.0	3.1	44	73	3.0
Japan	30	79	84	5.3	5.4	20	62	5.0
Canada	73	95	91	2.9	2.7	80	93	1.9
Greece	21	37	–	3.9	–	21	48	4.1
Norway	57	83	86	3.3	3.4	58	80	2.4
Portugal	19	41	–	4.6	–	20	45	4.1
Germany	66	79	82	2.6	2.7	57	80	2.5
Finland	**53**	**78**	**67**	**3.3**	**2.7**	**47**	**74**	**2.9**
Switzerland	95	91	89	1.9	1.7	82	89	1.6
France	59	77	78	2.9	2.9	55	83	2.7
Sweden	77	82	78	2.2	2.0	71	77	1.6
Denmark	68	77	79	2.4	2.4	61	68	1.7
Turkey	16	21	21	2.8	2.8	13	23	3.3
New Zealand	80	64	63	1.2	1.2	87	69	0.6
United States (USA)	100	100	100	2.0	2.0	100	100	1.4
Average (not including USA)	54	69	72	3.0	2.8	52	72	2.7

Source: Summers and Heston (1991).

these comparative figures are presented in relation to the development in the USA and as average growth rates.

In 1960 the standard of living in Finland was 53 per cent that of the USA, but by 1990 it had already reached 78 per cent. In the following two years, it dropped back dramatically to 67 per cent in 1992. This improvement in the standards of living was not, however, based on the productivity of labour, which was only slightly above average. Pohjola (1996) has shown that behind the growth of Finland has been a high rate of labour force participation in the economy and the 'world-record' levels of investments.

Finland's investment rate has been one of the highest in the world after the Second World War (Vartia and Ylä-Anttila 1996). At the aggregate national level these large-scale investments could be financed only by refraining from consumption. The high rate of savings was accomplished by allowing tax-exempt deposit accounts. The housing system, based on family ownership and not rental, also encouraged 'forced' savings by the great majority of the population (Lilja et al. 1992).

The newly established state-owned companies, especially in paper, metal, chemical, and energy sectors, offered national outlets for the use of increased savings. Overall, the Finnish national model of economic development after the war was based on the tight regulation of the labour and capital markets. The consent of employees was accomplished by introducing a centralised wage bargaining system. Moderate wage increases were exchanged for a gradual implementation of a welfare state and the benefits it provided for the population (Pohjola 1994). Finnish industrial policy after the war followed the Soviet model which gave the priority to the development of heavy industries and industrialisation of rural areas (Pohjola 1994). A capital-intensive industrial policy generated high pay-offs and fast economic growth, which provided a solid ground for the industrial expansion from the 1960s until 1980s.

All these accomplishments came into question in the 1990s. Finland's record of growth faltered, causing commentators to look again at the factors which had contributed to its success. How did these relate to the depth of the crisis in the 1990s?

3.   Labour and Capital Productivity at the Sectoral Level

The first observation from the evidence above is that although the Finnish growth performance has been strong, productivity performance has been below average. After controlling for the high share of investment in GDP the performance of Finland can even be regarded as weak (Pohjola 1996).

At the aggregate level the high growth figures of Finland after the war seem to have been based on the growth of the capital stock at the expense of productivity and efficiency. This kind of evidence were discussed in studies of the Finnish economy undertaken in the 1960s and 1970s, but recently this has also been confirmed by a number of cross-country comparisons (Crafts and Toniolo 1996).

Productivity comparisons can be extended to the sectoral level to get more insights into Finland's productivity puzzle. Such comparisons reveal the highly specialised structure of the Finnish manufacturing industry. In Table 3 the level of labour and capital productivity as well as that of capital intensity are compared between Finland and the USA.[1]

Table 3 reveals that labour productivity in the Finnish manufacturing sector was 68 per cent and capital productivity 60 per cent of the US level in 1990. Capital intensity was 13 per cent higher in Finland than in the USA. Pohjola (1996) shows that the high capital intensity is not only a unique feature of the

Table 3: *Relative Labour and Capital Productivity and Capital Intensity in Manufacturing Industries in 1990 (in %, USA = 100)*

Industries	Labour productivity	Capital productivity	Capital intensity
Food, bevarages and tobacco	58	51	113
Textiles, clothing and footwear	68	42	162
Wood and wood products	75	29	260
Paper, printing and publishing	95	44	213
Chemical products	65	65	100
Non-metallic mineral products	62	69	89
Basic metal and metal products	84	97	86
Machinery and equipment	62	86	73
All manufacturing	**68**	**60**	**113**

Source: Pohjola (1996).

manufacturing industry, but in the whole business sector the capital stock per worker was in Finland 19 per cent higher than in the United States.

In the wood and paper industries capital intensity is remarkably high in Finland. As labour productivity has not been any higher in these industries than in the USA capital productivity there must be lower. This is in fact confirmed in Table 3, which shows that capital productivity was, relative to the US level, only 29 per cent in the wood and wood products industry and 44 per cent in the paper, printing and publishing industry. These industries have been abundant in capital. This may reflect their perceived importance in the Finnish development strategy and industrial policy as well as the power of their lobbying organisations.

The productivity of labour has been rather high in the Finnish paper industry. It was 95 per cent of the US level in 1990. The performance was even better in terms of the value added per hour worked. Labour productivity measured in this way exceeded the US level by 6 per cent in 1990 because the number of hours worked per employee is lower in the Finnish than in the US paper industry (Pohjola 1996).

International comparisons have also identified productivity problems in the Finnish service sectors. Despite the great difficulties in measuring output and productivity in services the evidence suggests a relatively low level of productivity in the Finnish distribution, sales and, surprisingly also in the telecommunication sectors (Pilat 1996).

The paper and metal industries have been, and still are, internationally the most competitive sectors of the Finnish economy. In 1996, the largest industry was machinery, electrical and transport equipment, accounting for 34 per cent of the overall output. The paper and wood industries accounted for 27 per cent of the total value added in manufacturing, basic metal for 11 per cent, and food and textile together for 13 per cent. In recent years the electronics industry has outperformed the other industries both by output and productivity growth. It has been the fastest growing industry in the 1990s. Its production has increased annually 25 per cent and labour productivity by 15 per cent.

In a comparative perspective labour productivity has turned out to be low at the aggregate level, but the Finnish economy consists also of a few sectors with relatively high productivity. This is a rather typical outcome from an extensive growth strategy. However, high labour productivity, even in the Finnish paper and wood industry, has been achieved at the expense of capital productivity. This was not a problem in the period of financial regulation and credit rationing. The opportunity cost of capital was low because the real rate of interest was low; it was even negative for most of the time from the late 1960s to the early 1980s. The situation changed, however, quite rapidly in the mid 1980s when the financial markets were deregulated, capital movements were liberalised and the real rate of interest increased substantially. Then the low productivity of capital became a problem in Finland. This also contributed to the deep recession of the 1990s and resulted in industrial restructuring.

4.   Geopolitical Processes Behind the Unsustainable Success of Finland

Next we explore how the extensive growth policy emerged in Finland in the post-war period, and how it ran into difficulties in the 1990s when the political and economic environment changed in Europe.

In order to make sense of all this we need to understand the history and political context of post-war Finland. The reasons for 'inefficient capital' evidently have their roots in the centralised economic policies, preservation of national unity, and the experiences of the war. All these factors are related to the Finnish-Soviet relations after the Second World War.

After the Second World War the world was divided into the spheres of the two superpowers. The Soviet Union's neighbours in Europe became either part of the Soviet Union (e.g. the Baltic states) or closely linked to it politically, militarily and economically (e.g. Central European countries). Finland became a 'special case'.

The Treaty of Cooperation, Friendship, and Mutual Assistance (1948) became the political foundation for relations between Finland and the Soviet Union. It stated that Finland, in the case of military threat, was to defend both herself and the Soviet Union. This treaty also became the basis for economic relations between the two countries. But, in order to stay independent, Finland had to avoid crises, especially world-wide conflicts, and for its own part dispel the widespread mistrust and fear towards its recent war enemy and one of the world's greatest military powers. Finnish foreign policy was dominated by the President of the country and most other spheres of social and economic life in Finland became subordinated to the official foreign policy.

In a situation of great uncertainty about the survival of the nation this was widely regarded as justifiable. There became one truth in foreign policy and one interpretation of that truth; both were in the possession of Dr. Urho Kekkonen, who served as the President of Finland from 1956 until 1981.

This meant that economic policies, strategies of companies, and even industrial relations were submitted and adjusted to geopolitical realities. In decision making this required the formation of a tight 'inner circle' at the top level where major decisions were coordinated and made. This system also made the top management of the Finnish corporations especially sensitive to the foreign-policy implications of their strategic moves.

An example of the complexities involved in this Finnish foreign-policy driven economy was the process of securing ties with Western economies in the 1960s and 1970s.

Finland's EFTA agreement in 1961 was possible only because there were equal terms for Finnish-Soviet trade (negotiated in 1960). The major condition of the agreement was that Finland's trade with the West could not disturb trade or relations with the Eastern bloc. An even more difficult process culminated in Finland's trade agreement with the EEC a decade later, in 1973. After complex three-year negotiations, where President Kekkonen was a central figure, Soviet suspicions were finally allayed. Kekkonen personally guaranteed that the EEC agreement would not harm Finnish-Soviet relations or trade. Kekkonen's term as President was extended by a Special Act in January 1973.

Finland had thus a special position in the Soviet 'economic and welfare race' with the USA in the 1960s. Finland's foreign policy had turned out to be stable and reliable. This was guaranteed by friendly, confidential personal relations between the top leaders of the two countries. Finland was the most important Western trading partner of the Soviet Union until the end of the 1960s. West Germany, the USA, and Japan subsequently overtook Finland. In 1981 Finland again achieved the biggest market share in Soviet imports (Alho et al. 1986).

Government-driven centralised structures were established for Finnish-Soviet trade. A Permanent Commission for Cooperation was founded in 1967 to coordinate and develop trade between Finland and the Soviet Union. The Finnish members of the first Commission were high-ranking politicians and civil servants all approved by the President. Later on the representation of business, especially that of state-owned companies, increased. Finland mainly imported crude oil and raw materials from the Soviet Union. Therefore the major actor on the Finnish side became Neste, the state-owned oil-refining company. The Commission decided on the amounts and distribution of Finnish exports and to a large extent the companies which received the orders.

In general, the Soviet trade was a profitable business for Finnish firms — the margins were about double the ones gained in Western trade. Demand was high, prices were favourable, quality-standards moderate, and the planning periods long and stable. This favoured and reinforced production- and investment-orientation in managerial policies in Finnish firms. Many of the firms, even industries, became almost totally dependent on the Soviet trade, especially companies producing textiles, shoes, ships, foodstuffs, and machinery. At the same time they became sheltered from both domestic and international competition.

Finland developed a state-driven economy, where a great number of industries operated behind protective and regulatory barriers, and where pressures for efficiencies were relatively low. The influence of Finland's Soviet trade, which was constantly 15–25 per cent of the total exports, was extended far beyond these actual figures, because of its political weight. Finnish trade with the centrally planned economy was organised in a centralised, government-driven, way. The state and industry became 'organisationally integrated' in that particular sphere of economy. The Finnish industrial growth policy renewed and strengthened the specific Finnish production structure, i.e. the raw material based heavy industries. The Finnish economy became *locked-in* in an institutional setting, which had originated from the post-war period.

A typical Finnish firm remained a large, capital-intensive raw material processor, where the mobilisation of stakeholders for large-scale investments was a central feature (Lilja and Tainio 1996). All this favoured the development of competencies, which were based on engineering skills and production management capacities, and supplemented by the capabilities to lobby national level institutional support for business. Engineers achieved high positions in Finnish business life. The engineering background of the top management reinforced an orientation in which all kinds of problems of managerial motivation were solved mainly by growth and investing in the technological base (Lilja and Tainio 1996). In cross-national comparisons Finnish managers have been found to rely heavily on hierarchies and top-down decision making (Hofstede 1980). They are production-orientated engineers who constantly search for the most updated technological solutions and do not pay major attention to market or capital dynamics (Lilja et al. 1992).

Until the late 1980s Finland's economy as a whole was relatively specialised and composed of a few large companies among which internal competition was weak or non-existent. Even the competitive part of the economy was still cartellised and ultimately supported by the government policy. Under these conditions the production-oriented managerial competencies appeared successful, and yielded rewards during the period of extensive growth. This increased and spread their use, accumulated experience with old routines, and improved managerial skills in existing operations. This meant that managers became reluctant to search for new possibilities and alternative managerial practices. When the economic and political environment changed in the late 1980s Finnish managers had difficulties in adjusting to these changes, and to responding to them promptly.

An example of such an environmental change was the deregulation of Finnish financial markets, which was related to the liberalisation of the finance sector globally. When capital became free to move across frontiers to earn the highest interest, and international interest rates were high, the inefficiencies of investments in Finland could not be hidden any more. The high cost of capital lowered the investment share down to 15 per cent of the GDP and resulted in capacity reduction in industries where capital intensities have been high in comparison to other industries, such as construction, retail sales and finance. This contributed to the record-high unemployment in Finland in the early 1990s (Pohjola 1994).

In sum, after the Second World War, world-wide tensions together with Finland's desire for independence led to a centralised, foreign policy-driven economic system. This was based on a state-led policy of long-term investment in heavy industries with cartellisation, weak competitive pressures, and wide reliance on planned markets. The major emphasis in economic development was to invest in order to increase new capacities at the expense of improving the efficiency and productivity of existing capital stock. What was a successful expansion strategy under regulated conditions turned out to result in severe structural problems in the 1990s following the opening of the economy and the changes in the political context, which had occurred in the late 1980s and early 1990s.

5.   Concluding Remarks

In this paper we have explored the performance of Finland, which turned from an apparent success to apparent failure in the early 1990s. At the national level the performance of Finland was for a long time based on an extensive rather than intensive growth. Growth was achieved mainly through investments and not through increased productivity. The inefficiencies of the business system were revealed, when the business environment changed rapidly in the late 1980s.

In the light of our evidence most of the structural problems in the Finnish economy, and its vulnerability in the early 1990s, can be understood as a result of the post-war institutional setting, which originated from Finland's geopolitical location between the Eastern and Western power blocks. The Finnish economy and institutions gradually became *locked-in* to the expansion strategy, which hampered the development of competencies necessary for adaptation to new competitive pressures.

The post-war development of Finland can be described as a chain of centrally planned 'national projects'. They continued longer in Finland than in most west

European countries. This was due to the uncertain international position next to the Soviet Union and the priority given to national security and unity. President Kekkonen's vision was that close economic cooperation between Finland and the Soviet Union would increase mutual trust between the nations and thus stabilise political relations. The vision turned out to be politically successful. However, the institutionalised nature of Soviet trade had far-reaching economic consequences. It reproduced the central role of the state in the economy, built a strong reliance on stable and planned demand markets, retained close links between the major Finnish companies, and encouraged a production-oriented, centralised mode of governance within them. It also, from its own part, renewed large-scale, process-engineering based, heavy industrial companies as the economic engine of Finland.

Both the long lasting 'national projects' as well as the company-level policies relied on high, long-term investments, which resulted in a large capital stock, though with little pressure to utilise it efficiently.

Even though centralised national programmes and institutions do not automatically mean centralised management cultures, this seems to have occurred in Finland. The Finnish industrial structure required strong engineering skills, a production orientation at top management level, and widespread linkages between companies and banks. This amplified the top-down decision making and investment-driven growth mode in the Finnish companies.

The Finnish case is an example of how a distinct sector specialisation generated specific managerial practices and institutional structures. The Finnish systems created structural inertia and constrained the development of new managerial capabilities required for new business realities. The change away from investment- and production-orientation was only triggered by the experience of a deep economic crisis, which highlighted the importance of labour and capital productivity, and the international competitiveness of business operations. A restructuring of the institutional setting and a renewal of managerial practices has begun in Finland.

Notes

1. Labour productivity is measured by value added per worker and capital productivity by value added per capital stock. Capital intensity is defined as divided by the number of workers. Value and the capital stock are denominated in a common set of prices so that real international quantity comparisons can be made.

References

Ahvenainen, J. 1974. The competitive position of the Finnish paper industry in the inter-war years, *Scandinavian Economic History Review* 72(1): 1–21.

Alho, K., O. Forsell, J. Huttunen, M. Kotilainen, I. Luukkonen, J. Moilanen, and P. Vartia. 1986. Neuvostoliiton-kauppa Suomen kansantaloudessa, *ETLA*, sarja B 50, Helsinki.

Bairoch, P. 1976. Europe's Gross National Product 1800–1975, *Journal of European Economic History* 5: 273–340.

Crafts, N., and G. Toniolo. 1996. Post-war growth: an overview. In: N. Crafts, and G. Toniolo (eds.), *Economic growth in Europe since 1945*, 1–37. Cambridge: Cambridge University Press.

Hofstede, G. 1980. *Culture's Consequences*. Beverly Hills: Sage.

Kuisma, M. 1993. Government action, cartels, and national corporations — the develop-ment strategy of a small peripheral nation during the period of crisis and economic disintegration in Europe. (Finland 1918–1938). *Scandinavian Economic History Review* 91(3): 242–268.

Kuisma, M. 1996. Cooperation in competition; Finland's national development strategy 1918–1938, Paper presented in the Workshop on "Företagsledning och institutionella söndrag i Finlands industrialiseringsprocess — en egen finsk modell?", 23.11.1996, Helsinki.

Lilja, K., and R. Tainio. 1996. The nature of the typical Finnish firm. In: R. Whitley, and P. H. Kristensen (eds.), *The Changing European Firm: Limits to Convergence*, 159–191. London: Routlege.

OECD. 1998. *National accounts*. Paris: OECD.

Pilat, D. 1996. Labour productivity levels in OECD countries: estimates for manufacturing and selected service sectors, Working Paper no.169, OECD Economics Department, Paris.

Pohjola, M. 1996. *Tehoton pääoma*. Helsinki: WSOY.

Pohjola, M. 1994. Nordic corporatism and economic performance: labour market equality at the expense of productive efficiency?. In: T. Kauppinen, and V. Köykkä (eds.), *Transformation of the Nordic Industrial Relations in the European Context*, 223–241. Helsinki: The Finnish Labour Relations Association.

Porter, M. 1990. *The Competitive Advantage of Nations*. New York: Free Press.

Senghaas, D. 1985. *The European Experience*. Leamington Spa: Berg.

Summers, R. and A. Heston. 1991. The Penn World Table, (Mark 5): An expanded set of international comparisons, 1950–1988, *Quarterly Journal of Economics* 106: 327–368.

Vartia, P., and P. Ylä-Anttila. 1996. *Kansantalous 2021*, ETLA, Series B 126, Helsinki.

Whitley, R. 1992. Societies, firms and markets: the social structuring of business systems. In: R. Whitley (ed.), *European Business Systems: Firms and Markets in their National Contexts*, 5–45. London: Sage.

CHAPTER 14

Success without Shock Therapy in Eastern Europe
The Case of Slovenia[*]

Richard Whitley   Marko Jaklic   Marko Hocevar

1. Introduction

Both before and after Slovenian independence in 1991, Slovenia was the most successful of the state socialist economies in Eastern Europe. In 1989 its gross domestic product (GDP) per head was $ 5,869, almost twice as much as that of Hungary's, while in 1993 its gross national product (GNP) per head in terms of purchasing power parities was $10,585 compared to $7,550 in the Czech Republic and $6,050 in Hungary. In 1997 its GDP per head in purchasing power parity terms was estimated to be $12,629 (Bank Slovenije 1998; EBRD 1995). By 1992, 87.6 per cent of its trade took place with the developed market economies, while only 56.9 per cent of Czechoslovakia's, and 66.6 per cent of Hungary's did (Mencinger 1995). Furthermore, the value of Slovenia's exports to OECD economies continued to rise in the 1990s, from $6,083 million in 1993 to $8,410 million in 1997. According to Rojec et al. (1998), Slovenia's global competitiveness index value at the end of 1997 remained above that of the Czech republic and Hungary. At the corporate level, net operating profits of most Slovene firms, and especially those majority owned by internal and private external shareholders, increased strongly in 1996. Only those remaining in state hands continued to make operational losses.

The continued success of the Slovene economy in the 1990s relative to other Central European late state socialist economies was achieved without the sort of 'shock therapy' administered elsewhere in the region. Although high real interest rates stabilised the new currency, the tolar, quite soon after independence, the

* We are grateful for the comments of participants at the EMOT Workshop on Economic Performance Outcomes in Europe: the role of national institutions and forms of economic organisation, held at the WZB, Berlin, 30th January — 1st February, 1997 and the editorial suggestions of Sigrid Quack.

economy did not suffer significant falls in GDP after 1992 or in industrial output after 1993. Unemployment rose to 9.1 per cent in 1993, as measured by ILO standards, but declined to 7.1 per cent in 1997. Bankruptcies and liquidations were limited by the government moratorium in 1991, although they are starting to rise now it has been abolished (IMAD 1997; Novkovic 1996). Overall, then, state policy has not administered radical deflation to the Slovene economy and many enterprises have been able to adapt successfully to increasing competition in domestic and export markets, as well as the loss of the formerly protected domestic Yugoslav market.

In this paper we explore the major factors which have enabled much of the Slovene economy to manage the transformation period relatively successfully, and consider how many enterprises have been able to adapt to the changed environment without radical shifts in ownership and control or thoroughgoing restructuring. First of all, we outline five key features of the state socialist period in Slovenia and summarise the main characteristics of the enterprises that developed there. Second, we describe the key changes that occurred in the dominant institutions and markets of Slovenia in the earlier 1990s and their likely impact on enterprise structures and behaviour. Third, we report on the results of a study of eight Slovene enterprises designed to investigate these changes, and finally we consider the likely ways that such firms will develop in the future, given their relatively successful adaptation to market conditions in the early 1990s.

2.   The Legacies of Yugoslav State Socialism in Slovenia

There were five principal legacies of the state socialist period that differentiated Slovenia from other Central and Eastern European states and which had significant consequences for the sorts of firms that developed there. First, it was more oriented to Western markets and more engaged in trade with Western Europe than the other Yugoslav republics and the CMEA economies. In 1985, 46.1 per cent of the external trade of Yugoslavia occurred with the developed market economies, mostly from Slovene enterprises, while the similar proportion for Poland at the same time was 32.4 per cent and for Hungary 30.2 per cent (Mencinger 1995). On the other hand, trade with the economies of Central and Eastern Europe accounted for only 32.1 per cent of Yugoslavia's external trade then, and this was dominated by Croatian and Serbian enterprises, while it was 40.7 per cent in Poland and 52.4 per cent in Hungary. Furthermore, foreign trade with OECD countries in Slovenia was not monopolised by central state agencies but was carried out by registered firms and specialised import-export trading companies. As Kumar (1992) puts it:

"The (Slovene) state's involvement in foreign trade was indirect only. It was characterised by non-market restrictive regulation of foreign payments and by the extensive use of quantitative and other restrictive foreign trade measures."

The combination of this leading role in foreign trade with the protected domestic market enabled many Slovene enterprises to build up substantial surpluses for investment in new machinery and foreign distribution networks. By selling their outputs on OECD markets at bargain basement prices, and using the foreign exchange so gained to import scarce foreign goods during the period of high inflation in Yugoslavia, they were able to make considerable profits in dinars (Kristensen and Jaklic 1997). Some large firms also established foreign distribution networks which they made available to other enterprises and a few set up subsidiaries in parts of Austria and Italy where there were substantial Slovene minorities (Konjhodzic 1996).

Second, Slovenian firms had a dominant position in the highly protected Yugoslav market. In the late 1980s, Slovenian firms produced about 35 per cent of the total output of all Yugoslav enterprises with only 10 per cent of the population, and their sales to the other republics were considerably greater than their purchases from them (Zavod RS za Statistiko 1991). The combination of this domestic dominance with experience of competitive Western markets provided Slovenian firms with the opportunity to learn how to compete in capitalist economies while building up organisational competences and investment funds for product and technological upgrading to a greater extent than elsewhere in Eastern Europe.

Third, constitutional reform in Yugoslavia in the 1970s decentralised political power to the provincial republics and local communes which took on many governmental functions. This relatively high degree of political decentralisation in Yugoslavia enabled provincial governments to gain experience of economic policy formation and implementation. At the same time the large vertically integrated enterprises that dominated many parts of the domestic economy were decomposed into Basic Organisations of Associated Labour (BOALs) which were the smallest economic units capable of producing tradable commodities (Lydall 1989). While many of these subsequently recombined into larger Work Organisations (WOs) and Composite Organisations of Associated Labour (COALs), the political emphasis on workers self-management at the smallest feasible organisational units ensured that these latter groupings were rarely fully integrated into a coherent managerial hierarchy (Dyker 1990; Jaklic 1997). This decentralisation reinforced strong loyalties to particular localities and inhibited geographic and labour mobility (Kristensen and Jaklic 1997; Svetlicic and Rojec 1996).

Fourth, relative remoteness from the central government in Belgrade — both politically and ethnically — ensured that Slovenian managers were both quite autonomous from central state direction and limited in their dependence on state support. They did, however, benefit from provincial support and the peculiarities of the Yugoslav financial system which funded trade bills as a matter of course (Ribnikar 1989). At the local level, managerial autonomy from political pressures was greatly enhanced by commercial success that enabled enterprises to maintain or increase employment. As a result, Slovenian firms were accustomed to being more self reliant than their counterparts in the rest of Yugoslavia and in the CMEA countries, although by no means as dependent on market success as many western firms.

Fifth, the institutionalisation of social ownership and self-management reinforced existing strong attachments to local villages and geographical districts that were reproduced through local land and housing ownership. Slovenia had quite a high proportion of private house ownership outside the major cities of Ljubljana and Maribor before 1990, partly due to the decentralised, semi-urban polycentric nature of its industrialisation (Konjhodzic 1996). Historically, attachment to private ownership of homes has been strong in Slovenia and many families have built their own properties in villages and small towns, often with the help of relatives and friends. In conjunction with the shortage of housing in the cities, this has limited geographical mobility and increased the interdependence between many enterprises and their local communities (Jaklic 1997).

The combination of the important political role of the communes during the latter part of the state socialist period with the close connections between local banks and companies further increased the strength of local attachments to enterprises. In Slovenia, while many banks were politically controlled, they were also decentralised to the commune level and were often established to channel funds to 'their' local enterprises by coalitions of local politicians and managers. They were not, then simply agents of the central state or part of the central bank but rather integral units of local economies and under joint local political-enterprise control (Lydall 1989: 155–7), frequently indeed co-owned by leading firms. Enterprise managers were, then, highly integrated into their local communities rather than forming a separate stratum of cosmopolitan, mobile experts. Within these communities, their status and power rested to a great extent on their ability to maintain employment and ensure firm growth, and so this local embeddedness combined with decentralisation to focus managers' attention on improving companies' effectiveness within the system.

These features of the late state socialist system in Yugoslavia helped to generate particular kinds of enterprises and managerial competences that differed significantly from those elsewhere in Eastern Europe. First of all, Slovene enterprises had much more autonomy from party officials and state bureaucrats as long as they made few financial demands on local governments and maintained local employment levels (Kristensen and Jaklic 1997). The self management system, however, and the need to maintain union support in the decentralised Yugoslav economy meant that managers had to bear employee interests very much in mind when deciding priorities and allocating resources. The dominant priorities of Slovene managers, then, concentrated on maintaining or increasing employee numbers, ensuring financial independence and building up foreign currency surpluses.

Second, the ability of exporters to obtain imported supplies and the post 1974 break-up of the vertically integrated COALs, encouraged greater horizontal specialisation among the BOALs and increasing reliance on market contracting for inputs. COALs were more diversified but tended to concentrate on one industry, and often had quite limited product ranges, although they incorporated more varied activities in other parts of Yugoslavia. In many cases, the outputs of particular COALs were the result of power struggles between managers of different plants and organisations and local officials, as each BOAL tried to increase their independence from central control. Large vertically integrated combines were not as significant here as in most of the CMEA countries, although some did exist and were more common in other parts of Yugoslavia.

Additionally, the COALs were less centrally integrated than the large combines in many East European countries because of the separate nature and rights of their constituent BOALs, although their top managers were able to redistribute surpluses between subunits with political support and to centralise foreign trading and employee training. Decision making in the BOALs was shared between the top managers, worker representatives and local politicians, although the more successful managers were able to dominate these organisations in practice (Dyker 1990; Lydall 1989; Jaklic 1997).

Third, the greater involvement of Slovene enterprises in OECD markets and their greater autonomy in selecting suppliers and customers in the 1970s and 1980s meant that product upgrading and improvement were both feasible and encouraged. Markets — both domestic and foreign — were more competitive than elsewhere in the region, with localities promoting the success of 'their' enterprises in the protected Yugoslav market (Lydall 1989: 78–9). Innovation was here necessary to maintain demand since losses invited intervention by local politicians and union leaders, as well as the loss of one's local reputation as a good manager. Decentralisation and some limited competition between enterprises and communes thus encouraged incremental improvements.

Fourth, inputs and outputs were coordinated through quasi-market transactions often based on personal bargains and linkages that stemmed from previously developed networks (Kristensen and Jaklic 1997). Communes and other local bodies frequently encouraged enterprises to obtain their inputs locally and thus tried to develop considerable economic autarky at the local level (Lydall 1989: 79). However, connections across regions were less developed, with considerable reluctance to develop close ties to Slovene firms in other parts of the republic. Even within some regions, the highly enterprise-focused loyalties and commitments encouraged by the self-management system limited cooperation between them. It was also restricted by the success of many Slovene firms in the protected domestic Yugoslav market which encouraged the belief among many managers that they could compete effectively on their own (Konjhodvic 1996).

Finally, considerable de facto worker independence and flexibility in how tasks were carried out seems to have been the norm in many Slovene plants, not least because of the self management ideology and influence of worker representatives (Jaklic 1997). Similarly, supervisor-worker distance was quite low, partly because of the quite strong egalitarian ethos and partly because of the limited powers of supervisors. In general, their discretion over performance evaluation and rewards were quite restricted by the combination of easy worker representative access to top management and the need for managers to control personnel issues directly.

In summary, the late state socialist Slovene economy was dominated by insider controlled small enterprises amalgamated into larger units that had limited control over their activities. Keeping the confidence of worker representatives and maintaining employment levels were major priorities of managers, as was generating enough financial surplus to be largely independent of outsider direction. Vertical integration was relatively low and incremental innovation in narrow product lines quite common. Local networks were important, both within supply chains and with banks, officials and other managers. Production chains generally exhibited greater reliance on market contracting than in the CMEA countries, although this was often organised around personal ties and informal groupings based on previous associations. Beyond local networks, inter-enterprise connections in Slovenia were often adversarial and remote, with cooperation being difficult to achieve in the absence of personal ties.

3.   Institutional Changes in the 1990s

The key changes in enterprises' institutional environments in the early 1990s were, of course, the democratisation of the political system through multiparty elections and the increasing liberalisation of market relations between them, together with greater openness to both imports and exports and, later on, privatisation. Essentially, the state withdrew from the active management of enterprise strategies — both directly and indirectly — and also became more responsive to emerging interest groups. At the same time the CMEA system collapsed and the Soviet Union disappeared, together with much effective demand for Eastern European products. Additionally, of course, the break up of Yugoslavia and the outbreak of ethnic conflicts there meant that many Slovene enterprises lost suppliers, customers, factories and other assets. Overall, enterprises became much more isolated and left on their own to deal with a much tougher business environment and hard budget constraints.

These changes were less radical in Slovenia than in the ex-CMEA countries, although many firms were of course severely affected by the loss of the domestic Yugoslav market. Since Slovene enterprises were more used to operating as quasi-autonomous organisations separate from the state, they had more experience of managing commercial risks and were more able to respond proactively to the loss of domestic markets. In this, they were considerably assisted by state support in funding early retirements of their older and less skilled workers and, in general, appear to have managed much of their reductions in employment through such means.

Considering institutional changes in Slovenia in more detail, it is important to bear in mind that these are still continuing and the nature of the new 'rules of the game' remains to be firmly established. In general, the new state of Slovenia has been less dominated by the political executive than in other East European states and the legislature has had greater control over policy choices. Governments have changed more frequently since 1991 and are more fragmented in terms of ruling coalition membership and turnover. The bureaucracy is limited in its powers and capabilities because of the greater influence of parliamentary factions and their leaders, as well as the brain drain to the private sector (Rus 1994). This has meant that central control over the economy has, on the whole, been limited in Slovenia in the 1990s, not least because of the continuing strength of local government and local commitments.

Additionally, the ability of many enterprise managers to mobilise support against political control over organisational restructuring and their own appointments/dismissals has decentralised control over the economic transformation process to firms (Kraft et al. 1994; Kristensen and Jaklic 1997; Rus 1994). Because of this — and the broader political conflicts over privatisation methods and policies — the transfer of ownership and control to private shareholders has been relatively slow in Slovenia and most enterprises of any size remain effectively controlled by internal coalitions of managers and other. Where state ownership remains significant — as in many loss-making firms — this is usually vested in the Development Fund of the Republic of Slovenia that is responsible for restructuring and subsequently selling state enterprises.

A further reason for the continuance of substantial internal control of most Slovene enterprises has been the relatively low external debt burden, and the correspondingly limited role of the IMF and World Bank. Although Slovenia has had to assume responsibility for a significant part of the former Yugoslav central bank's debts, it inherited relatively limited foreign liabilities. The comparatively healthy macro economic position in 1991, and the later success of the Bank of

Slovenia in reducing inflation and managing the new national currency, the tolar, has meant that external pressures for radical shock therapy have been weak and largely ignored. On the whole, the enterprises have been left to cope with hard budget constraints and market loss on their own without also having to restructure their ownership and control relationships radically.

The reorganisation of the banking system has reduced the previously very close connections between local banks and enterprises but personal ties remain important and anecdotally seem to bypass formal rules and procedures. Competition from foreign banks has become more significant, but most firms continue to have substantial borrowings from domestic banks and have not developed close connections to foreign ones based outside the country. On the whole, financial institutions in Slovenia remained state owned and/or controlled up to the mid-1990s, continued to have substantial loans outstanding to many enterprises and have been reluctant to finance major new investment. This reluctance, or inability due to lack of capital, has been mirrored in many cases by managers' unwillingness to take on major liabilities during a period of political and economic uncertainty.

Similarly, changes to labour laws and institutions in the 1990s have had only limited effects on the system of labour supply and management in Slovenia. While managers have much more discretion in managing work and employment relations than in pre-1980 state socialism, they still have to deal with significant union strength in the large firm sector — and with works/enterprise councils — and with continued state intervention in wage policies. They also, of course, remain embedded in established conventions of fairness and appropriate standards of behaviour, especially concerning supervisor-subordinate relations and wage differentials. Additionally, the reformed and reorganised socialist unions have remained by far the largest and most important representatives of labour interests in the large firm sector. Most of the 'new' and 'independent' unions have gained little support outside narrowly defined interest groups such as professional white collar workers and other occupationally defined groups (Luksic 1994).

These changes in dominant institutional arrangements in Slovenia can be expected to affect enterprises in five major ways. First of all, the loss of the domestic Yugoslav market, intensification of competition in domestic and foreign markets and the imposition of hard budget constraints should encourage enterprises to search energetically for new customers — sometimes at any cost simply to keep cash coming in. They should also lead eventually to the development of new products and processes to attract and keep customers. Such innovations do, though, require resources, both technological and human, which are typically in short supply in many enterprises, especially in view of the speed with witch some markets collapsed.

Secondly, the withdrawal of state support and of state guidance of enterprise activities meant that managers and workers had both more autonomy in dealing with economic crises and more responsibility for doing so on their own. In principle, then, managers had much greater independence and discretion in deciding what to do. Given the legacies of the late state socialist period listed above, we would expect Slovene managers in the more successful firms to develop coalitions with employee representatives to manage their 'privatisation' and retain substantial internal control over strategic choices.

Third, these internal coalitions are likely to resist outside owners' demands for higher dividend payouts and to prefer to invest surpluses in new facilities and developing new markets. Particularly in the more profitable firms in Slovenia, where managers are most autonomous and able to control strategic choices in cooperation with employee representatives, such investments will probably be concentrated on the incremental improvement of existing products and markets. Radical changes in firms' technologies, skills and markets seem unlikely to be undertaken here.

Fourth, the delegation of substantial control over policies and resources to the BOALs in the 1980s and early 1990s enabled the more successful ones to secede from their 'parent' COALs. Because many managers of these units resented their formal subservience to the conglomerate top managers, as well as the transfer of their surpluses to less successful members of the group, they rapidly sought to become fully-fledged autonomous firms. As a result, many, if not most, of the conglomerates in Slovenia broke up and the typical Slovene 'firm' — or at least those that were profitable — became smaller and more narrowly focused on a limited range of products, often very narrow such as *Iskra Emeco* which manufactures electricity supply meters. The legacy of distrust and low cohesion within many of the COALs, then, will lead to many Slovene firms being quite specialised and wary of developing collaborative links with former group members.

Turning to consider employment policies and work systems, we might expect the strong position of worker representatives and local embeddedness of enterprises to limit redundancies. Increased competition and the need to export more to OECD markets, though, could encourage a move to greater managerial control of work processes as pressures to cut costs and improve productivity increase, and perhaps to reorganise production processes in a more flexible and responsive manner. While the influence of employees — both as owners and as recognised partners in company development — might restrict such reorganisation, the considerable employer-employee commitment resulting from low labour mobility and strong local attachments could also facilitate moves to enhance flexibility and the development of multitask, integrated jobs. Thus, overall in Slovenia we would not expect greatly increased supervisory control of work processes or over performance evaluation, but might well anticipate increased flexibility of production processes and willingness to trust skilled workers to manage changes in these and improve them.

4.   Enterprise Change in Slovenia: Evidence from Eight Organisations

These broad expectations were explored in a study of eight Slovene enterprises in 1995 and 1996, funded by the European Union's ACE programme (Action for Cooperation in the Field of Economics). These represented a wide variety of industries, reflecting the diverse nature of the economy, and of company sizes. Three companies were in the electrical machinery industry, one in pharmaceuticals, one in food and drink processing, one in timber products, one in distribution and retailing and one in tourism. While two employed over 3000 people — and one of these was among the largest five Slovene enterprises — one had fewer than 500 employees and three had between 500 and 1000. The remaining two had between 1000 and 3000 staff. Seven firms had made profits in 1993 and 1994, while the eighth was state owned, had made losses in those years and also had substantial debts. Most, then, were relatively successful financially.

In all, we interviewed 71 top managers from these companies. These interviews covered the ownership and control of these firms, their strategic priorities and choices, product lines, markets served, technologies, customers, suppliers and work organisation. Initially, we report on the relatively slow rate of change of ownership and control in these firms, and then discuss managers' perceptions of their strategic priorities, innovation strategies and cooperation with other enterprises. Finally, we describe changes in their employment structures and patterns of work organisation and control. Where appropriate we compare these results with those obtained from a three and a half year study of leading enterprises in Hungary, reported in a number of recent papers (Czaban and Whitley 1998; Whitley and Czaban 1998a, 1998b; Whitley et al. 1997). Twenty-seven Hungarian enterprises were studied in 1993 and 1994, with 18 of these also being analysed in 1996. They tended to be larger than the Slovene ones considered here, and more of them were in the capital goods sectors, reflecting the different structure of the Hungarian economy.

4.1 Ownership and Control

The Law on Ownership Transformation of Companies, finally passed by the Slovene Parliament in November 1992, introduced a combination of free distribution of shares and the commercial privatisation of companies. Typically, 10 per cent of shares of a company are transferred to the Compensation/Restitution Fund, 10 per cent to the Pension Fund, 20 per cent to the special Privatisation Investment Funds for free distribution to all Slovenian citizens via ownership certificates, and 60 per cent is available for internal free distribution to employees via ownership certificates. This is usually termed the 60:20:10:10 model. The certificates can be sold either on preferential terms to insiders under a special internal buy-out scheme, or on commercial terms through a public offering of shares, public tender or public auction at the discretion of managers.

The law is flexible in allowing modification of the basic transformation scheme, and therefore various combinations of methods can be used. Companies may also be transformed by raising new private equity on commercial terms and transferring the existing shares representing social capital to different financial institutions. As can readily be seen, this legislation grants top managers considerable discretion over the privatisation process. Additionally, to avoid a sharp drop in the value of shares on the capital market, and to diminish the risk of negative effects on interest rates and economic growth, shares from internal distribution cannot, by law, be transferred at least for two years. Shares acquired through internal buy-outs are transferable only between participants of the internal buy-out until the program is concluded. Privatisation to powerful external owners will therefore take place only gradually through the resale of shares by their initial owners.

The ownership structure of the eight firms we studied was quite varied. Three had adopted the 60:20:10:10 formula which meant that inside owners clearly dominated. One was 51 per cent owned by a foreign (German, later American) company, one almost entirely (92 per cent) by the State Development Fund following major financial restructuring of the parent group and the other three were owned by a combination of employees, the retirement fund, the composition/restitution fund and individual external investors with no single shareholder owning over 20 per cent.

Owner control and managerial discretion were assessed through a number of questions about owners' veto powers, their involvement in a range of major decisions, the frequency of formal and informal contact with owners, and the extent of managers' independence in making eight key strategic choices. With the exception of the state owned enterprise, external owners seemed to have remarkably little control over these Slovene enterprises. In two cases, owners had no formal veto powers over major financial or organisational decisions; in a further three they only had to give their formal approval to the appointment of the CEO. In the other three firms they also had veto powers over major expenditures — typically over 1 million DEM — and in the state firm they also had to approve new product introductions and business unit closures or openings.

Owners' involvement in 14 issues concerning suppliers, products, markets, technologies, work organisation, employment policies and financial decisions was likewise limited in these firms. Only in one firm, the state owned loss maker, were the outside owners involved to a large extent in more than two of these issues and in only two were they at all involved in half of them. Typically, it was the appointment of top managers and financial policies, such as dividend payments, which were the focus of owners' influence. Similarly, the overwhelming majority of these firms' top managers claimed they had a 'very high' degree of independence in deciding which products to make, which markets to serve and how to reach them, the selection of suppliers and machinery, the choice of organisation structures, employment policies and work control practices. Only one group of top managers said they had less than a 'high' amount of independence in any of these matters — in the state enterprise — and even here it was only for three decision areas.

In general, then, these Slovene top managers had considerable autonomy from owners in both strategic and operational matters, whether the largest owners were employees, foreign firms or investment funds, and certainly much more than their Hungarian counterparts (Whitley et al. 1997; Whitley and Czaban 1998b). This presumably reflects the high level of decentralisation in the self-management system, compared to the CMEA countries, and the high level of manager-employee interdependence and awareness of common interests.

4.2 *Strategic Choices, Innovations and Cooperation*

As might be expected from this high level of managerial autonomy, growth goals tended to dominate strategic choices in these Slovene companies. Six of the eight said that sales growth was more important than short-term profitability and that increasing market share and sales were very important objectives. None claimed that profitability was more significant than sales growth. However, productivity and cost cutting were also seen as very important objectives by five groups of top managers which indicates that competitive pressures were widely acknowledged to require improvements in the work system and labour costs despite substantial employee ownership. The considerable local embeddedness of these firms and employer-employee interdependence also influenced growth strategies. Growth was predominantly seen as a matter of internal development and expansion of current organisational skills and capabilities rather than radically changing them through acquisition and unrelated diversification. Relatedly, top managers of seven of the eight firms saw the development of employee skills and commitment as a key strategic goal.

Turning to consider how these firms have adapted to the loss of their markets in Yugoslavia and increasing domestic competition, the dominant pattern is one of product and/or process innovations in the same business area. All but one of the manufacturing companies in this group of Slovene firms had introduced new products since 1989 that contributed over 5 per cent of sales in 1994. In one case, a firm had developed 11 new products in 1995 alone that contributed 15 per cent of turnover in that year. While some of these had been developed jointly with suppliers or customers, or acquired through licensing, the majority had been developed internally, some by reverse engineering. In four firms, significant product innovations had been entirely developed within the enterprise, which demonstrates the considerable innovative capabilities of some Slovene companies. All of these product changes were closely related to existing product lines and/or markets.

Similarly, all but two of the 20 process innovations implemented since 1989 were closely connected to existing technologies, but rather fewer (seven) were entirely developed internally, with six being the result of joint work with suppliers. It is worth noting that the two firms with no significant product/service innovations since 1989 had implemented some changes in their technological systems, indicating a willingness and capacity to innovate. It is also worth pointing out that these Slovene enterprises had developed more product and process changes since 1989 than the 27 Hungarian firms interviewed in 1993/4 (Whitley and Czaban 1998b). They additionally appeared to have generated more of these innovations internally, indicating a higher level of organisational capabilities than those from the more centralised, CMEA dominated economy did.

Nearly all these changes were made within the existing range of products and markets, which tended to be dominated by quite narrowly defined and specialised outputs. In four cases, the major product line in 1990 contributed over 80 per cent of firms' sales turnover in that year, and in 1994 the same product lines still generated over 70 per cent of the same firms' sales. In only three firms did their largest product lines produce under 50 per cent of total sales in 1990, and the second largest lines in terms of turnover of these companies contributed over 20 per cent. Furthermore, these latter products were closely related to the most important ones, either technologically and/or in market terms. The proportions of sales produced by these lines in 1994 remained much the same as in 1990, so that these firms remained highly specialised in terms of product lines and markets served throughout the early 1990s.

These eight Slovene firms, then, had all innovated, albeit to varying degrees, during the early transformation period, but had remained in the same business field with the same product lines producing much the same proportion of total sales in 1994 as they had in 1990. In general, their top managers appeared to view their businesses and markets in terms of existing products and services, and to consider their competitors to be similarly bounded by the same limits. This rather conservative perception of markets and business domains is reinforced by the lack of risk sharing agencies and of cooperation between enterprises in Slovenia. Only the managers of the state owned firm said that they could share the risks of diversification and new developments with the state — and the innovation in question was an extension of existing facilities to serve a different kind of customer. All the other managers claimed they had to bear all business risks internally, with no help from banks, the state or business partners. Many commented that before 1989 they had been able to share risks with the state and the banks, but this was no longer the case.

This feeling of isolation and self-reliance was echoed in many responses to questions about cooperation and information sharing with business partners. Although six of the eight were members of trade associations organised by the Chambers of Commerce — as is legally required — only three found such membership of any use whatsoever and the common view was that they did not lead to any cooperation. As one CEO put it, the Slovenian producers in his sector behave: "Like small roosters on even smaller dungheaps". While four firms said they did discuss new developments with competitors, at least to some extent, only three engaged in joint lobbying of state and other agencies, only two shared any information on employment matters with competitors and only three collaborated in export markets. Overall, then, the bulk of these Slovene firms were not used to working together as members of the same industry, and did not expect to do so in the near future. This reluctance to collaborate with business partners in the same industry contrasts quite strongly with the experiences of large Hungarian enterprises which manifested more 'obligational' (Dore 1986) connections with suppliers and customers, probably as a result of their greater dependence on state agencies and shortages of supplies in the CMEA system (Whitley et al. 1996).

There was, though, some cooperation with major international customers in terms of technology transfer. Four firms' managers said that such customers made a high level of technical expertise available to them, while two claimed a medium level of technical transfer. Four companies also said that customers shared at least some commercial risks with them in the event of unforeseen events occurring. Overall, however, the majority perception was of being isolated and having to manage on one's own.

4.3 Employment Policies and Work Organisation

The combination of considerable interdependence between managers and workers with strong enterprise — community links and with the relatively successful financial record of many Slovene companies in the early 1990s was expected to limit the extent of organisational restructuring and employment reductions in these enterprises. This was reinforced by managers' need to maintain the support of workers' representatives during the pre-privatisation period if they wished to retain control (Jaklic 1997).

A further important factor limiting enforced redundancies in Slovenia has been their high cost to firms (Korze 1996) and the time taken to negotiate them with the unions. As a result, many Slovene companies have managed their problem of surplus labour by encouraging early retirements rather than through compulsory redundancies, helped by quite a generous level of state support. Particularly in 1991–1993, many firms bought 'extra years' pension contributions for employees they wished to retire, with funds both from the state budget and their own resources. Consequently, whereas 3.3 active workers supported each pensioner in Slovenia in 1981, by 1995 this figure was 1.7 active workers, and the average age of male retirement had dropped to 56 years and 2 months in 1993 (Simcic and Vidic 1995). According to Kukar and Stanovnik (1993), the percentage of GDP paid out in the form of pensions in Slovenia was the highest in Europe at 14 per cent.

Somewhat contrary to these expectations, Table 1 shows that three firms had reduced their total workforce quite significantly between the 1st January 1990 and the 1st January 1995, mostly within domestic plants. On the whole, employment reductions had not involved closing whole business units. While five firms had lost or closed subsidiaries in former Yugoslavia, these were only significant in terms of employees (i.e. over 100) in one case and that firm had also reduced employment in their 'core' activities in Slovenia. One of these was the state controlled loss maker, but two others were making profits in 1993 and 1994. Only two firms had closed or sold organisational units employing over 10 per cent of their workforces in the early 1990s, and only 13 units in total — mostly employing small numbers of people — had been disposed of.

Conversely, 16 new units had been established or acquired by these eight companies, some of them employing over 100 staff. Relatedly, two successful exporters had actually increased their employment total, one quite significantly but mostly through taking on 'temporary' contract staff. These changes in employment suggest that some Slovene firms have been able and willing to implement significant alterations to their workforces without the threat of imminent bankruptcy and have also been able to respond to market changes and opportunities for growth. This indicates the considerable trust established by managers and their capacity to act in a rapidly changing environment.

Unlike the Hungarian firms we studied, these reductions were not especially high among support workers as opposed to those engaged upon direct production tasks. It is, though, worth noting that the firm increasing employment most had reduced the number of non-workflow personnel. However, the link between workforce reductions and increasing supervisor proportions noted in many Hungarian companies (Whitley and Czaban 1998b) was also apparent in these Slovene ones. In all three firms where significant cuts in total employment had been made in the early 1990s, the number of production workers per supervisor had reduced by 20 per cent or more, and by over a third in the loss making enterprise. In contrast, this ratio had doubled in the expanding firm, partly because of workflow changes to stand alone workstations.

In terms of managerial turnover, it is worth noting here that whereas nearly two thirds of all Slovene firms had changed their CEO in the early 1990s (Pucko 1994) only three of the eight reported in this paper had done so and only two of these had come from outside the organisation. In six firms the top management

Table 1: *Employment Changes in 8 Slovene Companies, 1/1/1990–1/1/1995*

Company		Total Workforce	Production Workers	Supervisors	Total Non-Workflow	Support Staff	% Production Workers	Production/ Supervisor
A	1990	1544	723	145	306	165	47	5
	1995	1955	1145	109	254	194	59	10.5
B	1990	842	662	33	103	42	79	20
	1995	954	785	30	87	42	82	26
C	1990	1155	770	24	355	181	67	32
	1995	957	640	20	271	150	67	32
D	1990	1471	938	92	n.a.	n.a.	64	10
	1995	1228	855	81	n.a.	n.a.	70	11
E	1990	1134	524	35	361	29	46	15
	1995	687	297	24	251	12	43	12
F	1990	4815	3659	182	569	362	76	20
	1995	4045	3097	142	421	321	77	22
G	1990	3433	1183	133	1106	663	34	9
	1995	2749	847	121	881	618	31	7
H	1990	310	220	26	60	23	71	8
	1995	205	120	26	51	20	59	5

Note: n.a. = not available

Source: Own data from a survey of 71 top managers in 8 Slovene enterprises, 1995/6.

team had remained much the same since 1989, with any change in leading personnel being restricted to internal promotions and demotions. Only in one case had a significant proportion (50 per cent) of the new top management team come from outside the organisation — the loss making state enterprise — and the average length of work experience in different organisations of all these 71 top managers was under five years. The vast majority, then, had spent the bulk of their working lives in the same enterprise or group of organisations, and had little or no experience of managing different activities or dealing with different markets.

Relatedly, nearly all of their middle managers were internally promoted, with seven firms claiming that 90 per cent of these roles were filled this way. Only in the loss making enterprise was external recruitment important at this level of the organisation. Similarly, four firms appointed almost all of their supervisors from production workers, although two did rely much more on external recruitment to fill such posts. Overall, five of the eight firms considered here said that over a half of their staff had been with them since leaving full time education, with only the two service sector firms experiencing high levels of labour turnover. The predominant pattern, then, was to recruit at the bottom of the hierarchy and promote internally, with little or no external recruitment for non-production jobs and a strong preference for hiring locally. Quite often managers would volunteer their commitment to recruit local people, and five firms were continuing their traditional scholarship programmes for local people, albeit often at a reduced level and only for university degrees in some cases.

This reliance on internal development and promotion was paralleled by the considerable investment these firms were making in training their staff. They all provided systematic induction training for new employees, in some cases this lasted for several months, and had all provided some training for many staff in 1994. All but one company had provided some training for their manual workers in 1994, mostly externally as well as internally, and all of them had invested in training for at least one group of non manual employees that year. Six of the eight had sent clerical, technical and managerial staff on external courses during 1994, often lasting for several days, and most top managers claimed they believed in continuous training for most staff as a key part of their firms' strategies.

The significance given to personnel issues — but not necessarily to the personnel management function — in most of these Slovene companies was also manifested by the elaborate procedures used to select new staff, and the common involvement of the Chief Executive and other top managers in making hiring and promotion decisions. This was particularly noticeable in the more successful enterprises. Given the expected long term commitments of both employers and employees in Slovenia which have been both reflected in, and reproduced by, the low rate of geographical mobility of most people after the completion of their education (Jaklic 1997), this is not surprising.

This commitment, and the important role of many of these firms in their localities, might be expected to encourage managers to provide a wide range of non-wage benefits and services to their employees, as in some other former state socialist societies (Hirschhausen 1995; Whitley et al. 1997). However, only two of these eight firms provided more than one non-wage benefit to the bulk of their labour force in 1995/6, although most gave managers some extra benefits, and none provided welfare services even though many had done so previously. Where additional benefits were provided, they were seen as incentives to encourage higher performance rather than being part of a general policy of corporate paternalism or 'welfarism'. Rewards typically comprised a basic wage tied to job complexity, employee capabilities and behaviour and a bonus linked to individual, group and company performance.

The legacy of egalitarian values and political reluctance to tolerate high rates of overt income inequality in state socialist societies can be expected to limit reward differentials in these companies. Certainly, compared to some Western European countries, and even to other Central and Eastern European societies such as Hungary (Whitley et al. 1997; Whitley and Czaban 1998b), wage differentials seemed more limited in these Slovene firms. Seven paid their skilled workers no more than 50 per cent more than their unskilled ones, and five paid first line supervisors less than twice the wages of operators, with three restricting that differential to less than 1.5:1. In fact, three companies paid supervisors only a little more than skilled workers did. Similarly, the differentials between middle managers and operators exceeded 2.5:1 in only three cases, and the median difference between all white- and blue-collar workers was 2:1.

Chief Executives typically received less than 10 times the average operator's pay in five firms, with one being paid only five times as much, although CEOs probably received more in total rewards than these figures suggest. Given the high degree of managerial discretion in general in these firms, and their considerable size in most cases, these differentials do suggest quite strong conventions against highly unequal income distributions, and there have been a number of criticisms of the perceived high wages that top managers are receiving today in Slovenia, especially in the less well performing firms.

Few companies had made radical changes in their employment policies or organisation structures since 1990. Many managers claimed that they now had more independence in making employment decisions because the unions were less powerful, but most also acknowledged the importance of maintaining cooperative relations with the union. In the two firms which had taken on a number of new staff, they had put them on temporary contracts since this meant they could be dismissed without compensation, and one had developed a system of home-working for simple tasks, but on the whole most had not changed labour management strategies. Similarly, few had reorganised themselves to any significant extent, despite some rhetoric about profit centres and decentralisation, nor had they tried to improve cross-functional coordination. Generally, Slovene firms seemed to have quite rigid functional hierarchies and there was little cooperation between staff in development, marketing and production departments in many of the companies we studied.

Rather more companies had tried to increase worker flexibility and mobility between tasks. Most managers interviewed were keen to develop multiskilled 'parachutists' who could move between machines and locations as needed, and three firms had special groups of such staff, while one had managed to equip many of its production workers with multiple skills and another claimed that they could mostly undertake two different tasks. One firm had, though, successfully replaced its assembly line production system with stand alone integrated work stations, and two were currently implementing a move to production cells, following their success at a Renault subsidiary. In general, these Slovene firms seemed to be more aware of the need to encourage and reward worker flexibility than their Hungarian counterparts, presumably because they had been exposed to western markets for longer.

5.   Conclusions and Prospects

The dominant impression of the more successful Slovene firms gained from this study of eight companies confirms many of our earlier suggestions. They had adapted to the loss of the protected domestic Yugoslav market and increased competitive pressures since 1990 by implementing product and/or process innovations, often developed internally, and meeting changing customer demands from their own resources. However, they had also demonstrated greater willingness to restructure organisational units and reduce overall employment than we had expected, aided by a generous state supported early retirement scheme. Many of these firms had been able to close some small units and had also established or acquired new ones in dealing with hard budget constraints, as well as restructuring workflows and work systems in some cases. Proactive, flexible strategies seemed to be more evident in Slovenia than among many Hungarian companies.

These quite autonomous and independent managers did, though, seem rather narrowly focused on current product and service lines, and growth strategies remained concentrated within existing market boundaries. Growth was clearly the dominant objective and seen as best achieved through internal development. Considerable investment in training and concern with personnel issues were characteristic of many of these Slovene enterprises, as expected from their interdependence with local communities and manager-worker cooperation. Risk sharing and collaborative ventures between them were, though, neither significant at the moment nor expected to develop in the near future. Firms and their communities appeared to be rather isolated and internally focused in Slovenia, perhaps more so in the 1990s because the threat of privatisation had reinforced managers' concern to build strong coalitions with employee representatives and the local communes. It was notable that the one loss making company in this group had difficult relations with their municipal government — partly because the former parent company had been based in Ljubljana — and the new top managers were very keen to improve these connections as well as to develop cooperative links with its immediate local competitors.

The high level of political and economic decentralisation in Slovenia, coupled with substantial exposure to western markets and a dominant role in the domestic market, as well as close local ties and interdependences, have, then, helped to develop many relatively successful companies. These have been able to introduce new products and processes with a skilled labour force in rather narrow market segments, without radical macro- or micro-economic changes and without major inflows of foreign capital. This continuity and relative success are threatened by three possible environmental shifts in ownership, competition and the social and political system.

The most obvious and commonly voiced threat to the current pattern of firm and market organisation in Slovenia is the move from internal ownership and control to external interests dominating firms' policies. Already some of the new investment companies have complained about the low level of dividends being paid by Slovene firms, and many managers and union leaders told us of their concern that outside owners might insist on high financial outflows at the expense of future investments. This view was sometimes reinforced by the claim that since the new owners had not actually paid for their shares with their own money, they did not have strong rights to income streams from assets that had been developed through social ownership and common labour. This fear of outside controllers was especially marked in the larger successful firms where managers and workers had difficulties in raising the considerable amount of capital required to retain 50 per cent insider ownership. In such cases, managers were encouraging the formation of shareholder organisations that they could deal with, and perhaps control.

If external portfolio investors do come to dominate the ownership of financial assets in the manner of the Anglo-Saxon economies, the nature of Slovene firms could alter significantly. However, this seems politically unlikely at the moment given the influence of leading firms, their managers and unions, despite some vocal advocates of such a transformation. Additionally, the small size of the economy and low liquidity of the embryonic capital markets will inhibit the growth and influence of an Anglo-Saxon financial system.

Second, and perhaps more important in the short to medium term, is the threat to these firms' competitive positions. The high level of local interdependence and manager-worker commitment to their community have probably helped to develop organisational capabilities and flexibility within fairly narrow markets. However, they may also have inhibited broader cooperation and risk sharing within and between different regions of Slovenia which could render these firms vulnerable to increased competition and market changes. To remain rather specialised and focused in their product and service lines, these companies need to be able to share development and market risks with other organisations such as banks, customers, suppliers, and competitors if they are to remain competitive in both the former Yugoslavia and OECD markets. While some cooperation with international customers is evident in these eight firms, it could develop into dependent subcontracting relationships without broader support and collaboration at a regional and perhaps national level.

Third, the establishment of the new state, reorganisation of the banking systems and restructuring of local government may increase geographical mobility, especially to the capital, and reduce the significance of local ties. The creation of an independent state bureaucracy and national government in such a small country encourages centralisation of decision making and resources, and focuses ambitions on the capital. Together with the centralisation of the banking system as many local banks in financial difficulties are merged and/or closed, this centralisation may well lead to local communities losing their attractions for the younger, better educated workers and managers, in addition to enhancing the desirability of working in new service sector businesses, such as financial services. Over time these developments may result in the localised polycentric pattern of economic development in Slovenia being replaced by a more centralised political and economic structure in which local communities, specially in the economically weaker areas, become more peripheral to both the state and to leading firms. If this does happen, employer-employee interdependence will probably decline and perhaps firms' ability to adapt and develop new capabilities decrease.

This analysis of the transformation processes in Slovenia highlights three broader issues concerning the role of institutional arrangements in structuring enterprise type and behaviour. First, not only did the legacies of Yugoslav late state socialism generate distinctive kinds of enterprises in Slovenia that behaved differently to those in the ex-CMEA countries, but they also enabled top managers to play a significant role in the evolution of state policies. They therefore helped to constitute a particular organisation of interest groups and patterns of their collaboration and competition in Slovenia that affected how the transformation was managed.

The active role of many enterprise managers in this period of radical political and economic change developed from their position and influence under the late state socialist regime. The path dependence of firm nature and actions is, then, echoed by the path dependence of interest group formation and activities. During rapid social change, such interest groups may be able to affect how new institutional arrangements are developed, but they themselves are constituted largely by previous ones. The ability of Slovene managers to play a more significant collective role in the transformation process than most of their Hungarian counterparts resulted from the particular legacies of late state socialism they inherited.

Second, while the relatively favourable institutional environment for many Slovene companies helped them to respond effectively to the changes of the early 1990s, it may inhibit their future adaptability in a comparable manner to the institutional lock-in effects found elsewhere in Europe (Braczyk et al. 1995; Schienstock 1997; Tainio et al. in this volume). The very structures and connections that have led to economic success in particular circumstances can inhibit further innovative development as skills and capabilities become entrenched in organisational routines that are reinforced by institutional arrangements. The difficulties that many Slovene firms seem to have in developing cooperative relations with business partners other than employees may well exemplify this kind of lock-in.

Third, these difficulties, and their likely roots in both the pre-war structure of agricultural communities in Slovenia and the particular pattern of entrepreneurial development in the postwar period, highlight the significant differences in how economic transactions are organised between specialised new enterprises across Europe (Kristensen and Jaklic 1997). Just as variations in the nature of pre-industrial society and industrialisation processes in Denmark and Italy led to significant differences in firm type and behaviour in Jutland and Northeast and Central Italy, so too the idiosyncrasies of the Slovene region before the creation of Yugoslavia and during the twentieth century have resulted in a particular kind of economy based on specialised firms developing there. Contrary to the more well known types in Western Europe, this sort of economic organisation combines considerable cooperation between managers and workers, and usually between managers and local agencies, with largely adversarial connections to other business partners. Here, at least, 'obligational' linkages between some economic actors are combined with more arms' length ones between other ones. This exemplifies the general point that such relationships need not take the same form with all partners, and therefore cannot be the direct result of dominant cultural norms governing economic exchanges.

References

Bank Slovenije. 1998. *Monthly Bulletin*, January.
Braczyk, H-J., G. Schienstock, and B. Steffensen. 1995. The Region of Baden-Würrtemberg: a Post-Fordist Success Story?. In: E. Dittrich, G. Schmidt, and R. Whitley (eds.), *Industrial Transformation in Europe*, 2–3–233. London: Sage.
Czaban, L., and R. Whitley. 1998. The Transformation of Work Systems in Emergent Capitalism: The case of Hungary, *Work, Employment and Society* 12: 1–26.
Dore, R. P. 1986. *Flexible Rigidities*. Stanford: Stanford University Press.
Dyker, D.A. 1990. *Yugoslavia: Socialism, development and debt*. London: Routledge.
EBRD. 1995. *Transition Report 1995*. London: European Bank for Reconstruction and Development.
Hirschhausen, C. von. 1995. No Privatization without Capitalization: approaches to post-socialist industrial restructuring in Central and Eastern Europe. In: E. Dittrich, G. Schmidt, and R. Whitley (eds.), *Industrial Transformation in Europe*, 54–78. London: Sage.
IMAD. 1997. *Analysis of Economic Developments in 1997 and prospects for 1998*. Ljubljana: Institute of Macroeconomic Analysis and Development.
Jaklic, M. 1994. Odnosi med podjetji z vidika trzne strukture gospodarstva (Relationship Among Companies, Business Conduct and Market Structure), *Teorija in Praksa* 31(7–8): 655–661.
Jaklic, M. 1997. Changing Governance Structures and Work Organisation in Slovenia. In: R. Whitley, and P. H. Kristensen (eds.), *Governance at Work: The social regulation of economic relations*, 209–223. Oxford University Press.
Javni dolg (Public Debt), *Porocevalec drzavnega zbora republike Slovenije* (Journal of the Slovenian Parliament) 1994. 10: 74–86, Ljubljana.
Konjhodzic, I. 1996. The Patterns of Adjustment of Small Economies in the Process of Liberalisation: The Finnish and Slovene experience in comparative perspective, Paper presented to a conference "50th Anniversary of Faculty of Economics in Ljubljana" held at the Faculty of Economics, University of Ljubljana, September.
Korze, U. 1996. Prestrukturiranje podjetij v Slovenjiji v devetdesetih (Restructuring of Slovenian Enterprises in the 90s), *Zbornik referatov: 28. simposij o sodobnih metodah v racunovodstvu in poslovnih financah*, Zveza ekonomistov Slovenije and Zveza racunovodij, financnikov in revizorjev Slovenije (Proceedings from the 28th Conference of Contemporary Methods in Accounting), Portoroz, Slovenia, pp. 9–24.
Korze, U., and M. Simoneti. 1993. Privatization in Slovenia — 1992. In: Centre for East Europe Privatisation Network (CEEPN), *Privatization in Central and Eastern Europe 1992*, 208–235. Annual Conference Series, Ljubljana.
Kovac, B. 1991. Entrepreneurship and Privatisation of Social Ownership in Economic Reforms. In: J. Simmie, and J. Dekleva (eds.), *Yugoslavia in Turmoil: After self-management*, 134–146. London: Pinter.
Kraft, E, M. Vodopivec, and M. Cvikl. 1994. On Its Own: The economy of independent Slovenia. In: J. Benderly, and E. Kraft (eds.), *Independent Slovenia*, 201–224. London: Macmillan.
Kristensen, P. H., and M. Jaklic. 1997. Atlantis' Valleys: Local continuity and industrialisation in Slovenia compared to West Jutland, Denmark and the Third Italy, unpublished paper, Copenhagen Business School, October.

Kukar, S., and T. Stanovnik. 1993. Analiza osnovnih ekonomskih elementov sistema pokojninskega zavaarovanja v Sloveniji (The Analysis of the Economic Basis of the Social Insurance System in Slovenia), *IB Revija* 27: 8, Ljubljana.

Kumar, A. 1992) Transition, *Slovenian Business Report* 8: 10–13, Lubljana.

Kuzmanic, T. 1994. Strikes, Trade Unions and Slovene Independence. In: J. Benderly, and E. Kraft (eds.), *Independent Slovenia*, 159–179. London: Macmillan.

Lazarevic, Z. 1994. Economic History of Twentieth Century Slovenia. In: J. Benderly, and E. Kraft (eds.), *Independent Slovenia*, 47–68. London: Macmillan.

Luksic, I. 1994. *Liberalizem versus korporativizem.* (Liberalism versus Corporatism), Ljubljana: Znanstveno publicistino sredisce.

Lydall, H. 1989. *Yugoslavia in Crisis.* Oxford: Oxford University Press.

Mencinger, J. 1995. Odpuseanje in upokojevanje (Dismissal and Retirement), *Gospodarska gibanja* (monthly journal of the Macroeconomic Institute, Ljubljana) 264: 25–38.

Mrak, M. 1995. Zunanja zadolbenost Republike Slovenije in njeno urejanje odnosov v tujini (External Slovenian Debt and the Management of Relationships Abroad), *Baneni Vestnik* (Bank Journal) 44(7–8): 10–16.

Novkovic, G. 1996. Moc, ki temelji na tveganju (Power based on Risk), *Gospodarski vestnik* (The Economic Herald) 20: 16–17, Ljubljana.

Pavlin, C. 1994. Nas eaka steeajni vihar? (Is the bankruptcy storm in front of us?), *Gospodarski vestnik* (The Economic Herald) 11: 8–11, Ljubljana.

Prasnikar, J., and W. Bartlett. 1995. Small Firms and Economic Transformation in Slovenia, *Communist Economies and Economic Transformation* 7: 83–103.

Pucko, D. 1994. Restructuring Strategies in the Slovenian Firms, Paper delivered to the European International Business Association, 20th Annual EIBA (European International Business Academy), December 1994, Warsaw.

Rant, A. 1995. Instrumenti denarne in devizne politike po letu 1991 (Instruments of Monetary and Foreign Exchange Policy After Year 1991. *Slovenska ekonomska revija* (Slovenian Economic Journal) 5: 465–483, Ljubljana.

Ribnikar, I. 1989. *Uvod v financno ekonomijo* (Introduction of Financial Economics), Ljubljana: Pegaz.

Rojec, M., B. Jasovic, M. Rems, and M. Simoneti. 1998. Company restructuring: 1994– 1996, *Slovenian Economic Mirror* 2: 1–26.

Rus, A. 1994. Quasi-privatisation: From class struggle to a scuffle of small particularisms. In: J. Benderly, and E. Kraft (eds.), *Independent Slovenia*, 225–249. London: Macmillan.

Schienstock, G. 1997. The Transformation of Regional Governance: Institutional Lock-Ins and the Development of Lean Production in Baden-Würrtemberg. In: R. Whitley, and P. H. Kristensen (eds.), *Governance at Work*, 190–208. Oxford: Oxford University Press.

Simcic, M., and I. Vidic. 1995. Reforma pokojninskega zavarovanja zamuja (The reform of the Social Insurance System is Late), *Gospodarski vestnik* 19: 27–36, Ljubljana.

Svetlicic, M., and M. Rojec. 1996. Kolektor, Case Study of Foreign Direct Investment in Slovenia, Faculty of Social Sciences, University of Ljubljana.

Whitley, R., J. Henderson, L. Czaban, and G. Lengyel. 1996. Trust and Contractual Relations in an Emerging Capitalist Economy: The changing trading relationships of 10 large Hungarian enterprises, *Organization Studies* 17: 397–420.

Whitley, R., J. Henderson, and L. Czaban. 1997. Ownership, Control and the Management of Labour in an Emergent Capitalist Economy: the case of Hungary, *Organization* 4(1): 75–98.

Whitley, R., and L. Czaban. 1998a. Ownership, Control and Authority in Emergent Capitalism: Changing supervisory relations in Hungarian industry, *International Journal of Human Resource Management* 9: 99–113.

Whitley, R., and L. Czaban. 1998b. Institutional Transformation and Enterprise Change in an Emergent Capitalist Economy: The Case of Hungary, *Organization Studies* 19: 259–280.

Zavod RS za Statistiko (Office for Statistics). 1991. *Rezultati raziskovanj — Prodaja po republikah in poraba reprodukcijskega materiala v republiki Sloveniji* (Research Results — Sales in different republics and use of reproduction material in Slovenia) 523: 77–92.

Index

John Benjamins Publishing Company publishes Advances in Organization Studies as a reformulated continuation of the De Gruyter Studies in Organization.

1. ZEYTINOĞLU, Işik Urla (ed.): *Developments in Changing Work Relationships in Industrialized Economies.* 1999.
2. HENKE, Holger and Ian BOXILL (eds.): *The End of the 'Asian Model'?* 2000.
3. QUACK, Sigrid, Glenn MORGAN and Richard WHITLEY (eds.): *National Capitalisms, Global Competition, and Economic Performance.* 2000.
4. MAURICE, Marc and Arndt SORGE (eds.): *Embedding Organizations. Societal analysis of actors, organizations and socio-economic context.* 2000.